SELLING
HELPING CUSTOMERS BUY

ROGER DITZENBERGER

DIVISION CHAIRMAN, OCCUPATIONAL AND VOCATIONAL EDUCATION

NORTH TEXAS STATE UNIVERSITY, DENTON, TEXAS

JOHN KIDNEY

DEPARTMENT CHAIRPERSON AND INSTRUCTOR, BUSINESS AND MARKETING DEPARTMENT

WEBSTER CITY HIGH SCHOOL, WEBSTER CITY, IOWA

2D EDITION

S20

Published by

SOUTH-WESTERN PUBLISHING CO.

CINCINNATI   WEST CHICAGO, IL   DALLAS   PELHAM MANOR, NY   LIVERMORE, CA

PREFACE

Selling: Helping Customers Buy, Second Edition, is written to provide you with the knowledge and skills you need to be successful in a sales career. The major emphasis of the text is placed on the specific selling techniques needed by salespeople in retailing. However, these skills are also useful to salespeople in wholesaling, manufacturing, and industrial sales jobs.

Selling focuses its attention on serving customers. Effective salespeople take the time to learn their products or services. Salespeople are genuinely interested in customers, taking time to listen to them and working to select the product or service that is right for each customer. Selling is really a matter of helping people buy.

The focal point of the text is customer-oriented selling. The most important responsibility of today's salesperson is satisfying the needs and wants of customers and assisting customers in making wise buying decisions. *Selling: Helping Customers Buy,* Second Edition, provides the techniques, skills, and attitudes you will need to assist your customer in making a wise buying decision.

The textbook is divided into five units. Unit 1 provides an overview of selling. It includes information on the importance of human relations in selling, the functions performed by salespeople, how to develop the personality traits needed by salespeople, and the buying and selling process.

Unit 2 presents information on the preapproach. This unit includes information on types of customers, customers' needs and wants, customer buying motives, product information, and how to use product information in a sales presentation.

The major emphasis of this book — sales techniques — is contained in Unit 3, "Developing Sales Skills: The Steps of a Sale." This unit has seven chapters which provide a sequenced account of the feature-benefit system of completing a sale. The unit contains many practical examples of how to conduct a feature-benefit sales presentation. Each of the seven chapters relates to a step in the feature-benefit sales presentation: the approach, determining customer needs and wants, planning a feature-benefit sales presentation, making a feature-benefit sales presentation, handling customer objections, closing the sale, and suggestion selling and reassurance. The examples in each chapter illustrate the salesperson's correct performance of various sales skills during each step of the sale.

Special skills needed in selling are explained in Unit 4. The purpose of this unit is to provide information on sales forms and transactions, cash register operation, store losses, sales-supporting skills, and telephone selling.

The last unit in the text, "Selling: Your Future" presents information on improving your feature-benefit sales techniques, job opportunities in selling, and how to get a job in selling. This unit emphasizes developing skills needed for the job application process and improving your selling skills once you have a sales job.

The chapters contain learning goals, sales terms, sales questions, and sales activities to aid in your learning. A sales training manual has also been developed to assist you in reviewing the text material and developing the feature-benefit sales techniques you will need to be successful in selling.

In reading and studying *Selling: Helping Customers Buy,* Second Edition, you can learn the sales attitudes and sales techniques needed for job success. Once you have developed the basic skills of selling, additional practice and experience will provide you greater job satisfaction and sales success.

Roger Ditzenberger
John Kidney

CONTENTS

UNIT 1 *SELLING: AN OVERVIEW*

Chapter 1. Introduction to Selling 3
Chapter 2. The Salesperson and Human Relations 12
Chapter 3. The Buying and Selling Process 30

UNIT 2 *PREPARING TO SELL: THE PREAPPROACH*

Chapter 4. Your Customer 51
Chapter 5. Customer Buying Motives 67
Chapter 6. Product Information 87

UNIT 3 *DEVELOPING SALES SKILLS: THE STEPS OF A SALE*

Chapter 7. The Approach 107
Chapter 8. Determining Customer Needs and Wants 119
Chapter 9. Planning a Feature-Benefit
            Sales Presentation 143
Chapter 10. Making a Feature-Benefit Sales
            Presentation 163
Chapter 11. Handling Customer Objections 181
Chapter 12. Closing the Sale 206
Chapter 13. Suggestion Selling and Reassurance 231

UNIT 4 SELLING: SPECIAL SKILLS NEEDED

Chapter 14. Sales Forms and Transactions 253

Chapter 15. Cash Register Operation and Handling Money 289

Chapter 16. Store Losses 313

Chapter 17 Sales-Supporting Skills 338

Chapter 18. Telephone Selling 352

UNIT 5 SELLING: YOUR FUTURE

Chapter 19. Improving Your Selling Skills 371

Chapter 20. Career Opportunities in Selling 383

Chapter 21. How to Get a Selling Job 403

Index 428

1

SELLING:
AN OVERVIEW

1

SELLING:

AN OVERVIEW

CHAPTER 1: INTRODUCTION TO SELLING

CHAPTER 2: THE SALESPERSON
AND HUMAN RELATIONS

CHAPTER 3: THE BUYING AND
SELLING PROCESS

1

INTRODUCTION TO SELLING

Your Learning Goals

After studying this chapter, you should:

- *be aware of the importance of selling in your personal life.*
- *develop the attitude that selling is assisting the customer.*
- *understand that selling should result in a benefit or gain to the customer.*
- *understand how salespeople can assist the customer in making a wise buying decision.*
- *know the three phases of our economy.*
- *be able to explain the contribution of selling to our country.*
- *be aware of the importance of the customer to a business.*

Selling skills can be very useful in your personal life. Have you ever wanted to use your parents' car to go to a rock concert, a dance, or a football or basketball game? You probably used selling skills to persuade them to let you use the car. Have you ever applied for a job? You probably tried to persuade the employer that you would be a good employee. Have you ever run for elected office in an organization? You probably tried to sell yourself to others by convincing the voting members in the organization that you could provide the type of leadership needed. These are all examples of using selling skills in your personal life. Selling involves persuading others to accept your ideas, advice, and leadership.

Selling skills are also important in business. To stay in operation and to grow, businesses depend on the money earned from the sales of products or services. Business owners and managers must hire people who are creative, who work well with others, and who contribute to the success of their businesses. In the business world, selling is a very important function.

Salespeople are often called the *bread and butter* of a business. They perform a most important role. Successful salespeople use selling skills to assist customers in making wise buying decisions. Customers who are satisfied with salespeople return to the business to buy again and again. To be successful, businesses need customers who repeatedly return to buy.

WHAT IS SELLING?

Selling involves the art of communicating effectively with people — simply explaining how a product or service will benefit the customer. Customers will not purchase a product or service until they are convinced that they will benefit from owning that product or service. As a salesperson, you need to explain, advise, and generally help the customer. In fact, your most important job is to assist the customer in making a wise buying decision. The word **selling** is defined as:

1. assisting the customer, and
2. helping the customer make a wise buying decision.

Assisting the Customer

Businesses in America today are very competitive. In our free enterprise system, there are many businesses that sell similar products and services. For example, you can purchase a pair of jeans from a department store, a women's or men's apparel shop, a specialty store, or a discount store. Because customers can purchase

Salespeople Can Assist Customers By . . .

- asking questions to learn customer needs.
- showing benefits to be received from the product or service.
- understanding customer objections.
- helping customers buy to their advantage.
- being concerned about customer satisfaction after the sale.

the same product or service from more than one business, it is important that businesses provide courteous, friendly service to customers. If customers do not receive courteous and capable help from salespeople at one business, they may decide to purchase from another business. To be an effective salesperson, you need to provide the help customers expect.

Helping the Customer Make a Wise Buying Decision

The most important responsibility of any salesperson is to help customers make wise buying decisions. Customers make wise buying decisions when they receive benefits from the products or services they purchase. These benefits are called **buyer benefits**. Buyer benefits are the gains or personal benefits customers receive from the products or services they purchase. Your job as a salesperson is to make sure your customers purchase the products or services which will most benefit them.

ILLUSTRATION 1-1
Buyer benefits are the gains or personal benefits customers receive from the products they purchase.

THE CONTRIBUTIONS OF SELLING

Selling is important to our economy, to business, and to the American people. In order to understand its importance, you need to be familiar with some basic facts about each segment of the American economy. The economy of our country is divided into three phases: production, marketing, and consumption.

Production refers to the physical creation of goods and services. Farming, mining, fishing, lumbering, and manufacturing make up the production phase of our economy. Thousands of goods and services are produced each year. These goods and services, however, do not sell themselves. After goods and services have been produced, they must be made available to consumers for purchase.

Marketing is the process through which goods and services flow from the producer to the consumer. Wholesalers and retailers participate in the marketing phase of our economy. Selling is the most important marketing function performed by retail and wholesale businesses. **Wholesalers** buy from producers and sell to retailers. **Retailers** buy from producers and wholesalers and sell to consumers.

Consumers are the users of goods and services in our society. The process of using goods and services is called **consumption**.

What contribution does selling make to our economy? The role of selling in our society is to identify and provide the goods and services that will satisfy the needs and wants of the consumer. Manufacturers, wholesalers, and retailers all depend on customers to purchase products and services. When a business's sales decline, the company usually reduces the number of its employees. The jobs of the many people who produce and provide goods and services therefore depend on successful salespeople.

When customers purchase products and services, they help create employment in manufacturing, wholesaling, and retailing. Full employment in our country creates additional purchasing power for our consumers. Selling therefore assists in maintaining the high standard of living enjoyed in our country.

What contribution does selling make to a business? The role of business in society is to provide the types of products and services that consumers need and want. It is the job of the salesperson, as the business's representative, to satisfy the customers' needs and wants. Salespeople, and the manner in which they treat customers, can really determine the success or failure of most businesses.

What contribution does selling make to the American consumer? Salespeople are often the only contact a customer has with a business. Salespeople represent the business to the customer.

ILLUSTRATION 1-2
Salespeople save customers time and money by providing product information.

J. P. Stevens & Co., Inc.

They should offer sincere, honest, friendly, and courteous service to customers. The salesperson's job is to make sure the customer benefits from purchasing a product or service. Salespeople can save customers time and money by providing product information, showing how a product or service will benefit the customer, and making sure customers purchase the products and services that will best meet their needs and wants.

In Our Society, Selling . . .

- identifies the goods and services needed by consumers.
- assists customers in purchasing products and services.
- creates and maintains employment of people.
- satisfies the needs and wants of consumers.
- assists in maintaining a high standard of living.

THE IMPORTANCE OF HUMAN RELATIONS IN SELLING

Businesses depend heavily on **repeat customers.** Repeat customers are those who frequently return to shop at a certain place of business. Often it is the friendly, courteous salesperson that keeps customers coming back. Customers may stop shopping at a business because of high prices, lack of merchandise, or lack of proper facilities. However, lack of courtesy or help from salespeople is the major reason customers give for not returning. That's why well-trained salespeople are so important. Salespeople represent the business to the customers and are often looked upon by customers as experts to whom they can turn for help.

Your attitude and how you relate to others are two of the most important factors in job success. The main reason workers lose jobs is due to a poor attitude. A recent study of beginning workers who had been fired showed that 80 percent lost their jobs because they couldn't get along with other people. It is especially important for salespeople to develop positive human relations skills in order to get along with fellow employees, managers, and customers.

ILLUSTRATION 1-3
Your attitude and how you relate to others are important factors in job success.

Salespeople need to develop pleasing personalities. Most retail, wholesale, and industrial firms stress to their sales forces that the CUSTOMER IS KING. Businesses which attempt to satisfy the needs and wants of their customers are called **customer-oriented businesses.** These businesses will demand that their salespeople follow the "Eleven Commandments of Good Business."

Eleven Commandments of Good Business

Customers ...

- are the most important people in any business.
- are not an interruption of our work — they are the purpose of it.
- are not dependent on us — we are dependent on them.
- are people who bring us their wants — it is our job to fill those wants.
- do us a favor when they call — we are not doing them a favor by serving them.
- are part of our business — not outsiders.
- are not a cold statistic — they are flesh and blood human beings with feelings and emotions.
- are not people with whom to argue or match wits.
- are deserving of the most courteous and attentive treatment we can give them.
- are the people who make it possible to pay our salaries, whether we are salespeople, department managers, or owners.
- are the lifeblood of every business.

Selling is the process of helping customers purchase the products and services that will benefit them. As a salesperson, you are a problem solver, adviser, and most importantly a person who assists the customer in buying the right product or service. Your job as a salesperson can be very rewarding. If you develop effective selling skills, you can be a very valuable and important person to your business and your customers. A good salesperson enjoys satisfying the needs and wants of customers. Salespeople who sincerely help customers purchase needed products and services find their jobs enjoyable and rewarding.

OPPORTUNITIES IN SELLING

There are hundreds of different types of selling jobs. Jobs in selling may be classified in several ways. They may be classified according to the employer. You can sell for a retailer, a wholesaler, or a manufacturer. Selling jobs may also be classified according to the types of products or services sold. Some salespeople sell **tangible products,** or products which can be felt or touched, including clothing, furniture, houses, automobiles, computers, and machinery. Other salespeople sell **intangible products or services,** or products and services which cannot be felt or touched, such as insurance policies, banking services, advertising services, and consulting services.

Successful salespeople are often promoted into supervisory and management positions in business. Many sales managers, vice-presidents of marketing, and company presidents began their careers as salespeople.

ILLUSTRATION 1-4
Some salespeople sell intangibles such as insurance and investment services.

Courtesy of Sears, Roebuck and Co.

SALES TERMS

selling

buyer benefits

production

marketing

wholesalers

retailers

consumers

consumption

repeat customers

customer-oriented businesses

tangible products

intangible products or services

SALES QUESTIONS

1. How might you use selling skills in your personal life?

2. Why is selling important to most businesses?

3. What is a salesperson's most important responsibility?

4. Explain how salespeople can assist customers in making a wise buying decision.

5. Why are *buyer benefits* important?

6. Explain the difference between the three phases of our economy.

7. What contribution does selling make to our economy?

8. How does selling affect the jobs of other employees in a business?

9. What contribution does selling make to a business?

10. What contribution does selling make to the American consumer?

11. Why is human relations important in selling?

12. The main reason beginning workers lose their jobs is poor attitude. What specific attitudes have you observed which you thought were poor attitudes of salespeople?

13. What business practices reflect a customer-oriented philosophy?

14. Does a career in selling appeal to you? Why or why not?

SALES ACTIVITIES

A. Selling is the process of assisting the customer in making a wise buying decision. The process involves two major concepts: (1) the salesperson should assist the customer, and (2) the purchase should provide a benefit to the customer. In your own words, describe the purchases of goods or services you made recently. Tell how the salesperson assisted you and describe how you benefited as a buyer.

B. Selling is not tricking your customers into buying or using high-pressure sales tactics on them. Selling should be a process of helping the customer. List at least six types of help customers expect from salespeople.

C. Most customer-oriented businesses believe that the CUSTOMER IS KING. Salespeople need to develop a positive attitude regarding the importance of the customer. The statement, "The customer is the most important person in any business," is very true. Write eight statements that reflect the attitude that the CUSTOMER IS KING.

2

THE SALESPERSON
AND HUMAN RELATIONS

Your Learning Goals

After studying this chapter, you should:

- *know the functions performed by a salesperson.*
- *understand the difference between a salesperson and an order-taker.*
- *understand the concept of customer-oriented selling.*
- *know the personality traits important to a salesperson.*
- *be able to analyze your personality.*
- *be able to develop personality traits needed by salespeople.*
- *understand patronage motives.*
- *be aware of what customers expect from salespeople.*
- *be aware of what employers expect of salespeople.*

In Chapter 1 you learned that selling is the process of assisting the customer in making a wise buying decision. A **salesperson** is a person who sells products or services to customers.

THE SALESPERSON'S JOB

To assist customers and satisfy customers' needs and wants, salespeople must develop both selling techniques and human relations skills. In addition to their major responsibility of selling, salespeople must also perform sales-supporting functions. Let's look at both the selling and sales-supporting functions of the sales-person's job.

First, let's look at the selling function. Sometimes a customer will approach a salesperson and say, "I'll take this, please." While this occasionally happens in business, it should not be considered selling. When a customer comes to you with this type of request, you are simply acting as an **order-taker**, not as a salesperson. Since most customers have not made the decision to buy a specific product or service when they enter a store, it is your job to help customers make wise buying decisions. Selling is much more than just ringing up the sale on the cash register or completing a sales ticket; an order-taker performs these functions.

Selling—The Salesperson's Most Important Function

Selling involves considerably more than just order-taking. Since most customers are either undecided, uncertain, or unaware of what they specifically want to buy, it is your job as a salesperson to provide the customer with help in purchasing the right product or service. As a responsible salesperson, you can provide assistance to your customers in the following ways:

1. Ask customers questions to determine their interest in products or services.
2. Assist customers in determining which products and services will best fulfill their needs.
3. Demonstrate product features to customers.
4. Explain to customers the benefits they will receive from buying the product or service.
5. Answer any objections customers have concerning the product or service.
6. Ask customers to buy the product or service.
7. Suggest additional related merchandise which will benefit the customers.
8. Reassure customers that the purchase is a wise buying decision.

Obviously being a salesperson is more challenging than just being an order-taker. The functions performed by the salesperson are done with the customer in mind. To be effective in assisting customers, a salesperson must be skilled in human relations. As a salesperson it is important to show your customers that you like them, understand them, and want to help them. The key to satisfying your customers is to determine what they need and then select and sell them the right product or service. Each step of your presentation should be based on your customers' responses and

ILLUSTRATION 2-1
It is important to show your customers that you like them, understand them, and
want to help them.

questions. Simply stated, good selling involves effective human relations with your customers.

When selling is based on the needs and wants of customers, it is called **customer-oriented selling.** If you are a customer-oriented salesperson concerned about satisfying your customers' needs and wants, you should have many repeat customers. Let's see how the salesperson effectively uses customer-oriented selling skills to satisfy the customer's needs and wants in the following example.

A high school student comes into a stereo electronics store thinking about purchasing a stereo AM-FM radio or stereo tape deck. She will graduate in May and plans to go on a long vacation immediately after graduation. She is thinking about purchasing a tape deck so she can listen to her favorite music on the trip. In order to sell a stereo AM-FM radio, stereo tape deck, or combination radio-tape deck to this girl, you must:

1. Welcome the girl to gain her trust and respect.
2. Determine which of the product's features will best meet the girl's needs.

3. Assist her in selecting the product which best fulfills her needs.
4. Demonstrate the features of the stereo equipment and explain how these features will benefit her.
5. Persuade or convince her that she will receive many benefits by purchasing the stereo equipment.
6. Answer any objections she has about the equipment.
7. Ask her to purchase the stereo equipment which best benefits her.
8. Suggest any related items which would make her trip and listening more enjoyable.
9. Thank her for the purchase and reassure her that she has made a wise purchase.

In this example of customer-oriented selling, the functions performed by the salesperson center on the customer and what would benefit her most. This is also called **personal selling** because the salesperson is personally concerned with satisfying the customer's wants and needs.

Remember that without customers, there would be no need for the product or service you are selling. Without customers, there would be no need for salespeople. Effective salespeople are good sources of information, ideas, and suggestions for their customers. They provide products or services that will satisfy their customers' needs and wants. A salesperson should perform the following functions during the sales presentation:

1. Welcome the customer and gain the customer's trust and respect.
2. Determine which product best fulfills the customer's needs.
3. Provide friendly, courteous assistance in selecting the right product or service.
4. Demonstrate the product features.
5. Explain how the product or service will benefit the customer.
6. Answer the customer's objections.
7. Ask the customer to buy the product or service.
8. Suggest additional merchandise which may benefit the customer.
9. Reassure the customer that a wise buying decision was made.

Since selling involves satisfying the needs and wants of customers, salespeople must be certain they use effective human relations skills. Customers expect salespeople to be friendly, sincere, honest, and concerned. Selling begins and ends with the customer, and salespeople must use good human relations skills in dealing with customers.

Sales-Supporting Duties of the Salesperson

A salesperson spends about half the time personally assisting the customer. The other half of a salesperson's time is spent performing sales-supporting duties. These nonselling duties include stocking shelves, marking merchandise, building displays, maintaining adequate merchandise stock, studying merchandise, taking inventory, and keeping the selling area neat and clean.

These nonselling duties are very important. Customers expect to shop in a clean store which maintains a stock of quality merchandise. A good salesperson takes pride in the business and spends a considerable amount of nonselling time keeping the sales area neat and clean.

ILLUSTRATION 2-2
Nonselling duties, such as keeping the sales area neat, are important.

Courtesy of Sears, Roebuck and Co.

PERSONALITY TRAITS NEEDED BY SALESPEOPLE

Most career salespeople agree that to be successful in sales you must develop sound selling techniques. Few salespeople ever question the fact that sales knowledge and selling skills are important to their job. Salespeople would not expect to advance very far in a selling career without good selling skills.

But selling is more than just having good selling skills. In fact, very few salespeople lose their jobs because they do not have adequate sales skills. A recent business survey found that, of all the people who lost their jobs, only 10 percent were fired due to a lack of job skills. Ninety percent were fired because of poor personality traits. A pleasing personality is essential to sales success. Therefore, while you are learning how to sell, you also need to spend some time learning about your own personality and how to improve it.

What do the following comments mean? "Judy certainly is a charming salesperson. She is loaded with personality." "Ralph has a lot of ability, but he'll never get ahead in sales because he has a poor personality." When we talk about a person's personality, what are we really talking about?

The term *personality* comes from the word *person*. **Personality** is what people see when they look at you, what they hear when you speak, and what they feel when in your presence. Personality is the total of all your attitudes, habits, and feelings. It is the total of all your traits and it sets you apart from all others. Your personality is a combination of the responses and feelings you express in everyday life. Personality is the most important factor in determining whether you are liked or disliked by others. It determines your ability to obtain friendly cooperation from your employers, your fellow employees, and your customers.

ILLUSTRATION 2-3
Your personality is the total of all your attitudes, habits, and feelings.

The majority of your habits may be good, but if you have one particularly bad habit, it may give you the reputation of having a poor personality. It is very important for you to develop a pleasing sales personality.

Attitudes, habits, and feelings are the three factors which make up your personality. When combined, these factors form a **trait**. Fortunately, personality traits can be changed and improved. What personality traits are desirable for salespeople? Take a look at the following list.

Personality Traits Needed by Salespeople

ambition	initiative
professionalism	loyalty
cooperation	neatness
consideration	poise
courtesy	punctuality
dependability	self-confidence
empathy	self-control
enthusiasm	sense of humor
honesty	tact

To better understand each of the personality traits needed by successful salespeople, read the following descriptions:

Ambition

Having **ambition** means you are constantly trying to improve yourself. To advance in sales, you need to do more than the minimum required and be better than average.

Professionalism

Customers like salespeople who know about the products and services they sell. Having **professionalism** means that you treat customers with courtesy, honesty, and sincerity. Being professional also means that you make it your business to help customers.

Cooperation

Business is a team effort. To have a successful team, everyone must make a contribution. **Cooperation** is one of the foundations of business. If you are cooperative, you are concerned about the welfare of the business, your co-workers, your customers, and not just about yourself.

Consideration

To be liked by other people, you must have **consideration** or concern for the feelings and rights of other people.

Courtesy

Courtesy is shown in the respect you give to other people. A courteous person is considerate of the rights and ideas of others and is sincerely interested in what people are doing and saying.

Dependability

Can you be counted on to do the job you are assigned and carry it out to its completion? Dependable people can. **Dependability** at work means you are always on time, you always go to work unless an absence is unavoidable, and you always complete your assigned tasks.

Empathy

Empathy is concern for the interests and feelings of other people. In selling, empathy means being interested in your customers, listening to customers, and attempting to understand customers' feelings.

Enthusiasm

Enthusiasm about your sales job makes life more pleasant and rewarding than working only because you have to. Being enthusiastic means you like your job and the products and services you provide your customers. Enthusiasm is catching. If you're excited about your job, your customers will probably see that and become interested in what you have to sell.

Honesty

A basic requirement for success in selling is **honesty**. Being honest with your employer means giving a full day's work for a full day's pay. Being honest with your customers means that you don't make false claims about a product. Salespeople should never make promises they cannot keep.

Initiative

Initiative is the ability to take action on your own. Initiative involves knowing what needs to be done and doing it. Salespeople with initiative know what sales-supporting jobs need to be done and they complete them without waiting to be told.

Loyalty

If you work for a business, be **loyal** to it. When you talk about the business, speak well of it. Don't gossip about what happens at work or about your employer. If you learn something that should be kept confidential, don't discuss it with other people.

Neatness

Neatness in your personal appearance is very important. The way you dress and the clothes you wear will depend upon the kind of sales work you do. Appropriate dress usually is based on the image the business or store wants to create.

Poise

The salesperson who possesses the ability to remain calm and in control at all times has **poise**. Poise is developed through sales practice and learning all you can about your products and services. Customers enjoy buying from salespeople who are calm, confident, and poised. Salespeople who lack poise are easily frustrated and have a difficult time completing sales.

Punctuality

If you have an appointment with a customer, be on time. Customers and employers expect salespeople to meet promised deadlines with **punctuality**. A punctual salesperson arrives at work on time.

Self-confidence

Customers enjoy buying from salespeople who have **self-confidence**. Salespeople should display confidence in their business, in the products and services they sell, and in their own sales abilities. Customers need to be assured that they are doing the right thing. A salesperson's self-confidence should be demonstrated by a calm, enthusiastic, and business-like manner.

Self-control

There is no easy way to develop **self-control**—the ability to stay calm under trying situations—but it must be done. The salesperson must always have control of the sales situation. Never let a customer visibly upset you or make you angry. Successful salespeople understand that the customer is always right. Always avoid arguing with the customer. You may win the argument but lose the customer's business.

Sense of humor

Can you smile and enjoy a joke even if it is played on you? Or are you easily offended? Salespeople must avoid being too serious about themselves. Having a **sense of humor** means you can laugh when the joke is on you, and with others when the fun points elsewhere. You need to be understanding and tolerant of other people's actions even though they may differ from your own.

Tact

Tact is the ability to say the right thing at the right time. Customers can be easily offended, so think before you speak. Salespeople need to be considerate of their customers' feelings. Treat your customers with courtesy, sincerity, and honesty.

Do you possess all of these traits? Probably not. In fact, few people do. But that doesn't mean that you should not try to develop every desirable trait in your own personality.

DEVELOPING A SALES PERSONALITY

For those who need to improve certain personality traits, it is good to know that this is possible. The personality traits needed for a successful selling career can be developed. However, personality traits cannot be changed overnight. A person's existing personality has been formed over many years and it will take time and honest effort to make any basic changes.

How can you change or improve your personality? First, recognize that your personality traits belong to you. No one can change them without your consent and cooperation. Unless you are willing to admit that you can improve your own personality, no progress can be made.

To begin a personality improvement plan, have a good reason for wanting to improve. "I would like to be a happier person" or "I want customers or other people to like me a little bit more" are good reasons to make changes. If you don't have a good reason for improvement, it is unlikely that your personality will change.

The second step in your personality improvement program is to select one or two habits, attitudes, or feelings you want to improve. Don't attempt to change too many traits at once. Once you have identified what you want to improve, learn the desired trait and then practice it with customers and other people.

WHAT CUSTOMERS EXPECT FROM SALESPEOPLE

Today's customers are the best read, most informed, most intelligent, and most demanding in the history of our country. Today's customers are not just buying products — they are buying benefits. They want to know how they will benefit from buying certain products or services.

Businesses and salespeople must respond to customer demands by providing better products and improved services. Customers want the best and the most for their money, just as you do. To be successful, however, businesses need to offer more than just good products and services.

Customers Expect Salespeople To...

- be friendly and helpful.
- provide prompt service.
- have a neat appearance.
- be courteous and patient.
- show them the benefits of a purchase.
- listen to them and understand their desires.
- answer their questions.
- provide suggestions on products and services.
- give accurate information.
- help them buy to their best advantage.
- be interested in customer satisfaction after the sale.
- show an all-out determination to please.
- remember customer preferences.
- assist them in making a wise buying decision.

Why do people shop at one store rather than another? There are several reasons which are known as **patronage motives.** Patronage motives, or the reasons why people shop at a specific business, vary among customers. The following table gives examples of patronage motives.

Patronage Motives

- friendly, helpful salespeople
- a wide selection of quality merchandise
- a clean appearance and good displays
- the store's location
- product guarantees and warranties
- customer services
- the pricing practices of the store
- the business's advertising
- the reputation of the business

Although all of these factors are important to the customer, one stands out above the others. It is estimated that 90 percent of the customers who leave a store and do not return do so because of lack of courtesy shown by salespeople — not because of prices, lack of merchandise, or proper facilities. You, the salesperson, are the most important service a business can provide to customers.

Customers expect to receive friendly, courteous assistance from salespeople. If they don't, they may not complain but may never return to shop at the business again. The following story illustrates the feelings of a typical customer toward the importance of service received from a business.

The Customer That Never Returns

I'm basically a nice person. I have lots of friends and people like me. I'm also the customer who never argues or complains, regardless of the service I receive.

I'll go into a department and wait and wait while the salesperson talks to a friend and ignores me. Even when someone else who comes into the department after me is helped first, I don't complain. I just wait.

Last week I took a pair of slacks back to a clothing store. I had paid $35 for the slacks, but during the alteration of the pant legs, one leg was made longer than the other. Because I hadn't tried on the slacks when I picked them up, I agreed that it was my fault. I had been in a hurry that day, so rather than argue about the extra charge, I decided to take the loss myself.

It's seldom that I ever return merchandise or complain about service. People just get too upset when they have to handle complaints, and life is much too short to argue over minor inconveniences.

Once I bought a hair dryer that burned out the first week I used it. I hated to bother the store's sales staff, but thought they could give me an address of an electric appliance repair shop. I didn't even get a chance to explain this because the salesperson was so busy telling me that I had intentionally burned the dryer out. I politely said, 'Thank you,' and left the store.

I never argue or criticize and I never ridicule a salesperson in a store. I really am a nice customer. Do you know who else I am? I'M THE CUSTOMER THAT NEVER RETURNS!

That's my personal revenge for the treatment I receive. I will take anything you hand out, but I'll never come back. Sure, it would be easier to tell you exactly what I feel and release my emotions right away, but in the long run my satisfaction comes from your loss of my business. You might not think I'm such a nice person now. Even though I quietly listen to your accusations, I get even in my own way.

A large city newspaper conducted a survey of its readership to determine what makes a good salesperson. The results showed that the four most-mentioned characteristics were: (1) "The good salesperson has the ability to understand my desires"; (2) "The good salesperson is courteous and patient"; (3) "The good salesperson is friendly"; and (4) "The good salesperson has the ability to help me buy to my best advantage."

A major magazine conducted a similar survey to learn the ingredients that make up a successful retail salesperson. They found there were four primary areas in which a salesperson must excel to be successful in retail selling: attitude, merchandise information, techniques of selling, and human relations.

WHAT EMPLOYERS EXPECT FROM A SALESPERSON

Businesses are run to satisfy the needs and wants of customers and to make a profit. Profits are based on sales. The more goods and services a business sells, the higher the profits will be. Employers, therefore, expect their salespeople to be good at selling.

Employers also expect salespeople to have positive work attitudes. As a salesperson, you must be able to work with other people. Employers expect salespeople to practice good **human relations.** Attitudes such as cooperation, dependability, enthu-

ILLUSTRATION 2-5
Employers expect salespeople to have positive work attitudes, such as honesty and dependability.

siasm, empathy, honesty, and initiative have been mentioned as personality traits salespeople need. In addition to these traits, employers expect you to have additional character traits which specifically relate to your attitude toward your job. Employers, in return for a day's pay, expect you to be willing to learn more about selling, to follow directions, to accept criticism, and to be loyal to the store and its owner.

Willingness to Learn More About Selling

Since selling is your most important job, your employer wants you to be as effective as possible. Your employer will want you to spend time improving your selling skills. More specifically, your employer will want you to learn more about the business's products and services, how to handle customers according to store policies, and how to use selling skills to satisfy the customers.

Selling is hard work. To be an effective salesperson you must study your job, work on personality skills, and practice effective selling techniques. A good salesperson always analyzes selling skills and tries to improve sales performance. Employers want employees who are interested in and willing to learn more about selling. The results can benefit you both.

Willingness to Follow Directions

As a new salesperson, you will receive training and directions from other experienced salespeople as well as from the owner or manager of the business. When you are given directions, it is important to follow them to the letter. In most cases businesses have reasons for doing things in a certain way. After you have more sales experience, you may wish to suggest ways to improve doing things. However, as a new employee, you should hold your suggestions until you're absolutely certain they will improve sales procedures. Experience is a good teacher, and too many suggestions from new employees are met with resentment from experienced salespeople.

Ability to Accept Criticism

In most situations, criticism is given to let you know what is expected of you and to make you aware of the areas you need to improve. As a salesperson, you must be able to accept criticism. To improve as a salesperson, learn to benefit from the criticism you are given.

You should expect criticism from your employer; do not take the criticism as a personal insult. Accept criticism for what it should be — a means of becoming a better salesperson. Constantly try to improve your sales and human relations skills.

Loyalty to Your Employer

Loyalty is one of the most important qualities salespeople should possess because salespeople play such an important role in creating a business's favorable image. Often the salesperson is the only person the customer meets in the business. As a loyal employee, you should represent the business in a manner which pleases management and creates a good customer image.

Loyalty can be expressed in many ways. As a new employee, you will be expected to learn and follow business rules and policies. You should not publicly criticize the business or its policies. It is important that you accept these policies, and it is your responsibility to carry them out. As a loyal employee, you should avoid gossiping, spreading rumors, or criticizing fellow employees, managers, or owners. If a salesperson does not speak well of the business, the customer will not have a good image of the business.

SALES TERMS

salesperson	consideration	poise
order-taker	courtesy	punctuality
customer-oriented selling	dependability	self-confidence
personal selling	empathy	self-control
personality	enthusiasm	sense of humor
trait	honesty	tact
ambition	initiative	patronage motives
professionalism	loyalty	human relations
cooperation	neatness	

SALES QUESTIONS

1. Explain the difference between selling functions and sales-supporting functions.

2. What is the difference between a salesperson and an order-taker?

3. What does it mean for a salesperson to be customer oriented?

4. Explain the statement: "No one is a born salesperson."

5. Why are nonselling duties important?

6. Are selling duties or nonselling duties more important? Explain.

7. List at least seven sales-supporting duties performed by a salesperson.

8. Which personality traits do you believe are most important for a customer-oriented salesperson?

9. When you shop for school clothes, which patronage motives are important to you?

10. What is the most common reason customers give for leaving a store and not returning?

11. List at least four characteristics customers expect from salespeople. Which of these do you feel are most important? Why?

12. List at least five qualities an employer expects to find in a salesperson.

SALES ACTIVITIES

A. In stores where you shop, are most of the sales personnel "salespeople" or "order-takers"? Explain.

B. Think of a person you enjoy or consider a friend. List the personality traits which you think are strengths of that person. Of the personality traits listed, which do you think are most important? Why?

C. Which of the selling functions listed on page 13 do you think would be the most difficult to develop?

D. Jill Evers has just started her first job as a salesperson in the women's department of a large department store. Two employees, Betty Bennett and Stan Holmes, ask Jill to go to lunch with them at the end of Jill's second week on the job. During lunch Betty talks freely and critically about the department manager, about store policies, and about how hard it is to suggest any new ideas to the manager. Jill agrees with Betty and says: "He seems to know all the answers and doesn't encourage suggestions from anyone. Maybe he's afraid our ideas will be better than his."

The next day Jill is called into the store manager's office and is criticized by the department manager for her remarks. Jill immediately realizes that one of her luncheon companions reported her remarks to the department manager.

1. What did Jill do wrong?
2. If you were Jill, what would you have done differently in handling this situation?
3. How do you think the department manager feels toward Jill?

THE BUYING AND SELLING PROCESS

Your Learning Goals

After studying this chapter, you should:

- *understand the five stages of the customer's buying process.*
- *know how to lead the customer through the five stages of the buying process.*
- *know the seven steps of a sale.*
- *identify selling techniques which should be used in each step of the sale.*
- *understand the* you *attitude in selling.*
- *understand the importance of customer empathy.*

Two parties, the salesperson and the customer, participate in every sale. The selling process involves a customer buying a product or service from a salesperson. The salesperson's job in this process is to satisfy the needs and wants of the customer. Selling the correct product or service to the customer will satisfy those wants and needs.

The selling process begins and ends with customers. Before you can satisfy customers' needs and wants, you must understand their buying motives. An effective salesperson understands the reasons customers purchase products and services, then sells those products which have benefits that will satisfy the customers' needs. The customers' needs or wants are satisfied when a benefit or personal gain is received from the products or services purchased.

The selling process ends when customers purchase products or services which satisfy their needs and wants. As seen in Illustration 3-1, the buying and selling process is divided into two parts: (1) the customers' buying process, and (2) the selling techniques used by the salesperson.

ILLUSTRATION 3-1
The buying and selling process involves the customer and the salesperson.

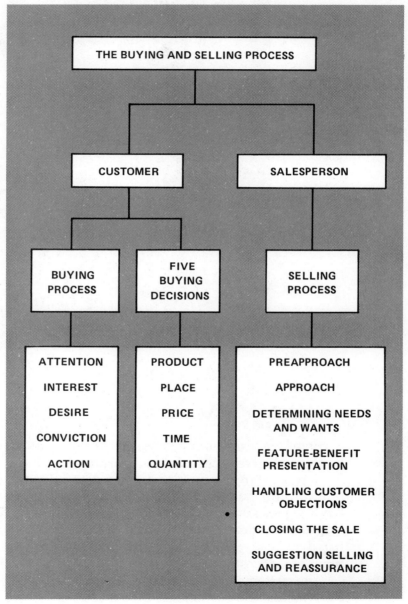

ILLUSTRATION 3-2
Customers' needs or wants are satisfied when a benefit is received from the product purchased.

THE CUSTOMERS' BUYING PROCESS

Before buying, your customer will consciously or unconsciously go through fives stages of self-persuasion. These five stages are fundamental to any purchase. They determine the customer's attitude toward buying a product or service. The five stages of the buying process are shown in Illustration 3-3. The five mental stages a customer goes through in making a buying decision are listed in a stepladder sequence because the customer normally completes the steps in order.

The customer's first mental stage in the buying process, **attention**, means the customer is aware of a need or want for a product

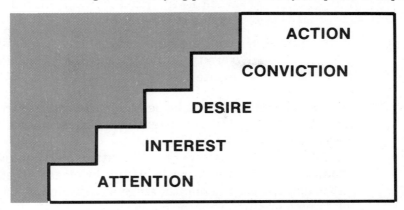

or service. The customer's attention to the product may be obtained by the salesperson's approach. For example, see how the salesperson directs the attention of this couple to a product which may satisfy their need for a graduation gift.

Salesperson: Good morning. Isn't it a beautiful spring day?

Mr. Johnson: It certainly is. We would rather be outside today, but at the moment we need a graduation gift for our nephew.

ILLUSTRATION 3-4
A salesperson directs customers' attention to a product which may satisfy their needs.

Salesperson:	We surely have been busy with graduation only a week away. Have you considered luggage or perhaps a briefcase for him?
Mrs. Johnson:	Well, he has an academic scholarship to the university, so maybe a briefcase would be an appropriate gift.

As you can see, the salesperson has gained control of the sale by directing the customers' attention to merchandise which may interest them.

Now that the salesperson has attracted the customers' attention, the customers' interest in the briefcase must be developed. **Interest,** the second mental stage a customer goes through in purchasing a product, is based on personal feelings. What the customer is thinking about is important. Remember, to develop interest in a product, you must find out what the customer personally feels is important, and then sell those benefits.

A customer's interest can be determined by asking questions. Note how this salesperson asks questions to determine the customers' interest in the product.

Salesperson:	My name is Deb Staton. I'll be happy to help you find a nice gift for your nephew.
Mr. Johnson:	Thank you. I'm Frank Johnson and this is my wife Barbara.
Salesperson:	You mentioned that your nephew received an academic scholarship to the university. You'll probably want a briefcase that will last him at least four years or longer.
Mrs. Johnson:	Yes, Dana will probably go on to graduate school.
Salesperson:	Well, we certainly have some quality briefcases for students and executives. For instance, let's look at this model. [*She hands Mrs. Johnson the briefcase.*] Mrs. Johnson, do either you or your husband carry a briefcase in your work?
Mrs. Johnson:	Yes, I'm a college professor and my husband is an engineer. We each carry a briefcase to work every day.
Salesperson:	Then I'm sure you know what features to look for in a briefcase. This particular briefcase has many features useful to a college student. But before I

	explain the features I think will most benefit your nephew, let me ask you what features you want in a briefcase.
Mrs. Johnson:	Well, I do a lot of traveling so I want a tough fabric and body. I also want a good lock and individual compartments for filing papers by different classes. Dana would probably want these same features.
Salesperson:	You're absolutely right, Mrs. Johnson. A good briefcase has all those features.

The salesperson has created interest in the briefcase by handing the briefcase to Mrs. Johnson and asking her opinion about it.

The next stage in the customer's buying process is **desire**. When customers reach this stage, they have already shown interest in the product and are considering purchasing the product. A salesperson can create desire for the product by demonstrating how the product will satisfy the customers' needs. It is important in creating desire for the product that the salesperson sell the features and benefits which are important to the customer. Notice, as the sale continues, that the salesperson creates desire by selling the benefits which Mrs. Johnson said were important.

Salesperson:	The features you listed — the tough body, good lock, and individual compartments — are all very important in buying a good briefcase. This briefcase has a quality lock which is guaranteed for the life of the briefcase. If Dana ever has trouble with this lock, we will replace it free of charge.
Mrs. Johnson:	I agree, the lock is very easy to operate.
Salesperson:	The guarantee is given on the handle as well. We also guarantee the body of the briefcase for ten years, so you don't need to worry about the toughness of the body. Tap the body of the case and I'm sure you'll note how sturdy, strong, and durable it is. Now open it up. This case features individual compartments. That means Dana could have one compartment for every class he takes. That will certainly make it easy to organize his homework for each course during the semester. Not many briefcases offer that benefit. Lift the briefcase, Mr. Johnson. Note how lightweight it is. It is designed

ILLUSTRATION 3-5
A salesperson can create desire for a product by demonstrating how the product will satisfy customers' needs.

with comfort in mind. Books can be heavy and if Dana's classes are far apart, carrying the case should be as easy as possible.

Salesperson: Mrs. Johnson, wouldn't you agree that the weight and comfort of the briefcase are important factors to consider?

Mrs. Johnson: Yes, there is certainly no need for the extra weight of a briefcase.

The salesperson has created desire by involving the customers in the sale. Desire is created by showing how the product will benefit the customer. It is important that the customer be actively involved in the sale by answering questions and using the product, if possible.

The next mental stage a customer goes through is **conviction.** Conviction is achieved when customers become convinced that the product will satisfy their needs. Customers are convinced about the benefits of the product when they agree that the product will satisfy their needs.

The salesperson can determine the customers' conviction to buy the product by getting positive responses to questions about the product's features and benefits. As this sale continues, notice how the salesperson determines the customers' conviction for the product.

Salesperson: Mrs. Johnson, you noticed how lightweight the briefcase is. That's a special bonded leather exterior with a full cloth innerlining. There is no lighter weight or tougher material available in a briefcase. You're certainly right about the important features, too. A good briefcase has good locks, a tough body, and individual compartments. Wouldn't you agree that this briefcase has all three of these features?

Mrs. Johnson: Yes.

Salesperson: Dana will not have to worry about the briefcase being damaged or destroyed. In addition don't you think this quality briefcase will make it easy for him to organize his course work by filing materials in these five compartments, one for each course?

Mrs. Johnson: Yes, that is certainly a nice feature.

Salesperson: And you both agree that the lightweight body makes it easy to carry?

Mr. and Mrs. Johnson: [*Nodding their heads, yes.*]

Salesperson: In fact, Mrs. Johnson, if someone were buying a briefcase for you, this one would probably fulfill your needs, wouldn't it?

Mrs. Johnson: [*Smiling*] Yes, it would.

The salesperson determined the customers' conviction by asking a series of questions. In fact, Deb asked her customers four questions to determine how strong a desire and conviction they had to purchase the briefcase. Receiving positive responses to these questions, she has determined that the customers are convinced that buying the briefcase would be a wise buying decision. The **action** stage is the one remaining stage in the customer's buying process. The customers have already shown attention, interest, desire, and conviction for the product. The action stage is the final step when the salesperson closes the sale. The sale concludes:

Salesperson:	Do you think Dana would prefer the black or the brown briefcase?
Mrs. Johnson:	Probably the brown case. He chose brown luggage for Christmas.
Salesperson:	We will also personalize the briefcase by sealing his initials next to the lock. What is the first letter of his last name?
Mr. Johnson:	It is J for Johnson.
Salesperson:	Thank you. Then DJ will be the initials you want on the case?
Mrs. Johnson:	Yes, that's fine.
Salesperson:	Would you like to use your credit card or will this be cash?
Mrs. Johnson:	No, I don't want to charge it. I'll pay cash.
Salesperson:	Fine. Dana certainly is a lucky graduate. This is a beautiful and very functional gift. You have made a wise buying decision.
Salesperson:	By the way, Mrs. Johnson, are you aware of the air travel regulation which states that you must have your name and address on carry-on luggage or briefcases? We have a half-price special on a matching name tag for people who purchase luggage or briefcases. Would you like a matching brown leather name tag for Dana's gift?

ILLUSTRATION 3-6
An effective salesperson suggests additional related items which
would benefit customers.

Mrs. Johnson:	How much are they?
Salesperson:	Regularly $5.95; but since you have purchased a briefcase, it will be only $2.98.
Mrs. Johnson:	Okay, that will make it even more personal.
Salesperson:	I'll bet you'd like this gift wrapped since it's a graduation present. You may take it to customer services in the back of the store for free gift wrapping.

ILLUSTRATION 3-7
Suggesting services, such as gift wrapping, adds to customer satisfaction.

The action stage is the last stage in the customer's buying process. It is important for the salesperson to understand when the customer is ready to purchase. Many sales are lost because salespeople simply fail to ask the customer for action to purchase. If the customer has gone through the mental stages of attention, interest, desire, and conviction, the action stage of closing the sale is merely a matter of asking the customer to buy.

As a salesperson, you must be aware of the customer's mental attitude toward purchasing the product or service. Once this has been determined, you can use specific selling skills to assist the customer in making a wise buying decision. Illustration 3-8 summarizes the selling skills you may use to lead the customer through the five mental stages to a buying decision.

ILLUSTRATION 3-8

Salespeople use specific selling techniques to lead customers through the five mental stages to a buying decision.

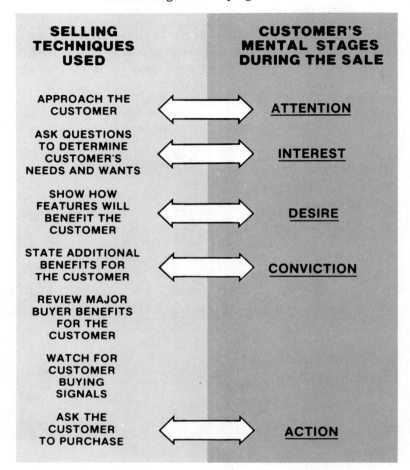

SELLING TECHNIQUES USED	CUSTOMER'S MENTAL STAGES DURING THE SALE
APPROACH THE CUSTOMER	<u>ATTENTION</u>
ASK QUESTIONS TO DETERMINE CUSTOMER'S NEEDS AND WANTS	<u>INTEREST</u>
SHOW HOW FEATURES WILL BENEFIT THE CUSTOMER	<u>DESIRE</u>
STATE ADDITIONAL BENEFITS FOR THE CUSTOMER	<u>CONVICTION</u>
REVIEW MAJOR BUYER BENEFITS FOR THE CUSTOMER	
WATCH FOR CUSTOMER BUYING SIGNALS	
ASK THE CUSTOMER TO PURCHASE	<u>ACTION</u>

SALES PROCESS — THE STEPS OF A SALE

The fundamentals of the selling process apply to all fields of selling. The techniques used by a retail salesperson may be used effectively by wholesale and industrial salespeople as well. In fact, every person involved in selling will use these techniques in some way.

The sales process can be divided into seven specific steps, as shown in Illustration 3-9. Certain selling techniques are used in each of these steps. You must learn to use these techniques to successfully sell a product or service.

ILLUSTRATION 3-9
The sales process can be divided into seven steps.

SUGGESTION SELLING
AND REASSURANCE

CLOSING THE SALE

HANDLING CUSTOMER
OBJECTIONS

FEATURE - BENEFIT
PRESENTATION

DETERMINING NEEDS AND WANTS

APPROACH

PREAPPROACH

Preapproach

The **preapproach** literally means "before the approach." It is the salesperson's preparation for a sale. As a salesperson, you need to spend time preparing to make a sale. According to some experts, selling is 90 percent preparation and 10 percent presentation. Time spent getting ready to sell is definitely time well spent.

What should you do to prepare yourself to sell your products or services to your customers? In order to make effective sales presentations, you must understand your customers' buying motives and your products' features and benefits. The salesperson, in addition to learning about products and customers, should be personally ready to sell. Since first impressions are so important, make sure your personal appearance is pleasant and businesslike.

Approach

The **approach** begins when you greet the customer. The purpose of the approach is to create a favorable impression of yourself to customers and to direct customers' attention to your product.

ILLUSTRATION 3-10
The approach creates a favorable impression on customers and directs their attention to the product or service.

Your goal is to convince the customers of your sincere interest in assisting them. You are trying to show the customers that you like them, understand them, and want to help them.

Determining Customer Needs and Wants

Once you have directed a customer's attention to a product, your next step is to determine the customer's needs and wants. Since many customers may not know exactly what they are looking for, it is important that you ask them well-chosen questions to determine their personal interests about a product or service. Listen carefully to their responses. Your customers' responses and reactions will help you select the right product or service for their needs. After selecting a particular product or service to sell, you now need to sell the customers on how the product or service will benefit them.

Making a Feature-Benefit Presentation

When your customers have expressed an interest in a product or service, your job is to sell the features, advantages, and benefits of that product or service. Remember that a benefit to you may not be a benefit to your customers. Ask your customers questions to determine what they really want. You can get them to reveal what they want by asking opinion questions. Questions such as: "What do you expect from this service?" "Does this suit you better?" "Would this feature be better for you?" are opinion questions. An **opinion question** is a question asked of customers to determine their attitudes or feelings about a product or service. Your job is to create interest by translating product features into buyer benefits. In order to do this, you need to know the customers' personal opinions about the product features.

How do you create desire in customers to purchase a product or service? Have you heard the phrase, "Seeing is believing"? It is much easier to convince your customers how a product or service will benefit them by showing them the product. Don't just talk about it. If it is small, hand the product to the customer. Have the customers try the product. If possible, demonstrate to the customers how the product works. Since it is your job to create desire, show your customers the product's benefits or help them visualize the benefits they will enjoy after purchasing the product. When you have shown the customer how the product features will benefit them, you have given a **feature-benefit presentation.** Effective salespeople appeal to as many of their customers' five senses — touch, sight, hearing, taste, and smell — as possible. Continue to stress all the benefits that the customer said were important.

Handling Customer Objections

Customer objections are reasons customers hesitate in purchasing a product or service. Objections may come at any time during a sale. Experienced salespeople view objections as a natural part of most sales and aren't alarmed when customers raise objections. Customers may raise objections because they don't really understand the product or its benefits.

In handling objections, you should:

1. listen for the real objection.
2. pause before answering the objection.
3. show empathy — don't evade or minimize the objection.
4. restate the objection.
5. answer the objection completely and concisely.

Remember, never argue with customers. Remain poised. Never downgrade your competition. Turn your customers' objections into positive selling points.

Closing the Sale

The **close** may come at any time during the sale. When you sense that customers have a strong desire for the product and have a positive attitude toward buying, try to close the sale. Your customers may give you buying signals as clues. A buying signal may be a facial expression, a "yes" answer to a series of questions, or a nod of the head. Many sales are lost because salespeople fail to ask for the sale. Be ready to close the sale. If you have effectively completed the previous steps of the sale, you should feel confident that your attempts to close the sale will be successful. Each customer has different needs and wants. Some customers will want a lot of product information, others will want less information. Base the timing of your close of the sale on the customer's reaction to your sales presentation.

Suggestion Selling and Reassurance

Suggestion selling is the process of selling customers an item to go with what they have already purchased. Once customers have decided to purchase a product or service, the salesperson should determine if the customers have other product needs by suggesting items which are directly related to the originally purchased item. Use suggestion selling as a sincere method of helping customers. For example, when customers buy paint, make sure they have brushes, cleaner, or other painting supplies needed to complete their painting job.

The sale ends when the salesperson reassures the customers that they have made a wise buying decision. Customers will feel even better about their purchase decisions if they receive sincere reassurance from the salesperson.

Summary of the Steps of a Sale

The outline on page 45 reviews the seven steps of a sale and lists the techniques you should use in performing each step. The techniques are the selling skills which salespeople should use in assisting customers. They are presented in this chapter as an overview to the selling process. Each of these steps will be discussed in detail in later chapters.

DEVELOPING THE YOU ATTITUDE IN SELLING

To be an effective salesperson, you must be able to get and keep customers. One way of doing this is by determining and using the customer's point of view. When you can do this, you are developing the *you* attitude.

Seven Sales Steps and Techniques

1. THE PREAPPROACH
   - Learn the features and benefits of your products or services.
   - Study your customer and the customer's buying motives.

2. THE APPROACH
   - Greet the customer with a warm, friendly welcome.
   - Gain the customer's confidence.
   - Direct the customer's attention to the product or service.

3. DETERMINING CUSTOMER NEEDS AND WANTS
   - Ask the customer questions.
   - Listen to the customer's answers.
   - Observe the customer's reactions.
   - Analyze the customer's responses and comments.
   - Select products for the sales presentation.

4. MAKING A FEATURE-BENEFIT PRESENTATION
   - Learn the features of products or services.
   - Translate product features into buyer benefits.
   - Create customer interest in the product or service.
   - Involve the customer in the presentation.
   - Get the product into the customer's hands.
   - Appeal to all five of the customer's senses.
   - Demonstrate the product's features and buyer benefits.
   - Develop customer desire for the product or service.

5. HANDLING CUSTOMER OBJECTIONS
   - Welcome customer objections.
   - Answer and overcome each customer objection.
   - Provide additional buyer benefits.
   - Repeat or review major buyer benefits.
   - Develop customer conviction for the product or service.

6. CLOSING THE SALE
   - Get agreement from the customer.
   - Watch for buying signals.
   - Attempt trial closes.
   - Assist the customer in making buying decisions.

7. SUGGESTION SELLING AND REASSURANCE
   - Suggest items to go with the purchase.
   - Demonstrate use of suggested items.
   - Ask the customer to purchase suggested items.
   - Reassure the customer that a wise buying decision was made.
   - Thank the customer and invite the customer to return.

Part of your sales job is to make your presentation acceptable from the customer's point of view. The sale, therefore, should be based on the customer. If you want a customer's business, remember that the *U* comes before the *I* in *business*.

This seems like a very easy approach to selling, doesn't it? First, learn your customers' needs and wants; then sell them the products or services which will benefit them by satisfying those needs and wants. Although this may sound simple enough, researchers claim that 85 percent of the sales made today are not based on the needs and wants of customers.

Despite the fact that customers buy the benefit or personal gain received from a product rather than the product itself, most salespeople continue to sell only the product and its features. Customers do not buy a product for what it is or for its features. Customers buy benefits. Products are bought after customers have answered the basic question, "How will I benefit from this purchase?"

When you understand your customers' buying needs or what benefits they will receive from their purchases, you are developing the *you* attitude. The more you learn about your customers and their buying needs, the easier it will be for you to sell to them. Remember, what may seem like a benefit to one person may not seem like a benefit to another. For example, one customer may be interested in saving money on clothing purchases while another may not care about any savings. The other customer may be more interested in being a fashion leader. This person will gladly spend more money on clothes to win such recognition. To attempt to sell this customer clothes based on saving money will not work.

Make sure that when you are making a feature-benefit sales presentation, you are selling the benefits customers want from the product. Don't sell what you think is important or what you would want from the product. Too many salespeople attempt to sell what they regard as benefits. The key to developing the *you* attitude in selling is to find out the specific benefits your customers feel are important. Ask questions. This will allow your customers to tell you what they want in the product or service you are selling.

As a salesperson, you can use the following techniques in developing the *you* attitude approach to selling:

1. Understand customers' buying motives.
2. Ask the customers questions.
3. Listen to their responses.
4. Analyze their responses to determine their individual buying needs.
5. Sell the benefits or gains which fulfill the customers' specific buying needs.

Remember the term *empathy?* For salespeople, **customer empathy** means having a sincere concern for the interests and feelings of the customer. It means salespeople are interested enough in the customers to find out their specific buying needs and the benefits they hope to receive from purchasing the product or service. The result of customer empathy is selling products or services which best fulfill customers' wants and needs.

SALES TERMS

attention

interest

desire

conviction

action

preapproach

approach

opinion questions

feature-benefit presentation

customer objections

close

suggestion selling

customer empathy

SALES QUESTIONS

1. What are the five stages of a customer's buying process?

2. What selling skills can you use to:

   a. direct a customer's attention to a product?

   b. interest the customer in the product?

   c. create customer desire for the product?

   d. develop customer conviction for the product?

e. get the customer to take action to buy the product?

3. Why should you ask the customer questions during your sales presentation?

4. Why is it important to prepare for selling before meeting your customers? What should you do to prepare for selling?

5. What are the steps of the selling process?

6. What is the purpose of:

   a. the approach?
   b. the feature-benefit presentation?
   c. suggestion selling?

7. What is the *you* attitude in selling?

8. Customers will not purchase a product until they can answer the question, "How will I benefit from this purchase?" Explain this statement.

9. Explain this statement: "The selling process is really the buying process."

SALES ACTIVITIES

A. Using a recent purchase you've made as an example, describe how you made the five buying decisions.

B. Describe the selling techniques used to lead a customer through each of the mental stages which make up the buying process.

C. A customer has entered your store and is looking at a new lawn mower. How can you use the *you* attitude in serving this customer?

PREPARING TO SELL:
THE PREAPPROACH

PREPARING TO SELL:
THE PREAPPROACH

CHAPTER 4: YOUR CUSTOMER
CHAPTER 5: CUSTOMER BUYING MOTIVES
CHAPTER 6: PRODUCT INFORMATION

YOUR CUSTOMER

Your Learning Goals

After studying this chapter, you should:

- *be aware of the importance of customers to the business.*
- *treat the customer as a friend.*
- *understand what influences customers before they make a purchase.*
- *understand the wants and needs of customers.*
- *understand the different types of customers.*
- *recognize the different customer moods.*
- *know the five customer buying decisions.*

Customers—without them, businesses could not exist. Our whole economic system revolves around customers buying goods and services. Customers are a vital part of the buying and selling process. Therefore, salespeople must recognize that customers are their most important responsibility. Salespeople need to understand the factors which influence customers to buy, the different types of customers, the different types of customers' shopping moods and how to respond to them, and the five buying decisions customers must make.

THE CUSTOMER, YOUR BOSS

Customers are vital to a business. They are responsible for the salesperson's employment. Without customers, the salesperson would not have a job.

The goal of every sale is to satisfy the customers with the merchandise they purchase and the service they receive. To satisfy a customer, the salesperson must know and understand the product or service; but more importantly, the salesperson must treat the customer well. Every salesperson's efforts should center on satisfying the customers' needs and wants. Satisfied customers feel they are important.

The needs of the customer come before the needs of the salesperson. A good salesperson will help customers feel they are important. Treat the customer as you would treat a friend. Don't downgrade competitors and their products, don't rush the customer in order to make a sale nor tell the customer how knowledgeable salespeople are. Treat customers as individuals with special interests, special likes and dislikes, and special wants or needs. All customers are not alike, and it would be a mistake to treat them all alike.

ILLUSTRATION 4-1
A good salesperson helps customers feel they are important.

Customers today are quite knowledgeable and generally will not hesitate to ask questions. Customers like to feel that their business is appreciated. They don't want to feel that every sales dollar just means profit and that profit is the salesperson's only concern. Remember, the customer provides both your salary and your position as a salesperson.

Treat Your Customer Like a Friend...

- welcome each customer with a friendly smile.
- greet each customer promptly. .
- treat each customer as a special individual.
- show interest and concern to help customers find the product or service they need or want. Don't just stand by or be too casual.
- avoid casual conversation with other salespeople while waiting on a customer. Focus your attention on your customers.
- always use good manners.

INFLUENCES ON TODAY'S CUSTOMERS

To understand customers, you must understand people. People are not alike and do not always react in the same way. People's actions are determined by their feelings and emotions as well as their wants and needs. A successful salesperson must understand that customers are influenced by many things before making a purchase.

Store Image

One factor which influences customers is store image. **Store image** is the attitude customers have toward the business.

"I really like shopping at Diamond's Department Store. I always find what I'm looking for, and the salespeople are very helpful." This customer obviously has a good feeling about the store. The management and salespeople in this store have paid close attention to good customer service. They have created a good store image.

Previous Experience

Without a doubt, customers' attitudes are strongly influenced by how they have been treated in the past. Customers want to feel welcome. They want prompt, courteous service as well as a wide selection of merchandise or services from which to choose. If the customers have had good experiences with the business and the salespeople, they will want to do business there again.

Advertising

Customers are influenced by advertising—whether radio, TV, newspaper, magazine, billboard, or other forms. Advertising informs and persuades people to try a new product, service, or store. Advertising also reminds customers of what merchandise and services are available at a business.

Customers are exposed to advertising every day. Advertising plays a leading role in getting customers to come into a business to buy.

Displays

Customers are influenced by window displays and interior displays. A well-designed, colorful display helps to develop a customer's good attitude toward a business. Some businesses feel that

ILLUSTRATION 4-2
Interior displays enhance the merchandise and help to develop a customer's good attitude toward the business.

displays are not important. This is unfortunate because displays may be the customer's first impression of the business. Just as customers may enter a business because of an effective window display, so may they be discouraged by dirty or poorly arranged displays.

Interior displays are also important in selling. They can help the salesperson sell merchandise. These displays enhance the merchandise and show how it can be used. They also add to the internal appearance of the business.

Store Interior

Customers are influenced by the interior of a business. As a customer walks around looking at the selection of merchandise in a retail store, the customer develops an attitude toward the store. "This store sure seems junky." "I can't find what I'm looking for." "It's so crowded, I can hardly walk down the aisle." Do these comments sound familiar? The store interior should allow the customer to shop in a pleasant environment. Customers like to walk freely around the store, looking at merchandise.

The Store's Interior . . .

- should not be overcrowded with merchandise.
- should have wide aisles for comfortable movement.
- should be comfortably warm in the winter and cool in the summer.
- should provide good lighting. People want to see what they are buying.
- should have an interior design which is coordinated in both color and style.

Services

The services a business offers are important in getting and holding customers. Competition for customers means that businesses must provide better and more complete customer services. The following are a few examples of the services offered by some businesses:

1. delivery service provided by a pharmacy or drugstore.
2. a home interior consultant employed by a furniture store.
3. branch banks located in hotels, office buildings, and shopping centers.

ILLUSTRATION 4-3
The services a business offers are important in getting and holding customers.

4. gift wrapping done at a candy shop.
5. tennis courts and a pool available for use by motel guests.
6. ample parking and long store hours featured at a shopping center.
7. charge accounts, gift wrapping, layaway, elevators or escalators, and public rest rooms available at a retail store.

Store services vary. If the management feels that customers will shop at a store because of a special service, the store will generally offer it. For example, a supermarket in a large suburb may provide customers with a small post office, an electronic banking machine, a pharmacy, a greeting card display, and a flower shop in addition to the more conventional bakery, delicatessen, grocery, and meat department. Such a store offers the customer **one-stop shopping.** This convenience is sure to attract customers.

Merchandise Available

The products available for sale are important to customers. Customers want to select the product or service that will best fit their needs or wants. For instance, when a customer buys a shirt or blouse, the selection of color, style, price, quality, and pattern is important. A barbershop or beauty salon is expected to offer convenience; a comfortable, relaxed atmosphere; and personal, yet professional service.

Customers have different wants and needs. This is the reason why a variety of products or services are available. Customers want merchandise or services to be available at the right time, at a fair price, in the desired quantities, and in up-to-date colors, styles, and materials.

Most customers base their purchases on quality rather than just on price. After a product or service has been used for several months, price — not quality — is often forgotten.

There are many other ways in which customers are influenced to buy. People are influenced by the opinions of friends, coworkers, or family members. Customers often base the selection of a store and the merchandise or service they purchase on these influences.

YOUR CUSTOMERS' WANTS AND NEEDS

Customers are vital to every business. Customers' needs and wants are the basis of all economic activity. For example, research showed that consumers wanted a device that would add, subtract, multiply, and divide quickly and accurately. Consumers wanted calculators and were willing to buy them. A manufacturing company used the technology available to put together a calculator at the most economical price.

This basic economic example shows that merchandise is manufactured because of consumers' needs and wants. This process provides us with products while it also provides jobs and improves our standard of living.

As a salesperson, you must understand your customers' needs and wants. Although people are alike in many ways, they are all individuals. Recognize customers as individuals with special traits. Their personalities, interests, and values are important. People buy out of fear and for affection, pleasure, variety, curiosity, convenience, acceptance, recognition, and prestige. It's easy to understand why people buy merchandise and services when you understand their reasons for buying.

With the money we earn, we try to improve ourselves and to be successful and happy. A husband may buy life insurance for the protection and security of those who are financially dependent on him. A wife may encourage her husband to buy life insurance because she is afraid of what might happen to her and her children should her husband die. In this example, the husband's reason for buying insurance is protection for his family; the wife's reason is fear of the future.

Learn about customers' attitudes and their motives toward buying. Know their likes and dislikes. Learn how they react under different situations. Salespeople should learn everything they can about customers.

MEET YOUR CUSTOMER

Customers are the most important people to your business. As a salesperson, you want to make them feel welcome. An alert salesperson will give prompt, courteous attention to customers. When a salesperson meets a potential customer, the salesperson should determine the best way to help the customer buy.

Customers are predictable. They are either decided customers, undecided customers, or just-looking customers.

The Decided Customer

Decided customers know what they want to buy. You can identify decided customers by the way they walk, the expression in their eyes, the tone of their voices, and their facial expressions. They are positive in their movements. Decided customers like to make buying decisions.

Before they enter the store, decided customers are often already convinced of the item they want to buy. A friend may have recommended a certain product or the customer may have already satisfactorily used the product or service. Perhaps the customer wants to buy a specific product because that customer shopped around and read all the available literature. Decided customers consider the merits of the product and are well informed before buying.

Decided customers come into a store looking for a specific item. Usually customers ask where the item is located. Decided customers are often irritated in a self-service store or in a store where the salesperson is of very little help. Because they know what they want to buy, they want immediate, friendly service.

As you show decided customers the item, they may ask a few questions and then make the purchase. Give them the information they need. You should be more knowledgeable about the item than are your customers. There is no need to give decided customers a complete sales presentation unless they request it. Let them do the talking. You may want to ask a question or two, but don't sell them your ideas.

Agree with your customers' opinions and listen to what they have to say. Decided customers like salespeople who listen to them. Acting as if the customers are teaching you about the product helps build your customers' confidence. In fact, they may tell you something about the product that will be of help to you in a future sales situation.

Finally, never rush the customer into making an immediate decision. Decided customers do not like to be sold. They want to make the decision after they have considered all the facts about the item.

ILLUSTRATION 4-5
A decided customer may give you product information that will be useful in a future sales situation.

The Undecided Customer

Undecided customers do not know what to buy. It is the salesperson's responsibility to help undecided customers make up their minds. Some undecided customers worry about making purchases. It takes them a long time to decide. Salespeople can easily confuse undecided customers about what to buy. Show them only a few items. If you show them too much, they will become even more confused.

A common mistake some salespeople make is to continue to show more and more merchandise or give more and more information about too many products. These salespeople believe that they will eventually find a product that undecided customers will like. But this will only confuse these customers more. Rather than show undecided customers more merchandise, you need to ask questions about their needs, the use of the product, and their likes and dislikes. Then you can better select one or two products you feel will satisfy their needs. By selecting one or two products and by setting aside others they will not like, you will help the undecided customers to avoid further confusion.

Rather than offering undecided customers a choice, make small, positive statements to them about the product. This helps undecided customers to decide. You may have to assume that the undecided customer has made a decision. For example: "The white shirt will look best for all occasions" rather than, "Do you like the blue or white shirt better?" Or "We could deliver the stereo tomorrow morning" rather than, "Would you want the stero delivered tomorrow?" Don't offer the undecided customer a choice. Avoid confusion by helping undecided customers to make a decision. Limit their selection of merchandise. If you have made the wrong assumption and they tell you they prefer the other product, you still have helped them to select a product. Offer undecided customers just one course of action and assume they have made a decision.

The Just-Looking Customer

How often have you heard a salesperson ask, "May I help you?" and the customer answer, "No, I'm just looking"? The **just-looking customers** are the most difficult to sell. They may be a decided customer or an undecided customer, but they do not want the assistance of a salesperson. This seems to be a trend today. Customers are hesitant to tell the salesperson what they are looking for. However, just-looking customers are not to be ignored.

When a customer comes into the store, avoid saying, "May I help you?" Say, "Hello" with a warm, friendly smile, then pause for the customer to say something. Since today's customers tend to say, "I'm just looking," you should ask the customer, "Is there anything special you are looking for?" This question may bring out a decided or undecided customer's desire for a particular product or service. The customer may say, "Where are your sweaters located?" or "I'm looking for an inexpensive wedding gift," or "I'm interested in a new set of golf clubs."

A just-looking customer may also be a **casual looker**. These customers really have nothing in mind to buy when they come into a store. They may not have been in the store for a long time and want to see what is new. Many people go shopping just to have something to do. Don't ignore customers who tell you they are just looking. Invite them to look around your store. You may want to direct them to items of special interest. Make them feel welcome to shop in your store. Remember, customers who feel welcome in a store will return to shop again. They may be casual lookers today, but buyers tomorrow.

After you have invited customers to look around, don't forget them. Be alert. Don't get so involved in stock work and other duties that you forget your customers. Customers become irritated by salespeople who offer assistance and then cannot be found when needed.

ILLUSTRATION 4-6
Casual lookers may just want to see what is new in the store.

If you see just-looking customers pause to look at an item, don't run over to them and begin a sales presentation. Customers who want to look around resent this. An alert salesperson carefully observes customers. If customers show an interest in an item by picking it up and looking around for a salesperson, you should then approach them. When you approach them, make a positive statement about the item. By talking about the merchandise, you will likely make a sale.

ILLUSTRATION 4-7
An alert salesperson approaches a just-looking customer when the customer shows interest in an item.

CUSTOMER MOODS

While we have categorized customers as decided, undecided, or just-looking, you should be aware of their different moods. You need to be aware of these moods in order to better serve these customers. Customers' moods can change quickly. At one moment customers may be friendly and decided, and at the next moment they may become impatient and dominating. Customer moods change based upon what they are buying, how they are being served, what their values are, and even what has happened earlier in the day.

You should constantly be alert for the different customer moods. Advance preparation in handling different customer moods often results in a successful sale and a satisfied customer.

Customer Moods and How to Respond to Them

Customer Moods	Salesperson's Response
Talkative	Try to direct the conversation to the merchandise. Don't allow the conversation to wander off to other topics.
Silent	Get the customer to start talking. Ask questions that require more than a "yes" or "no" response.
Friendly	You can help this customer by giving information needed to make a wise buying decision. Talk with rather than at the customer.
Disagreeable or Argumentative	Listen to them. Don't argue. Agree with minor points of the conversation and base your presentation upon these points of agreement.
Timid or Sensitive	Be patient. Don't rush them. Support them by using empathy. Show evidence of factual information. Don't ridicule. Help them feel comfortable about purchasing the product or service.
Impatient	Serve them promptly. Answer questions. Don't try to oversell. Speed up the sales presentation by giving the basic features and customer benefits of the item being sold.
Dominating or Superior	Let them do the talking. Make them feel important. Present information quickly. Let these kinds of customers sell themselves.
Procrastinating	These customers want to delay buying. Get them to agree to key selling points. You may have to assume they will buy. After you have determined their needs, don't offer a choice of products.

CUSTOMER BUYING DECISIONS

Before a purchase is made, each person must have a need or want for a product or service. Based upon this need, the customer must answer these five questions.

1. What product should I buy?
2. Where should I buy?
3. What price should I pay?
4. What time should I buy?
5. What quantity should I buy?

No purchase is ever made until the customer has made all five decisions. All customers must make these buying decisions even though they may not be aware of them. These buying decisions are based on the needs and wants of customers. When customers become consciously aware of a need, they make the five buying decisions in order to purchase a product or service to satisfy that need.

The Product to Buy

"What product or service should I purchase?" The brand, convenience, reputation, size, model, color, quality, and style must all be considered when making a purchase. Today there are many similar kinds of products and services available to satisfy the different needs and wants of customers.

The Place to Buy

"Where should I buy?" Consumers select a place to buy for various reasons, such as service, salespeople, store atmosphere, and selection. For some consumers the place to buy is very important. The fact that a customer is proud to say a product or service was bought at a particular store reveals the importance of the store's image to the customer.

ILLUSTRATION 4-8
Consumers may shop at a store because of its atmosphere and selection.

The Price to Pay

"How much should I spend?" The price of products or services is considered when making a purchase. Customers want to buy a product that they feel is the best value for their money. The benefits of the product must be worth the price.

The Time to Buy

"When should I buy?" Consumers must ask how soon they need to make a purchase. Some purchases need to be made immediately while others can wait. A person who needs only routine dental care may put off a visit to the dentist until a more convenient time. But a toothache could quickly change the time to buy dental service.

The Quantity to Buy

"How many should I buy?" With some products, usually single-purpose items, customers buy just one—a camera, a set of golf clubs, a tennis racket, a television set. However, even if some merchandise is purchased in a single unit, it may need related products in order to function. For example, a camera needs film. If a store has film on sale, then the customers must decide how many pictures they want to take to determine how many rolls of film to buy. The decision of how many to buy is often based on cost. Salespeople can often increase their sales by suggesting items to go with an original purchase.

All five buying decisions are not of equal importance at every sale. For example, a person who is about to run out of gasoline will find time and place to be most important. What brand, how much to pay, and how much to buy are not as important. The important thing for this customer is to buy the product as soon as possible.

Customers have different wants and needs, are influenced by various factors, and have different moods. The better you understand your customers, the better the salesperson you will be.

SALES TERMS

store image	decided customer	just-looking customer
one-stop shopping	undecided customer	casual looker

SALES QUESTIONS

1. Around what group of people is economic activity centered?

2. Explain the goal of every sale.

3. What can a salesperson do in order to treat a customer like a friend?

4. List and explain the things that influence customers before they make a purchase.

5. What are the three types of customers a salesperson will meet?

6. Give a few suggestions on how to help each of the three types of customers to buy.

7. Explain the importance of understanding the moods of customers.

8. Explain the five buying decisions customers make before purchasing a product or a service.

SALES ACTIVITIES

A. Conduct a short survey by asking a few of your friends this question: "In general, what has been your attitude, as a customer, towards salespeople?" Write a short paper to explain the results of your survey.

B. Describe a recent purchase you made and how you were treated as a customer.

C. Think of a time when you entered a store as an undecided customer and left the store after making a purchase. What influenced you to become a decided customer?

D. As a just-looking customer, how would you like to be treated by a salesperson?

E. Your store manager has just asked you to conduct the sales training meeting for this week. The topic for this meeting is, "Focus Your Attention on Your Customer." What would you say at this sales meeting?

5

CUSTOMER BUYING MOTIVES

Your Learning Goals

After studying this chapter, you should:

- *understand what motivates customers to buy a product or service.*
- *know the seven most common buying motives.*
- *know the difference between the following classifications of buying motives:*

  primary and selective
  rational and emotional
  product and patronage

- *understand why a customer chooses to shop at a particular store.*
- *be aware that different buying motives are present in every sale.*
- *be aware of the importance of buying motives in every sale.*
- *understand the importance of appealing to the customer's strongest buying motives.*

Why do people buy the things they buy? Why do customers select one product or service over others? Whether consciously aware of them or not, people have reasons for their actions. Every buyer has a reason for trading money for a product or service. Sales are made because customers are motivated by the desire to make purchases.

All purchases are made because of a need or want for something. In fact, the needs and wants of customers are the basis of all economic activity. Whether customers have decided upon an item

ILLUSTRATION 5-1
The needs and wants of customers are the basis of all economic activity.

of merchandise or they are just looking around, all customers have one thing in common — trying to satisfy a need or want.

Sometimes it is difficult to separate the meanings of the terms *needs* and *wants*. The terms are often used interchangeably. "I need the car tonight." "I want a new pair of shoes." "Do you need to buy another record?" Actually, a **need** is something that is considered a basic necessity, such as food, clothing, and shelter. A **want** is something that is not essential, but is desired.

Why do some people buy expensive, name-brand clothes? Why does a homemaker purchase an expensive self-cleaning spray and steam iron rather than a less expensive iron? Why does a beginning golfer buy a well-advertised brand of golf balls rather than an unknown brand? Salespeople must know what motivates customers to satisfy their wants or needs.

BUYING MOTIVES

People do not make purchases without reasons. Salespeople must be aware of the reasons that motivate customers to buy products and services. A successful salesperson must understand why customers act as they do.

Customers come from different backgrounds with different interests and values. You must learn to recognize what influences customers when making a purchase. These influences are called **motives**. The reasons customers are influenced to purchase a product or service are called **buying motives.** Buying motives are based upon the customers' needs and wants.

Buying motives are of interest to salespeople because salespeople want to know how to assist customers in making wise buying decisions. For example, it would be a serious error for a tire salesperson to keep emphasizing low prices if the customer is more interested in mileage or safety. The customer would feel that mileage and safety might be sacrificed for low prices. A sale is made in the mind of the buyer—not in the mind of the salesperson. The major reasons that motivate most customers to make a purchase go beyond the desire to own a product. The customers' main concern is how the product will benefit them.

A good salesperson realizes that people and their reasons for making purchases are different. Two customers may purchase the same product or service for different reasons. Also, the same customer may have different buying motives at different times. For example, read the following story:

Sara Diaz wants to purchase an electric can opener. She tells the salesperson that she wants a basic white one that is small and easy to store when not in use. A few days later Sara receives an invitation to her sister's bridal shower. Sara likes her can opener so well that she decides it would be a good shower gift. Sara goes back to the store to buy another electric can opener, but this time she wants a green one with a knife sharpener. It will cost a little more, but it is for a special occasion. This is the same customer in the same store buying the same product, only this time for a different reason.

Buying motives are present in every sale. The customers' buying motives ultimately decide the outcome of every sale. Although not every customer buys the same product or service for the same reasons, salespeople must learn to recognize why customers buy.

WHY CUSTOMERS BUY

It is important to be able to recognize the most common buying motives and to learn how to respond to them as a salesperson. The most common, and the most powerful, buying motives are listed here.

Gain or Economy

All customers want to make money, save time, or save money. Many products and services are available today in order to help customers get more for their money. Customers are interested in products that last a long time, are reduced in price, and are a good value. A customer might buy a subcompact car because it is economical and easy to park. Another customer might buy electric woodworking tools because it is less expensive to make and repair furniture than it is to buy new furniture. A person might make airplane reservations in advance in order to get reduced ticket prices. A business person might purchase a telephone answering device in order not to miss important phone calls. To earn money, a student might buy a lawn mower to mow lawns during the summer. Can the customer make a profit, save time, or save money? Gain or economy is a very basic, yet powerful, buying motive.

Health

A customer's desire for products or services that help maintain one's physical well-being is an important buying motive. This desire for good health is especially strong if the customer is ill or injured.

Customers purchase many products and services to improve or maintain their health. For example, they enroll in physical fitness classes, purchase memberships in local health clubs, and buy weight-lifting or exercise equipment. Parents buy vitamins for

ILLUSTRATION 5-2
The desire for good health is a powerful buying motive.

their children. Consumers buy cold and flu medications. Warm winter clothing is often bought for health reasons. Customers may purchase an extra-firm mattress thinking it will provide a good night's sleep which is important to good health.

All people want to live a healthy life. Feeling physically fit is a strong desire for customers. Because health is important, it is a powerful buying motive.

Comfort and Convenience

People like to be comfortable. They also want products and services that are convenient. Comfort and convenience are buying motives that play a dominant part in the sale of almost every product. A customer may say, "This chair is really comfortable." What the customer is actually saying is, "I like this chair. I feel relaxed when I sit down."

Comfort is an individual preference. "Air conditioning would be nice in the summertime." "These shoes don't pinch my feet." "There seems to be plenty of legroom in the back seat of this car." "The dress fits just right." "I like a mattress that is firm." "These plastic framed glasses are so easy to wear." In each example, the statement given may indicate comfort for one person but not for another. Yet, everyone wants to be comfortable.

Convenience is also a powerful buying motive. People want products that are convenient, easy to operate, and readily avail-

ILLUSTRATION 5-3
Comfort and convenience are buying motives present in the sale of most products.

able. Manufacturers are constantly working to produce time-saving products that require little effort to use. For example, a cake mix that comes with its own cake pan and ready-made frosting is convenient for a busy homemaker. Permanent press fabrics, microwave ovens, disposable diapers, frozen dinners, checking accounts, and credit cards are all convenience items.

Lodging services for travelers recognize comfort and convenience as buying motives of customers. Motels are usually built near major highways where they will be convenient for travelers. Many provide advanced reservation service, restaurants, laundry facilities, and free ice. A special effort is made to assure comfort by providing soundproof rooms, television sets, comfortable beds, and pleasant surroundings.

Safety and Protection

The desire for safety and protection is a strong motivating factor when making a purchase, whether it be for one's own safety or for the protection of others. Customers want product information that demonstrates the product's safety features. If a customer is afraid a product is unsafe, a sale may not be made.

Many products today are tested by the Consumer Product Safety Commission, Underwriters Laboratory, and other interested consumer organizations. These groups help manufacturers and consumers determine if products are safe for use. Many toys for children are much safer today because of the involvement of the Consumer Product Safety Commission. Toys that were considered dangerous because of sharp edges, small metal pieces, poor construction, or possible electrical problems have been improved and made safe or are no longer sold.

Businesses are also interested in the safety features of their merchandise. Consumer safety and satisfaction are important to them. It is poor business to carry unsafe merchandise.

The automotive industry has become quite safety conscious, partly due to prodding by the federal government. Automobiles are now manufactured with seat belts, safety glass, padded dashboards, and energy-absorbing bumpers. For home protection, customers can buy smoke alarms, fire extinguishers, electrical fuses, security lights, burglar alarms, and nonslip guides for stairs. Flame retardant clothing and medicine with child-proof caps are available, too. People also buy life insurance, homeowners' insurance, car insurance, and health insurance for protection.

The main concern of customers is to avoid loss, reduce the chances of injury, or protect themselves or others from possible danger. The freedom from worry and risk is a powerful buying motive.

Affection and Love

Affection and love are emotional buying motives. Many products and services today are purchased because of someone's special feelings for another person. A parent may buy a new color TV because of a feeling of affection and love for the family. Books and magazines may be bought for the same reasons.

ILLUSTRATION 5-4
Gifts purchased for no special occasion are purchased because of affection and love buying motives.

There are many ways for someone to express affection. Flowers, greeting cards, candy, jewelry, and toys are all purchased out of love and affection. It is especially nice when gifts are purchased for no special occasion. Sending an "I'm thinking of you" greeting card in the mail can make someone's day a little brighter.

Many times customers will not reveal their true motives for making purchases. It will take careful observation and listening to determine customers' motives. Simply because a customer doesn't tell you the reason for buying, don't overlook affection and love; these are powerful emotional buying motives.

Prestige and Recognition

Prestige is the desire to be important and to have influence and control. We all like to feel important. A pool table for a game room, even though the person buying it doesn't play pool, is an example of an item bought for prestige. Another person may purchase a limited edition painting. The customer can take pride in the fact that the painting is a limited edition. Prestige can come from the feeling of distinction through ownership of an item that most people do not have.

Recognition is the desire for acknowledgement. People want to be noticed and to gain approval from others. A woman may purchase a wig to wear to work. She likes the recognition she receives from her co-workers and the customers she serves. Fashionable clothing, art objects, home furnishings, jewelry, and items of luxury may also be purchased because of the recognition a customer wants to receive. Recognition helps the customer to feel successful and popular.

Of course, the customer is looking for items that will gain positive recognition. Don't try to sell an unacceptable item; for example, an item that is out of date. The customer will soon realize that it was a poor purchase. This is a sure way to lose a good customer.

There are many motives that describe how people feel about themselves and their relationships with others. Some people want to be popular, well known, and have many friends. Others seek wealth, success, conformity, nonconformity, approval, imitation, or power. Most of these motives are included in the buying motives of prestige and recognition. Although many customers are not willing to openly admit to these buying motives, they are present in almost every sale.

Variety and Recreation

Most people want variety in their daily routines. Recreation and variety are a desire for refreshment or change. They help people to change their daily routines. For example, a person who

Common Buying Motives . . .

- gain or economy
- health
- comfort and convenience
- safety and protection
- affection and love
- prestige and recognition
- variety and recreation

has concert tickets will look forward to enjoying the concert. This means variety and recreation for the person. For recreation, a customer may purchase a tent, a sleeping bag, a camp stove, and a lantern to enjoy a weekend of camping. For variety, another customer may purchase a piano and begin taking piano lessons.

There are many products and services available that help customers achieve the desire for variety and recreation. Travel equipment, sporting goods, camping equipment, luggage, trips, cameras, clothing, and entertainment are all examples of items purchased for variety and recreation.

ILLUSTRATION 5-5
Outdoor sports help satisfy the desire for variety and recreation.

Outward Bound USA

CLASSIFICATIONS OF BUYING MOTIVES

Buying motives are *why* customers buy. A product's features and benefits are *what* they buy. Buying decisions result from the action taken based on buying motives.

Buying motives and buying decisions are present in every sale. The sale is made when customers take action on their buying motives. In many cases, it will be necessary for a salesperson to appeal to several buying motives in order to obtain the desired action.

There is no specific order to follow when appealing to different buying motives. Not all buying motives are used in selling every product. Certain buying motives may be more dominant than others in some customers' minds. When selling, never emphasize a buying motive which has no appeal to the customer.

A useful way for a salesperson to understand buying motives is to classify them. The following classification of buying motives should give the salesperson a general guideline for assisting customers.

Classification of Buying Motives

- primary buying motives
- selective buying motives
- rational buying motives
- emotional buying motives
- product buying motives
- patronage buying motives

Primary Buying Motives

Primary buying motives cause a customer to select one type or class of merchandise or service rather than another. The first decision of the customer is *what* to buy. Customers may decide to buy a sewing machine rather than a stereo, a car rather than a riding lawn mower. The salesperson should be aware of the customer's primary reason for buying. This primary buying motive—the right product or service—must be satisfied before a sale can be made.

Even though primary buying motives may seem obvious to you, customers may not always have the same primary reason for buying. For example, a customer who suffers from hay fever may want an air conditioner for the home. The primary reason for the purchase of the air conditioner is to remove pollen from the air in order to give relief from the symptoms of hay fever. In this case, keeping cool in hot weather is not the primary buying motive.

Selective Buying Motives

Once the customer has decided what type of merchandise or service to buy, the next decision is *which product or service* to buy. **Selective buying motives** cause the customer to choose a specific product or service. There are many reasons for selecting one item over another: color, style, price, quality, versatility, convenience, durability, or use of the product or service, to name a few. This selection by the customer is made after the primary buying motives have been determined.

COURTESY KIDDE, INC.

For example, a customer must be sold on the idea of shaving with an electric razor before comparing brand, price, or product features of electric razors. When a customer buys an electric razor, the primary buying motive may be the desire to shave without the risk of being cut (safety), to shave quickly without a mess (convenience), or to shave with the same electric razor rather than buying disposable blades (economy). Whatever the primary buying motive is, it must be strong enough to keep the customer from selecting another class of goods, such as a disposable blade razor. Selective buying motives would include the price of the electric razor, the ease of cleaning the shaving heads, the number and style of shaving heads, the closeness and quality of the shave, and the quality of the specific brand of electric razor. These selective buying motives help to determine the choice of a specific electric razor.

The following situation demonstrates primary and selective buying motives. Mr. and Mrs. Jack Ferrell went shopping in a department store. They looked at a lawn mower, a TV set, and a washer and dryer. Later they discussed the items and decided that the family had the greatest need for a new washer and dryer. This decision was based on primary buying motives. Mr. and Mrs. Ferrell returned to the home appliance department. The salesperson approached them.

Salesperson: Hi, my name is Dan Willard. May I show you a new washer?

Mr. Ferrell: I'm Jack Ferrell and this is my wife, Joyce. We are interested in a washer and dryer.

Salesperson: We have a fine selection of washers and dryers in your choice of four colors.

Mrs. Ferrell: Maybe we should just get a white one. It probably isn't as expensive.

Mr. Ferrell: That's a good idea. White is fine with me.

Salesperson: Well, Mr. and Mrs. Ferrell, two of the most important considerations with a new washing machine are the motor and size of tub. The machine should give you years of dependable service. This particular brand has a solid guarantee and if and when you need service, we have a highly trained technician here in the store.

Mrs. Ferrell: That's nice to know. How big is the tub?

Salesperson: This particular brand has two tub sizes. The regular size and a larger size for larger families. Which size do you think you would like, the regular or larger size?

Mr. Ferrell: I would like the larger size if it isn't too expensive.

As you can see, the salesperson has the sale well under control. The salesperson was able to determine that the Ferrell's primary buying motive was to purchase a new washer and dryer. The selective buying motives in this example were the price, model, brand, size of tub, a guarantee, and repair service availability.

Rational Buying Motives

Rational buying motives are based on the customers' logical reasoning. Customers who plan their purchases are using rational buying motives. These customers will evaluate their purchases: "What are the advantages and disadvantages of this purchase?" "Is the value of the product or service worth the asking price?" The most common rational buying motives include safety, simplicity, quality, reliability, economy, convenience, service, durability, knowledge, money gain, and ease of operation.

Customers who use rational buying motives will make a purchase only after they have given it careful thought. They will weigh the facts and determine if the product will benefit them. When selling, all salespeople should help customers make wise buying decisions.

Appeal to the customer's sense of logic. For example, a customer interested in a new vacuum cleaner may rationalize that the old one is no longer effective. Although the customer's old one could be repaired, it would still be old and might not last. The customer may also rationalize that with a new vacuum cleaner, cleaning will be easier and the new cleaner will do a better job in less time.

Emotional Buying Motives

Emotional buying motives are based on a desire to have a specific product or service. Customers buy specific items because of their personal feelings. Customers often act on impulse. Most buying motives are emotional. In fact, emotional buying motives may have more of an influence on the customers' buying decisions than rational buying motives.

A salesperson must understand people and why they buy specific merchandise or services. In the case of sporting goods, the customer may be affected by the following emotional buying motives: excitement, adventure, recreation, recognition, and variety. Emotional buying motives such as protection, fear, affection, and safety can enter into the sale of smoke alarms, for example.

There are many emotional buying motives. The most common are fear, protection, appearance, recreation, improved health, comfort, recognition, variety, pride of ownership, adventure, affection, imitation, prestige, and popularity. Salespeople must be able to recognize these emotional buying motives in their customers. These motives tell the salesperson the reason the customer is shopping. Because most items are sold to customers based upon their personal feelings, the salesperson must appeal to these emotional buying motives. These motives are very important in selling.

Some of these buying motives may be rational as well as emotional. The category of the buying motive would depend upon the reason or intent of the customer. For example, the desire to improve one's health may be rational as well as emotional. Because of a desire for good health, a customer may use rational buying motives to purchase natural health foods. However, the emotional buying

ILLUSTRATION 5-7
Emotional buying motives such as protection, safety, and love may have more
influence on customers than rational buying motives.

motives could be a desire to feel better, to look better, and to live
longer.

Not all customers are consciously aware of their reasons for
buying particular products or services. Such hidden motives are
frequently caused by a person's feelings about him- or herself or
about other people. The salesperson must determine the reasons for
the purchase and then appeal to them. Consider the parent who
takes the child into a shoe store to buy a pair of boots.

Customer:	I want to see a pair of boots for my son.
Salesperson:	What style did you have in mind?
Customer:	A rubber boot with buckles, size 9. I want a pair that will last several years.
Salesperson:	These are the finest rubber overshoes on the market. [*Salesperson helps the boy try them on.*] Notice the reinforced heel. This is where most boots rip after only one season of wear. These boots are made to withstand rugged use.
Customer:	Does he have enough room in them so he can wear them next year?
Salesperson:	Yes, there is extra room without being too large. Of course, it will be hard to determine how much

his feet will grow over the next few years. These overshoes are a fine value for the money. They will keep your son's feet dry all winter and should help prevent sore throats and bad colds.

Customer: Well, I didn't think of that. I'll take them.

ILLUSTRATION 5-8
A customer may be motivated to purchase boots because of an emotional desire for good health for her child.

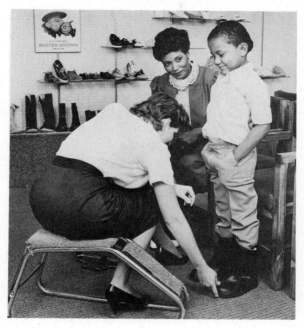

What was the motive that helped the customer make a wise buying decision? Was it a rational buying motive — quality, comfort, buckles that won't jam, a good fit, or reinforced heel? These were important to the customer, but it was the emotional appeal of good health that sold the boots. Determine the buying motives which have the strongest appeal to your customers and use them in your sales presentation.

Product Buying Motives

If the product itself is more important than where it is purchased, the customer will buy the item based on **product buying motives.** It doesn't really make much difference to the customer where the merchandise is bought. Product buying motives cause a customer to buy one specific product in preference to another. The customer's buying decision is often influenced by a specific feature or characteristic of the product or service.

Product buying motives are similar to primary and selective buying motives. It is the product that the customer is more interested in. Based on product buying motives, a customer buying a set of steel-belted radial tires is most interested in size, features, and price of the tires. Where the tires are bought is of little interest. The salesperson who is selling to a customer with a strong conviction toward the product must have extensive product knowledge. The customer will expect detailed information and the salesperson should be able to give it.

Patronage Buying Motives

Customers who prefer to buy from one business or store rather than from another do so because of **patronage buying motives.** It is where they buy that is most important to them. These customers may have several reasons for selecting one business over another. Important patronage buying motives include helpful salespeople, store image, assortment of merchandise, merchandise quality and price, store services, and store location.

Helpful Salespeople. This is the most important reason why customers return to a particular store. Salespeople influence customers more than any other single patronage buying motive. Customers like to feel important. It is the salesperson who can make customers feel like preferred customers. Customers want salespeople who are courteous, helpful, friendly, sincere, and knowledgeable, and who show a personal interest in them and their needs. Salespeople who know their merchandise and the customers they serve will be successful salespeople.

Store Image. The image of the store influences customers to shop there. The store image is the feeling customers have about the store. While salespeople contribute to the store image, the store's layout, design, color, roominess, and general interior give customers an image of the business. Store image also includes fairness in dealing with customers, truthful advertising and service, satisfaction with goods and services, and reasonable return and adjustment policies. If aisles are cluttered, window and interior displays are messy, or merchandise is dusty or unorganized, the image of the store is not inviting to customers. However, if the store is attractive, clean, modern, well-lighted, uncluttered, and the merchandise is well displayed and organized, the customer will feel more welcome to shop there.

Assortment of Merchandise. Customers may elect to shop at a particular store because of the assortment of merchandise available for sale. Customers like a choice of merchandise. They will select a store that can offer a wide variety of merchandise in many styles, brands, colors, and sizes. While it is more costly for a store to carry many items, store owners realize the importance of merchandise assortment to customers when they are selecting a place to shop.

Merchandise Quality and Price. Many businesses offer a wide selection of prices and quality of merchandise. Broad selection is aimed at securing a larger share of shoppers. However, some businesses offer either lower quality and prices or more exclusive merchandise in order to reach a more limited buying market.

Store Services. Almost every business offers store services, but some offer more than others. Customers may shop at a particular business because of extra store services. Services are important. For example, one customer may purchase clothing at a store that will gift wrap; another customer may purchase prescription drugs from a pharmacy because they will deliver to the home.

ILLUSTRATION 5-9
Shopping malls offer customers one-stop shopping and a variety of businesses.

Common store services are: credit, layaway, delivery, repair services, gift wrapping, and free parking. Some businesses offer more specialized services: a bank with a drive-up window, a delicatessen with a lunchroom, a flower shop with out-of-town telephone service, or a store with an elevator. When selecting a place to shop, customers will consider store services, such as a rest area, trading stamps, and a public rest room.

Store Location. Another important reason customers shop at a particular business is location. Customers shop at businesses that are convenient to them; for example, a grocery store or drugstore that is in the neighborhood. A business must also offer plenty of parking for its customers. Some businesses are located together in a shopping center. This offers the customer one-stop shopping with many businesses to select from, as well as ample parking.

USE BUYING MOTIVES TO SELL

Products or services seldom appeal to only one buying motive. The customer usually has several buying motives when making a purchase. A talented salesperson will appeal to the greatest number of motives possible.

Determine which of the buying motives seems most important to your customer. Mention several motives without going into detail. As you mention them, watch and listen to your customer for reactions. This will help you to determine which buying motives are most important. Devote the remainder of the presentation to these dominant buying motives.

The more knowledge you have about the products you sell and the reasons customers buy your products, the better salesperson you will become. Help the customer make a wise buying decision. Remember, your selling process is helping the customer to move through the buying process.

SALES TERMS

need	prestige	rational buying motive
want	recognition	emotional buying motive
motive	primary buying motive	product buying motive
buying motive	selective buying motive	

SALES QUESTIONS

1. Explain why customers' needs and wants are the basis of all economic activity.

2. Explain the difference between a need and a want.

3. Why might a beginning golfer buy a well-advertised brand of golf balls rather than an unknown brand?

4. Why must salespeople be aware of the reasons that motivate customers to buy products or services?

5. Explain and give an example for each of the following powerful buying motives:

   a. gain or economy
   b. health
   c. comfort and convenience
   d. safety and protection
   e. affection and love
   f. prestige and recognition
   g. variety and recreation

6. Why should you try to determine the customer's strongest or most dominant buying motives?

7. Explain and give examples for the following classification of buying motives:

   a. primary buying motives
   b. selective buying motives
   c. rational buying motives
   d. emotional buying motives
   e. product buying motives
   f. patronage buying motives

8. Often customers will not tell you the true motive for their purchases. Why?

9. When selling, why should the salesperson appeal to a combination of buying motives?

10. Explain the difference between emotional and rational buying motives.

11. Should a salesperson appeal more to a customer's rational buying motives than to a customer's emotional buying motives?

12. Give several examples of patronage buying motives.

SALES ACTIVITIES

A. For the following products, list some of the rational and emotional buying motives that salespeople might use to sell a bed, a radio, fingernail polish, shoes, car insurance, lawn-care service.

B. Write down the following products: lawn mower, blender, movie camera. Below each product, write a sales statement based on each one of the following seven buying motives:

   1. gain or economy
   2. health
   3. comfort and convenience
   4. safety
   5. affection and love
   6. prestige and recognition
   7. variety and recreation

C. What selective buying motives might a customer use to select the following products: car, newspaper, haircutting shop, travel agency, microwave oven?

D. Identify the buying motives in the following customer statements:

1. "I'd like a pair of new shoes just like the ones I have on now. These were expensive but they lasted a long time and I didn't have to break them in."
2. "I want a pair of prewashed jeans that will fit right and won't shrink — you know, the kind everyone is wearing."
3. "I need a new typewriter. I thought my office could get along with the portable I brought in, but it isn't electric and it doesn't make good carbon copies. Every now and then the 'L' key sticks, too."

PRODUCT INFORMATION

6

Your Learning Goals

After studying this chapter, you should:

- *be aware of the personal benefits of product or service knowledge.*
- *understand that product or service knowledge is more than just information about the product.*
- *understand what to learn about your products or services.*
- *be able to identify the sources of product information.*
- *understand how to present product information.*

You may think that product knowledge is becoming less important for salespeople. Today many retail businesses are largely self-service and product information is often plainly printed on the product's package. However, if salespeople do not know about their products or services, they cannot be effective and productive salespeople. They cannot give the sales assistance that customers demand. Whether the business is self-service or gives personal service, customers expect salespeople to be knowledgeable about their products.

Many of today's customers have a general knowledge of what they are purchasing. They often rely upon their own experience or on a friend's or relative's experience with the product or service. Customers may read literature about the product before they buy. Customers may have observed an advertisement that convinced them to stop and see the item.

New products, new materials, and new uses for products make product information increasingly important to salespeople. Salespeople must be able to provide the customer with more product information than the customer already has. Salespeople must be knowledgeable in order to reassure the customers about the customers' product knowledge and beliefs.

BENEFITS OF PRODUCT OR SERVICE KNOWLEDGE

Salespeople who are well informed about their products or services receive several benefits. (1) They find their jobs to be more enjoyable. (2) They develop confidence in themselves, and their customers have confidence in them. (3) They are better able to organize effective sales presentations. (4) They can overcome sales resistance. (5) They increase their chances for promotion.

You Will Enjoy Your Job More

Knowledgeable salespeople find their work more enjoyable. Trying to sell without adequate product or service knowledge is stressful. Unprepared salespeople fear every objection raised by the customer. They hesitate to help customers for fear the customer will ask questions that they cannot answer.

Unprepared salespeople worry that the customer will not buy. To avoid these feelings you must be prepared. You must be an expert on the products or services you sell. With preparation you will enjoy serving your customers. By giving product or service information that will help customers make a wise buying decision, you will receive the personal satisfaction necessary to make your work more enjoyable.

You Will Gain Confidence

Sometimes the salesperson makes a sale just because the product or service is superior. However, in most cases it does not work this way. When customers are shopping, especially for expensive items, they want to deal with a confident, knowledgeable salesperson. They will look for confident salespeople who know their products or services. Salespeople who have confidence in themselves inspire confidence in their customers.

Customers want to be helped by salespeople who believe in their products or services. Customers seek out confident salespeople who will answer their questions and who will understand their problems. For example, a salesperson who has helped to lay carpet and

ILLUSTRATION 6-1
Customers want to deal with knowledgeable salespeople, especially when
shopping for expensive items, such as cars.

has toured a carpet manufacturing plant will be better able to
understand the problems and concerns of the customer looking for
quality carpeting.

Don't destroy your customers' confidence by giving uninformed,
misleading, or exaggerated statements such as: "It's better because
it costs more" or "All you have to do to operate it is read the
directions." Customers don't want to be helped by salespeople who
lack product or service knowledge. This is the reason product or
service knowledge is important. With this knowledge you can be
confident when you sell. When your customers observe your confidence in your products or services, they will also gain confidence
in your ability to help them buy the product or service that will
meet their needs.

You Can Organize Your Sales Presentation

A well-organized sales presentation is the result of a salesperson's knowledge of the products or services available. The organized salesperson is better able to talk intelligently about the
products or services that will meet the needs of the customer. If you
are organized, you won't feel as if you need to bluff customers or
just stand there while your customers sell themselves. With prod-

uct or service knowledge you can plan an enthusiastic sales presentation.

Because you will probably sell many items, don't try to memorize every possible feature. Learn the important facts and features. It is a mistake to spend too much time studying facts and features without understanding their purpose or benefits to your customers. Ask yourself, "Why is this feature important to the customer?" Knowledgeable salespeople can be enthusiastic about what they sell if they fully understand the products or services and the benefits to their customers. In planning an enthusiastic sales presentation, use interesting facts about the product or service, how it is made, how it operates, and how the buyers' wants and needs will be satisfied by the purchase.

You Can Overcome Sales Resistance

Customers like to shop for similar products or services in different businesses. With a thorough knowledge of products or services, salespeople are able to answer objections raised by customers, such as: "It was less expensive in the other store." "But their suitcase is lighter weight." "They can dry-clean my drapes tomorrow." Unless salespeople understand their customers' problems and know how their products or services are better, the sale will be lost.

By knowing your competition you will be better prepared to meet your customers' objections. Many products and services look alike to customers, but often there are hidden features and benefits that you need to point out to customers. For example, when the customer says, "They can dry-clean my drapes tomorrow," the salesperson might say, "Yes, that is fast, but if you brought your drapes in to us today, we not only would have them dry-cleaned tomorrow, but we would have them neatly pressed and delivered to your home so your drapes would be less likely to wrinkle before they are hung." This salesperson recognized the customer's problem and was able to overcome sales resistance by selling the customer on the store's services.

You May Earn a Promotion

Product or service knowledge is important for salespeople who want to be successful. When considering a salesperson for promotion, management looks at a salesperson's relationship with customers and his or her knowledge of the products or services sold. When evaluating the sales staff, several questions must be considered: Do they thoroughly know their products or services?

Are they friendly and helpful? Do they have a good attitude toward their work? Are they enthusiastic when they sell? Are they constantly learning about new or improved items? Are they productive workers?

It is easy to see the difference between salespeople with minimal background information and salespeople who have taken the time and effort to learn complete information about their products or services. Promotions are based not only on how long salespeople have worked for the company or on attendance. Of course these are important, but salespeople who have learned about their products or services and how to help customers buy are often considered first for promotions.

KNOWLEDGE MAKES A DIFFERENCE

Most salespeople know far too little about what they sell. Too often a person is put on the sales floor without much sales training. Without the techniques of selling and a basic understanding of the people to be served, most salespeople soon learn that to be effective, a little product knowledge is not enough. Product or service knowledge is the foundation for any successful salesperson. Before salespeople begin selling, they should:

1. **Know what merchandise is carried by the store.**
   What brands, colors, sizes, styles, and prices of merchandise does the store carry? Without this information, you can't help your customers.
2. **Know the location of merchandise within the store.**
   Don't lead the customer around the store looking for a requested item. Know where the merchandise is kept. Know the location of items that are not frequently sold. Also, know how the items are arranged on the shelf or rack.
3. **Know reserve stock and its location.**
   Often extra quantities of merchandise are stored until needed. Merchandise that is out of season may be put away until next season. Know where it is located.
4. **Know merchandise in other departments.**
   Customers may ask whether another department carries a certain brand, size, or kind of item. Know what products other departments carry.
5. **Know merchandise *not* carried by the store.**
   When a customer asks for a specific item by brand, know whether you have it. Know the products and services sold by your competition.

6. **Know what merchandise can be special ordered.**
A customer may want an item that is not in stock. Know if it can be ordered and how long it might take to receive it. If you don't know, ask the store manager or store buyer.

7. **Know the merchandise being promoted.**
Know what items are being featured in the store's advertising. You should also know what items are in the display window. When a customer asks to see the displayed item or the one featured in a newspaper advertisement, you should know which item the customer is requesting.

ILLUSTRATION 6-2
A successful salesperson should know what items are being featured in the store's advertising.

8. **Know how to care for the merchandise or equipment.**
The salesperson needs to know the housekeeping responsibilities within the store. Stop and look at your counters and display racks as a customer would look at them. Are the counters clean? Is the merchandise neatly straightened? Do all the items have price tickets? Is your equipment clean and in good working order? The care and treatment of merchandise and equipment is important in selling.

A factor which sets some salespeople apart from others is their amount of product knowledge. Impress your customers by knowing all there is to know about what you sell. Be informed before you begin selling.

WHAT TO LEARN ABOUT YOUR PRODUCTS OR SERVICES

As a salesperson, you must learn everything there is to know about the products or services you sell. Without preparation, you can't expect to make many sales. As you analyze the facts and features of a product or service, ask yourself, "Why was this product or service created?" All products or services are developed with the customer in mind. If you know why a product or service was created, you know why your customers will want to buy it. The more you can see from the customers' point of view, the better you will be able to organize sales presentations that will appeal to them. Learn everything possible about the products and services you sell. Customers like to buy from experts. Be one!

Know Your Products

Salespeople should know the appearance, the material composition, the manufacturing process, uses, performance, service, care, brand, price, competition, and related items of the product.

Appearance. The appearance of products is very important to customers. Customers are concerned about selecting items that appear appropriate for them. Once the customer has decided on the general item such as furniture, clothing, appliances, or home furnishings, the selection is based on the choices available to the buyer. Style, color, shape, size, and design will influence the final decision of the customer.

Customers will appreciate your help in selecting the right item. You will build the customers' confidence in you when you ask them about the appearance of the item desired. When organizing your sales presentation, consider questions that will help you to select a product for the customers. For example, when customers are looking for a new kitchen sink, ask the color of their counter tops or the color of their kitchen appliances. Ask if they would prefer enamel or stainless steel. If the customers are looking for a lamp, ask if they want modern, early American, or Mediterranean. Ask if they want a hanging lamp or a table lamp.

Material Composition. The material the product is made from should be given as a part of every sales presentation. The customer should not have to ask, "What is this made of?" Don't assume your customers already know this information.

Learn about the differences in materials. What is the difference between redwood, maple, and walnut, for example? What is the difference between polyester and rayon? Tell your customers the reason why a particular material was used. You should know exactly what materials the product is made of as well as the advantages of each material. State the advantages which make your products superior to other products. For example, if a customer is looking at a permanent press dress shirt, you might say, "You will find this permanent press dress shirt to be very comfortable. It always looks neat and fresh and it seldom needs ironing because the fabric is a blend of polyester and cotton."

Manufacturing Process. Because salespeople sell so many items, they generally don't take the time to learn how their products are made. But this knowledge often helps salespeople improve their sales ability. The manufacturing process will often determine the quality and performance of the product. Manufacturing companies have conducted research to determine what materials will give the best performance at the most reasonable cost to the customer. There are standards of production and quality control as well as testing and inspection of the final product.

Salespeople use this knowledge to explain to their customers why an electric saw has a three-prong plug, why a freezer uses two inches of pressed-foam insulation, or why a mattress uses independently pocketed coil springs.

Salespeople who know how a product is made can better appreciate the value and quality of the item. They will believe in the product and its value to their customers. With this knowledge, salespeople can be more excited and enthusiastic about what they sell.

Uses. The confidence of your customers will depend upon your ability to explain or demonstrate the use of your products. Salespeople must know how to use the product. Customers expect it. It is extremely important to learn this before you start selling. You will be of no help if you have to read the directions along with the customer. Even if the directions are printed on the product, your customers will appreciate being told how to use the product.

Knowing how to use a product is especially helpful during a product demonstration. Customers want to know how to operate it, wear it, prepare it, or arrange it. Of course, if there is more than one use for the product, be sure you show this to your customers.

ILLUSTRATION 6-3
A customer's confidence depends on the salesperson's ability to explain or
demonstrate the use of the product.

For a customer looking at a riding lawn mower, the salesperson
should demonstrate how to start and operate it. The salesperson
should explain how many gears it has, whether the oil has to be
premixed with the gas, and how wide it cuts. In addition, if the
riding lawn mower has any other purposes such as being used as a
rototiller or a snowplow by adding attachments, the salesperson
should be able to explain or demonstrate these uses of the product.

Performance. Too often salespeople become so involved with
product features that they fail to tell the customer what the product
does or how long it will last. Many products look alike to customers
and are sold for the same basic purpose. In order for customers to
make wise buying decisions, they need to know the advantages of
one product over another.

The performance of the product is an important consideration to
the customers. How long will the paint last? How fast will the
moped run? How often might it need repair? Will this material
wear well? Salespeople must be able to truthfully answer the customers' questions. For example, an income tax office needs a photocopy machine that is reliable and that can handle a high volume of
photocopy work without the need for frequent service. The most
important factor for this customer is performance, not the appearance of the product, how the product is made, or how it operates.

Service. Many products may require service. Customers want to know if the product will be easily serviced should something go wrong. Many appliance and TV businesses have service representatives who will repair their products. It is important for you to know how the product can be repaired or replaced if it fails to perform to the customer's satisfaction. Guarantees are usually attached to the product. In addition, if your store offers a guarantee, make sure the customers are aware of the conditions of the guarantee. Are parts replaced at no charge? Are pickup or delivery and labor charges covered? These are important questions to customers. If you only mention that the product is guaranteed without explaining the guarantee, misunderstandings may result when the product needs service. Be sure to learn about all service agreements, guarantees, and additional charges for services available to your customers.

Care. Salespeople need to inform customers of how to take care of products. This important subject is often forgotten. Many times a customer's decision to buy is based on the amount of care necessary for the item. Customers will appreciate a salesperson who shows them how to take care of the product. Proper care will usually increase the performance of the product and reduce the cost of repair or replacement.

Customers will gain confidence in your sales ability and in the reputation of the company you represent if you take the time to show them how to take care of the product. For example, show the customer that a hedge trimmer should be cleaned and oiled after a season of use. Inform the customer that when an automatic drip coffee maker is cleaned occasionally with hot white vinegar solution, the coffee will taste fresher and the coffee maker will give many years of good service. Tell your customer how to care for the products you sell.

Brand. Products with well-known brand names are often requested by customers. By selling brand-name items, businesses can build repeat business because the brand has earned a reputation for good performance. Businesses carry brand-name merchandise for this reason. Once customers buy a particular brand, they are hesitant to buy a different, less familiar brand. These customers generally feel that a well-established brand will give them the repeated quality they desire. Know and learn about the brands of merchandise you sell. Mention these brand names as you sell.

Price. Most businesses handle several price lines of merchandise. Some customers are interested in low-priced items, while others are interested in medium- or high-priced items. You should become familiar with the price of your products. Be able to justify the price to yourself and to your customers. Learn the reasons why your products are worth the asking price. Is the value of the product worth the price to the customers? Remember, it is value that interests customers the most. If your customers feel they are receiving a product that is valuable to them, it will be worth the price.

Competition. Some businesses carry several brands of merchandise while other businesses may specialize in one brand. Generally customers like to compare products before making that final decision to buy. Whether the customers ask you or not, they are interested in knowing how your products compare to those of your competitors. This is why you should become familiar with your competition. What brands do they carry? How are the products similar? What are the differences between product features? How is one product superior to its competition?

As a salesperson, you will need to compare use, performance, quality, color, style, size, price, convenience, care, and other important features and benefits of each competing product. With this information you will be able to better prepare and organize your sales presentation.

Related Items. Having product knowledge is important. It is also important to know what related items are available. For example, a customer buying a microwave oven may need special cookware because metal pots cannot be used. An electric drill is of little value without the additional purchase of drill bits. In fact, there are a number of products that require the purchase of related items. This is the reason salespeople need to know all related items as well as their own products.

Knowledge of items that are required with the original purchase is especially important if the customer cannot operate or assemble the product without that additional purchase. Consider how you would feel toward the salesperson who sold you an electric drill if, when you wanted to use it, you found that the electric drill had no drill bits. Whether related items are required or not, all salespeople should be familiar with the products they sell and the related items.

Know Your Services

Retail stores are in business primarily to sell products. Still, the sale of many products requires supporting services. Few people can alter the ready-made clothes they buy, so clothing stores provide alteration services. A fabric store may measure, make, and properly hang draperies. A hardware store may assemble merchandise for its customers. A real estate firm may provide free baby-sitting service while the parents look at a new home. Salespeople need to be aware of the services their companies offer to customers. Services to customers are important. Sell services along with your merchandise.

There is an increasing demand for service businesses. These are businesses that will perform an important service for their customers. Examples include travel agencies, health-care facilities, hairstylists, pest exterminators, TV repair shops, coin laundry facilities, dry cleaners, and wedding consultants, to name just a few. Service salespeople must know their services as well as retail salespeople must know their merchandise. Customers want to know how the service is performed, how long it will take, how much it will cost, when the service can be given, and where the service is to take place. Ask yourself why the service was created and how it will benefit your customers.

If you are selling a service, you must be able to explain or demonstrate the service's benefit to your customers. The more you know about your services, the more accurately you will be able to talk to customers about what can or cannot be done and why. This will help you to avoid promises that your service cannot fulfill. There is no excuse for poor service. Service businesses are highly competitive and require knowledgeable, skilled salespeople. People

ILLUSTRATION 6-4
Service businesses, such as travel agencies, are highly competitive and require knowledgeable, skilled salespeople.

want services to make their lives easier, more enjoyable, and more successful.

SOURCES OF INFORMATION

It is important for beginning salespeople to receive product or service information before they actually start to sell. Most store managers or buyers will show new employees around the store. Usually they will show new employees the location of the merchandise before they sell. Store managers may briefly explain the services offered or give new employees some information about several products. But this is not enough to make the new employees the experts they need to be.

As a new employee, learning about the products or services is your responsibility. It is your responsibility to learn everything you need to know to help your customers make wise buying decisions. Because you may sell many products, it is necessary to have a wealth of information ready when you need it.

Just memorizing and giving facts about products or services doesn't sell your customers. These facts must be interpreted so that the customers will completely understand. Learning the facts and features of your products or services and how they will benefit customers is essential background information. These facts and features will help you to become an expert — an authority on what you sell. Salespeople can learn this information from several sources.

The Merchandise

Examining the merchandise itself is the best source of product information. When you are not selling, take every opportunity to look over new items and those items with which you are not familiar. While unpacking, pricing, or putting merchandise on the shelves, become familiar with your products. When few customers are in the store and selling is slow, take some time to examine what you sell. The product's appearance, its unique features, how it is used, how it will perform, and its style, color, design, brand, price, guarantee, and safety features are all important information to know.

Much of this information can be found on the product's labels and tags attached by the manufacturer. During the sales presentation you can point out this information to your customers. They are interested in the special instructions on how to use and care for the product as well as any safety or precautionary features. Whether reading labels and tags or examining the merchandise you sell, look for selling points that are not obvious to your customers.

Salespeople

A new salesperson will find that experienced salespeople are a good source of product or service information. You can learn from their experience. If a label or tag is too technical and you don't understand it, don't hesitate to ask the people you work with. They have the benefit of sales experience. They know the limitations as well as valuable selling points of the item or service. In fact, if you sell a service, other salespeople are probably the best way to learn the service business. They can show you the special secrets that have made them successful. Ask them questions when they are not busy!

Customers

Generally, salespeople are more knowledgeable than customers. However, customers who have used a product or service can be an excellent source of information. Customers often know more than salespeople about performance, usage, and how the product compares to other brands. Let your customers tell you how well it wears, how it was used, if it was the quality they expected, and what they liked best about the product or service. Listen carefully. You will be able to understand your products or services better. In fact, when selling, you can tell your customers about other people who have successfully used your product or service. Learn from the experiences of others.

Personal Experience

To better understand performance, usage, and care, learn first-hand by using the product or service yourself. As a paint salesperson, for example, it would be worthwhile to learn that paint applied by spraying will dry faster and spread more evenly if it is slightly thinned before use. You could learn this fact if you used the paint yourself. Travel agents often go on the same tours that they sell to their customers to learn about the tours firsthand.

Generally customers don't want to hear about your personal experiences with products or services when such experiences reflect personal taste, such as experiences with clothing or cosmetics. But when the product or service is not a matter of personal preference, such as the use of appliances or the repair of a car, some customers appreciate a salesperson's explanation of knowledge gained from personal use. Of course, if a customer asks your personal opinion, your answer will mean more if you have actually used the product or service. Personal experience is a good way to learn information that will help you when selling, regardless of whether or not you tell the customer about your experience.

ILLUSTRATION 6-5
Personal experience with the products you sell is a good way to gain understanding of performance, usage, and care.

Publications

There are a variety of publications, magazines, pamphlets, booklets, and sales bulletins containing product or service information. Sales representatives from manufacturing companies will often make this information available upon request. These publications give detailed information along with helpful illustrations on how the product is manufactured. Only a personal tour of a company could better illustrate the manufacturing process. Many publications will also explain tests that the product has undergone. These tests will help you understand the manufacturer's standards of quality and concern for the customer.

Check your public library. There are books and other publications that give facts on such topics as fabrics, glass, plastics, woods, and other materials. Reference books and encyclopedias also contain product information. For information on current subjects not found in books, check magazines and other periodicals. Ask your librarian to help you check in the card catalog for specific and general headings. The public library has many books and periodicals that can give you a wealth of background information.

Magazines are available on almost every occupational interest. Magazines are published by trade associations, consumer groups, and government agencies. Many news stories, editorials, and advertisements give the salesperson useful information. These publications not only give information on how a product or service was developed, but also on testing and consumer reaction. While some of this information can be rather technical, you may learn why it is important and how it benefits your customers.

Another source of information about a variety of merchandise is in the mail-order department store catalogs. While the product information is very basic, it is a good reference for a beginning salesperson to study. These catalogs give information that is of interest to customers. Learn to use the key words and phrases that are given in these catalogs.

Other Sources of Information

Other sources of product or service information are available to salespeople. Some salespeople take special training courses offered by manufacturers, while others may enroll in correspondence courses or evening college courses. Comparative shopping is a valuable way to learn about the products you sell. Shop in similar businesses and ask the salespeople about their products or services, read competitive advertisements, and look at similar businesses' window displays.

Some salespeople have the opportunity to visit the company that manufactures the products they sell. These tours are educational. Salespeople can then appreciate the work it takes to make the product.

It takes a great deal of planning, effort, and patience to prepare yourself to sell. Regardless of what methods you use to learn about your products or services, develop your personal knowledge to become an expert on what you sell. Your customers expect it.

DON'T BE A KNOW-IT-ALL

You have spent a great deal of time learning your products or services. You have become the expert — the specialist. Now think like a customer. What would you want to know if you were buying your product or service? Your customers want to know the specific facts and features that make your product or service worth the

ILLUSTRATION 6-6
Salespeople may tour a manufacturer's plant to learn more about the products
they sell.

asking price. Learn all you can. Be confident, but not overbearing.
Believe in what you are selling. But be careful not to develop the
attitude that you know it all. Customers want information, but
they don't want to feel stupid. Don't develop the attitude that the
salesperson is always right and the customer is always wrong. Your
customers won't listen to you and they won't take your advice. If
your personal manner irritates them, they won't accept you and
they may leave without buying.

Customers want to be respected. Remember to treat customers
the way you would treat a friend. Work with your customers to
select the right product or service for them. Make them a partner
in the decision.

SALES QUESTIONS

1. "Today product knowledge is becoming less important." Explain why this statement is false.

2. Explain the five personal benefits salespeople gain by knowing about their products or services.

3. How can a customer tell if a salesperson lacks personal confidence?

4. What are the dangers of a salesperson lacking product or service knowledge?

5. When learning about products, salespeople should not try to memorize every possible product feature. Why?

6. How can product or service knowledge help you to organize a better sales presentation?

7. "Promotions are NOT always based on how long salespeople have worked for a company or attendance." Explain this statement.

8. Before you begin selling to your customers, what information would you want to know?

9. Why should a salesperson stress service when selling merchandise?

10. What is important for you to know about services provided by the business?

11. Explain the relationship between price and value. Why is it important in selling?

12. What is the best way to learn about the products you sell?

13. What is the best way to learn about the services you sell?

14. Explain why salespeople can gain product and service knowledge from customers.

15. Do you think beginning salespeople should listen to people who find fault with the products or services they have purchased? Explain.

16. When should salespeople give their customers information about their personal experiences with a product or service?

17. Explain how you can use the library to gain product or service knowledge.

18. Can salespeople know too much about what they sell? Explain.

19. Describe the attitude salespeople should have when selling.

SALES ACTIVITIES

A. List several specific facts or features about the following items. Then list what particular benefit the customer will receive from each feature.

1. AM radio
2. electronic calculator
3. watch
4. shoes

B. You are employed as a salesperson in an automotive service center. A customer looking at tires asks you, "What is the difference between this radial tire and this steel-belted radial tire?" Unfortunately you don't know. What should you say?

C. Select an item of merchandise that interests you. Using the school or public library, find information about the item; then write a report. List the information you found and the sources where you found it. For the final part of your report, tell how a salesperson could best use this information in a sales presentation.

D. Joe Malek is a new salesperson. Your store manager has asked you to show Joe around the store and to help him become familiar with the products he will be selling. Explain to Joe what information he should know *before* he begins selling the store's products.

3

DEVELOPING SALES SKILLS: THE STEPS OF A SALE

3

DEVELOPING SALES SKILLS: THE STEPS OF A SALE

CHAPTER 7: THE APPROACH

CHAPTER 8: DETERMINING CUSTOMER
NEEDS AND WANTS

CHAPTER 9: PLANNING A FEATURE-BENEFIT
SALES PRESENTATION

CHAPTER 10: MAKING A FEATURE-BENEFIT
SALES PRESENTATION

CHAPTER 11: HANDLING CUSTOMER
OBJECTIONS

CHAPTER 12: CLOSING THE SALE

CHAPTER 13: SUGGESTION SELLING
AND REASSURANCE

7

THE APPROACH

Your Learning Goals

After studying this chapter, you should:

- *be aware of the importance of the approach.*
- *be able to welcome the customer to the store.*
- *be able to take control of the sales presentation.*
- *know how to introduce yourself and learn the customer's name.*
- *be able to select and use the appropriate customer approach.*
- *know how to get the sale off to a good start.*

Selling is serving customers, not pushing customers into buying. Selling is really a matter of helping people buy. The ability to sell successfully means satisfying customers, not only with the merchandise or service you sell, but also with the service you give. Satisfied customers will want to come back to the store and to you.

The step in the selling process when the customer and the salesperson first communicate is the approach. The approach involves greeting the customer to gain attention and then directing the customer toward the merchandise available for sale. In every selling situation, the salesperson should be prepared to meet or approach the customer. The salesperson must understand the customer, the customer's buying motives, and the buying decisions the customer will make during the sale.

The salesperson must also understand that the customer will be analyzing the salesperson. The customer's attitude toward the business and the salesperson depends upon the sales attitude the salesperson projects when approaching the customer. The appearance and personality of the salesperson, plus the interest shown in the customer, are all part of the approach. Having the proper sales attitude is important in getting the sale off to a good start.

THE IMPORTANCE OF THE APPROACH

The sale begins when the salesperson approaches the customer. The impressions salespeople make during the approach help to determine the buyer's attitude toward salespeople and their sales presentations. When you are selling, make your approach warm, sincere, genuine, and friendly. Welcome your customer with a positive attitude and a smile on your face.

Although you might feel hesitant to approach a customer, show confidence in yourself and in your ability to sell. Don't be reserved and shy. It may take extra initiative to overcome your initial hesitation. At first you may feel self-conscious, but the more you approach and sell to customers, the more self-confident you will become. Relax and enjoy meeting and selling to your customers.

ILLUSTRATION 7-1
As you approach the customer show confidence in yourself and in your ability to sell.

FOCUS THE APPROACH ON THE CUSTOMER

It is important to welcome the customer. The customer's first impression of the business and its sales staff is often a lasting impression. The salesperson's approach, appearance, and attitude combine to make a strong impresssion that affects the outcome of the sale.

A Good Approach ...

- gains the customer's attention and acknowledges that customer's presence in the store.
- puts the customer at ease with a warm, friendly welcome.
- places the emphasis on the importance of the customer by using words like *you, your,* and *yours,* or by using the customer's name.
- creates a favorable impression toward the business and its sales staff.
- gains the customer's confidence in the salesperson's ability to select the right merchandise or service.
- allows the salesperson to begin to analyze the type of customer (decided, undecided, or casual looker) to be served.
- sets the stage for a successful sales presentation.
- directs the customer's attention to the mechandise or service available for sale.

As a salesperson, when should you approach the customer? This will depend upon where you are when the customer arrives. Obviously if the customer comes in and you are at the back of the store, you would not shout across the sales floor. For **proper timing**, salespeople must allow the customer time to come into the store and then make a prompt approach. Customers consider their time to be valuable. For those who are ready to be served, it is frustrating to wait or look for a salesperson to help them. Salespeople need to be alert and aware of customers who need assistance. Consider these examples of poor approaches:

1. The customer who comes into the store during the lunch hour looking for a gift and finds no salesperson in sight.
2. The customer who enters a restaurant and is not promptly served because the waiter or waitress is too busy cleaning off other tables.
3. The customer who drives into a service station and has to wait because the salespeople are too busy doing stock work or talking to other employees.

4. The customer who comes into a shoe store for a pair of shoes and the salesperson is too busy reading the newpaper to offer assistance.

Unfortunately these situations happen often. Sales are lost when salespeople think the customers will come to them for assistance.

Take Control

As a salesperson, you must take control of the sales presentation with a prompt approach. Forget the stock work, the conversation with other employees, or other nonsales activities. When customers come into your area, your job is to serve them. **Sales control** begins the first few minutes a customer comes into the store. Getting the sale off to a good start depends on your ability to analyze the sales situation quickly. Choosing an appropriate greeting will help the customer to be receptive to your assistance.

If the customer comes into a clothing store, quickly walks over to the shirts and picks up a white dress shirt, the salesperson should recognize that this is probably a decided customer. The salesperson might say, "Did you find the correct size?" "Did you want a long-sleeved or a short-sleeved dress shirt?" or "This dress shirt requires no ironing." However, if another customer comes into the clothing store and strolls through the store looking at a variety of merchandise, the salesperson might say, "Good morning." This approach lets the customer know that the salesperson is standing by, ready to help. Or, "Good morning. You may want to look over here at these sale items" is a more specific approach and guides the customer to special merchandise.

Sales control is important. The salesperson wants to guide the customer through the five stages of the buying process — attention, interest, desire, conviction, and action. Taking control is easy when the salesperson observes and listens carefully to the customer. The salesperson who is genuinely interested, uses good selling techniques, and is sincere in serving the customer will have sales control.

Sales control is also needed when a customer walks into the store and the salesperson is busy with another customer. Be sure to acknowledge the presence of all customers who come into the store. Do not ignore customers who are nearby. If the store is not very busy, the salesperson might say, "Hi, someone will be with you in just a moment." The salesperson then might excuse him- or herself from the first customer to show the second customer where a particular kind of merchandise is located or to get another salesperson.

However, use care and caution in this particular situation. Your response to the second customer will depend upon the kind of merchandise you are showing, how involved you are with the first customer, both customers' attitudes, and your position in the store in relation to the customers.

When a store is very busy and all the salespeople are helping customers, it is the salesperson's responsibility to serve as many customers as possible. Be tactful and courteous; never abruptly leave one customer to wait on another!

Use the Customer's Name

It is beneficial for salespeople to attempt to learn their customers' names. Customers like to hear their own names used during the sale because it makes them feel important. By knowing the customers' names, the salesperson can make the sales presentation seem more personal. At the same time, salespeople who care enough to introduce themselves to their customers will also gain their customers' confidence. This shows that the salesperson cares about the customers' wants and needs. By knowing and using each others' names, customers feel more comfortable during the sale. For example, a customer is sitting in a restaurant and the waitress approaches:

Waitress: Good evening. My name is Linda. I'll be your waitress. Would you like a few more minutes to look at the menu?

Customer: Yes, I would. Thank you, Linda.

The customer gained a feeling of confidence from the waitress. The customer can now use the waitress's name when more assistance is needed. By introducing herself, Linda established a personal relationship with her customers.

In another example, the sale may already be under way and the salesperson, in order to develop a closer relationship with the customer, will exchange names. In the following example, the salesperson is showing a suit to a customer in a men's clothing store:

Salesperson: By the way, my name is Ken Reynolds.

Customer: I'm Rick Sanchez.

Salesperson: Do you wear a suit often, Mr. Sanchez?

Customer: Yes, I do. I'm an accountant and need to wear a suit every day.

Salesperson: Well, Mr. Sanchez, do you have a particular color or style in mind?

In this situation the salesperson learned the customer's name and occupation. This is valuable information that can be used throughout the sales presentation.

Sometimes it is not convenient to ask a customer's name during a sales presentation. A salesperson may learn customers' names from personal checks used for purchases, alteration tags, layaway slips, charge cards, or by asking other salespeople in the store. When a repeat customer comes into the store, that person can be greeted by name. Learn, remember, and use your customers' names whenever possible.

Select the Appropriate Approach

The first few words of a sales approach set the mood for the sale. The salesperson should begin the approach with a smile, a positive attitude, and a genuine interest in serving the customer.

As a customer, have you ever been approached by a salesperson who asks "May I help you?" You probably responded, "No, I'm just looking." Obviously this is a poor way to start a sale. The approach, "May I help you?" draws a negative response from the customer. What can a salesperson say to "No"? Not much!

By using this approach, salespeople paint themselves into a corner with no acceptable way out. Salespeople who use this approach show neither enthusiasm for selling nor any personal interest in their customers.

It is difficult selecting an effective and appropriate greeting to use with a customer. No single approach should be used in every situation. Selecting the most effective approach depends largely upon the customer. Observe the person carefully. Is the customer walking quickly through the store, perhaps looking for something special? Is the customer examining specific products? Does the customer appear to be decided or undecided? By close observation, the salesperson can usually choose an appropriate approach.

TYPES OF CUSTOMER APPROACHES

Several types of customer approaches are used in selling: the merchandise approach, the welcome approach, and the service approach.

The Merchandise Approach

If the customer is looking at an item of merchandise, the salesperson can approach with a comment about that particular product. **The merchandise approach** is considered to be the most effective approach. It directs the customer's attention and interest to a specific item. For example: "That blender you are looking at is the best high-speed blender available" or "That sport coat has been one of our best-selling wool sport coats this fall." The major advantage of this approach is that it doesn't give the customer a chance to reply, "I'm just looking." The merchandise approach gives the salesperson the opportunity to begin selling the product.

It takes time and practice to use the merchandise approach effectively. You must know the major product features and how to turn those features into buyer benefits. The merchandise approach should be changed to fit the needs of each customer.

ILLUSTRATION 7-2
When using the merchandise approach the salesperson must know the major product features and how to turn those features into buyer benefits.

If a customer is lifting a piece of luggage, the salesperson might use the following approach: "This luggage is very light and easy to carry because it is molded polyurethane over a light aluminum frame." If the customer is examining the sides of the luggage, the salesperson might say, "You'll find the finish will repel water. This case is also dustproof." If the customer is looking at the built-in rollers on the bottom of the luggage, the salesperson might say, "Now you won't have to carry a heavy piece of luggage when you travel. You simply pull this one behind you."

The merchandise approach is most effective when the product features relate to the customer's need. Use this approach as often as possible. Customers appreciate a salesperson who knows the merchandise and how it will benefit them. Using the merchandise approach will give you confidence in your selling ability, and you will sell more merchandise as a result.

The Welcome Approach

The **welcome approach** is used to greet customers on an informal basis and its purpose is to welcome customers to the store. Sometimes "Good morning," "Good afternoon," or "Good evening" followed by a pause is enough to encourage customers to tell you about their needs.

If you know the customer's name, make the welcome approach more personal by using the customer's name: "Good morning, Miss Miller" or "Good afternoon, Mr. Komuro. Those tires you looked at the other day are on special this week."

If you know your customers have recently taken a trip, purchased a car, or had their name or picture in the paper, mention that when you greet them. "Hi, Jack, did you take a lot of pictures during your trip to Florida?" or "Good morning, Ms. Bell. Congratulations on being elected to the city council." Always be on the alert to pick up and use bits of personal information about your customers. That shows you think of your customers as individuals and not just as people with money to spend.

The welcome approach is also used to acknowledge the presence of a customer when you are busy with another customer. By simply acknowledging the second customer, that person will not feel neglected or overlooked. The customer will realize that you are busy, but that you or someone else will be of service as soon as possible.

Remember, the customer is the most important person to any business. Use the customer's name if possible. A customer who shops at a store and feels welcome will return.

ILLUSTRATION 7-3
The welcome approach is used to acknowledge the presence of a customer when the salesperson is busy with another customer.

The Service Approach

The **service approach** offers assistance to the customer. The service approach is probably the most widely used and most overused approach in selling. Common questions include: "Is there something I can show you?" "Has someone helped you?" "May I help you find your size?" "May I help you?"

How many times have you been approached with, "May I help you?" and you've responded, "No, I'm just looking." Unless a customer wants immediate sales help, the service approach generally encourages a negative response. This overused approach tells customers that you are not really interested in them.

The service approach can best be used for customers who are obviously in a hurry. Hurried customers want and expect quick and friendly service. Very little selling can actually be done. Hurried customers may ask only one or two questions before the sale is completed. For example, this customer is holding two white shirts as the salesperson approaches:

Salesperson: May I help you?

Customer: Yes, I need a 15½ × 33 inch long-sleeved dress shirt.

Salesperson: This white dress shirt is 65 percent polyester, 35 percent cotton and needs no ironing.

Customer: That's what I'm looking for, a dress shirt that needs no ironing. I'll take it.

In this example, "May I help you?" did not draw a "no" response as it usually does. This customer needed help and said so. When a customer obviously needs help, the service approach is useful.

GETTING THE SALE OFF TO A GOOD START

Every selling situation must have a beginning. That beginning is the approach. As the salesperson, you must select the most appropriate approach with which to greet your customers. Use the merchandise approach, the welcome approach, the service approach, or a combination of approaches to most effectively welcome the customers to shop in your store.

Approach your customers with a positive attitude and a smile on your face. Make your approach warm, sincere, genuine, and friendly. Focus your attention on your customers, use names if possible, and take control of the sale. Greet your customers, determine their wants or needs, then direct their attention toward the appropriate merchandise. Remember, getting the sale off to a good start is the most important thing you can do at this point.

Carefully observe and listen to other salespeople—their customer approaches, their attitudes, and their methods. How do customers react and respond to their approaches? By doing this, you can learn to avoid mistakes that lose sales. Select your approach with care, evaluate your customer's reaction, and then practice the winning technique of getting the sale off to a good start.

SALES TERMS

proper timing	merchandise approach	service approach
sales control	welcome approach	

SALES QUESTIONS

1. Explain the importance of a good approach.

2. When should the salesperson approach the customer?

3. Explain how the salesperson can take control of the sales presentation by using the proper approach.

4. What important facts should salespeople consider before leaving one customer to help another?

5. Why might it be beneficial for a salesperson to learn customers' names?

6. How can a salesperson obtain the customer's name?

7. Salespeople should not use the same approach for all customers. Why?

8. Explain and give an example of each of these sales approaches:

   a. merchandise approach
   b. welcome approach
   c. service approach

SALES ACTIVITIES

A. For each of the following situations, write an example of a merchandise approach, a welcome approach, and a service approach.

   1. Jeff and Sue are looking at a laser-disc player.
   2. You are at the back of the store doing stock work. A customer who seems to be looking for something enters your department.
   3. Mr. Canfield comes into your store and walks quickly over to the camera department. He seems to want to buy some film.
   4. You are busy showing a customer a personal computer when you notice another customer looking over to observe the sale.

B. Read the following situation and answer the questions.

   Situation: Two salespeople, Joyce and Dan, are standing behind the sales counter talking. A customer enters their department.

   Joyce: I can't believe it. Ron Swenson worked all afternoon yesterday. I told him to put away this stock but he was too busy.

   Dan: Yeah. The part-time help think that all they have to do is sell, and we get stuck with the stock work.

   [*After waiting for help, the customer walks closer to the salespeople.*]

   Joyce: [*under her breath to Dan*] One of these important customers. [*aloud*] Yes, I suppose I can help you.

   Customer: I'd like to see a set of golf clubs, please.

   Joyce: All we've got is just what you see.

Customer:	Well, I'm just learning how to play golf. Which set would you recommend?
Joyce:	I don't know. This set looks cheap.
Customer:	Well, sorry to bother you. I think I'll just look around.

Questions:

1. Why did this sale get off to a poor start?
2. What could have been said to make a better approach?
3. If the situation had begun with a good approach, do you feel a sale could have been made? Why or why not?
4. If you were the store manager and you observed the conversation, what would you do?
5. As the store manager, how could you prevent a situation like this from happening in the future?

DETERMINING CUSTOMER NEEDS AND WANTS

Your Learning Goals

After studying this chapter, you should:

- *know how to observe customers.*
- *understand how to qualify customers by giving a selling statement or asking questions.*
- *be able to observe and listen to customers' reactions.*
- *be able to ask well-chosen questions.*
- *know how to use effective listening skills.*
- *know how to select the right product to show to the customer.*
- *recognize the customers' buying motives.*
- *be able to listen and look for buying signals.*

After you have approached the customer, the next step in the selling process is to find out what the customer wants or needs. This step keeps the attention you gained through your good approach and directs the customer's interest to the merchandise or service for sale.

It is the salesperson's responsibility to learn what merchandise or service the customer wants. Customers who come into a retail store are usually in the mood to buy. They may not buy today, but each customer is a potential buyer—a valued customer. Which customer becomes a buyer depends upon you and your ability to create a sincere person-to-person relationship. Don't get upset if a customer says, "I'm just looking, thank you." Make them feel comfortable to shop in your store and see what's new.

You and the store need customers. Chances are the store has spent a great deal of money on advertising and sales promotions to attract customers to shop there. Make customers feel welcome to shop in your store.

Customers who enter a store are there for a reason. Customers may already know what they want, they may want to see what is new, they may be looking for ideas, or they may just be "browsing." No matter what the customers' reasons for entering the store, it is your responsibility as a salesperson to help them determine their wants and needs. Customers will only buy when they find what they want or need. Help them to buy by showing them merchandise that will interest them.

HOW TO SELL TO DIFFERENT TYPES OF CUSTOMERS

All customers have needs and wants to be satisfied, yet all customers are different. Learn the needs and wants of each customer and be prepared to meet them. No matter what type of customer you are helping, treat each customer like a buyer. Show your customers that you are determined to work toward their interests.

People buy products for different reasons, but they still have the same basic needs and wants. For example, a customer who has just purchased a house will need to purchase a lawn mower. Another customer may purchase a lawn mower because the old one won't run anymore. In both cases the customers have the same need—cutting the grass—but their reasons for purchasing the lawn mower are different.

The ability to recognize the needs and wants of customers is one of the characteristics of a good salesperson. In Chapter 4 you learned that there are three types of customers the salesperson needs to be aware of: decided customers, undecided customers, and just-looking customers.

Decided Customers

When decided customers come into the store, they know exactly what they want to purchase. There is no need to go into detail about the product, its use, or its benefit to them. These customers are presold. Be of service to them by finding the desired item as quickly as possible.

Three Types of Customers

Decided
Customers . . . . Customers who know exactly what they want or
need.

Undecided
Customers . . . . Customers who have an idea of what they want, or
customers who want something later but are shopping around now.

Just-Looking
Customers . . . . Customers who have nothing definite in mind but
just want to look around.

If the customer is not in a hurry, ask a few questions. Talk to your customers and learn from them. Have they used the item before or was it recommended by a friend? Why were they satisfied with the product? What was it about the item they liked best? Customers are an excellent source of product information. For example:

Salesperson:	Hello.
Customer:	Hi. I want to buy that camera. [*The customer points to the display.*]
Salesperson:	Yes, that camera is a good value. [*The salesperson hands the camera to the customer.*]
Customer:	I know my brother will like it. I have one just like it. It takes great pictures.
Salesperson:	[*Noticing the customer is not in a hurry.*] Is there something special about this camera you like best?
Customer:	The built-in flash! Before I bought this type of camera it seemed like I could never find my flash attachment when I wanted to take a picture. The film cartridges this camera uses are a nice feature, too — easy to reload so I won't miss an important picture.
Salesperson:	It's nice to have a reliable camera. I'm sure your brother will enjoy it. Will you need any film?
Customer:	Good idea! Thanks.

While it is easy to serve decided customers, take the time to learn from them. Reassure them about the products they are buying and suggest additional items.

ILLUSTRATION 8-1
A salesperson can ask questions of and learn from a decided customer.

Undecided Customers

Undecided customers are customers who want to buy, but don't know exactly what they want. They may have something in mind, but are willing to listen to suggestions. Undecided customers want to buy but they will not purchase a product or service until they have had a chance to shop around. You must use selling techniques to determine the undecided customers' wants and needs. Then you can suggest the correct product or service to the customers for complete satisfaction.

The following couple recently purchased an older home. They plan to remodel their kitchen. They are uncertain about the color of their appliances. They are undecided customers.

Customer:	We are beginning to remodel our kitchen, and we need to select new appliances.
Salesperson:	That sounds like a big project. Have you selected a color scheme for your kitchen?
Customer:	Yes, we decided on soft earth-tone colors and oak cabinets. But we can't decide what color appliances we should consider.
Salesperson:	That is an important decision.
Customer:	What do you think? Should we choose basic white or purchase colored appliances?
Salesperson:	Most customers prefer to select a color that will compliment their kitchen. Our appliances are available in gold, green, bronze, and almond. Which color do you like best?
Customer:	I don't know. What would you recommend?
Salesperson:	Because you are using earth-tones, the gold, green, or almond colors would be good selections. However, I think I would recommend the almond appliances. Almond is a soft, neutral color that will enhance the other colors in your kitchen.
Customer:	I think you might be right, but how can I be sure?
Salesperson:	Satisfied customers are important to our business. Let us deliver an almond-colored stove so that you can see how it looks in your new kitchen.
Customer:	Oh, that would be great!

The salesperson recognized that the customers needed direction. The customers had a general idea of what to consider, but just couldn't decide. The salesperson helped the customers make a selection. The salesperson recognized that the customers wanted to make the right decision. After all, this is an expensive decision and one that the customers must be happy with for a long time. The salesperson took the time to explain the choices and then offered a suggestion based on the color scheme for their new kitchen. It is this sincere interest in helping customers that will make this salesperson successful.

Some undecided customers may be shopping now for something they want later. In the winter, a travel agency will display travel posters of summer trips to encourage shoppers to begin planning for a summer vacation. This method allows customers to develop a desire for something and it allows them time to shop before making a decision.

You must sell undecided customers on the value of the merchandise or service being offered. Give them as much information as you can about the benefits of your products or services. Although you should encourage them to buy, they may not buy right away. However, if you have been courteous and helpful to them, they will most likely be back later to buy.

Just-Looking Customers

Just-looking customers have nothing definite in mind to buy; they just want to look around. These customers may not be aware of an immediate need for anything. However, when customers make an effort to shop around, they are generally in the mood to buy.

What do you say to a customer who tells you, "I'm just looking"? You might say, "Thanks for coming in. I'll be nearby if you need me." One word of caution—be nearby. If a customer does find something and wants your assistance, be there to help. If you are gone, customers will become irritated or angry and may leave without buying.

Another response might be, "Go right ahead and look around. Don't miss our special on dress shirts. They are located right over here." If something is new, unique, or a good value, point it out to them. Customers will appreciate your concern.

Keep your eye on customers but don't run over to them every time they stop to look at an item. Let them look around without the feeling that you are watching their every move. If you feel they want your help, walk over and ask them.

Another example of a just-looking customer is one who is looking at an item of merchandise but doesn't want any help. If a customer returns your greeting and goes on examining the merchandise, make a positive statement about the merchandise. Say, "That black-and-white TV will run on batteries as well as house current," or "The nice thing about this crock pot is that it comes apart for easy cleaning," or "These short-sleeved dress shirts are a fine value." Don't just start asking questions at this point.

By using short statements rather than questions, the customer will respond with a statement that will give you a clue to that person's reason for shopping. The customer may respond, "Do you have a small, color portable TV that isn't too expensive?" or "I want an appliance that is easy to clean," or "I'd rather have a long-sleeved dress shirt." Customers' responses give you a clue as to their needs.

ILLUSTRATION 8-2
If something is new, unique, or a good value, point it out to your customers.

Too many salespeople stop trying to sell when a customer says, "I'm just looking." Many customers say this automatically, so don't pass up an opportunity to make a sale. Ask the customer, "Is there anything special you are looking for?" If the customer says no, at least you have made an attempt to begin the sale. You would be surprised how many times customers would tell you what they are looking for if they were asked.

QUALIFY YOUR CUSTOMERS

Before you start selecting merchandise to sell to your customers, you will need to qualify them. To **qualify** your customers means to determine what products or services will best satisfy their wants and needs. You can best qualify your customers by closely observing them, by giving a selling statement or asking questions, and by carefully listening to your customers. These techniques in qualifying customers are not a step-by-step plan. As you improve your selling skill, you will learn to combine these techniques to better serve your customers.

- by observing the customer.
- by giving a selling statement or asking questions.
- by listening to the customer.

To be successful in person-to-person selling, you must have a clear picture of your customers' wants and needs in order to help them make wise buying decisions. Unless you understand your customers from the very beginning of the sale, you will probably never really close the sale. Of course the customers might buy, but only because they sold themselves. You really didn't sell to them. You should not sell to any two people in exactly the same manner. You need to build your sale around a personal concern for the customers' individual wants and needs.

Your sales success largely depends on your control of the sale. Take the initial step in establishing control by qualifying every customer before you attempt to sell anything. By determining the wants and needs of your customers, you will be able to determine the best way to sell to them.

Continue to determine the wants and needs of your customers throughout the sale. Don't ever stop observing, questioning, or listening. The key to selling to customers is for you to determine what they need and then to select and sell the right product or service. Question your customers and listen to what they say. This will shorten the time you spend with individual customers and will help you satisfy your customers' wants and needs.

Observe Your Customers

Observing your customers is an important method of communication. Pay close attention to them. This can help you to select the right selling approach for each individual customer. All of your customers' observable actions should communicate something to you. By watching the behavior of your customers, you will be better able to serve them.

What information can you obtain by watching them? Are they in a hurry? Are they walking about the store quickly, looking for something they can't find? Or are they casually walking around? Do they pick up the same item two or three times, or walk away and later return to it? Notice their mannerisms — hurried or relaxed — so you can get in tune with their moods.

Watch the customers' faces. Do they show satisfaction, disapproval, or doubt? Are they smiling? Do their eyes show interest or do they have that "lost look"? Are they showing interest in an item of merchandise? When you are talking with a customer, is the customer looking at you and your merchandise or being distracted and not paying attention? Use eye contact. It is important to look at your customers when speaking or listening to them. It shows customers that you are concentrating on their needs.

Never judge customers by their outward appearance. A customer with a poor appearance may be able to afford quality merchandise and may prefer an expensive item. On the other hand, a customer who is well dressed may select a low-priced item because it is a "good buy" or "good enough" for the situation.

Treat every customer with respect. Regard every customer as an individual. People's values are different. One customer may purchase clothes at a discount store but wouldn't think of cutting costs on tires for the car. Another customer may value quality clothing but will purchase the least expensive gasoline for the car.

Throughout the sales presentation, continue to observe your customers' actions. Judge the interest of your customers by their reactions to what you say or to the merchandise they are considering. Observe their behavior. Watch their facial expressions. Listen to their comments. Do they need help or further information on your merchandise or services? Are they friendly or irritable? Are they listening to you?

ILLUSTRATION 8-3
Observe your customers' actions and facial expressions throughout the sales presentation.

Communicate with your customers. Listen to them and use eye contact. Through observation you will be able to better determine your customers' wants and needs.

At this point, you will have to decide whether a selling statement or a question is appropriate. Both methods are attempts on your part to get your customers to talk about themselves and their wants and needs. Customers' participation in a selling situation is essential. It will help you to understand the customers' points of view. It should also help to develop a good person-to-person selling relationship. A good **conversation** shows a genuine interest in communicating with customers about their wants and needs. It should not become just a matter of taking turns talking.

Make a Selling Statement

When you are trying to determine customers' wants or needs, the main question is, "Do your customers know exactly what they want or will you have to ask them questions to determine their needs?" For example, a customer is looking at a car battery. You observe the customer's interest as you approach. If the customer does not say something to you after your greeting or simply returns your greeting, you should try to qualify the customer by giving a selling statement.

Salesperson: I see you are interested in a new car battery.

Customer: Oh, I'm not sure. My car hasn't been starting. I was late to work again this morning.

Salesperson: That is a problem no one needs. I'm sure we can find something that will help you to solve that problem. Now this battery will...

When the salesperson gave a selling statement, the customer responded with a need. The salesperson went on to say, "That is a problem no one needs." This shows the customer that the salesperson is listening and understands the problem. After the sale is started, the salesperson may need to ask a few questions to determine the type, price, and quality of car battery that would satisfy the customer's needs.

What might have happened if the salesperson had started with a question?

Salesperson: May I show you a car battery?

Customer: No, I don't think so. I'm just looking right now.

Salesperson: That's fine. I'll be over here if you need any help.

While this question is better than, "May I help you?" or "Is there something I could help you with?", it did not draw out any clues as to the wants and needs of the customer. In the first example, the salesperson correctly assumed the customer was interested in a car battery. If the customer had not been interested in a car battery, the customer most likely would have stated that fact. In the second example, the salesperson doesn't know why the customer turned down the offer to show merchandise. It may be because the customer was uncertain about whether to buy a new heavy-duty car battery, a less expensive battery, or a used battery. The salesperson will probably never know.

This situation happens every day. Unfortunately some salespeople fail to qualify their customers. They use the same approach and procedures for every customer. It doesn't work. Customers want to be served by salespeople who show a genuine interest and concern for their needs, their wants, and their problems.

Ask Questions

There are times when a few well-chosen questions are appropriate. Questions are one of the best techniques a salesperson can use to determine the customer's wants and needs. In a conversation, skillful questioning accomplishes the following: it obtains useful information from the customer, it encourages person-to-person communication, it brings the wandering attention of the customer back to the sale, and finally, it helps the salesperson to check the customer's understanding of the sale. Questions bring the customer's needs, desires, or problems out into the open. This permits the salesperson to deal directly with these needs.

Too often inexperienced salespeople begin a sale by telling a customer all about an item or a service before they understand what the customer wants. The salesperson tells and shows and tells some more until the customer becomes bored and makes up an excuse to leave.

Don't start a sale with a constant flow of talk. If your customers are willing to talk early in the sale without being questioned, listen to them. Save questions until you need them. If you need questions to identify the customers' wants or needs, develop them around the use of the product or service. By asking a few well-chosen questions, you can quickly discover the customers' real buying motives. Emphasize these motives during the sale, and you will be able to sell the customers on the need for the item they are considering.

Some salespeople ask too many unimportant questions. This is a serious mistake. A salesperson can overpower a customer by asking one question after another. Too many questions tell the customer that the salesperson is lazy. In fact, customers resent being pinned down. This error in questioning makes the customer feel committed to the item. This does not allow the customer to look at other items or allow the salesperson to show items of better quality. Customers like to choose among products. For example, a customer comes into the store looking for a shirt.

Customer: I need a shirt.

Salesperson: A dress shirt or sport shirt?

Customer: A dress shirt.

Salesperson: What size?

Customer: 15½.

Salesperson: Short sleeved or long sleeved?

Customer: Long sleeved.

Salesperson: What length sleeve?

Customer: 33 inches.

Salesperson: What color?

Customer: White.

Salesperson: Do you have a certain brand in mind?

Customer: Not really.

The salesperson, who may have good intentions of being helpful, is being rude to the customer. This salesperson should have asked one or two questions and then selected the merchandise to be shown. Get merchandise into the customer's hands as soon as possible. Give the customer something to do, something to look at, something to touch.

Notice how the following salesperson skillfully uses selling statements and questions to determine the customer's wants and needs. The same customer comes into the store looking for a shirt.

Customer: I need a shirt.

Salesperson: The shirts are located over here. [*Salesperson walks with the customer to the shirt counter.*] Were you interested in a dress shirt or a sport shirt?

Customer: A dress shirt.

Salesperson: Well, we have a fine selection of long- and short-sleeved dress shirts in your size.

Customer: Oh, I want a long-sleeved dress shirt, size 15½.

Salesperson: And I would guess with a 33-inch sleeve?

Customer: That's right. [*The salesperson helps the customer to select several shirts from the counter.*]

Salesperson: [*The salesperson observes that the customer has picked up a white shirt several times.*] Were you thinking of a white dress shirt?

Customer: Yes. I've been wearing light blue, but I want a change.

Salesperson: I've noticed more customers are buying white dress shirts. They seem right for almost every occasion.

Notice how this salesperson was more helpful to the customer. The salesperson asked one or two questions and then started to show the customer a few shirts. Also, rather than just asking questions, the salesperson made several statements that brought a response from the customer. "We have a fine selection of long- and short-sleeved dress shirts in your size." Actually the salesperson was asking if the customer wanted long or short sleeves and the correct size.

This salesperson communicated with the customer. The salesperson observed, questioned, listened, and analyzed the customer. The salesperson and the customer didn't just take turns talking. Their conversation showed a genuine person-to-person relationship that is very important in selling.

Certain questions must be asked before a salesperson can begin showing merchandise. For example, a customer comes in and asks to see a stove. As you take the customer over to the stoves, ask if the customer prefers gas or electric. For a customer who wants to look at a bike, ask, "What size?" or "Do you want a boys' or girls' model?" These important questions get you started. You can now begin to discuss the customers' specific needs and wants.

Don't cross-examine your customers. The wise use of questions will put the buyer in a talkative mood, arouse interest, and create a desire to become involved in the sale.

The timing of your questions is important. Questions help you to control the sale. Is the sale going too fast or too slow? Does the customer understand what you are saying? Are you asking too many questions? Is the customer's attention wandering? What is the customer thinking?

The best way to determine if you are communicating with the customer is to ask questions, listen to the customer's answers, and observe his or her behavior. The questions must be skillfully worded and presented at the proper time to keep the presentation in tune with the customer. Let the customer's understanding serve as your timing guide. You can then adjust the timing of your sale to a pace that will best serve your customer.

A salesperson's questions must come from honest concern for the customer, not attempts at flattery or obvious efforts to manipulate the customer. Develop your skill in asking the right questions at the right time. Ask the customer who, what, where, when, how, and why. The answers to these and other questions serve as your key to fully understanding your customer's needs, wants, and buying motives.

Be a Good Listener

Effective salespeople are good listeners. They enjoy listening to customers because they are sincerely interested in satisfying their customers' needs and wants. Customers think more highly of salespeople who listen to them. This is one of the best methods salespeople can use to establish their customers' confidence. When salespeople listen, it encourages customers to listen to what the salespeople say.

Observing, questioning, and listening are important in helping the salesperson qualify customers. They provide a means of effective communication on how the sales presentation is progressing and the direction it should take. Look and listen for clues from your customers. Too often, however, salespeople feel that they must constantly talk in order to remain in control of the sale. This is not so! Customers quickly retreat when under verbal attack by a salesperson. Instead, let the customers talk.

It is important that the salesperson listen actively. If a salesperson's attention is wandering, the customer will sense this. If the salesperson has a blank stare or is looking at everything but the customer, it becomes obvious that the salesperson isn't listening. Salespeople who automatically keep nodding their heads or repeatedly say, "I see," "yes," or "oh" are letting their minds wander from the sale.

Good listening is a skill. Good listening is important to effective communication. Listening actively takes concentration.

Take the time to listen to your customers. It is not easy to listen when you want to talk about the products or services you know so well. But be patient! Help customers to talk by asking a few questions and then listen attentively to what they have to say. Don't interrupt or overpower the customers with your product knowl-

ILLUSTRATION 8-4
Effective salespeople are good listeners.

edge. Salespeople who listen to their customers will accomplish the objective of selling — helping customers make wise buying decisions.

Many people do not know how to listen. If you want to learn to sell, if you care about your customers, if you want to be a successful salesperson, you must learn to listen effectively and respond to your customers' needs. Here are some basic principles on how to become an effective listener.

1. **Prepare to listen.** First of all, be prepared to sell. Know the policies and procedures of the business. Be knowledgeable about the products or services you are selling. Anticipate the questions customers may ask. With good preparation, you can free your mind to listen.

2. **Stop talking and listen.** Take time to listen. Don't be in a hurry. Let the customers tell you about their wants, needs, and desires. You can learn a lot by getting the customers to talk. Inexperienced or poor salespeople feel that if they are not talking, they are not selling. Salespeople cannot listen until they stop talking.

3. **Pay attention.** There are many things that can distract salespeople from listening. But to be good listeners, salespeople need to concentrate fully on the immediate customers and their needs. Listen carefully and with an open mind.

4. **Look and act interested.** Being a good listener is not just a matter of being attentive. It is also a matter of appearing and acting attentive. Don't just stand there. Listen with your eyes by looking at your customers. Smile. Raise an eyebrow. Occasionally nod your head. Interject a word of agreement. Ask a question from time to time. Be enthusiastic. These actions will show that you are a good listener.

5. **Don't interrupt.** Be patient. The salesperson who listens with a half-open mouth, ready to say something every time the customer pauses, is not really listening. Let the customer finish talking before you say anything. Some salespeople make hasty judgments before a person has finished talking. Even if what they are saying is favorable, don't cut them off. Interrupting is rude.

6. **Give customers time to think.** Give your customers time to think. They may be talking and then pause. Don't start talking just because nothing is being said. Even if customers pause, this doesn't mean they are finished saying everything they want to say. However, don't stand back like you don't care—carefully observe your customers. Give them time to think.

7. **Give listening responses.** Let your customers know you are listening. Encourage them to keep talking by using reflective phrases: "Let me see if I understand." "Did you say..." "You mentioned..." "That is a good point." "Sure." Even an occasional, "yes," "I see," or "oh" shows customers that you are listening.

8. **Practice listening.** In every conversation with friends, members of your family, and the people you serve, practice active listening. Use the techniques of listening. Sharpen your listening skills. You can learn a great deal about people by listening to what they say.

To determine customers' wants and needs, the salesperson must observe, question, and listen to customers. The salesperson has to time and pace the sale. Person-to-person communication requires time to talk, time to listen, time to think, and time to take action. By listening and letting the customers talk, salespeople will learn the customers' buying motives for a particular product or service. Casual conversation directed toward the desires of customers will make you an effective salesperson.

SELECTING THE ITEM TO BE SHOWN

Successful selling requires the salesperson to get a clear picture of the needs and wants of the customer. After carefully observing, questioning, and listening, the salesperson can use the information to select an item that will satisfy the customer's needs and wants. From what salespeople see, question, and hear, they can quickly diagnose each customer's interests and needs.

Decided customers are sure of what they want. They quickly ask for an item, pay for it, and leave. It only takes a few minutes to properly select the item and serve these customers. However, many other people need help making the proper merchandise selection. Some people have a vague idea of what they want, while other people are unable to recognize their own needs.

Salespeople cannot wait for the customer to say, "I'll take it." Some people need help in selecting merchandise and taking action to buy. Without it, these customers may decide to leave the store rather than make a purchase.

Notice in the following example how this salesperson helps the customer who has stopped to look at a little girl's dress.

Salesperson: Did you find the correct size?

Customer: I think so. These dresses are all cute. It makes it difficult to select just one. I can just see my granddaughter in this dress. [*Pauses to consider it.*] This dress is so pretty. But I don't know which one I like best. Maybe I'll just look around a little more before I decide.

Salesperson: You seem to like the dress. Is there a reason you think it isn't right for her?

ILLUSTRATION 8-5
Some customers need help in selecting merchandise.

Customer:	My daughter has to be able to put it in the washing machine. This dress looks too delicate to machine wash.
Salesperson:	It does look delicate, but actually it's easy to take care of. Your daughter can put it right into the washing machine. The instructions for washing are here on the label.
Customer:	Oh, that's great.
Salesperson:	It is very practical. May I gift wrap this for you?
Customer:	Yes, thank you. To think, I almost didn't buy this dress because I thought it wasn't machine washable.

Even though this customer needed to buy a child's dress, the salesperson helped the customer to select a dress that was just right for her granddaughter — a dress that was practical and washable. To do this, the salesperson observed, questioned, and listened.

Unless you understand your customers from the beginning, you probably will never be able to select the right item or close the sale. Find out what your customers want and then try your best to satisfy them. If you show a low-quality, inexpensive item when the customer really wants a higher quality item, the customer may be offended. If you show a high-quality, more expensive item, the customer may say "No, thank you," and walk away.

The merchandise to be shown depends upon your customers' desires. Select questions based upon the item to help you qualify your customers' needs and wants. Don't ask useless questions. Ask one or two key questions and then select the quality and style of merchandise you think your customers want. In this way you can start showing merchandise. If you are wrong, your customers will tell you.

Don't show customers too much merchandise. This will only confuse them. The more confused customers become, the more difficult it is to help them sort out their needs. On the other hand, don't passively stand back and wait while they serve themselves. Customers want guidance — help them!

Think about a customer who comes in to look at a pair of shoes. The customer wants to be helped, but the salesperson keeps showing the customer one pair of shoes after another. The customer, who only wants one pair of shoes, becomes confused.

Salesperson:	Now, how does this one feel? Stand up and try it.
Customer:	[*walks on shoe*] This feels pretty comfortable. They might do.

Salesperson:	[as the customer sits back down] Now here is one that just came in.
Customer:	They're nice, too.
Salesperson:	Let's try it on the other foot. [customer walks on it—long pause to consider the shoe] This one is imported. [The salesperson picks up another shoe.] Can't say we don't have a fine assortment in your size.
Customer:	I just don't know which one feels the most comfortable. I'm on my feet all day, so what matters most to me is comfort. [takes off shoes] Maybe I'll just . . .
Salesperson:	[interrupts] Here is a nice looking pair we haven't tried on yet. Aren't they good looking shoes?
Customer:	Yes, I guess so. [Customer puts on the old shoes.] My own fit the best. [Stands up to leave.]
Salesperson:	Wait. I may have more in stock if you'll wait just a minute.
Customer:	No, thanks. I'm just looking today. [Customer leaves.]

This salesperson made several errors in selling. The salesperson didn't try to qualify the customer; didn't observe, question, or listen; missed the real buying motive; and was more preoccupied with showing shoes than with trying to satisfy the customer's needs. The salesperson showed the customer too much merchandise. The salesperson probably felt insulted because after the salesperson brought out almost every shoe in stock, the customer still didn't buy. At the end of the day, this salesperson will probably say, "Why do I get all the customers who are just looking?"

Avoid making these mistakes. Help the customer select the right item. Learn the customer's preferences by asking a few well-chosen questions. Listen. Present an assortment of merchandise, but not everything in stock. Remove the items the customer doesn't seem to care for. You not only want to help your customers buy, but also to help them buy the quality and quantity they need.

RECOGNIZING CUSTOMER BUYING SIGNALS

When presenting merchandise, salespeople need to watch and listen to their customers for buying signals. **Buying signals** are clues that the customer is ready to buy. By looking at and listening to the customer, a salesperson should be able to determine if the customer is showing signals of approval of the item. If the customer keeps coming back to an item or repeatedly picks it up, this is a sign of interest in the item. Customers' buying signals can be a comment or a question about the item. The customers' actions and expressions are also signs of their likes and dislikes.

Buying signals may be given by the customer at any time. Watch and listen for them. When a salesperson makes an effective selling point that is aimed directly at a benefit to the customer, the customer usually responds with a buying signal. For example, a customer walks into the small appliance department and is looking around when the salesperson approaches.

Salesperson: Hello.

Customer: Hi. I'm looking for a gift for our son who will be attending college this fall. Can you help me find something that he might like?

Salesperson: I've got an idea I think you might like. [*Salesperson walks over to a selection of microwave ovens.*] Here is a compact microwave oven that doesn't take much counter space.

Customer: Oh, maybe that's the answer to my problem. How does it work?

ILLUSTRATION 8-6
Salespeople need to watch and listen to their customers for buying signals.

Salesperson:	It's very easy. You simply select the correct setting from this front panel and push the start button. He can prepare meals or warm up leftovers. It's safe and very easy to operate.
Customer:	That sounds perfect.
Salesperson:	I'm sure he will enjoy it. It also comes with a quick meal recipe guide that he will find useful.

In this example, the salesperson listened for the buying signals. "Maybe that's the answer to my problem." "How does it work?" "That sounds perfect." The salesperson also stressed the space-saving size, ease of operation, and safety features. There was no need to discuss other facts or benefits of the microwave oven. The customer seemed happy with the merchandise selection.

There are times when salespeople miss buying signals. This indicates the salesperson is not concentrating or listening to the customer. When a salesperson misses the buying signals, often the sale is lost. In the following example the customer is looking for a billfold.

Customer:	I'm looking for a thin billfold.
Salesperson:	What do you mean?
Customer:	You know, one that folds up neatly so it won't bulge my pants pockets.
Salesperson:	Here is a beautiful black leather billfold.
Customer:	Yes, that is nice leather.
Salesperson:	Maybe you would like this other style. It has been popular. [Customer looks at it and then picks up the first billfold.]
Customer:	Does this come in brown?
Salesperson:	I think so. [pause] Maybe you would prefer a tri-fold billfold. You can put more into it.
Customer:	No, I don't think so. I'll look around.

This salesperson missed the sale. The salesperson tried to qualify the customer with a poor opening question, "What do you mean?" The customer ignored the insult and asked to see a billfold. The salesperson didn't properly determine the customer's wants or needs and just started showing billfolds. The salesperson missed the customer's buying motive—a thin billfold that would be comfortable in the pocket. The buying signals were also ignored when the customer returned to the original billfold and asked, "Does this come in brown?" To really prove to the customer that the salesperson was not listening, the salesperson said, "You can put more into it." This salesperson showed no interest in helping the customer make a wise buying decision.

THE TRIAL CLOSE

Buying signals are clues to close the sale. If a salesperson fails to listen to or recognize these clues, it will cause an unnecessary delay in closing the sale. The sale may even be lost. In fact, if you continue to discuss the sale when your customers are ready to buy, you may actually talk them out of buying.

The time to close the sale is when the customer is ready to buy. You should try to close the sale at the earliest, most convenient point. This is called the **trial close**, and it takes practice. Don't be abrupt or awkward. Close the sale with: "Do you like the black or brown better?" "Will this be cash or charge?" "Is there any additional information I can give you before I write this up?" "I'm sure you will receive many years of service from this purchase." Closing statements should be given in a normal, conversational manner.

Carefully study your customers to determine if they are ready to buy. From the very beginning of the sale, observe, question, and listen to what your customer does and says. When a customer gives you a buying signal, attempt to close the sale.

SALES TERMS

qualify   buying signals   trial close

conversation

SALES QUESTIONS

1. Give several reasons why people enter a store.

2. Define the three types of customers.

3. Why should a salesperson ask customers about products or services they have used and have been satisfied with?

4. When should you try an approach on a customer who is just looking around?

5. When selling to just-looking customers, how can you get a clue as to what they might want?

6. Why is it important to have a clear understanding of the customer's wants and needs?

7. How can you establish control of the sale?

8. What techniques are used to qualify customers?

9. What can you learn by closely observing your customers?

10. Why should you avoid judging your customers on their appearance?

11. How do you decide if a selling statement or a question is appropriate in determining the customer's wants or needs?

12. What can skillful questioning of customers accomplish for salespeople?

13. Why is it a mistake to ask too many questions?

14. By listening to your customers, what can you gain?

15. What is required to establish person-to-person communication?

16. Why can't you wait for the customer to say, "I'll take it"?

17. How will you determine what merchandise to show the customer?

18. What happens in a sale when you show customers too much merchandise?

19. How do customers communicate their buying signals?

20. Why do salespeople miss customer buying signals? What is the general result of the sale?

21. Explain the trial close.

SALES ACTIVITIES

A. You are to give selling tips at a store meeting. The manager has asked you to help four new salespeople learn ways to determine the customer's wants and needs. What information and suggestions will you give them? Be detailed.

B. For each product listed, write three good questions to qualify customers.

1. bookcase
2. tablecloth
3. video tape recorder
4. pen and pencil set
5. sweater
6. hiking boots

C. In the following situations, which response would a salesperson give to the customer to best determine that customer's wants or needs?

1. Customer: [looking at a picture frame]

   Salesperson: a. Nice weather today, isn't it?
                  b. What size picture frame did you need?
                  c. How about this early American picture frame?

2. Customer: I saw the robes in the display window. May I see them?

   Salesperson: a. We don't have too many left, but what size do you need?
                  b. Would you like a long or short robe?
                  c. Is this a gift?

3. Customer: I'm looking for a graduation gift.

   Salesperson: a. How much would you like to spend?
   b. What did you have in mind?
   c. Let me show you a few ideas. Is the gift for a boy or girl?

4. Customer: I need some film for my camera.

   Salesperson: a. Do you know the correct size to fit your camera?
   b. Black and white or color?
   c. How many cartridges would you like?

D. Read the following situation and answer the questions.

   Situation: The salesperson, who has worked in an office supply store for about four weeks, approaches a customer.

   Salesperson: May I help you?

   Customer: I'm just looking.

   Salesperson: Looking for anything special?

   Customer: I was thinking of a file cabinet for my office, if they aren't too expensive.

   Salesperson: With or without a lock?

   Customer: I really don't think I need a lock.

   Salesperson: For your office at home or at work?

   Customer: It is for my home — to hold tax records, bills, and things like that.

   Salesperson: What color?

   Customer: How about black?

   Salesperson: I'm not sure we have black. How about light grey?

   Customer: No thanks, I want black. I'll look around.

   Salesperson: Thanks for stopping in. If I can help you find anything else, let me know.

Questions:

1. What errors in qualifying the customer did the salesperson make during this sale?

2. What advice would you give this salesperson?

3. At what point in the above sales presentation should the salesperson have stopped asking questions and started showing merchandise?

4. Do you feel that another salesperson could have sold this customer a file cabinet? Explain.

PLANNING A FEATURE-BENEFIT SALES PRESENTATION

Your Learning Goals

After studying this chapter, you should:

- *be aware of the importance of planning a sales presentation.*
- *understand how to plan a feature-benefit sales presentation.*
- *understand the difference between a product feature and a buyer benefit.*
- *understand the common types of buyer benefits.*
- *be able to use the following formula in developing a sales presentation: feature + performance = buyer benefits.*
- *be able to translate product features into buyer benefits.*

Have you ever gone into a business to buy a specific product and left without buying anything? Have you ever asked for help and found that the salesperson didn't know what to say or do? Remember how you felt? You were probably disgusted or disappointed in the salesperson and the business.

If you're like most customers, you expect salespeople to give you friendly, courteous assistance. Customers appreciate salespeople who provide them with information in order to make a buying decision. Information about product features, how a product works, and what benefits customers will receive from owning that product is very helpful to customers.

THE IMPORTANCE OF THE SALES PRESENTATION

Product presentation plays an important role in helping the customer make a buying decision. An organized presentation allows the salesperson to maintain control of the sale and create customer desire for the product. A good feature-benefit sales presentation based on solid product knowledge also reassures the customer that the salesperson is knowledgeable. From which of the following salespeople would you rather buy?

Sales Situation 1

Customer: The sticker on this hair dryer lists 1250 watts. What does that mean?

Salesperson: I believe that has something to do with the power of the hair dryer.

Customer: How does it work?

Salesperson: I'm not sure. Let me check the instruction book.

Sales Situation 2

Customer: The sticker on this hair dryer lists 1250 watts. What does this mean?

Salesperson: That's a good question! The 1250 refers to the resistance rating of the heating element. Heating elements in hair dryers range from 600 to 1500 watts. The heating element produces the hot air. Is this dryer for yourself or are you buying it as a gift for someone else?

Customer: It's for me.

Salesperson: Most beauticians prefer the 1250-watt dryer so they can dry hair faster. With your length of hair I would recommend this 1250-watt dryer. It also has two speeds which allow you to dry your hair quickly or slowly. This is our most popular hair dryer. Let me show you how it works.

The second salesperson has a definite edge over the first salesperson who seems uncertain. A well-planned presentation of a product based on features, benefits, and customers' needs gives customers the assurance that they have come to the right place to buy.

Another important reason a feature-benefit presentation builds desire in customers is that the customers can personally experience those features and benefits of a product which will satisfy their needs. After you determine the customers' needs, you select a product to meet those needs. As a salesperson, you must know which features and benefits of a product will best meet a given customer's needs.

When customers can experience the benefits of a product firsthand, they know that the product will meet their needs. All customers have a certain amount of the *show me* attitude. It's up to the individual creativity of the salesperson to plan and organize the sales presentation so that the customers can experience the benefits in which they are most interested.

ILLUSTRATION 9-1
A feature-benefit presentation builds desire in customers by letting them personally experience those features and benefits which will satisfy their needs.

WHAT CUSTOMERS BUY

As a salesperson, it is your job to help satisfy the needs and wants of your customers with the products or services you sell. Before you can satisfy those needs, you must first understand the buying motives of customers. A buying motive is the reason customers purchase a product or service. You can determine customers' buying motives by observing customers' actions, asking customers questions, and listening to their responses. Listening to what your customers say will help you to emphasize the buyer benefits they need. The other half of your job is to show how your particular product or service will satisfy that need better than any other product or service available.

To be a successful salesperson, you need to understand why people buy. Researchers have found that people spend 90 to 95 percent of their time thinking about themselves. They buy or act only when they get the answer to the question: "How will I benefit?" If customers buy products or services because of the benefits they receive rather than the product features, then it is important that you sell them what they want to buy. In other words, sell them benefits!

The technique of selling benefits applies to both product and service selling. Each customer's buyer benefits may be different, but the fact remains that all customers buy personal benefits rather than product features. Salespeople who stress only product features in their sales presentations are not selling what customers want to buy. Customers will not buy until they answer the following questions: "How will I benefit?" "What will the product or service do for me?" "What can I gain from the product or service?"

PLANNING A FEATURE-BENEFIT SALES PRESENTATION

It has been said that selling is 90 percent preparation and 10 percent presentation. Therefore, a good way to introduce the concept of feature-benefit selling is to explain how to plan a feature-benefit sales presentation. A feature-benefit sales presentation is based on the needs and wants of your customer. This sales presentation is centered on the customer and the customer's buying motives rather than on the product and the salesperson. When the buyer benefits of a product or service are explained and demonstrated to a customer, the salesperson is making a feature-benefit sales presentation.

To be able to plan and complete a feature-benefit sales presentation, you should understand the parts of the presentation, what to say, and what to do during the presentation. The planning phase should be completed during the preapproach or before the actual sales presentation. The outline at the top of page 147 explains how to plan and make a feature-benefit sales presentation.

DETERMINING WHAT TO SAY

The sales presentation is that part of the sales process in which the salesperson explains and demonstrates how a product or ser-

A Feature-Benefit Sales Presentation

I. PLANNING THE SALES PRESENTATION

A. Determine What to Say

    1. Identify the features of your product.
    2. Learn how your product performs and what the product features will do for your customers.
    3. Translate your product features into buyer benefits.
    4. List at least five qualifying questions you should use to determine your customers' buying motives.

II. MAKING A FEATURE-BENEFIT SALES PRESENTATION

A. Determine What to Do

    1. Approach your customers.
    2. Begin your feature-benefit sales presentation with questions to qualify your customers.
    3. Listen to your customers and analyze their responses.
    4. Select a product and involve your customers in the demonstration.
    5. Appeal to your customers' buying motives and buyer benefits.
    6. Demonstrate the product stressing your customer's buyer benefits.
    7. Close the sale.
    8. Use suggestion selling and reassure your customers that a wise buying decision has been made.

B. Analyze, practice, and improve your sales presentation.

vice will benefit the customer. As the salesperson, you must know what you are going to say and do to encourage the customer to buy.

To organize a feature-benefit presentation, the salesperson must have an understanding of product features and buyer benefits. This understanding will help the salesperson determine what to say about a particular product or service.

Even though people buy benefits, product features are still important to the salesperson. Why? Because buyer benefits come from product features. A very important part of your job as a salesperson is to know your product features, be able to explain how your product performs, and know what benefits your customer will receive from the product or service. Before you can understand and perform these selling skills, you must understand what a product feature is and what a buyer benefit is. Once you have learned this, you can easily translate a product feature into a buyer benefit for your customer.

What Is a Product Feature?

A **feature** is a physical characteristic or quality. A **product feature** is a specific quality or characteristic of a product or service. It is something that you can see, feel, hear, smell, or taste. Product features are those facts which describe the product and answer the question: "What is it?"

The following are examples of product features and how to express them as feature statements in your sales presentation:

Product	Product Features	Feature Statement
Winter coat	• Treated with fabric protector • Down-filled • Zip-out lining	"For a winter coat to do its job, it should be *treated with fabric protector* and *down-filled*. This one is made even more versatile by having a *zip-out lining*."
Stereo receiver	• 50 watts • Headphone jack • AM-FM tuner • FM-muting switch	"A good stereo receiver should be power-rated for at least *50 watts*, have a separate *headphone jack*, and contain a quality *AM-FM tuner* with a separate *FM-muting switch*."
Sports car	• Four-speed transmission • Turbo-charged V8 engine • T-top sunroof	"Sports cars really need a *four-speed transmission* to deliver the power of a *turbo-charged V8 engine*. The *T-top sunroof* is an added feature of this model."
Hair dryer	• 1250-watt heating element • Two speeds • Two temperature controls • Six-foot heavy-duty cord • Unbreakable case	"An efficient hair dryer needs the heat available from a *1250-watt heating element* as well as the versatility of *two speeds* and *two temperature controls*. This dryer even has a *six-foot heavy-duty cord* and an *unbreakable case*."

The feature statements for the four product examples listed above describe physical characteristics or facts about the product. Chapter 6 on product information explained how and where a salesperson can obtain information about product features. To be a good salesperson, you need to develop the ability to arrange the product's features into an order of importance.

Let's return to the sales situation used earlier in this chapter in which a customer was looking at a hair dryer. The hair dryer had many product features. The features included a 1250-watt heating element, two speeds, two temperature controls, a heavy-duty six-foot cord, and an unbreakable case.

ILLUSTRATION 9-2
Product features are physical characteristics of a product.

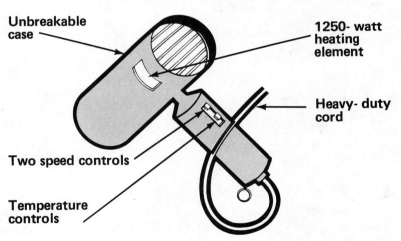

Unbreakable case

1250- watt heating element

Heavy- duty cord

Two speed controls

Temperature controls

Determining which product features are important will depend upon your customer. If the customer has long hair, you might want to stress the fact that the 1250-watt heating element will dry hair faster. To decide which features and benefits to stress in your sales presentation, you must determine your customer's needs. You determine needs by observing, by giving selling statements, or by asking your customers questions and then listening to and analyzing their responses.

What Is a Buyer Benefit?

A buyer benefit is anything that promotes the well-being of the buyer. It is the gain, the satisfaction, or whatever else the product or service means to the customer. The buyer benefit is the personal benefit the customer receives from using the product or service. Buyer benefits answer the customer's question: "How will I benefit by making this purchase?"

A Buyer Benefit . . .

- is the gain, satisfaction, or personal benefit received by the customer.
- answers the question: What does it mean to me? or How will I benefit?

Customers purchase products or services to receive buyer benefits. The following list contains the most common types of buyer benefits.

Buyer Benefits Include . . .

- money savings
- time savings
- pride of ownership
- convenience
- enjoyment
- comfort
- prestige
- security
- acceptance
- safety
- appearance
- pleasure

Notice that the relationship between customer buying motives (Chapter 5), the process of determining customer wants and needs (Chapter 8), and buyer benefits is a narrowing process which leads to the satisfaction of the customer's needs. Notice also that this relationship doesn't include product features. Why? Because customers do not buy just the product or service; they buy benefits. They buy what the product *means* to them — the satisfaction, the gain, and the benefits which go beyond the product or service itself.

Remember the last time you bought new clothing? Did you buy the merchandise for what it was or for what it meant to you? Weren't you really buying it for fashion, style, comfort, convenience, or warmth? When you buy the services of a barber or a

ILLUSTRATION 9-3
Customers buy what the product means to them.

March of Dimes

hair stylist, what are you really buying? When you buy a new purse or new billfold, what are you buying? In all cases, you purchase products and services because of the benefits you receive.

To make certain your customer understands the benefits that will be received by owning the product or service, state the benefits in specific terms. Do not assume that the customer understands the benefits. Make the benefits specific enough so the customer does not have to translate or interpret your selling statement. For example, if you think the customer is buying a washing machine because it is economical, don't say, "The machine is a good buy because it is economical." Rather, tell the customer, "You will save money by buying this machine because it uses less energy to operate than other models." Be specific. Help the customer understand the benefit by stating it in very specific terms.

If you feel that saving time may be the buyer benefit, state the benefit so that the customer understands what you mean. Whenever possible, explain how saving time is a benefit. If you are selling a lawn mower to a customer who has a large lawn, explain that by buying a riding mower, the customer can reduce mowing time by one hour. Tell the customer that by buying a riding lawn mower the one hour saved can be spent in playing tennis or a round of golf with friends. You are really selling the customer the added benefit of personal enjoyment.

However, it is also important to keep in mind that not all benefits appeal to all customers. Saving time may be the most important benefit to one customer yet another might be more interested in saving money or in fashion. Even though the features and benefits of a product or service don't change, the degree of importance placed on each feature-benefit will not only change with each customer, but may change each time the same customer buys.

Here are four examples of buyer-benefit statements that could be used in a sales presentation.

Product	Buyer Benefit	Buyer Benefit Statement
Winter coat	• Save money	"Because this coat is treated with fabric protector, it will wear longer, which means you will *save money.*"
Stereo receiver	• Listening enjoyment	"This stereo will provide you with many hours of *listening enjoyment.*"
Sports car	• Impress your friends	"The turbo engine and sunroof will really *impress your friends.*"
Hair dryer	• Save time	"This hair dryer is used by many professional beauticians. The two temperature controls and the two speeds will allow you to dry your hair faster. These features will *save you time* every morning or when you're in a hurry."

When a salesperson talks in terms of benefits, an appeal is made to the customers' buying motives. Benefit statements show customers how they will personally benefit from a product or service.

When you sell benefits, you are selling what the customer wants to buy. You are not talking about what you want to sell. There is a difference. The salesperson must be aware of this difference and develop the ability to transform product features into buyer benefits in order to complete a successful sale.

For example, how would you react if a salesperson said to you that a hair dryer had a 1250-watt heating element, two speeds, and two temperature controls? A typical customer would probably think, so what? By just stating the product's features, the salesperson is simply talking about the product. This does not assist the customer in understanding the personal benefits to be received from the product.

The only way you can be sure customers understand how they will benefit from the product is to tell them. Customers are more likely to buy a product when the salesperson explains the benefits to be received from owning the product. The 1250-watt heating element becomes important to customers when the salesperson explains that hair will dry faster and that because of this, the customers will have more time for leisure activities.

Translating Product Features into Buyer Benefits

Features alone have very little impact on the customer. Features become meaningful only when the customer can relate the feature to something that will be of personal benefit. Unfortunately, too many salespeople try to sell product features and assume the customer can translate those features into buyer benefits. In most cases, the customer is unable to mentally change the feature into a personal benefit and the sale is lost.

To be successful, you need to explain the feature in an easy-to-understand manner. Then you must be able to translate the feature into a buyer benefit for the customer. There are three steps in successfully translating product features into buyer benefits:

1. List the product feature(s).
2. Determine what the feature(s) will do for the customer.
3. Explain how your customer can benefit from the product feature(s).

The following example illustrates the use of this three-step process. To sell jogging shoes, the first step is to list as many product features as you can. The product features tell the customer about the physical features of the shoes and explain what the product *is*.

Step 1. List the product features for jogging shoes.

Feature		
• Cushioned arch support		
• Leather upper		
• Reinforced toe		
• Rubber sole		
• Tongue-hook for shoestrings		
• Cushioned insole		

The second step in translating product features into buyer benefits is to list **product performance**—what each feature *does*. Customers are interested in what the product or service will do for them.

Step 2. Determine what each feature does for the customer.

Feature	Performance	
• Cushioned arch support	• Provides foot support for running	
• Leather upper	• Provides durable wear	
• Reinforced toe	• Protects toes	
• Rubber sole	• Grips the surface better	
• Tongue-hook for shoestrings	• Holds the tongue up	
• Cushioned insole	• Helps prevent blisters	

ILLUSTRATION 9-4
Customers are interested in what the product or service will do for them.

Now you are ready for step three. In this step the salesperson changes the product features into something the customer will understand and appreciate — buyer benefits. During the sales presentation, your customer has been thinking about one basic question: How will I benefit? By changing product features into buyer benefits, you can answer your customer's question. The buyer benefit explains how the feature and the feature's performance will benefit the customer. The buyer benefit is what the feature *means* to the customer.

Step 3. Explain how your customer will benefit from the product features.

Feature	Performance	Buyer Benefit
• Cushioned arch support	• Provides foot support for running	• You will have more personal comfort.
• Leather upper	• Provides durable wear	• Because they wear longer, you will save money.
• Reinforced toe	• Protects toes	• You will be less likely to injure your toes.
• Rubber sole	• Grips the surface better	• Your feet will be more comfortable and you will be less likely to slip and fall.
• Tongue-hook for shoestrings	• Holds the tongue up	• Your feet will be more comfortable.
• Cushioned insole	• Helps prevent blisters	• Your feet will be more comfortable and you won't be so tired.

By selling buyer benefits, you are explaining the personal gain or personal benefits your customer will receive from owning the jogging shoes.

If you want your customers to understand how they will benefit from buying your product or service, you must sell them buyer benefits. When translating product features into buyer benefits, a simple formula to remember is:

Feature	+	Performance	=	Buyer Benefit
(What the feature *is*.)		(What the feature *does*.)		(What the feature *means* to the customer.)

Several examples of translating product features into buyer benefits using this formula are shown in the feature–benefit charts on pages 156–161.

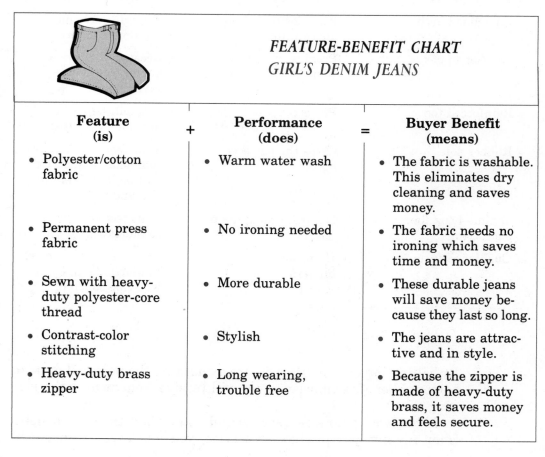

FEATURE-BENEFIT CHART
GIRL'S DENIM JEANS

Feature (is)	+	Performance (does)	=	Buyer Benefit (means)
• Polyester/cotton fabric		• Warm water wash		• The fabric is washable. This eliminates dry cleaning and saves money.
• Permanent press fabric		• No ironing needed		• The fabric needs no ironing which saves time and money.
• Sewn with heavy-duty polyester-core thread		• More durable		• These durable jeans will save money because they last so long.
• Contrast-color stitching		• Stylish		• The jeans are attractive and in style.
• Heavy-duty brass zipper		• Long wearing, trouble free		• Because the zipper is made of heavy-duty brass, it saves money and feels secure.

ILLUSTRATION 9-5

Buyer benefits show the gain customers will receive by owning the product.

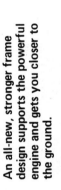

Progressive spring rear suspension means a more stable, comfortable ride.

Cast aluminum full disc wheel holds the industry's widest V-rated tire providing more stability and traction which means more safety for you.

A virtually maintenance-free, fully enclosed shaft drive saves you money while providing tremendous power.

An efficient megaphone exhaust system provides a high-performance sound for the ultimate ride.

An all-new, stronger frame design supports the powerful engine and gets you closer to the ground.

The four-gallon fuel tank located beneath the seat lowers the center of gravity for a safer ride.

The 40 mm air-assisted front forks for stable cornering provide a smoother, more comfortable ride.

The ventilated triple disc brakes with opposed-piston calipers provide more safety for you.

Photo courtesy of Yamaha Motor Corporation U.S.A.

FEATURE-BENEFIT CHART
QUARTZ WATCH

Feature (is)	+	Performance (does)	=	Buyer Benefit (means)
• LCD readout		• Shows seconds, minutes, hours, day, and date		• The watch is exact and easy to read with a prestigious look.
• Stopwatch function		• Can be used to time activities and sports events		• The stopwatch makes it easy to time activities.
• Alarm function		• Provides a reminder for a meeting or wake-up time		• With the alarm you will not be late for an important function.
• Quartz movement		• Provides unexcelled accuracy with no winding		• You have an accurate time-keeping watch which requires no winding.
• Water resistant		• Keeps watch in good operating condition		• You need not remove your watch when swimming, bathing, and the like.
• Stainless steel		• Protects watch from rust		• The watch will have a longer life and save you money.
• Flexible, adjustable band		• Provides perfect fit		• You will enjoy a perfectly fitting watch that is comfortable and attractive to wear.
• Calendar readout		• Automatically adjusts for odd- and even-day months		• The calendar will serve as a quick reference for dates.

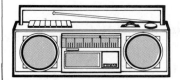

FEATURE-BENEFIT CHART
PORTABLE AM/FM STEREO
CASSETTE RECORDER

Feature (is)	+	Performance (does)	=	Buyer Benefits (means)
• Two-way speakers		• Provides broad stereo sound		• The speakers provide you with louder and better quality sound.
• Two built-in microphones		• Can tape "live" or directly off the radio		• You can tape whatever you want.
• LED indicators		• Provides easy search for tape selection		• You save time in playing and recording tapes.
• Battery operated		• Can play the radio or recorder anywhere		• You can enjoy music anywhere.
• Auto reverse		• Allows continuous playback		• The recorder is easy to rewind. You will save time.
• Auto-search music		• Advances tape to specific selection		• You can find special selections quickly.
• Lightweight		• Easy to carry		• The stereo/recorder is convenient for you to carry and you will enjoy music without becoming tired.
• Telescoping antenna		• Provides powerful receiver		• You will have clear reception and more listening enjoyment.
• Variable monitor		• Allows you to listen to music at any volume as you record		• You will enjoy uninterrupted listening while recording.

FEATURE-BENEFIT CHART
35mm SLR CAMERA

Feature (is)	+	Performance (does)	=	Buyer Benefit (means)
• 50mm 1.8 lens		• Gives normal vision pictures		• This lens will provide you with very natural and lifelike pictures.
• Automatic self-timer		• Takes time-delayed pictures		• With this automatic timer, you have the convenience of taking a picture of yourself.
• Automatic aperture control		• Sets aperture automatically		• This automatic control saves you time and gives you correct exposure for a good picture.
• Battery test button		• Tests battery		• You won't miss good shots because of a dead battery.
• Automatic focus		• Focuses camera		• Camera will always be focused so you don't waste film.
• Bayonet mounted lens		• Lens removes very easily		• Easy lens removal saves you time and effort.
• Through-the-lens light meter		• Measures light coming in		• Pictures are never under- or overexposed, so you save film and money.
• Leather carrying strap		• Easy to carry		• You won't get tired of carrying the camera, and the camera will be out of your way.
• Screw-in tripod mounting		• Can mount on tripod		• The tripod provides steadiness for a sharper image.

FEATURE-BENEFIT CHART
STEREO RECEIVER

Feature (is)	+	Performance (does)	=	Buyer Benefit (means)
• 65 watts per channel		• Provides more power		• You will have louder, clearer music for your listening enjoyment.
• .05 distortion rating		• Provides cleaner reproduction		• The low distortion provides you more listening enjoyment.
• Tape/auxiliary jacks		• Record from cassette, eight-track, or reel-to-reel recorder		• Record in any manner, which means you save time and money.
• FM channel lock		• Eliminates interference from CB's, airplanes, or other stations		• This feature provides you with better quality sound.
• Calibrated pre-amp control		• Provides a well-defined control of the music		• You can listen to the music however you prefer.
• Class A operation		• Provides maximum DB's with lower wattage rating		• You will save money because the possibility of blown-out speakers is prevented.

You begin an effective sales presentation by planning what you want to say and what you want to do. You should now understand product features, buyer benefits, and how to translate a product feature into a buyer benefit. With this information, you should be able to prepare an effective sales presentation stressing buyer benefits. The next chapter provides information on how to complete a feature-benefit sales presentation to motivate your customers to buy.

SALES TERMS

feature   product feature   product performance

SALES QUESTIONS

1. What types of information do customers want from salespeople?

2. What benefits do salespeople receive from having an organized sales presentation?

3. List three ways to determine your customer's buying motives.

4. Explain this statement: Customers buy benefits.

5. Why are product features important?

6. Explain the difference between a product feature and a buyer benefit.

7. List at least seven common types of buyer benefits.

8. Explain this statement: Not all benefits appeal to every one of your customers.

9. List the three steps in translating product features into buyer benefits.

10. Explain the formula: feature + performance = buyer benefits.

11. Explain this statement: Salespeople use product features to tell the customers about the product or service.

12. Explain this statement: Salespeople use buyer benefits to sell the customers what they want to buy.

SALES ACTIVITIES

A. Select a product and list at least five features and buyer benefits for that product.

B. Using the feature-benefit charts provided on pages 156–161, select the buyer benefit for each product that is most important to you. Ask two other people to select the most important buyer benefit for each product. Were the buyer benefits the same? Why is it important to understand the importance of the buyer benefits of each customer?

C. Select three products from the following list and complete a feature-benefit chart for each of the three products.

1. jeans
2. pen
3. heavy-duty tennis balls
4. home computer
5. golf balls
6. 35mm camera
7. alarm clock
8. billfold
9. backpack
10. tires

MAKING A FEATURE-BENEFIT SALES PRESENTATION

Your Learning Goals

After studying this chapter, you should:

- *know how to begin the sales presentation by asking qualifying questions.*
- *be able to get your customer's opinion.*
- *be able to check your customer's understanding.*
- *be able to determine your customer's buyer benefits.*
- *be able to present the product's features as buyer benefits.*
- *know how to involve your customer in the sales demonstration.*
- *be able to appeal to your customer's senses.*
- *know how to handle the product properly.*
- *be able to base the sales demonstration on your customer's buyer benefits.*

A good salesperson not only knows what to say to customers, but also knows how to present an effective sales demonstration. Although every step of the sales presentation is important, it is the salesperson's ability to creatively demonstrate or present the product or service to the customer that will result in a sale. Yet, too often the importance of this step is overlooked and the products are left to sell themselves. It is true that some products are easier to sell than others; but a creative, experienced salesperson knows how to demonstrate a product's features and benefits to keep customer interest and to motivate customers to buy.

In the last chapter you learned the importance of the sales presentation. You also learned that customers buy benefits—not product features. You learned how to plan a feature-benefit sales presentation and what to say in a sales presentation. Now that you understand your role, you should learn how to involve your customer in the presentation. Involving your customer and selling buyer benefits will help you to close more sales.

Let's briefly review the steps of a sale to identify the sequence of the sales presentation. The selling process may be divided into seven steps: the preapproach, the approach, determining needs and wants, the feature-benefit sales presentation, handling customer objections, closing the sale, and suggestion selling and reassurance.

ILLUSTRATION 10-1
The sales presentation follows a sequence of seven steps.

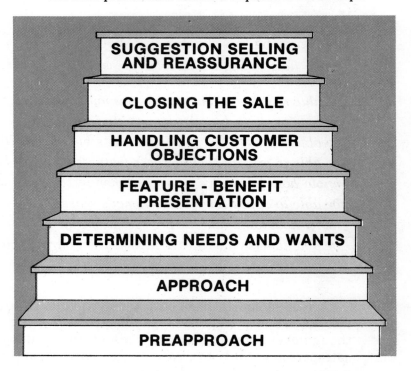

SUGGESTION SELLING
AND REASSURANCE

CLOSING THE SALE

HANDLING CUSTOMER
OBJECTIONS

FEATURE - BENEFIT
PRESENTATION

DETERMINING NEEDS AND WANTS

APPROACH

PREAPPROACH

DETERMINE WHAT TO DO

The first thing a good salesperson does is prepare for the sales presentation. This is called preapproach. Remember that the purpose of the preapproach is to study customer buying motives, product features, and buyer benefits. By studying these areas, you are learning information needed for the sales presentation. When you understand this information, you are ready to develop your sales presentation.

The first step in the actual sales presentation is the approach. The purpose of the approach is to welcome your customer, gain your customer's confidence and trust, and direct your customer's attention to the product.

The next step in the sales process is to determine your customer's needs and wants. This is done by asking **qualifying questions**. Good salespeople should not present a product to the customer until they understand what the customer wants. The product you decide to present, as well as your actual feature-benefit presentation, should be based on your customer's responses to qualifying questions.

It is important to realize that the success of your feature-benefit presentation will depend on how well you determine your customers' buying motives and needs and wants, and how well you are able to involve your customers in the sales presentation.

BEGIN THE FEATURE-BENEFIT SALES PRESENTATION BY QUALIFYING YOUR CUSTOMER

After you have approached the customer, begin the sales presentation by qualifying your customer. Selling involves gaining information from the customer. Successful salespeople don't sell what they like about a product or service, they sell what the customer likes. In order to find out what your customer really likes, you need to ask questions, listen to your customer's answers, and watch your customer's reactions to your sales presentation.

Asking good qualifying questions gets your customer involved in the sales presentation. It is the first step in determining your customer's wants, needs, likes, and dislikes about a product or service. The more you find out, the easier it will be to continue the presentation by selecting the product which meets your customer's needs and wants. Additional qualifying questions should be used throughout the sales presentation.

The timing of your questions is important. Questions will help you control the sale. Is the sale going too fast or too slow? Does the customer understand what you are saying? Are you asking too many questions? Is the customer's attention wandering? What is the customer thinking?

The best way to determine if you are communicating with the customers is to ask questions, listen to the answers, and observe the customer's behavior. The questions must be skillfully worded and presented at the proper time to keep the presentation in step with the customer. Let the customer's understanding serve as your timing guide. You can then adjust the timing of your demonstration to a speed that will best serve your customer. Here are a few examples of types of questions to ask while giving your sales presentation.

Get the Customer's Opinion

Your customer's opinion is important. If you don't understand your customer's opinion, you will most likely lose the sale. To better understand your customer's opinion, ask these types of questions: What is your opinion? Have you ever tried this? Do you like this feature? What do you think of that?

Check the Customer's Understanding

During the sale it is important to check your customer's understanding. You may be showing the customer the wrong merchandise. Use these kinds of questions: Is this right? Does this make sense to you? Is this clear? How does that look to you? Do you understand? Should I go over the procedure again?

ILLUSTRATION 10-2
During the sale, check your customer's understanding by asking questions.

Give Selling Statements As Questions

Sometimes it is best for customers to draw a conclusion for themselves. Instead of giving a direct selling statement, put it in the form of a question. For example: Don't your think the blue goes well with the silver? Isn't this feature nice? Doesn't this fabric feel soft? When asked these questions, the customers are actively participating in the sale. This is a desirable way for customers to sell themselves.

Check for a Wandering Mind

Sometimes customers' minds wander. They may be thinking of their answer to your last question. They may be distracted by someone or something. An alert salesperson will observe when customers' minds are wandering. Bring them back to the sale by asking a question about the item being shown. For example: "Have you noticed the safety features?" "Will you open this for me?" "Would you like to try it on?"

A salesperson's question must come from honest concern for the customers, not attempts at flattery nor obvious efforts to manipulate the customers. Develop skill in asking your customers the right questions at the right time. Ask your customers *who, what, where, when,* and *how* questions. The answers to these and other

ILLUSTRATION 10-3
An alert salesperson observes when customers' minds are wandering and brings them back to the sale with questions.

Ask Questions to Determine . . .

- who will use the product.
- what your customer expects from the product.
- what your customer likes and dislikes.
- where the product will be used.
- when the product is needed
- how the product will be used.

questions serve as clues to understanding your customers' needs, wants, and buying motives.

The following sales example illustrates a selling technique you may use to approach customers and begin the sales presentation.

The Approach

Salesperson: Good morning. I see you're looking at our new 13″ portable color TV set. This set has several unique features. Let me show you how it works. [*The salesperson turns the set on.*]

Customer: OK.

The salesperson opened this sale by using a merchandise approach. The approach directed the customer's attention to the product and led the customer right into the sales presentation. Since the salesperson has the customer's attention, the next step is to determine the customer's needs and wants.

Now that the sale has started, the salesperson needs to ask qualifying questions in order to base the sales presentation on the customers' needs. (Remember, good qualifying questions ask the customer *who, what, where, when,* and *how.*) Qualifying questions get the sale started and keep the customer involved in the sales presentation. They also provide the salesperson with needed information about the customer. Notice the questions used to qualify the customer in the following sales example.

Qualifying the Customer

Salesperson: This portable TV is an excellent set. As you can see, the picture is sharp, bright, and clear even under our fluorescent lights. The picture adjusts

	to any light level automatically. Will you be using the set in the living room, family room, or bedroom?
Customer:	I'm not sure. I may use it in my study or it may be used in my son's bedroom.
Salesperson:	I see. Do you have any TV sets in your home now?
Customer:	I have a 21″ color TV in the living room.
Salesperson:	Are you happy with your set?
Customer:	I sure am. I haven't spent much in repairs over the last five years and the picture is still good.
Salesperson:	That's good! It seems TV repair bills, like everything else, are going up. Who will be using this set?
Customer:	Probably Dave, our youngest son, and myself. I'm making one of our bedrooms into an office and study and would like a TV for it.
Salesperson:	So you're probably looking for a set that can be moved easily from a bedroom to your study?
Customer:	Yes, that's very important.

ILLUSTRATION 10-4
The salesperson must ask qualifying questions in order to base the sales presentation on the customer's needs.

The salesperson has asked several good qualifying questions:

1. Will you be using the set in the living room, family room, or bedroom?
2. Do you have any TV sets in your home now?
3. Are you happy with your set?
4. Who will be using this set?

By asking these questions, the salesperson is qualifying the customer and determining the customer's needs and wants. By listening to the customer's replies, the salesperson finds out what the customer wants. The actual sales demonstration can now be based on the customer's buying motives and buyer benefits. When qualifying the customer, don't get so wrapped up in your questions that you forget to listen to your customer's responses.

INVOLVE THE CUSTOMER IN THE DEMONSTRATION

Asking questions is only a small part of the necessary communication between customers and salespeople. Listening to the customers' answers is as important as asking the questions. The customers' responses will let you know which benefits to stress. Customers can communicate their feelings by the way they react to a question or feature-benefit statement. Always observe the customers' movements, facial expressions, and tone of voice.

Once you have qualified the customer with good questions, keep the customer involved in the sale by demonstrating or showing the product's features and benefits. It is very important that the customer be actively involved in the **product demonstration.** Think about yourself for a moment. Which of the following activities do you enjoy most: listening to a lecture, reading a book, watching a movie, or actually participating in an activity? Your answer may vary depending on your mood, but most people prefer to participate in activities rather than to listen, read, or watch an activity. Psy-

Involve the Customer in the Sales Demonstration to . . .

- increase customer interest in and create desire for the product or service.
- help the customer develop a sense of ownership.
- get the customer to answer questions to determine additional needs and wants.
- demonstrate specific buyer benefits of interest to the customer.

Colorado Department of Public Relations

chologists say that people remember 90 percent of what they participate in, 50 percent of what they see, and 10 percent of what they hear.

This principle also holds true in selling. Most customers learn more and enjoy the sales presentation more if they are involved in it. Customers go through five mental stages in their buying process—attention, interest, desire, conviction, and action. Keeping the customers actively involved in the presentation will maintain their interest and create desire for the product or service. The effective salesperson gets customers to actually experience how the benefits of the product or service will meet their needs. As customers handle the product, try it on, or see how it works, they begin to develop a sense of ownership as they mentally see themselves possessing the product.

You learned earlier in this chapter that a good way to involve your customers in the sale is to ask them questions. The next step in keeping customers involved is to get the product in their hands, or to demonstrate how the product works. An effective salesperson gets customers to actually experience how the product works and how the benefits of the product will meet their needs. The salesperson should make certain that the customers handle the product or see how it works.

Appeal to Your Customer's Senses

People use the five senses of touch, smell, taste, sight, and hearing to gather information about things around them. A successful salesperson will attempt to appeal to as many of these senses as possible during a sales presentation. The purpose of this appeal is to familiarize the customer with the product and to develop a sense of ownership of the product. For example, a customer may think a pair of shoes look great. If buying the shoes satisfies a fashion need, then the sight of shoes is enough to develop a sense of ownership. But if the customer has a need for comfortable shoes, just looking at the shoes and listening to the salesperson talk about the shoes will probably not satisfy this need for comfort. The customer will want to try the shoes on to experience the comfort personally. Trying on the shoes will give the customer the opportunity to decide if the product will satisfy this need for comfort.

To understand how to appeal to your customer's senses, you must start with the product itself. Determine how many ways the customer can experience the product. Lipstick, for example, can be experienced through the senses of sight, touch, taste, and smell. Clothing can be experienced through sight, and touch. Clothing being purchased for personal use should be tried on and viewed in a mirror, if possible. A radio or stereo receiver can be experienced through the sense of hearing. By listening to the sound of a radio or stereo receiver, your customer can personally experience and judge the quality of the product.

When trying to determine to which of your customer's five senses to appeal, ask yourself the following questions:

Hearing — Are there sounds created by the product that would appeal to a customer?

Touch — How does the product feel? A pleasant texture will increase the value of the product in the customer's mind.

Smell — Does the smell or fragrance of the product reveal the product's desirable qualities?

Taste — Does the product have an appealing taste or will the product produce a good taste which the customer can imagine?

Sight — Will the appearance of the product improve the customer's self-image or gain the approval of other people?

You can have the customer actually look at, listen to, touch, smell, or taste some products. However, another way to appeal to the senses is through the customer's imagination. If the product will produce a result which cannot be demonstrated, help the cus-

ILLUSTRATION 10-6
The sense of touch can help the customer develop a sense of ownership in the product.

tomer to imagine or sense the satisfaction by making selling statements such as:

"Wouldn't it be great to come home after a hard day at work and jump into a pool for a refreshing swim?"

"Think how nice it would be to have 9 percent more money in your savings account by the end of the year."

"With the long-lasting qualities of these cosmetics, you'll look great all day!"

Use Showmanship or Dramatization

A good demonstration should make a favorable impression on your customer. To accomplish this, you may want to dramatize your product by using **showmanship**. Showmanship, or **dramatization**, involves using descriptive words, hand and body gestures, enthusiasm, change in your tone of voice, and props to create customer desire for your product. For example, a jeweler will use a special light to bring out the sparkling qualities of a diamond ring when showing it to an engaged couple. The ring may also be placed elegantly on a velvet pad to dramatize the richness or value of the ring. The jeweler will also use terms like exquisite, everlasting, unique, finest, and extraordinary to describe the ring. Showmanship is used to dramatize the ring to make a favorable and lasting impression. Even if the customers decide to shop around, the favorable impression made by the salesperson will usually bring the customers back to buy. The following examples describe how salespeople dramatize certain products.

Luggage — The luggage is placed on the floor; the salesperson then stands or jumps on it to dramatize its strength and durability.

Wrinkle-free dress or shirt — The salesperson crumples the dress or shirt, places it in a sack, and leaves it there while explaining other feature-benefits of the product. The salesperson then takes it out of the bag to dramatize its "just-ironed" look.

China cup — The salesperson carefully places a delicate china cup on the floor and then stands on it to dramatize its strength.

Smoke alarm — The salesperson holds a match near it to set off the alarm.

Microwave oven — The salesperson places a cup of water in the oven and shows how the water can be brought to boil in about a minute.

Handle the Product Properly

There are two points that you, as a salesperson, must think about when handling products. One is to remember that, while you are watching and observing the customer, the customer is also observing you. The customer will notice right away how you handle the merchandise. The product, regardless of its price, deserves the respect of the salesperson. If you handle it roughly and carelessly, it gives the customer the impression that the product is not very valuable — and who wants to buy something that's not valuable? On the other hand, if you handle the product with care, the customer will see the product as a more valuable investment.

Don't be confused about handling a product carefully to show respect and treating a product roughly in order to demonstrate a feature. In a previous example, a salesperson placed a china cup on the floor and stood on it. This dramatized the feature of strength. The cup, however, should have been handled carefully before placing it on the floor and after standing on it. When this demonstration was over, the salesperson should have picked up the cup, wiped it clean and carefully placed it into the customer's hands for inspection.

Always handle the product so that the customer can see the product and the feature you are trying to point out. Small items should be brought as close as possible for the customer to see. A salesperson's hands should not cover up important features of the product. With larger products, the salesperson should make sure that the customer is following the sales demonstration by pointing clearly to the product features being discussed. Improper handling of the product by the salesperson could result in the loss of a sale.

Use Selling Aids

There are times when the product the salesperson is trying to sell is too large, too noisy, or otherwise impossible to demonstrate. In these cases, the salesperson must rely on the use of **selling aids.** Selling aids are visual tools the salesperson uses to provide the customer with more information about the product. Selling aids, of course, can be used anytime, even if the product can be effectively demonstrated in the presence of the customer. In fact, most people who work in nonretail sales occupations use several types of selling aids.

Selling aids can include models of the product, brochures, flip charts, display boards, pictures, graphs, slides, films, overlays, and anything else salespeople can find to help sell their products. Many selling aids are produced by the manufacturers of the products and are made available to salespeople. When these selling aids are not provided, creative salespeople can put together their own. Successful salespeople often carry pictures of businesses and people who have bought and used their products.

In the previous sales example, the salesperson began the sales presentation with good qualifying questions. The customer's responses to the qualifying questions provided the information the salesperson needed to start the sales demonstration. The salesperson can now base the demonstration part of the sales presentation on the customer's buying motives and buyer benefits. The sale continues with the salesperson starting the actual **feature-benefit sales demonstration.**

Demonstrating Buyer Benefits

Salesperson: I mentioned that this portable TV set has several outstanding features. Let me explain the benefits of owning this set.

Customer:	OK, but my study isn't completed yet, so I have plenty of time before I buy.
Salesperson:	That's fine. When you do buy a set, you said it may be used in a bedroom or your study.
Customer:	Yes, that's right.
Salesperson:	Well, this set is lightweight and portable. It only weighs 33 pounds. It will be very easy for you to move from room to room. The handle makes it easy to lift and carry. Here, lift it to see how light it is.
Customer:	[*lifting TV set by the handle*] Yes, it sure is a lot lighter than our 21″ TV set. It should be easy to move.

ILLUSTRATION 10-7
The salesperson may be able to prove certain benefits by involving the customer in the sales demonstration.

Since the customer mentioned the need to move the TV from one room to another, the salesperson demonstrated that the set was lightweight and portable by having the customer lift the TV set. The salesperson was able to prove a benefit by involving the customer in the sales demonstration. The sales demonstration continues with the salesperson providing additional feature-benefits, asking more qualifying questions, and involving the customer in the demonstration.

Feature-Benefit Demonstration

Salesperson: You mentioned that you were happy with your present set because it didn't cost you much in repairs. I'm sure you'll be interested in learning that this 13″ portable is the same brand as your 21″ and has one of the lowest frequency-of-repair records in the entire TV industry. That means that you'll certainly save repair costs by purchasing this set. It will give you many hours of trouble-free viewing enjoyment. That's certainly a very important benefit, isn't it?.

Customer: Yes, it sure is.

Salesperson: What other features do you want in a TV set?

Customer: I want a good, bright picture and a set that gets good reception with just an indoor antenna.

Salesperson: That makes sense. Just look at the type of picture you get with this set on several channels. [*Salesperson has customer switch the channel selector and view several channels.*] There are two good reasons this set gets such an excellent picture.

Salesperson: This was one of the first manufacturers to have 'automatic fine tuning.' Push that AFT button right there and see what happens to the picture. The picture is locked in by an "electronic video-guard tuning system." Because this tuner is electronic, it has no internal moving parts to wear out or cause picture problems. The picture will stay sharp for years. Isn't that picture bright and clear?

Customer: It sure is.

Salesperson: The second feature which guarantees you a high-quality picture is our solid-state, automatic fringe-lock circuit. This means that your picture will be excellent even in fringe reception areas. You also will not be bothered by airplane flutter, electronic interference, or other reception problems. You'll enjoy many hours of clear viewing.

Customer: If the picture stays like that, I'll be very pleased with the reception.

Salesperson: Now, let me be sure I understand what you've told me. You've said that you wanted a set to be almost

maintenance free, to be portable, to have a good, bright picture, and to get good reception. This set will certainly deliver all those benefits to you and more. Now don't you think this 13″ portable is what you're looking for?

Customer: It seems to be what I need. I don't particularly care for this white, modern finish though. Dave's bedroom and my study have dark walnut paneling and brown carpeting. I think we'd prefer a dark brown cabinet.

The salesperson has continued to involve the customer in the sales demonstration by: having the customer *use* the channel selector and *view* several channels, and having the customer *push* the AFT button to *view* the clear picture. These techniques are used to involve the customer in the sales presentation and to present the buyer benefits which the customer said were important. The salesperson has increased the customer's desire to own the TV by having the customer use the product. The customer in our sales situation has shown an interest in and desire for the TV and has even given the salesperson several buying signals. The salesperson can now close the sale based on the choice of cabinet finish.

Closing the Sale

Salesperson: Yes, I think a dark walnut cabinet would probably look very nice in your bedroom and study. [*Taking the customer to a TV in a walnut cabinet, the salesperson closes the sale.*] Would you like to put this on your account or will this be cash?

Customer: Well, I guess I'll charge it.

Salesperson: [*Reassuring the customer.*] You've made a good purchase. You'll get the same good picture and service from this set as you receive from your 21″ set.

ILLUSTRATION 10-9
By being customer-oriented, a salesperson will close more sales.

In summary, to be an effective salesperson, you need to carefully plan what you are going to say and how you are going to make a feature-benefit sales demonstration. In planning the sale, you should list your product's features and buyer benefits, and develop qualifying questions to determine the customer's buying motives.

After your approach, begin the actual sale by using qualifying questions. Once you determine your customer's needs and wants, stress the buyer benefits that will satisfy your customer's buying needs. Involve your customer in the sales demonstration, appeal to the customer's five senses, and provide a sales demonstration centered on your customer. A customer-oriented salesperson will effectively close many sales and bring the customer back to the business to buy again.

SALES TERMS

qualifying questions   showmanship   selling aids

product demonstration   dramatization   feature-benefit sales demonstration

SALES QUESTIONS

1. List the seven steps of a sales presentation.

2. List three things a salesperson should study in the preapproach step of a sale.

3. What are three purposes of the approach in a sales presentation?

4. Explain how qualifying questions will help you gain control of the sale.

5. List at least four types of information you can obtain from the customer by asking good qualifying questions.

6. List four reasons why salespeople should involve the customer in the sales demonstration.

7. What are the five senses a salesperson should appeal to in a sales presentation?

8. What questions can you ask yourself about a product to determine which of the five senses to appeal to?

9. Why are selling aids used in a sales presentation?

10. List at least seven types of selling aids.

11. Should your sales presentation center on the product or selling aid or on the customer? Explain your answer.

12. How can you center your sales demonstration on the customer?

SALES ACTIVITIES

A. Select any two products and list at least five buyer benefits for each product. Also list five qualifying questions to ask a customer for each product.

B. For the two products you selected in Part A, list the customer senses you would appeal to for each product.

HANDLING CUSTOMER OBJECTIONS

11

Your Learning Goals

After studying this chapter, you should:

- *be able to welcome customer objections.*
- *understand the necessary attitude to accept objections from customers.*
- *know the difference between an excuse and a real objection.*
- *be able to listen to customer objections.*
- *have skill in pausing before answering customer objections.*
- *be able to show empathy for your customers.*
- *be able to restate customer objections.*
- *be able to answer customer objections.*
- *be able to check the customer's reactions to your response.*

Up to this point in the sale, you have determined the customer's wants and needs, helped the customer to select the right product or service, and made your sales demonstration. You have presented the features and benefits that you think will appeal to your customer's buying motives. You have watched and listened for signs of approval or disapproval. Your customer seemed interested. But now, the customer raises an objection. The customer seems to resist buying.

It is at this point that many salespeople stop selling because they feel that the customer is no longer interested in the sale. This is not true! Customer sales resistance is normal. If you have attracted the customer's attention, aroused interest, and created desire, then why shouldn't the customer ask questions or raise objections? This shows that the customer is interested in the product or service.

WELCOME CUSTOMER OBJECTIONS

Salespeople should welcome objections. They are an important part of the selling process and should be expected. Few sales happen without customer objections. An **objection** is a customer's concern or hesitation when considering the purchase of products or services. Objections are not roadblocks or barriers in completing the sale. If customers aren't interested in your products or services, chances are they won't bother raising objections. Objections show that customers are interested in buying but that they lack certain information.

Why, then, do customers raise objections? Objections are a natural way for the customer to weigh value against price. "Am I getting my money's worth?" "Should I buy now?" "Is this the right product or service for me?" A good salesperson must be able to show the customer that value outweighs price. Value exists in the mind of the customer, and this is the value the salesperson should stress. If the customer feels that the product or service is a good value, your chances of making a sale are good.

Too many salespeople feel insulted if a customer raises an objection, but they shouldn't feel this way. The customer may have missed a point the salesperson made during the presentation. Instructions about how to operate or care for the item may have been misunderstood. Perhaps the customer doesn't feel the right selection of product or service was made.

Whatever the reason for customer objections, the salesperson must not show a feeling of annoyance or bother. An objection may seem small or unimportant to the salesperson. However, if objections are raised by customers, those objections are important to them. At no time should a salesperson show disinterest or lack of concern. A disinterested attitude often turns the customer's attention away from what is being sold. The customer will quickly develop a disinterested attitude, too, and will probably go elsewhere to shop.

The importance of the proper attitude in answering objections cannot be overemphasized. As a salesperson, you must control the sale by being courteous. Answer objections in a pleasant voice.

ILLUSTRATION 11-1
The value of a product exists in the mind of the customer.

Courtesy of Allis-Chalmers

Don't shake your head, roll your eyes, or raise your voice. Show your customers that you are sincere in helping them make a wise buying decision. When your customers give objections, listen carefully and show concern. Respect their opinions. Your attitude should be positive and should demonstrate to your customers that you are ready and willing to answer any objections they might have. By having the proper attitude in handling sales resistance, you will find more success in selling.

Welcome objections. They are a sure sign that the customer is thinking about the sale. Turn every objection to your sales advantage. Do not argue. Customer objections will give you an opportunity to measure the customer's interest and to select those features and benefits that will make your presentation more appealing to the customer's buying motives. Your customer may say "no" several times during your presentation and may say "yes" only once to become a buyer. Remember, customer objections show the customer's interest in the sale, and an interested customer usually makes a purchase.

OBJECTIONS OR EXCUSES

Good salespeople realize that customers often display **sales resistance.** The most common forms of customer sales resistance are real objections and excuses. It is important for salespeople to learn the differences between them. Sales resistance is a natural part of the buying process. In order for a customer to buy, all forms of sales resistance must be answered.

Real objections are concerns or hesitations the customer has when considering the purchase of products or services. Generally real objections are based on the merchandise. The customer is uncertain about a merchandise feature or service. The customer may express a genuine concern about the price of the item, when to make the purchase, or how many to buy. Real objections will tell you what is keeping the customer from buying. You may hear these common real objections: "Does this come in a different style?" "I really don't like this color." "It seems hard to repair." "I can't operate that; it's too complicated!" "I'm not familiar with that brand."

Customers also give **excuses** to delay making a purchase or to avoid becoming involved in the sale. Customer excuses are seldom related to the merchandise or service. They are generally insincere reasons. A few common excuses include: "I just want to look around." "I don't need any today." "I can't afford it." "I'll think about it." "No, thanks, not today." "I never buy before I shop around."

Your customers will vary in the ways they reveal or conceal their sales resistance. Some customers do not hesitate to express their feelings. They are direct and straightforward with their objections. If their objections are sincere, the customers will be interested in your response.

However, some customers do not readily voice their objections. Their concerns are called **hidden objections.** Obviously, if customers do not tell you their objections or concerns, it is much more difficult to determine whether or not they are interested in the product or service. Skillful questioning, observation, and customer participation may give you a clue to the customers' real objections. One of the best techniques for bringing out hidden objections is to try to close the sale. If customers are not ready to buy, they will usually give objections or excuses. When objections or excuses are expressed, they are much easier to answer.

Sales resistance that comes at the beginning of the selling process is usually an excuse, but not always. For example, the customer might say, "Oh, no! I don't like slip-on shoes." In this example the customer is objecting to the product. When the customer raises an objection about the item at the beginning of the sale, remove that item, if possible, and bring out another. You may not have properly determined the customer's needs or wants. You will need to ask a few more well-chosen questions to determine the desired item.

Most real objections are given later in the sales presentation when the customer has learned more about the product or service. If excuses arise later in the sale, it means that you are losing the customer's interest or the customer has a hidden objection. For example:

Salesperson:	This propane camping heater is an excellent buy.
Customer:	Yes, but I want to think it over first.

At this point, don't give up. By saying "yes" to your sales statement, the customer has agreed that the propane camping heater is an excellent buy. This is a buying signal. The customer's remark seems like an excuse, but it may really be a hidden objection. Continue the sale.

Salesperson:	You seem to like this camping heater. Why don't you feel it is right for you?
Customer:	Well, I'm not sure I like a propane heater. It doesn't seem safe to me.
Salesperson:	I can understand your concern. Let me show you a special safety feature that is built into this particular camping heater.

What seemed to be an excuse was actually a hidden objection. The concern for safety was not adequately covered during the sales presentation. The customer needed more information and reassurance that the product was safe. Had the salesperson said, "Thanks for looking. Stop back again," the sale would have been lost.

In order to handle sales resistance, a salesperson must turn the customer's negative attitude into a positive one. It is very important that a salesperson be able to distinguish between real objections and excuses. This can be difficult because objections and excuses may sound similar. With experience a salesperson will be able to determine if the customer's attitude shows indifference or a sincere interest. Remember, real objections generally relate to the product or service, while excuses are used by customers to delay a decision to buy.

What should you do if you feel the customer has given you an excuse? The best way to handle an excuse is to treat it like a real objection — because it might be. Answer or acknowledge the excuse and continue to sell. However, don't spend time with a customer who is truly disinterested. Here is an example of how a positive-minded salesperson helped a customer who kept making excuses.

Salesperson:	That set of luggage is lightweight molded polyurethane. It is great for trips.
Customer:	I really can't afford it. [*Customer lifts a piece of luggage.*]
Salesperson:	That is a problem for many people who wish to invest in quality luggage. We have several payment plans. I'm sure you will find one of them to be satisfactory.
Customer:	No, thanks, I don't like to charge things. Besides, I'm not planning a trip right now.
Salesperson:	Many customers like to begin a set by buying just one piece of luggage at a time. It is less expensive, and they can add a matching piece of luggage later when they might need it.
Customer:	I never buy anything before I shop around. [*Customer sets the luggage down but hesitates to leave.*]
Salesperson:	I can see you are a wise shopper. Let me point out a few important features you will want to look for in any piece of luggage. It should be light in weight and should have a key lock for protection of your belongings. I would also recommend that it be rugged and scratch resistant. Be sure and ask if other pieces of the set will be available several years from now, so you can add an additional piece later. Shop and compare. I'm sure you will find our luggage to be a fine value for your investment.
Customer:	I'll do that! Thank you for your help.

Three times the customer gave the salesperson an excuse not to buy. The customer gave excuses, yet the salesperson noticed that the customer seemed interested. The customer picked up a piece of luggage and set it down but did not walk away. It would have been easy for the salesperson to quit selling and help another customer, but with a positive attitude, this salesperson wanted to help this customer make a wise buying decision. The salesperson showed concern for the customer by suggesting features to look for when buying any piece of luggage. The salesperson had a good knowledge of the merchandise. Chances are this customer will come back to buy the luggage.

Always show a sincere concern for your customer. Don't stop selling until you are sure that the customer is no longer interested in your products or services.

PREPARE TO ANSWER CUSTOMER OBJECTIONS

As you sell, you will notice that many customers will have the same objections or questions about the merchandise or service you are selling. The best way to prepare answers to objections is to expect certain objections from your customers. You know that customers have similar buying motives. If you understand why people buy and you are completely knowledgeable about your merchandise features and their benefits to customers, you should be able to prepare answers for your customers' objections before the sale begins. Be prepared! By anticipating objections, you will be able to build a more effective sales presentation around the buying motives of your customers.

Learn everything you can about what you sell. Customers expect salespeople to have a complete knowledge of the merchandise or service they sell. If you attempt to bluff or are not prepared to answer objections about the item for sale, the customers will quickly lose confidence in your ability to sell. Most likely, the customers will give you excuses and will leave without any further consideration.

ILLUSTRATION 11-2
Salespeople should take the opportunity to study the merchandise or service they sell.

The merchandise you sell has value to your customers. Objections must be overcome with value. More facts, clarification, and review of all the advantages the product or service offers will help strengthen its value to the point where value can overcome the objection. Because of its quality, your merchandise will vary greatly in price. You should be able to find reasons to justify the price by the value of the merchandise. Be able to explain to your customers the difference in value between the differently priced items.

The best method of anticipating objections is to plan a sales presentation that includes all the information the customers will need to make a wise buying decision. Be prepared to answer objections! You will find it helpful to make a list of the most common objections or questions about the merchandise or service features you are selling. By writing such a list, you will be better able to anticipate many objections before you begin selling. List the product or service feature and the frequently asked objection to the feature. Then write a positive sales statement for each objection. Give the customers benefits for each feature you have listed. Even if you feel the objection is not a real objection, attempt to answer it.

Be critical of what you sell. Look at your items through your customers' eyes. When attempting to answer objections or to list benefits for each feature, ask yourself *why?* "Why is this blouse made of 45 percent dacron and 55 percent cotton?" "Why does this iron use tap water and others do not?" "Why do some tennis rackets have aluminum frames while others have wooden frames?" Take the most important features and benefits as well as the most frequently asked objections and develop a more effective sales presentation. Prepare for sales resistance before you greet your customers. By working these features and benefits into your sales talk, you eliminate many objections customers might have. This will strengthen your sales presentation.

When selling, the customers' objections may be slightly different from ones you are prepared to answer. Don't let this surprise you. Give the customers clear, logical, and complete answers. This shouldn't be difficult if you have anticipated objections. However, if you are not prepared to answer objections or questions, don't bluff or try to make up answers. This can get you into serious trouble.

As you prepare your sales presentation, don't raise objections unnecessarily in order to answer them. This is the wrong way to anticipate or answer objections. Avoid mentioning objections just for the sake of answering them. Statements which point to possible negative features in what you are selling may raise the customers' doubts about the product. For example, don't say, "Most people think that microwave ovens are not safe because too much radiation escapes from around the door." Instead, emphasize all the positive features about what you are selling. "I'm sure you would like to know that these microwave ovens have been tested for radiation leakage to insure that they are perfectly safe." This is a positive way of handling the possible objection concerning radiation.

By anticipating objections, you will build the confidence of your customers in your ability to understand their needs and wants and their buying motives. Of course, not all objections can be anticipated. When selling, if you receive many objections from your customers, you may need to change your sales presentations. Add to your list any new, unexpected sales objections that a customer raised during the last sale. Use this information to better overcome the sales resistance of your next customer. The better prepared you are, the fewer objections you should receive.

BUYING DECISION OBJECTIONS

Before customers make a purchase, they must make five buying decisions — what to buy, where to buy, what price to pay, when to buy, and how much to buy. Customer objections will usually fall into these same five general areas: product, place, price, time, and quantity.

Product

Your customers may raise objections dealing with the products or services. They may not like the style, color, size, model, quality, or other features of the product. Salespeople must know their merchandise and be able to *tell the features* and *sell the benefits* of the product. Product knowledge is a must. You must know your merchandise or service better than the customers do. Show confidence in what you sell. Obviously if you don't have confidence, the customers won't either.

Place

When customers object to the business, they are usually reflecting on a negative experience they may have had in the past. The image of the business is very important! Salespeople, advertising, store design and layout, merchandise, and treatment of customers all contribute to the customers' image of the business. Salespeople have a key responsibility in improving the business's image to customers. Assure the customers that you and the business firm are there to serve them. Point out those positive aspects of the business that will convince the customers of their importance to you and to the business.

Price

Sometimes it seems as if price is the biggest obstacle a salesperson has to overcome when selling. Price is probably the most talked about objection, but many customers don't really treat it as an objection. Instead, price is often a frustration for customers because higher prices have become a way of life.

If price is an objection, show the customer that the merchandise or service being offered is priced right. Point out special features or high quality which make the product worth the price. Merchandise that is reduced in price will also help salespeople in selling. Alert salespeople can use a special promotion to sell other merchandise as well as the merchandise being promoted. If the merchandise is sale priced, emphasize the value and show how much the customer will save. Sell value — not price. Show value received from the product. Don't make up excuses for price; be ready to defend the price. If the price is too high for the customer, show a less expensive item.

Time

Customers often ask themselves, "When should I buy?" This is a real problem that many customers will not express. Customers who say they do not want to buy are, in many cases, simply saying, "I need you to reassure me to buy now." A salesperson has to look at this objection positively.

There are several ways a salesperson can reassure the customer that now is the time to buy. For example, a salesperson may talk about price if it will increase soon. A salesperson may talk about the product's high quality, features, dependability, warranty, or appearance. A salesperson may talk about the business — the store or company's reputation. The salesperson may also reassure customers about making a wise buying decision. The salesperson should follow up after the sale is made to determine if the customers are satisfied with the purchase. Make customers feel they are important to you. They are!

Quantity

Objections to the quantity needed usually are given by customers who feel that they are overbuying. Also, many objections to quantity are given for those additional or extra items needed with the main purchase. For example, with the purchase of a sewing machine, the customer may need extra needles, machine oil, or several bobbins. With the purchase of a camera, the customer may need extra film, batteries, flash cubes, or a case. Point out the benefits of having the quantity needed. Customers will appreciate the fact that you recommended enough of an item so they won't run short and have to make a special trip to buy more. Help your customers buy the necessary items and in the right quantity.

ILLUSTRATION 11-3
Customers will appreciate that you recommended enough of an item so they won't run short.

WHEN TO ANSWER OBJECTIONS

Most salespeople feel they have three possibilities when addressing an objection: answer it, postpone it, or ignore it. When customers raise objections, they are expressing a concern over the purchase of the product or service. They are hesitating to make a decision.

When your customer presents an objection, you should at least acknowledge the objection. Let your customer know you have heard the objection. Generally the best time to answer a customer's objection is when the objection is raised. Don't be abrupt. Pause to show the customer that you are giving the objection some thought before answering it. A salesperson with a poor attitude toward objections will answer the objection abruptly and carelessly. This shows the customer that the salesperson is annoyed by objections.

Customers feel their objections are important — no matter how large or small they seem to you. Customers want an immediate answer to their objections. They don't want to wait until later in your presentation for an answer. If you want the customers to forget about the objection, answer it. If you promise to answer the objection later, the customers will generally not be attentive to the rest of your sales presentation. By postponing the objection, the customers will be concentrating on the objection and will lose confidence in your ability to sell. This will make the objection seem more important to the customers than it really is. By not answering the objection immediately, the customers may feel that you are just reciting a speech and cannot be interrupted until you have finished.

Always acknowledge the objection. If you are coming to a selling point that will answer the customer's objection, you should quickly finish the point you are discussing and answer the objection. Don't delay your answer or ignore the objection. Answering objections as they are raised will show your customers that you have concern for their wants and needs. Remember, the best time to answer objections is when they are given. The sooner the objection is answered, the sooner you can continue the sale by showing other features and benefits.

GENERAL PROCEDURE FOR ANSWERING OBJECTIONS

Every salesperson should be prepared to answer objections or excuses. Exactly how and when to answer depends largely upon the circumstances of the sale and the mood of your customer. However, there is a general procedure by which most objections may be answered. Learn this procedure so you will be able to more easily and effectively answer customer objections.

Listen to the Customer's Objection

An important principle to follow in answering customer objections is to listen. Listening to the customers will help you to understand their hesitations and concerns. It is difficult to answer an objection unless you fully understand it. Let the customers talk. When customers have an objection, let them state it completely.

Don't interrupt or answer the objection abruptly. Listen with sincere interest before answering.

Too often salespeople are in a hurry to prove the customer wrong. This will irritate the customer and perhaps start an argument. At this point each of you wants to be heard, but neither of you wants to listen. The only way to understand the customer's objection to the sale is to listen carefully to what the customer is saying. While you are listening, as the customer finishes stating the objection, ask yourself, "Why is this particular customer raising this objection and how can I respond to it?"

Pause Before Answering

When the customer has finished stating the objection, pause for a moment. Don't be in a hurry to answer. Relax and show the customer that you are not surprised or disturbed by the objection. An answer given too quickly shows that you can hardly wait to prove the customer wrong. If you pause before you answer, the customer will listen attentively, and the pause will give you an opportunity to form an appropriate response. Even if the objection is very common and you can answer it immediately, pause long enough to weigh it carefully in your own mind.

Show Empathy for Your Customer

Showing empathy for your customers means that you understand their feelings and appreciate their points of view. It does not mean that you completely agree with them. Instead, it shows you understand why they feel the way they do. When customers raise objections, they usually are involved emotionally in the sale. Show your customers that you understand their feelings. Use reflective statements such as: "I know just how you feel." "It often seems that way." "I'm glad you asked that question." "You've made a good point." "Yes, that is important." "I can understand how you might get that impression." "I can appreciate why you said that." "I understand your concern."

Respect your customers' opinions. By giving reflective statements, you help customers realize that you share their concerns and that they are important to you. It tells customers that you consider their objections important. If you use reflective statements, you will find that your customers will be more open and honest with you. Thus, you avoid a possible argument. Show your customers that you understand them. They will be more positive and receptive to your answers.

Restate the Objection

When a customer gives you an objection, be sure you understand it. You don't want to answer an objection that the customer never really stated. Be sure the customer knows you understand the objection. Rephrase or restate the objection in your own words. By restating the objection, you will demonstrate to your customer that you understand it. It is important for customers to know that you share their concerns. In addition, by rephrasing or restating the objection, you are giving yourself more time to develop a better answer.

Whenever possible, change the objection into a question. For example, the customer may object to buying a set of new tires because a previous set did not wear well. You might respond: "I can appreciate your concern and you have brought up a good point. Can you be sure these tires will wear well over the next several years?" Pause, then answer your own question. By rephrasing the objection before answering it, you show that you appreciate the customer's point of view. You have listened and you understand the objection. The customer is now more open-minded and receptive to your answer.

If a customer gives you several objections at once, don't restate all of them. Use a variety of responses. Avoid meaningless replies. Use reflective empathy statements. The customer will then feel that you are not giving a memorized speech on the product or service.

Answer the Objection

All objections must be acknowledged or answered before the sale can continue. Of course, you can postpone the objection until later, but from then on, the customer will be concentrating on the objection, not on the sale. Soon the customer will believe that the objection is more important than it really is. The customer might think, "Something must be wrong if this salesperson won't answer my objection." You will hurt your chances of making the sale by ignoring or lightly passing over the customer's objection.

Now is the time to use your product and service knowledge and advanced preparation. Select those benefits that will appeal most to your customer's buying motives. With empathy, answer the objection in a sincere, straightforward manner. Answer it completely and then continue your sales presentation. Some salespeople make an error by repeating the objection and its answer several times later in the sales presentation. This will only magnify the objection and its importance in the customer's mind.

After you have answered the customer's objection, check to see if the customer understood your answer. Watch facial expressions. Ask, "Have I answered your question?" or "Is this more clear?" and then continue the sale. If you pause too long before continuing, the customer may feel that you have finished selling.

By following this important procedure for answering objections, you will show your customers that you appreciate their points of view, that you have really listened to them, and that you understand their objections. Once you have accomplished this, you will be better able to use the following special techniques for handling and answering objections.

To Answer Objections . . .

- listen to the customer's objection.
- pause before answering.
- show empathy for your customer.
- restate the objection.
- answer the objection.

TECHNIQUES FOR ANSWERING OBJECTIONS

There are several techniques salespeople use to answer objections. Not every objection can be answered in the same manner. Each objection should be considered individually. Some may require long answers while others may be answered with short statements. Keep in mind that as long as your customers are questioning or raising objections, they are still interested in buying.

The following special techniques will assist you in helping your customers to make a wise buying decision.

Special Techniques for Answering Objections

- *Yes, But* Method
- Direct-Denial Method
- Superior-Point Method
- Boomerang Method
- Question Method
- Demonstration Method
- Third-Party Method
- Close-on-an-Objection Method

Yes, But Method

The **yes, but method** is probably the most widely used method of answering objections. It is very simple, yet effective. With this method the salesperson acknowledges the customer's objection, and then gives the customer an answer to the objection.

Most customers are emotionally involved in the objections they give. This method will calm their emotions. It will bring the customers back into the selling conversation without an argument or without proving the customers wrong. This method is useful when a customer has a misunderstanding about the product or service. Use it often. For example, a customer is looking at new carpeting for the family room.

Customer:	I like the color, but the price seems high.
Salesperson:	Yes, the price does seem high, but this carpeting has more fabric per square inch than less expensive carpeting. The dense pile is perfect for a high-traffic area of your home like the family room.

ILLUSTRATION 11-4
The "yes, but method" allows the salesperson to acknowledge the customer's objection and then give the customer an answer to the objection.

What has the salesperson accomplished? The salesperson used empathy in acknowledging the customer's point of view. The salesperson showed that he or she was listening and understood the customer's objection by restating it. As a result, the salesperson was able to select those benefits that would best answer the customer's objection. By using the *yes, but* method, the salesperson calmed the customer's emotions so that the customer would listen with more interest to the answer.

Direct-Denial Method

When the customers' objections are questions based on incorrect information or a misunderstanding, use the **direct-denial method** to deny the objection. However, this is the poorest method of answering customer objections. In reality, you are telling your customers that they are wrong. This method is a direct attack on the customers' opinions or points of view. The following responses are all *poor* examples of the direct-denial method: "Now wait a minute. You don't expect me to believe that, do you?" "That's where you're wrong, and I'll prove it." "You don't seem to understand what I'm talking about." "Where did you ever get that idea?" Responses like these do nothing more than start arguments. The customer will be offended and may leave.

Instead, use empathy to help soften the customer's emotions. Use the direct-denial method only after you have prepared the customer for your response. For example, a customer is looking at a circular hand saw:

Customer:	They sure are making them cheap these days. Why don't they make the case out of metal rather than plastic?
Salesperson:	I understand your concern. However, this plastic is very strong and is just as safe as metal. In addition, this case is shockproof. We have found that the occasional user prefers this style. It is lightweight and less expensive to manufacture, yet it is just as reliable.

Imagine if the salesperson had said, "Where did you ever get that idea?" The customer probably would have become offended or angered. However, it is a far different story when the customer raises an objection and you use a response based on empathy and a sincere concern for your customer. Your customer's reaction to the direct-denial method will largely depend on how you use this method. Use the direct-denial method only when it is necessary.

Superior-Point Method

Using the **superior-point method,** the salesperson listens to the objection and then offers the customer a superior point to overcome the customer's objection. When the objection is a valid reason for the customer to express a concern, use the superior-point method. Admit that the customer has made a good point; then offer a superior reason to buy. For example:

Salesperson:　　How do you like the jeans?

Customer:　　I like the style of these jeans, but I'm afraid they will shrink.

Salesperson:　　Several years ago that would have been a problem, but today these jeans are prewashed to prevent further shrinkage. The washing instructions are sewn on the inside of the waistband. By following these instructions you should have no shrinkage problem with this pair of jeans.

Boomerang Method

When an objection is based on the product or service, use the **boomerang method** to turn the objection into a selling point. By using this method, the salesperson is actually tossing the objection back to the customer as a reason to buy. In this example, the customer is looking at a marble vanity.

Customer:　　I don't like the double sink in this vanity.

Salesperson:　　It does seem unusual to have a double sink. However, because this vanity top is six-feet long, a double sink would fit nicely and still give you plenty of countertop area to use. It is surprising how many times two people want to wash their hair, brush their teeth, or wash their hands at the same time. Mornings are usually hectic in most homes. This double sink would help to eliminate some of the confusion.

The customer's objection was given back to the customer as a reason to buy — like a boomerang. One word of caution: don't appear too confident in showing the customer that you or your company is better than your competition. Don't put your competition down; customers resent this. Rather, be friendly and sincere. Talk to customers in a conversational manner about the positive features and benefits they will receive from you and your company.

Question Method

Sometimes the **question method** is useful in helping customers examine their own objections. Use a few questions to explore the customers' objections. This will involve the customers in considering their objections. Often this method can be more effective than directly answering the objection. Also, asking a few questions will allow you time to think before you discuss the objections with your customers. For example, this customer is looking at a new snow blower:

Customer: I think I can get a snow blower cheaper at another store.

Salesperson: A less expensive snow blower is usually smaller. Is this what you are looking for?

Customer: No, but the discount store has a snow blower for a few dollars less.

Salesperson: How does it compare to our snow blower?

Customer: Well, their snow blowers are . . .

By asking a few questions, the salesperson has the customer comparing the two products. The salesperson is letting the customer examine the facts. By listening carefully, the salesperson will learn what features and benefits are important to the customer. This method has also allowed the salesperson extra time to think out the responses for this particular customer. This salesperson should be knowledgeable about all brands of snow blowers. With this product knowledge, the salesperson can help the customer examine both machines. The salesperson can then describe the features and benefits that make this snow blower the best value for the customer.

You can also ask questions that begin with *why*. Many times questions that begin with why will remove an excuse or a hidden objection and will give you the customer's real objections. Read the following example:

Customer: I don't think my mother would like this dress.

Salesperson: Why don't you think she would like it?

Customer: The dress length seems too long.

This salesperson was able to determine the real objection by asking the customer a question that began with the word why. Avoid saying just the word "why" without further comment because the customer may become insulted and may not reveal the real reason for the objection. As a result, the sale is lost.

Demonstration Method

A **demonstration** is a test which allows the salesperson to show the customer that the objection is wrong without having to say it. The **demonstration method** is very effective in overcoming customers' objections. Once you have given the brief demonstration, make a positive sales statement and then go on with the sales presentation. The demonstration offers proof that the product will do what you claim it will do. For example:

Customer:	My daughter thinks I should buy a dishwasher, but I don't think I need one.
Salesperson:	Why do you feel a dishwasher is a poor investment?
Customer:	I don't see how the dishes can be as clean as when I do them by hand. The top rack of dishes can't be as clean.

ILLUSTRATION 11-5
The demonstration method is very effective in overcoming customers' objections.

Salesperson:	I see what you mean; you want to be sure your dishes get clean. Look at this model with the see-through door. See that white shaft in the middle. It carries the hot water to the top rack and this [*points to the bottom rotor*] delivers the hot water to the bottom rack. This water will not only clean your dishes, pots, and pans, but will also sterilize them to be sure they are perfectly clean. That is important, isn't it?

There is probably nothing more effective in overcoming a customer's objection than showing or demonstrating that the product can do something that will answer the objection. Also, you can use company literature, visual displays, or product reports to show the customer those features and benefits that will help overcome objections.

Third-Party Method

The **third-party method** uses the testimonial of another person. A **testimonial** is an example used by the salesperson of someone who has used the product or service and found it to be satisfactory. With this method the salesperson can prove the answer to the customer's objection without offending the customer. Customers have a tendency to believe a neutral third party. These testimonials are very effective in helping you to sell. For example:

Salesperson:	You could install your own telephone and save money.
Customer:	I couldn't install it myself.
Salesperson:	I can understand how you might feel. Jean Liang bought a new telephone just a few weeks ago and thought she would have trouble installing it. I received a letter from her the other day saying that she couldn't believe how easy it was to install. She said that while it took a little time, the instruction booklet we gave her was very simple and easy to understand. Take a look at this instruction booklet and I'll explain how you can do the telephone installation yourself.

Close-on-an-Objection Method

Be alert throughout the sale for every opportunity to close. If the objection is a buying signal, answer the objection and close the sale. This is the **close-on-an-objection method.** When a customer gives you a statement or a question that has to do with ownership, this is a clue that the customer is ready to buy. After the objection is answered, try to close the sale. In this example the customer is looking at a new suit:

Customer:	I like the suit, but the pants are too big and the sleeves need to be shortened.
Salesperson:	Don't worry! We employ an excellent tailor. After this suit is altered, it will fit you perfectly. Let me call the tailor to show you how well the suit will fit after it is altered.
Customer:	That sounds fine. I'll take it. Thank you.

CUSTOMER OBJECTIONS—MAKE THEM WORK FOR YOU

Answer objections properly and promptly. You will find that if you give a response based on empathy, it will be easier for your customers to accept your answers. Remember this general procedure: listen to the customer's objection, pause before answering, show empathy for your customer, restate the objection, and answer the objection.

Practice the special techniques used by salespeople to more effectively answer objections. Use one or more techniques that will help you overcome customer objections. By taking these important steps, you will show your customers that you appreciate their points of view, that you really listen to them, and that you understand their objections. Answer customer objections honestly. Once objections have been overcome, you can help the customers to make wise buying decisions.

SALES TERMS

objection	*yes, but* method	demonstration
sales resistance	direct-denial method	demonstration method
real objections	superior-point method	third-party method
excuses	boomerang method	testimonial
hidden objections	question method	close-on-an-objection method

SALES QUESTIONS

1. Salespeople should welcome customer objections. Why?

2. Why do customers raise objections?

3. What attitude should salespeople have when answering objections?

4. Describe the two most common forms of sales resistance.

5. How can a salesperson determine the customers' concerns if the customers will not express their hidden objections?

6. When a customer objects to the product at the beginning of the sale, what should the salesperson do?

7. When are most real objections given by customers?

8. What does it mean if the customer gives excuses after the salesperson has given most of the sales presentation?

9. When customers give several excuses, how should the salesperson handle them?

10. What is the best way salespeople can prepare for customer objections?

11. What should you do if a customer gives you an objection that you are not prepared to answer?

12. Why should you avoid mentioning objections just for the sake of answering them?

13. Customer objections to a purchase generally relate to five general areas. What are these areas?

14. Why should salespeople answer objections promptly?

15. Why is it important to carefully listen to customer objections?

16. Even if you can respond immediately, why should you pause briefly before answering an objection?

17. Explain the purpose of using reflective statements.

18. What is the purpose of restating a customer objection?

19. Why is it important to check the customer's understanding of your answer to an objection?

20. Explain the method that is useful when a customer has a misunderstanding about the product or service.

21. Which method is considered the poorest technique for answering objections? Why?

22. When the customer has raised a valid objection and you offer a better reason for buying, what method are you using to overcome the objection?

23. Which method turns an objection into a selling point?

24. Which method of answering objections will help your customers examine their own objections?

25. Explain the value to the salesperson of asking a question that begins with the word "why."

26. Give an example of the demonstration method of answering an objection.

27. Explain the method that uses the testimonial of another person.

28. If the objection contains a buying signal, what method of answering the objection should you use?

SALES ACTIVITIES

A. For each statement below, write whether you think the objection is a real objection or an excuse.

  1. I'll think it over.
  2. I don't like that color.
  3. I don't have time today.
  4. How about something that costs about $4?
  5. This doesn't seem heavy enough.
  6. I'll talk it over with my wife.
  7. I always shop around before I buy.
  8. That's not for me.
  9. Your repair service is too slow.
  10. I've never heard of that brand before.

B. Read the following objections and select the best response and the poorest response that a salesperson could make to the customer.

  1. I don't think I care for the color.
     a. But it is a nice, neutral color.
     b. What color did you have in mind?
     c. This color has been very popular.
     d. You will learn to like the color.

  2. It's too big for the room.
     a. I think we can order it in a smaller size.
     b. Couldn't it fit in another room?
     c. Not really.
     d. What size is your room?

  3. It will be hard to keep clean.
     a. It's machine washable.
     b. You will only want to wear it for dress-up occasions.
     c. Don't you worry about it. There is a special cleaner you can buy.
     d. The cleaning instructions are on the tag.

  4. I have always bought another brand.
     a. I understand that brand isn't as good as it used to be.
     b. Then you may want to consider a change.
     c. Yes, that is a good brand, but this one is also recognized as a quality product.
     d. The brand of the product isn't important.

C. For each of the following objections, determine which buying decision the customer is objecting to: product, place, price, time, or quantity.

  1. I've never bought anything from your company before.
  2. I don't think I can justify buying any more.
  3. It's a handy gadget all right, but I don't think I should buy one right now.
  4. No, thanks, it seems too complicated.
  5. That's your most expensive model!

D. For each of the following customer objections, give a reflective empathy statement and restate the objection.

1. The price of this lawn mower is just too high.
2. This television is not a major brand.
3. I like the stereo, but I don't need an amplifier quite that powerful.
4. This winter coat is beautiful, but I'm afraid it isn't heavy enough.
5. The case looks as if it were made of plastic. Won't it break rather easily?

CLOSING THE SALE

Your Learning Goals

After studying this chapter, you should:

- *understand that a well-planned sales presentation will result in a natural close.*
- *know how to make the buying decision seem easy for the customer.*
- *be able to narrow the customer's choice of product selection.*
- *be able to talk about customer ownership of the product or service.*
- *be able to ask the customer to buy using an appropriate closing technique.*
- *be able to watch and listen for customer buying signals.*
- *be able to give a trial close.*
- *be able to develop the close based on the customer's response to the sales presentation.*
- *be able to provide reassurance to the customer after closing the sale.*
- *understand the importance of analyzing unsuccessful closings.*

Every customer you approach is a potential buyer. Which customer becomes a buyer depends upon you and your ability to close the sale. Most people enter a store because they want to buy something. It is your responsibility to help them. It is up to you to turn possible sales into actual sales by making the most of every customer contact.

Up to this point in the sale, you have presented a well-planned and organized sales presentation. Your approach was personal. You asked a few well-chosen questions to determine the right items to show the customer. You directed your presentation toward your customer's buying motives. You demonstrated the product's features and explained how the customer would benefit from the features. You answered all of the customer's questions and objections. All the time and effort you have put into this sale should now pay off.

A NATURAL CLOSE

The goal of every sales presentation is to close the sale. This means that the customer accepts the merchandise or service and buys it. With a well-planned sales presentation, the closing should become a natural part of the sale. It does not involve tricking the customer nor putting pressure on the customer to buy. The closing process helps the customer to make a wise buying decision.

Skillful salespeople are problem solvers—not product pushers. Selling is not pressuring the customer to buy. The customer will make the final buying decision. Too many salespeople feel they

ILLUSTRATION 12-1
The goal of every sales presentation is to close the sale.

have to trick customers to get them to buy. This is just not true. If you sincerely feel that you have selected a product or service that is right for the customer, it is your responsibility to convince the customer of this.

As your sale progresses, bring it to a natural close. During the sale, seek agreement from the customer on the product's obvious benefits. Ask questions that make it easy for the customer to agree. When your customer is convinced through a series of several small decisions that you are offering the right product or service, try to close the sale. Reaching several positive agreements, rather than just one final agreement, is the way to close the sale naturally. For example, this salesperson has been showing shoes to a customer. The salesperson feels that the customer is ready to make a decision.

Salesperson:	You have already mentioned that you prefer the black shoes rather than the brown, is that correct?
Customer:	Yes. Black seems dressier. It will go with almost everything I wear.
Salesperson:	You also said that the first pair you tried on was comfortable.
Customer:	Yes, and I must have shoes that are comfortable. I'm on my feet all day.
Salesperson:	That certainly is important. [short pause] The pair you found comfortable is available in black. You will not only find these shoes comfortable but you will also find that these quality leather shoes will wear well.
Customer:	I certainly want quality shoes. They may cost a little more, but to me they are worth a little extra.
Salesperson:	I'm sure you will like this pair of black shoes. They seem to fit you perfectly. Excuse me for just a minute and I'll put them in a box for you.

MAKE THE BUYING DECISION EASY

From the beginning of the sale, you must be ready to close. Some people know exactly what product or service they want. These decided customers quickly ask for it, pay for it, and leave with it. The sale only takes a few minutes. However, there are just as many people who may have only a vague idea of what they want. These undecided customers need your help. Without it, they may leave without buying.

To create acceptance and close the sale, you must build understanding between you and your customers. Concentrate on the needs of your customers. Then help them select the product or service they want. Use a sales presentation that is directed at their buying motives. Help them learn about the features and benefits of your product or service. In other words, help make the buying decision easy for them and the close easy for you.

Stop Showing New Merchandise

When you are attempting to close the sale, do not show additional merchandise. This will only confuse your customers. They may begin to wonder what other items you have not shown them. If you have asked well-chosen questions to determine your customer's wants and needs, you should have been able to select appropriate items to show. Don't show the customer too much merchandise. After you have presented several items for consideration, you should be able to tell which items are the most interesting to your customer.

Narrow the Selection

Remove the items of merchandise which do not interest the customer. Set these items off to the side or put them back in stock. As a general rule, you should narrow the selection to two, but never

ILLUSTRATION 12-2
After you have presented several items for consideration, you should determine which items are the most interesting to your customer.

more than three, items. If you feel that the customer wants to see additional items before deciding, remove one or two items the customer doesn't like. Then bring out a few more, but don't be in a hurry. You don't want the customer to feel rushed. By placing these unwanted items of merchandise back in stock or removing them from the customer's view, you will have helped to narrow the selection. By narrowing the selection, the sale will be easier to close.

Talk About Customer Ownership

Always try to use the words *you* and *yours* when talking to your customers. Help your customers picture themselves as the owners and users of your product or service. Always talk and demonstrate the product or service in terms of the customer's ownership. For example:

When *you* use this lawn mower, *you* will like how easy it is to start.
You will find so many uses for *your* new food processor.
Your family will really like the sound of this new stereo.
Owning this microwave oven will save *you* time preparing meals.

Ask Your Customers to Buy

It is amazing how many salespeople give a fine sales presentation, but then fail to close the sale. Too often salespeople feel that the customer must say, "I'll take it." They seem to be afraid to ask the customer to buy. They continue to talk and demonstrate until the customer interrupts to say "I'll take it" or gives an excuse to leave without buying. When you are asking customers to buy, you are not pressuring them to make a decision. Instead, you are giving them the opportunity to make a purchase. If you are confident in the buyer benefits of your products or services, then wouldn't it seem only natural to ask your customers to buy?

There are several reasons why salespeople hesitate to ask customers to buy:

1. Salespeople who are not well trained lack the knowledge and skill of selling.
2. Some salespeople give a poor sales presentation.
3. Some salespeople are afraid to receive a negative answer. They are afraid to be turned down.
4. The customer, not the salesperson, may be in control of the sale.
5. Some salespeople do not believe in the value and benefits of the products or services they sell.

6. Some salespeople have no self-confidence; they almost expect their customers not to buy.

Don't approach the closing of the sale with any trace of fear that you may fail. If you are afraid you will fail, you probably will. Instead, expect to be successful!

Be Confident

Probably the greatest cause of failing to close the sale is lack of confidence. Salespeople often lack confidence in themselves, their sales ability, and the products or services they sell. They must believe in their products or services and in the buyer benefits in order to be successful.

Don't be embarrassed to ask your customers to buy. Your product or service should be worth every penny being charged. If you don't believe it is, then you are selling the wrong thing. Be proud to offer your customers the opportunity to invest in a product or service that will benefit them. Be confident. Talk with conviction. Speak with authority. Show enthusiasm for what you sell.

If you feel confident that you have selected the right product or service to benefit your customer, ask the customer to buy. The important thing to remember is to keep trying. Welcome the close as your opportunity to help your customer make a wise buying decision.

Find Out Why Some Customers Resist Buying

To guide a sale to a successful close, you have to build up to that moment of decision from your first greeting of the customers. Pay attention to your customers' likes and dislikes. Customers may not always tell you their opinions. If customers give some resistance, they are not convinced that the product or service is right for them. Perhaps they want the product but feel that now is not the time to buy or that a less expensive product would be more appropriate. Remember, salespeople are problem solvers — not product pushers.

When customers cannot make up their minds, don't be afraid to ask a *why* question. "You seem to like this pair of shoes. Why don't you feel they are right for you?" or "Why don't you care for this style?" Customers will usually tell you. Listen to your customers. Unless you understand them from the beginning of the sale, you will probably never close the sale. If you know the reason the customer is resisting, you will be better able to adjust your sales presentation to bring the sale to a natural close.

- stop showing new merchandise.
- narrow the selection.
- talk about customer ownership.
- ask your customers to buy.
- be confident.
- find out why some customers resist buying.

WHEN TO CLOSE THE SALE

From almost the beginning of the sales presentation, you are looking for an opportunity to ask your customers to buy. When you have reason to believe that the customers' needs have been determined and the right item has been selected to meet those needs, it is time to try to close the sale. This doesn't mean that customers will automatically buy. They may raise an objection or ask more questions. But, at this point, you should begin trying to close the sale.

There is no one exact time to close the sale. The best time to try for a close is when customers seem ready to make a buying decision. Customers will often indicate when such opportunities arise.

Throughout the sales presentation, customers who are satisfied with the product or service will give you buying signals. Buying signals are signs of approval from customers who are ready to make a buying decision. When customers give you buying signals, it is time to stop selling additional merchandise. Learn to watch and listen to your customers. Watch your customers rather than the merchandise. Don't become so preoccupied by the sales presentation that you forget who you are selling — the customer.

Carefully observe the customer for signs of approval. Do the eyes show signs of acceptance? Did the customer show interest in one item? Does the facial expression show interest? Is the customer smiling? Has the customer stopped to look at the same item several times? Does the customer seem to show more interest in a particular item by reading the guarantee, the operating instructions, or the care instructions? These are examples of buying signals.

Salespeople must be able to recognize buying signals. Salespeople who do not observe or listen to their customers may oversell

ILLUSTRATION 12-3
Customers who are satisfied with the product will give you buying signals.

by talking and demonstrating long after the customer has decided to buy. When this happens, the customer may decide against the purchase. Salespeople need to be alert so they are ready to close the sale when the customer is ready to buy. Close when the opportunity seems logical: after stressing a feature that interests the customer, after the customer seems sold on the benefits of the item, after showing the customer that the item will satisfy a need or want, or after proving the item's advantages over another item. Use every buying signal as an opportunity to close the sale.

Customers give many buying signals during the sale. Listen carefully to your customers. They may make a favorable comment or ask a question. For example: "Does your company install the carpet?" "How many yards of fabric will I need?" "Those are beautiful flower pots." "Are the attachments to the vacuum cleaner expensive?" There are many other buying signals, but they all say the same thing: "I like it. I'm ready to make a buying decision." When these signals are given, it is time to try to close the sale.

During the sale, be aware of your customers' reactions to your demonstration and to the product or service being sold. The customers' questions, comments, expressions, and actions will give you clues to their readiness to make a buying decision. It is time to attempt a trial close if a customer wants a selling point clarified ("What size batteries would I need?") or when the customer is hesitant ("I like it, but...") or if the customer implies ownership ("I've always wanted one of these.").

THE TRIAL CLOSE

When the customer gives a buying signal, you should ask for a buying decision with a trial close. The trial close is your first attempt to find out if the customer is ready to buy. Trial closes are usually given in the form of a question. Some typical trial closes might be: "Will one be enough?" "When should we deliver?" "Will this be cash or charge?" "Do you want the blue or green sweater?" "We can install this on Friday morning. Will that be all right?"

In the following example, the customer has tried on several pairs of boots. Notice the customer's buying signals and how the salesperson follows up with a trial close.

Customer:	Well, leather boots will probably last longer, but they surely are expensive.
Salesperson:	Of course, you're right. Quality boots may cost a little more, but leather boots are durable as well as comfortable. I'm sure you will like them — don't you agree?
Customer:	It just seems like a lot of money to spend for boots.
Salesperson:	Think of it as an investment. These boots will last longer than a less expensive boot that may not be as comfortable. You want a good fit. There's nothing worse than having sore feet. [*The salesperson picks up the boot the customer seems to prefer.*] Do you like this boot best?
Customer:	Yes, I think so.
Salesperson:	Would you like to wear them or shall I put them in a box?
Customer:	I think I'll wear them.

The customer gave the salesperson a buying signal: "Leather boots will probably last longer." The salesperson made a favorable comment and then tried to close the sale. Notice the salesperson did not avoid price talk but tried to establish the value of the product.

The customer did not buy at first because the price was still a concern. But the salesperson didn't give up or stop selling. Instead, the salesperson continued the sales presentation by justifying the price and trying to close again. Notice that the salesperson assumed the customer was buying a pair of boots and recognized that the question in the customer's mind was which pair to select rather than whether to buy or not to buy.

A trial close will also help you to determine customers' interest. It will help you find out what they are thinking. If the decision to buy has not yet been made, you can then adjust your sales presentation accordingly. Use the trial close often. It is a safe way to ask your customers to buy. If customers are ready to buy, it will result in a purchase. When customers give you a buying signal, attempt a trial close.

TECHNIQUES TO CLOSE MORE SALES

Salespeople must realize that they are not going to close every sale. However, they will close more sales if they know the proper techniques.

Knowing the techniques of closing the sale is important. But to be a successful salesperson, you must also understand how to sell to customers as you would want a salesperson to sell to you. For example, when you are shopping, you want a salesperson who can answer your questions and demonstrate the merchandise. A salesperson who stands there saying nothing is irritating. It is just as annoying to have a salesperson rush you into making a decision before you are ready to decide.

Sell to your customers as you would want a salesperson to sell to you. Be helpful and understanding. Show concern for your customers' wants. Help them make a decision, but don't rush them. When they seem ready to decide, ask a trial closing question. The question should be given as a matter of normal conversation; it should not be abrupt or awkward. The close is easy when you understand the techniques of closing the sale.

The techniques successful salespeople use to close a sale are listed on page 216. You may use several techniques throughout the sales presentation. You may also want to combine two closing techniques to close the sale.

Ask-Your-Customers-To-Buy Close

Don't be afraid to ask your customers to buy. Too many sales are lost because the salespeople continue to sell when they should try

Closing Techniques

- ask your customers to buy.
- present a choice.
- assume they are buying.
- give advantages and disadvantages.
- offer a premium.
- use the last-chance-to-buy method.
- use the standing-room-only method.
- give a narrative or testimonial.
- close on an objection.
- suggest related merchandise.

to close. Salespeople who ignore or miss buying signals and are hesitant to ask the customers to buy will not close many sales. In fact, to close the sale, some customers may interrupt a salesperson and say, "I'll take it."

Use the **ask-your-customer-to-buy close** when customers show buying signals. Customers know that the salesperson expects to close the sale, so don't make them feel uncomfortable by letting them just stand there. Ask your customers to buy. They expect it.

A good way to lead into asking the customers to buy is to review the major selling features and benefits of the product or service. This involves summarizing the reasons the customers should make the purchase. Then when you ask them to buy, the close will be part of your natural conversation.

Salesperson: This color TV is a good value. It comes with a black matrix picture tube found in your best quality TV sets. It has a silent remote control, stereo sound, and is cable ready. It is completely electronic and is available in walnut, oak, or pecan trim. You can feel confident that you will be purchasing a quality color TV that will be reliable for many years. Wouldn't you agree?

Don't attack your customers by saying, "Do you want to buy it?" or "Have you made up your mind yet?" or "Are you going to buy this or not?" These questions are too blunt. The customer will feel pressured and will probably not buy.

Choice Close

The **choice close** is probably the best and most widely used closing technique. Presenting a choice is a safe way to help your customers select the item they want to buy. At this point, you have helped them narrow their selection to two items. By offering a choice you are asking the customers which item they want to buy. Notice that it is a choice between one item or the other — not a choice whether to buy or not to buy.

When offering a choice, you are asking your customers for a commitment on a minor buying decision. You are taking it for granted that the time is right to make a decision. Instead of a major decision, you offer a choice on a minor decision. Instead of asking your customers if they want a new dishwasher, ask them if they want their new dishwasher in a gold or an avocado finish. If possible, never give them more than two choices. Keep the choice simple. With more than two choices the decision becomes difficult.

Here are a few examples of choice closes: "Do you want drawers on the right or left side of your new desk?" "Will you want this delivered tomorrow morning or afternoon?" "Do you want the 21- or 24-inch bike?"

Sometimes a customer may ask your opinion. Offer your opinion only when requested, and of course, be honest. Customers can tell if you are giving false flattery.

The customer may ask, "Which do you think looks better on me?" The customer is obviously having a difficult time coming to a decision. Don't say, "It's up to you" or "Whatever you think looks good." Remarks like these are of no value to the customer. If the customer asks your opinion, then and only then should you give your personal preference. Tell the customer why you prefer one item over the other. Be honest, yet tactful.

Base your comments on your customer's needs and wants. For example, don't say to a customer looking at a dress, "Green was never my favorite color, so I would buy the brown one." The customer is not interested in what you prefer for yourself. The customer wants your opinion about the item and how it looks. Instead say, "They are both attractive, but I guess I do like the brown one just a little better. Brown has been a very popular color this season and it does look good on you. Do you like the brown one better than the green?" In this situation you have tactfully given the customer your opinion. You have also tried to close the sale with the choice close. If the customer agrees with you and prefers the brown, remove the green dress and close the sale.

There are many questions you can ask your customers in closing the sale with a choice close. Consider color, model, size, material,

ILLUSTRATION 12-4
When the customer selects an item, remove the other items.

or other product features. Try to close your sales with an appropriate choice close. When the customers make a choice, remove the other items. The choice of an item represents the closing of the sale.

Assume-They-Are-Buying Close

Throughout the sales presentation you should be asking questions that seek agreement from your customers. When your customers seem interested and have agreed on minor points during the sale, it will seem natural to close the sale by using the **assume-they-are-buying close.** Ask a leading question or give a leading statement that will get a commitment from the customers. For example: "We'll schedule your car into our service area this morning to mount these new tires." "With only 10 percent down we can set up a payment plan for you." "Shall I gift wrap this for you?" "Do you want to charge this?" "How many do you want?"

As a logical continuation of the points of agreement established during the sale, close on the assumption that the customers will buy. In this method of closing, your final questions or statements are not about the product but on matters having to do with delivery, method of payment, service, care for the item, or other items of business. Act as though the customers have made the purchase. Start to write up your sales slip or write out a service ticket. If your customers are not ready to make a decision, they will tell you.

Don't pressure your customers to buy. If they are not ready to buy, continue with your sales presentation. You can use a different closing technique after you have better established the value of the product in the customer's mind.

Advantages-and-Disadvantages Close

When selling to customers who are having a difficult time making a decision, use the **advantages-and-disadvantages close.** With this method you can summarize or review for the customers the reasons to make the purchase. Appeal to the customers' rational buying motives. Customers want to feel they are being logical about their purchases.

As a salesperson, you might say, "Let's consider all the reasons in favor of buying." Then you and the customer will summarize the advantages. The customer will usually give you a few reasons for not buying. As a knowledgeable salesperson it is up to you to turn a disadvantage into a selling point—a reason for buying. There should be more advantages than disadvantages. If you have a good product and have given a good sales presentation, you should be able to turn any disadvantage into an advantage, and then close the sale. Sometimes it is helpful to write down these advantages and disadvantages. Make a list so the customer can see the advantages, point by point.

Consider the customer who is shopping for a portable gas grill. The salesperson and the customer have discussed all the advantages and disadvantages. Now the salesperson is going to turn a disadvantage into an advantage for buying.

Customer:	I really don't like the idea of having to refill the propane gas tank.
Salesperson:	I would agree that's a small inconvenience, but a full tank will last a long time. There is a gauge right here [*points to it*] that will tell you when you will need to refill it. That way you won't run out of gas while you are grilling. Besides, it only takes a few minutes to refill the tank.
Customer:	I guess you're right. I also like the idea of being able to move the grill if I want.

From this point the salesperson assumes the customer is satisfied with the purchase. In order to close the sale, the salesperson might say, "Shall I have the propane tank filled for you?" If the customer is still concerned about the disadvantage, the salesperson should admit there is nothing that can be done about it. If you are not able to find an item to satisfy the needs of your customer, there is no reason to try to sell the customer something not wanted. If the customer isn't convinced of the value of the product or service, it isn't possible to close the sale.

Premium Close

In using the **premium close,** the salesperson offers a bonus — something extra — to persuade the customer to make the purchase. Guidelines are given to salespeople by store management so that, if it becomes desirable, the salesperson may use this closing technique. The technique is used more in specialty stores and for expensive items than it is in department stores and for less expensive items.

It is much better to offer something extra than to offer a reduced price on a purchase. By reducing the price, the salesperson is opening price negotiations with the customer. This implies that the original price may have been inflated. Instead, offer the customer something in addition to the purchase. For example, you may be authorized to offer a free box of disks with the purchase of a computer, or a box of paper with the purchase of a printer.

Premiums are designed to persuade the customer to buy now. Don't emphasize giving the customer something extra. Offer a premium as a matter of being helpful to the customer, not to show your importance or power.

ILLUSTRATION 12-5
Premiums are designed to persuade the customer to buy now.

Last-Chance-To-Buy Close

The **last-chance-to-buy close** is a method used to inspire customers to take prompt action to buy. The last chance to buy means that the quantity of the item is limited or that a special offer is limited. Customers won't want to miss such an opportunity. This method is used to encourage customers to buy now for fear of not being able to buy later. For example:

Customer: I like this car but I want to think it over first.

Salesperson: This is the last car of its kind on the lot. I can see you like it. Is it the right color?

Customer: Yes. [*pausing to think about the purchase*]

Salesperson: I know you would be disappointed if the car were sold before you returned. Shall I go ahead and write up a contract for the loan?

Be honest! Don't tell your customers that this is the last product in stock if it is not. Talk with the customers about their needs and the benefit of buying now, rather than how important it is for you to make the sale.

The last-chance method is often used by salespeople when a special offer or sale is about to expire. The salesperson might say, "Today is the last day of our half-price sale. If you buy today you can buy two for the price of one." Customers want to be informed about special offers, but don't overuse this method as a means of persuading a customer to buy.

Standing-Room-Only Close

The **standing-room-only close** is based on the idea that customer demand for the product is high while the supply of the item is limited. Generally, people want what other people want. The standing-room-only close is being used when a salesperson says, "This has been our most popular selling item this season," or "I only have three more items in stock, and I don't know if we can get any more," or "This is the last one in stock."

Many items have a special appeal to customers, such as special styles, an item which is one of a limited number manufactured, or a product whose price is increasing. The idea of the standing-room-only close is to buy now for fear it won't be available later, or if it is available, it will cost more. Salespeople should be careful in using this emotional closing appeal. Customers may feel that the salesperson is using a scare tactic in order to make the sale.

Narrative or Testimonial Close

Testimonials are an excellent way to close a sale. People like to hear stories about other people who have successfully used a product or service. It helps your customers believe what you have already told them. The **narrative or testimonial close** can be a gentle way to encourage your customers to buy. In this example the customer is looking at a microwave oven:

Customer: I'm not sure I'd like to cook with a microwave oven.

Salesperson: I understand just how you feel. Many customers have said the same thing. I was talking to Julia Fernandez earlier today. She bought the same brand and model of microwave oven you are considering and she just loves it. She said she can bake a potato in a few minutes rather than an hour, and her kitchen isn't hot in the summer because she doesn't use her regular oven very often. She told me that when they use their outdooor grill, they grill a few extra pieces of meat and put them in the freezer. Then, when the weather isn't good for outdoor grilling, she takes them out of the freezer and heats them in her microwave. She said they are just as tender and juicy as if they had been just grilled.

Customer: Well, I never thought of that. It surely would be nice to cook a fast meal for company so I wouldn't have to spend all my time in the kitchen.

Salesperson: I think you would enjoy using a microwave oven. Do you like this model?

Don't use the narrative or testimonial close to frighten your customers. Customers resist this method of selling, even if what you say is true. For example, a salesperson might say, "Those tires don't have much tread on them. You had better replace them soon. Just last week a family was seriously hurt in a car accident because they blew a tire. You don't want to take chances." Although fear may sometimes be a reason for buying, it is never good to use fear as a basis for closing a sale.

Objection Close

Sometimes the following situation occurs: Throughout the sales presentation, the salesperson has asked questions and the customer has responded favorably. The customer seems interested, but there seems to be one objection that is keeping the customer from buying. If the salesperson can use the **objection close** method to overcome the objection or make it seem incidental, the sale can be closed.

In order to close on an objection, the first thing the salesperson must do is to get the customer to agree that the objection raised is the only thing holding up the purchase. In other words, if the objection were removed, the customer would buy.

Customer:	I like this piece of luggage, but it will be heavy to carry.
Salesperson:	Heavy luggage is a problem. Is this the only reason you hesitate to buy?
Customer:	Yes, I think so.
Salesperson:	One of the optional features on this brand of luggage is the attachment of small wheels to the bottom, so you can simply pull your luggage rather than carry it. Many customers who buy this larger piece want this feature. Shall I have these wheels put on the bottom of your new piece of luggage?
Customer:	That sounds great—thank you!

When the objection is removed or minimized, the customer no longer has a reason not to buy. When using this method, it is important to ask if this is the *only* reason for not buying. If the customer says "yes," then the customer is committed to buying if the objection can be overcome. Ask the question as part of the normal sales conversation—never act as if you have trapped the customer.

Suggest-Related-Merchandise Close

When a customer is considering an item but is not sure about it, try using the **suggest-related-merchandise close.** If you detect that the customer is concerned about the limited use of an item, use related merchandise to show the customer the possibilities of the item. For example:

Customer:	I like the color of this tablecloth. This shade of green is perfect for my kitchen, but the tablecloth seems too plain. Do you have anything fancier?

Salesperson:	Let me show you how easy it is to dress up this tablecloth. What other colors do you have in your kitchen?
Customer:	A soft yellow.
Salesperson:	With these yellow place mats and matching cloth napkins, you can add a touch of color to your dinner table. The place mats will help keep your tablecloth clean and looking new for years. Do you like the color combination?"
Customer:	Yes, it does make a beautiful table.
Salesperson:	How many place mats and napkins would you like to go with your new tablecloth?

ILLUSTRATION 12-6
Suggesting closely related merchandise is a good way to close the sale.

Suggesting closely related merchandise that will protect the original item or enhance its value is a good way to close the sale. This method can also give you an additional sale. But more importantly, by using this method you have been helpful to your customers. Suggest a special picture frame to enhance a family portrait, cooking utensils to go with a microwave oven, a storage box for VCR tapes, furniture for a computer system, or accessories for a few clothing outfits. Be helpful to your customers. Show them related merchandise.

Other Closing Techniques

There are several other closing techniques that salespeople can use to close a sale. Most of these use the basic techniques already given. For example:

The *credit close*:	"May I add this to your charge account?"
The *delivery close*:	"When would it be convenient to have this delivered?"
The *conditional close:*	"As soon as your credit application is approved, we can begin the addition to your home."
The *exclusive-line-of-merchandise close*:	"We offer this brand exclusively because people like you want the best quality."
The *price close*:	"If you put a down payment on it today, I can give you 5 percent off the list price." Or, "When you buy this, you can buy another one for half the price."
The *trial order close*:	"Try it for two weeks and then tell me how you like it."

Remember that in using any closing technique you are not asking a favor of your customers to buy from you, and you should never make the customer feel pressured into buying. Closing techniques are used by skilled salespeople to guide their customers into making wise buying decisions. These techniques should be a natural part of the sale and should not be abrupt nor awkward. Successful closing takes practice. As you sell, develop your closing skills.

ERRORS IN CLOSING A SALE

The most obvious mistake made by some salespeople is to ask the customer to buy using a negative close, such as: "You wouldn't want to try it, would you?" Questions like this show that the salesperson has no confidence in the product or in his or her ability to sell. Customers generally have no confidence in these salespeople, either. Consequently, they say "no" to the salesperson's question.

Another serious error is offering the customer an unsatisfactory substitute item, suggesting that it can be returned later for the desired item. For example, a customer wants to purchase a set of king-sized sheets as a wedding gift based on information in the bridal registry. The salesperson says, "We have sold all of the king-sized sheets in this pattern. Just take these queen-sized ones and then, after the wedding, the bride can return them for the correct size. We should have more in by then." This sales tactic causes many problems. The first problem is that the bride will be expecting king-sized not queen-sized sheets. Thus, the customer looks ignorant for purchasing the wrong item. Second, the bride must return the item without a sales slip to the place it was purchased in order to exchange it. The whole process is an unnecessary inconvenience. Third, another customer may want the merchandise which was taken out of stock; thus, another sale could be lost. If merchandise selections are correct when sold, there will not be as many problems with returned merchandise. Attempting to close by offering an unsatisfactory substitute item is not very considerate of the customer.

Another common error in closing is trying to scare the customer or to panic the buyer into making a purchase. Appeals to fear should be avoided. For example: "If you don't take my advice, you could end up spending a fortune in repair bills," or, "I'm afraid I can't hold this item for you. There was another person looking at it earlier," or "If you wait, there won't be any left."

Some salespeople make an error in thinking that an immediate sale is more important than a satisfied customer. When you sell, be honest with your customers. If you are convinced that the item will not be satisfactory, be ready to admit it. It is better to lose one sale than to have a dissatisfied or irritated customer. For example, a salesperson is waiting on a customer who is just learning to sew. The customer has selected a pattern and fabric and is excited about making the item. It is the salesperson's responsibility to explain to the customer if the pattern selected is rather difficult and will require more skill and patience than most beginners have. The customer may still buy it or may select another pattern that will not be as difficult. By pointing out the difficulty of the pattern selected, the salesperson has shown a genuine concern for the customer, and in the future, the customer will regard the salesperson as knowledgeable and honest.

Another error often made in closing the sale is that of rushing the customer. Salespeople should not try to force the customer to buy. Don't push a sales form or contract at the customer; explain it first. Salespeople who ignore major objections and try to close too early, who try to sell items which will not satisfy customers' needs, or who passively stand by while their customers sell themselves have poor selling techniques.

IF YOU CLOSED THE SALE

Don't stop selling after you have closed the sale. Consider those extra items the customer might need or want: batteries for the radio, refills for the pen, shoe polish for the shoes, or an extension cord for a new power saw. It is your responsibility to see that the customer buys not only the item he or she came to purchase, but also other related items that the customer will need.

During the close, while you are removing tags, filling out a sales slip, using the cash register, making change, and packaging the item, continue to talk with your customers. When the sale is final, be sure to sincerely thank your customers. Make a positive comment about their purchases. Compliment them on their selection. Words of reassurance will help your customers realize that you were sincere in helping them make a wise buying decision.

IF YOU DIDN'T CLOSE THE SALE

You will not be successful in closing every sale. If you become rude or insulting because the customer didn't buy, you will lose more than the sale—you also will lose a customer! The customer will feel that you were thinking only about making a sale.

Even if you fail to close, be courteous to your customers. Don't turn away or leave too quickly. Tell your customers that you en-

ILLUSTRATION 12-7
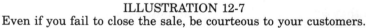
Even if you fail to close the sale, be courteous to your customers.

joyed showing them the merchandise. Invite them to shop at your store again. After the customer is gone, think back over the incompleted sale. Did you make a mistake somewhere in the selling process? By reviewing lost sales, you will learn ways to improve your selling skills.

The successful completion of a sale doesn't just happen. A successful sale is a carefully planned presentation of a product or service. This includes approaching the customer, determining the customer's wants and needs, demonstrating the product, answering customer objections, and then closing the sale.

The closing of the sale is not the final step in selling. You really don't stop selling until the customer has gone. From the time you first greet the customer until the customer leaves your business, you should be selling yourself, your business, and your merchandise or services.

SALES TERMS

ask-your-customer-
to-buy close

choice close

assume-they-are-
buying close

advantages-and-
disadvantages close

premium close

last-chance-to
buy close

standing-room-
only close

narrative or
testimonial close

objection close

suggest-related-
merchandise close

SALES QUESTIONS

1. What is the goal of every sales presentation?

2. Why shouldn't you apply pressure to get a customer to buy?

3. Explain the following statement: Salespeople are problem solvers— not product pushers.

4. As the sale progresses, why is it important to frequently seek customer agreement?

5. How should salespeople build up to the closing of the sale?

6. At what point should salespeople stop showing new merchandise?

7. What is the general rule for narrowing the selection of merchandise?

8. How can you help your customers picture themselves as the owners of the item you are demonstrating?

9. Why should you ask your customers to buy?

10. What is the greatest cause of failing to close a sale?

11. When is it time for the salesperson to close the sale?

12. Explain the following statement: There is no one exact time to close the sale.

13. Customer buying signals indicate the customer is ready to buy. Give several examples of customer buying signals.

14. Explain the purpose of the trial close.

15. A good way to close the sale is with questions. Give several examples of closing questions.

16. What closing technique is considered the safest and the more widely used method?

17. Give an example and explain how to use each of the following techniques of closing the sale:

   a. ask-your-customer-to-buy close
   b. choice close
   c. assume-they-are-buying close
   d. advantages-and-disadvantages close

e. premium close
f. last-chance-to-buy close
g. standing-room-only close
h. narrative or testimonial close
i. objection close
j. suggest-related-merchandise close

18. Which closing techniques strongly appeal to the customer's rational buying motives?

19. Explain the difference between a trial close and the techniques of closing a sale.

20. When using the premium close, why is it better to offer something extra rather than to offer a reduced price?

21. When using the objection close method, what questions should you ask your customer?

22. Describe several common errors in closing the sale.

23. Explain the following statement: You don't stop selling after you have closed the sale.

24. If you have given a closing and the customer does not make a purchase, what should you do?

SALES ACTIVITIES

A. Write several examples of physical buying signals and verbal or spoken buying signals for three products of your choice.

B. Write an example of a testimonial close for a product or service you purchased and were very satisfied with.

C. The following are comments a customer might make to a salesperson during a sale. What key word or phrase in each comment is a customer buying signal?

   1. The stereo I have now needs a lot of repair, but the new ones are so expensive. Do you have any that are less expensive?

2. I like the size and shape, but doesn't it come in a different color?
3. Do you sell many of these refrigerators with the freezer on the bottom? I think I like the side-by-side freezer-refrigerators.
4. What kind of a guarantee do you give on this washer and dryer? I don't want to get stuck with a lot of repair bills.
5. Well, I'm no mechanic, but I think I could change the oil. What do you think?

D. Write a *choice close* for each of the following products or services:

1. a clock radio
2. carpet cleaning
3. food processor
4. motorcycle
5. backyard fence
6. a purse
7. electric drill

E. Poor salespeople sometimes use negative closings. Rewrite the following negative closings to make them positive.

1. You probably don't want to buy a lawn mower today, do you?
2. Most likely you aren't interested in this more expensive calculator.
3. I doubt that you would want to buy four bath towels and washcloths.

SUGGESTION SELLING AND REASSURANCE

Your Learning Goals

After studying this chapter, you should:

- *know why suggestion selling is important.*
- *understand how suggestion selling increases the business's profit.*
- *be able to suggest related items, new merchandise, or larger quantities of merchandise.*
- *be able to use trading-up selling skills with your customers.*
- *be able to suggest items from the customer's viewpoint.*
- *be able to suggest items which will benefit the customers.*
- *be able to demonstrate the suggested item.*
- *be able to provide reassurance to the customers.*

Have you ever entered a store intending to buy a specific item and left with more than one item? Have you ever known exactly what you wanted to buy, but a salesperson convinced you that another item would be a better purchase?

No doubt all of us have had experiences like these. What caused us to change our minds when we thought we knew exactly what we wanted? Chances are it was a talented salesperson who knew how to use a sales technique called suggestion selling. Remember, that's what selling is all about — helping customers buy. If a salesperson suggests additional logical purchases, customers will often increase the amount of their purchases. And, best of all, the salesperson is appreciated for suggesting the added items!

WHAT IS SUGGESTION SELLING?

Suggestion selling is a service you should provide for your customers. It can take many forms. Suggestion selling is simply suggesting merchandise that relates to your customers' original purchase or suggesting other items your customers may need. Your suggestions should be sincere and should be made as a helpful reminder to your customers. Suggestion selling should not be done to push something off on your customers that they don't want or need. The suggestions you make should be based on what the customers tell you during the sale.

Suggestions from salespeople are well-received by customers when the suggestions remind them of needed merchandise or when the merchandise suggested will benefit them. Suggestion selling should not be high-pressure selling. It is offered as a service to your customers to help them satisfy their needs and wants.

Suggestion selling is simply asking customers to buy merchandise based on their needs and wants. This may be additional merchandise beyond the original purchase or it may be merchandise totally unrelated to the original sale. It is one of the easiest and most effective sales-increasing techniques any salesperson can learn. It really works!

IMPORTANCE OF SUGGESTION SELLING

Suggestion selling is important because, if done correctly, it benefits the customers, the salespeople, and the business. If customers don't know what they want to buy, then how will a suggestion from a salesperson help them? Well, that's where the salesperson's product and service knowledge becomes most useful. By having a complete understanding of the products or services they sell, salespeople can suggest purchases the customers may have never even considered. For example, when you buy a new pair of jeans, you may need a new shirt or blouse, sweater, or pair of shoes to complete your outfit. An effective salesperson may save you an unnecessary return trip to the store by suggesting this related merchandise.

Customers appreciate the expert advice of salespeople in selecting the right merchandise. For example, when customers buy fashion items, they appreciate the sincere advice and opinion of the salesperson. Customers expect salespeople to provide expert advice. When you buy a new dress or sport coat, aren't you really trying to improve your appearance? A sincere, courteous salesperson can assist you in selecting the fashion items which look best

ILLUSTRATION 13-1
Effective suggestion selling may save your customer unnecessary return trips to the store.

on you. Salespeople who sell fashion merchandise are often expected to be fashion experts, and customers seek their help in buying clothes which are stylish, attractive, and appropriate for the occasion.

Suggestion selling also benefits the salesperson. If you offer good suggestions to customers, they will return to buy from you again. Customers appreciate a salesperson who has a sincere interest in helping them. The increased sales you make from suggestion selling can improve your wages if you work on a commission basis. Even if you're not on commission, increased sales from suggestion selling will make you a valuable salesperson at your business. Pay raises and job promotions often go to the most productive sales employees first.

Suggestion selling is very important to a business. The additional sales which result from suggestion selling increase a business's gross sales and net profit. **Gross sales** are the amount of dollars a business receives from the merchandise or services it sells. **Net profit** is the amount of profit left after subtracting the cost of the merchandise and operating expenses from gross sales.

Let's look at a typical example of how suggestion selling can increase the net profit of a business.

	Initial Sale		Suggestion Selling— Increased Quantity	
1 pair of shoes	$39.95	2 pair of shoes	$79.90
Cost of item	−19.95	Cost of items	−39.90
Gross profit	20.00	Gross profit	40.00
Operating expenses	−14.45	Operating expenses	−14.45
Net profit	5.55	Net profit	25.55

This example shows that almost five times more profit can be made by selling only twice as much merchandise. Similar results occur when you sell your customer a related item to go with the original purchase.

	Initial Sale		Suggestion Selling— Related Item	
1 white shirt	$14.95	1 white shirt	$14.95
Cost of item	− 9.75	1 dress tie	+10.00
Gross profit	5.20	Total sales	24.95
Operating expenses	− 4.83	Cost of items	−14.75
Net profit	$ .37	Gross profit	10.20
		Operating expenses	− 4.83
		Net profit	$ 5.37

By selling a dress tie to go with the white shirt, the salesperson has increased the net profit of the store by 14 times. Although the operating expenses may be slightly higher in selling two items rather than one, the result is still a much larger net profit. It's certainly easy to understand that suggestion selling, when done properly, is very important to the business as well as to the customer and salesperson.

WHAT TO SUGGEST TO YOUR CUSTOMERS

Now that you understand the importance and the value of suggestion selling, the next step is to know what items to suggest to your customers. Deciding what to suggest to your customers should be very easy. The products within a department or store are usually organized as they relate to each other. The displays within your store or department are often built to display related merchandise.

For example, when you purchase a new skirt in the women's department of a department store, that department also carries merchandise which goes with your original purchase. You could choose from sweaters, blouses, or jackets. A man who buys a new pair of dress pants may find, in the same department, a dress shirt and tie or a sport coat to go with the pants. Here are some other examples of related-merchandise sales:

1. A customer buying an AM-FM cassette stereo for a car may buy new speakers, cassette tapes, a tape storage case, and a cassette head cleaner tape.
2. A person interested in jogging may purchase jogging shoes, sweat socks, jogging shorts, T-shirts, and a jogging suit.
3. A man buying a sport coat will naturally want to look at a new shirt, tie, pants, and maybe a new pair of shoes.
4. When you wash and wax your car, you'll need a bucket, a sponge, chamois, car wax, tire cleaner, upholstery cleaner, and glass cleaner.
5. If you plan to paint a room in your house, you'll need brushes or a paint roller, a paint tray, a trim brush or trim roller, masking tape, and a floor cover.
6. A girl interested in taking up tennis will need a racket, tennis balls, tennis shoes, tennis shorts, a tennis shirt, sweat socks, a wrist band, a sun shade or hat, and a racket press.

These are just a few examples. It's not hard to suggest merchandise to go with the customers' original purchases. The chart below identifies the types of merchandise you may suggest to your customers.

Types of Merchandise to Suggest to Your Customer Include...

- related merchandise.
- new merchandise.
- a larger quantity of merchandise.
- better quality merchandise.
- merchandise specials.
- merchandise for special occasions.

Suggest Related Merchandise

Certain products and services require that **related merchandise** be purchased at the same time. Only a sleepy salesperson would forget to suggest paint rollers and brushes to the customer purchasing six gallons of interior paint!

Buying a microcomputer is a new experience for many customers today and it opens up a whole host of suggestion–selling opportunities. For example, although many microcomputers come with a limited guarantee from the manufacturer, stores offer extended warranties once the manufacturer's warranty has expired. Because the microcomputer is a relatively new product, customers need to be educated on how it may be used. The microcomputer is versatile; it has many, many uses. It can be used for business purposes, entertainment, schoolwork, personal and household tasks.

Once customers purchase the microcomputer they may need several related products to enjoy their personal computer. An obvious need would be a computer table. A printer for the microcomputer is a second related product. Software is a definite need. Software to prepare for the SAT (Scholastic Aptitude Test), to learn how to type, or to plan your budget are just three of thousands of software options. There are software games for people of all ages. The salesperson might even suggest that the customer enroll in classes offered by the store on how to use the microcomputer.

The following example illustrates a salesperson using related-merchandise suggestion selling with a customer who has just purchased a tennis racket.

Salesperson:	I'm sure you'll enjoy your new tennis racket. The imperial gut strings will really help you control your serve and forehand. Are you planning to try out your new racket today?
Customer:	Yes, I'm anxious to see how well I hit with it.
Salesperson:	You'll probably want to use new tennis balls with that racket. Do you like regular or heavy-duty tennis balls?
Customer:	Either one's okay.
Salesperson:	Let me suggest a couple of other items for your racket. Since you wanted the gut-string racket, I would suggest that you buy some conditioner to put on the strings to keep them from wearing out. The conditioner puts a thick lacquer coating on the string and prevents it from wearing or raveling. It is inexpensive and will make your strings last longer.
Customer:	How much is it?
Salesperson:	This six-ounce bottle is $4.95 and it will last for at least two years.

ILLUSTRATION 13-2
Suggest related merchandise that your customers may need to go along with their original purchases.

Customer:	Okay.
Salesperson:	The second item I think you might like is the new adhesive racket tape. This is a new product which I think is really effective. I guarantee that it will improve your grip.
Customer:	How?
Salesperson:	The racket tape is wrapped around your racket handle like this. The adhesive on the tape locks your grip on the racket handle. You won't have to worry about your grip slipping. Even when you're really sweating, it works great! Here, feel how the adhesive provides a sure-lock grip.
Customer:	It sure gives you a strong grip. How much is it?
Salesperson:	It's only $3.25.
Customer:	That's fine. I'll take it.

It's really quite easy to suggest related merchandise. Your own alertness and initiative allows the possibilities to be nearly limitless. No sale should be considered complete without the suggestion of related items. Just think about what your customers may need to go along with their original purchases.

Suggest New Merchandise

Have you ever noticed a friend wearing something new and wished you had some new clothes, too? As a salesperson, you can benefit from your customers' wants. By knowing your customers, you will know which customers are usually interested in new merchandise. A smart salesperson will keep a list of customers who like to be kept up-to-date on new merchandise. These customers should be called and told when new merchandise they either have asked about or would enjoy looking at, is delivered. **Want lists** are kept by salespeople who sell real estate, cars, clothing, art, antiques, furniture, and recreation and sports equipment.

The following examples illustrate the effective use of suggesting new merchandise:

Car-Stereo Salesperson:	Hi, Dave. I'm glad you came in today. I was planning on calling you. Our new car stereos came in last week, and I really think you'll like our new high-power car stereos with automatic reverse cassette players. Let's listen to this one with the graphic equalizer first.
Clothing Salesperson:	Miss Evers, I'm telephoning to let you know that our spring shipment of women's sweatsuits has just arrived and there are several tri-color sweatsuits I think you'll be interested in.
Hardware Salesperson:	Well, you should be ready for this spring with the lawn mower you just purchased. You'll like its magnesium body. It is extremely lightweight and will be very easy for you to push. Since you're thinking about lawn care now, let me show you the new lawn fertilizer that we received yesterday. This is an excellent time to put down nitrogen fertilizer. The spring rains and this fertilizer will give you a beautiful thick, green lawn.

Suggest Larger Quantities of Merchandise

Nothing aggravates some customers more than having to make another trip to a store because they didn't purchase enough of a product to complete a job. For instance, wouldn't you be irritated if you bought a gallon of paint to paint a bedroom and after painting for two hours, find out that you need to drive several miles back to the store to buy more paint to finish the job?

An alert salesperson doesn't miss an opportunity to tactfully suggest to customers additional items that they may ultimately need. For example, a customer approaching a salesperson at the counter of a sporting goods store asks:

Customer:	Do you have a heavy, cushioned pair of sweat socks? I need them for jogging. The socks I'm wearing now are much too thin. I'm getting blisters!
Salesperson:	Yes, we have some very nice cushioned sweat socks. How does this pair feel? Is it heavy enough?
Customer:	I think so. They are certainly soft. I'll try a pair.
Salesperson:	You're right; they are soft. They are our best selling brand. Have you been jogging long?
Customer:	About two months.
Salesperson:	How often do you jog?
Customer:	I jog every evening with my daughter. She's an electrician and doesn't get much exercise at her job.
Salesperson:	Well, if you jog every day, you'll probably need more than one pair. They are $3 a pair or three pair for $8. May I suggest you get three pair and save yourself a dollar.
Customer:	They sure feel comfortable. I guess three pair will be all right.

This example illustrates how a tactful and honest suggestion can benefit your customer. Suggestion selling should benefit the customer as well as increase the sales and profits of a store.

Suggest Better Quality — Trading Up

When a salesperson shows the customer one item and then shows a higher priced item, this technique is called **trading up**. You should use trading up when you determine that your customer would benefit from better quality merchandise. It is important when using trading up that you explain to your customers the benefits they will receive from purchasing the better quality merchandise. You should use trading up when the customer will receive a better value from purchasing the higher priced merchandise. The following example illustrates a salesperson using trading up to assist the customer in making a wise buying decision.

Salesperson:	That is one of our newer nonreflex 35mm cameras.
Customer:	It sure is easy to operate. My friend has one and he really likes it.
Salesperson:	We have received good comments from our customers about its performance.
Customer:	My friend took great pictures on his vacation in the mountains. How much does it cost?
Salesperson:	It's $129.95.
Customer:	Sounds like a good buy. He said he paid about $150.00 for his. That's $20.00 more than this price.
Salesperson:	You're right. That is a good price. Are you interested in a camera mostly for family pictures and vacation shots?
Customer:	Yes, I want to take some pictures of my daughter and son in their activities. My daughter is a varsity tennis player and my son plays football and basketball in 8th grade. I am also a high school distributive education teacher and would like to use the camera for taking slides for classroom instruction.
Salesperson:	So you probably would like to take fast-action pictures of your children playing sports. What types of pictures will you be taking for use in your class?
Customer:	Probably slides of stores, displays, ads, and business scenes. I will also be doing some title slides.
Salesperson:	Sounds as if you have a much greater need for a camera than your friend did. I think you will be using the camera for many things.
Customer:	Yes, my son also is interested in photography, and he wants to build a darkroom in our basement.
Salesperson:	Now, to take action slides of your daughter and son you will need fast shutter-speed capabilities. To take your own slides for classroom use, you will need a close-up lens. Let me show you a 35mm SLR camera that will take both action shots and close-up title slides.

ILLUSTRATION 13-3
Use trading up when your customer will benefit from purchasing better
quality merchandise.

The salesperson used qualifying questions to find out what the customer really needs in a camera. Based on the customer's responses, the salesperson suggests that the customer trade up to a higher priced, better quality single-lens reflex (SLR) 35mm camera. The salesperson, after qualifying the customer, has identified the benefits needed by the customer and has shown a camera that provides those benefits. The trading-up sale concludes:

Salesperson:	Let me explain why this 35mm SLR is a better camera for you.
Customer:	It looks complicated and expensive.
Salesperson:	First, let me assure you that this camera is very easy to use and will take pictures as good as almost any camera you can buy. Let me recap what you want in a camera. First, you said you wanted to take pictures of your son and daughter participating in athletics. Is that right?
Customer:	Yes, Jill plays tennis and Scott plays football and basketball.
Salesperson:	I enjoy sports myself. Let me show you why this camera will take good pictures of your children playing tennis and football. This camera has a

shutter-speed range from one second to 1/1000th of a second. This will allow you to take stop-action pictures. You can capture your daughter hitting her serve or your son making a tackle. You will be able to take pictures of them which you will all appreciate for many years.

Customer: How about the slides for my classroom?

Salesperson: Many schools have purchased this camera for their audio-visual staff's use. We have some very inexpensive close-up lenses to make your title slides — something you couldn't do with the other camera.

Customer: I'll bet this camera is really going to cost me a fortune.

Salesperson: No. In fact, it is very reasonable considering everything you want it to do. It sells for $249.95 and the only accessories you need are the close-up lenses.

Customer: Ouch, that's $120 more.

Salesperson: Well, that may seem like a lot of money. But let me ask you a question. How long do you think this camera should last?

Customer: It better last 10 to 15 years!

Salesperson: There's really no reason it shouldn't last 20 years or more. What's 20 into $120?

Customer: Well, that's $6.

Salesperson: That's right. For $6 more per year you can own one of the best cameras on the market. When you buy a camera, you're much better off paying slightly more money and getting what you really need. When you buy this camera, you'll never need to spend money on another camera. This camera will do everything you want it to do. Don't you agree?

Customer: Well, if it does what you said it will, I guess you're right.

Salesperson: This camera will take all your pictures — your family and vacation pictures, pictures of Jill and Scott participating in athletics, and your slides for classroom teaching. If it will do all these things,

	wouldn't you agree it's a reasonable price for the camera you need?
Customer:	I guess so. All right, I'll take it!
Salesperson:	That's great. If Scott wants to build a darkroom, I'm sure he is really interested in photography. This camera is the start of a system. He can build on to it and become an excellent amateur photographer. You're actually saving money when you purchase this camera rather than the first camera you mentioned. Now, would you like some color film?
Customer:	Yes, I'll need two rolls of 36 exposures.
Salesperson:	Prints or slides?
Customer:	Prints. I thought I'd take some pictures of Jill at tennis practice today.
Salesperson:	Well, you've certainly bought an excellent camera. You'll enjoy the pictures of your family and it will take excellent slides for your classes. Would you like to look at a close-up lens today?
Customer:	No, not today.
Salesperson:	Okay. When you are ready to start taking slides for your class, come back to see me. I'll show you how to use a close-up lens for title slides to give your slide presentations a professional look. Will this be cash or would you like to open a charge account today?
Customer:	I'll write a check for it.

Suggest Merchandise Specials

Have you ever been in a large discount store when a voice over the public-address system announced that, for the next 30 minutes, all lawn chair prices would be reduced by 20 percent? That was a form of suggestion selling—suggesting to everyone in the store that a **merchandise special** was available.

You, as a salesperson, can do the same thing with an individual customer. Make sure your customer knows about any current special offers. The merchandise may not be related at all to the customer's current purchase, but because it's a good deal, you want to make sure your customer knows about it. The decision to buy or refuse still rests with the customer. But do your part as a competent salesperson to make your customer aware of the merchandise specials through suggestion selling.

Many stores will feature merchandise specials. Some shoppers will visit stores to find out what is being featured. Retail stores often build special displays of featured items to assist salespeople in making suggestions to shoppers. It is your job as a salesperson to know what your department and other departments in the store are featuring. Merchandise specials and sale merchandise should always be mentioned to customers. Even if the merchandise doesn't relate to the original purchase, most customers appreciate learning about good buys. Here are some examples of statements to use in suggesting merchandise specials:

"Did you notice our special sale this week? We're featuring our two-piece swimsuits at 25 percent off. That's a great buy! This is a good time to buy your swimwear for this summer."

"Diana, did you know that we are having a special sale on blouses? We will give you 40 percent off any blouse in stock when you buy a pair of fashion jeans."

"May I suggest the Chicken Monterey? It is our chef's specialty. I had it yesterday and the sweet and sour sauce was excellent."

"Hi, Jim. Did you see our special sale on sweaters? Several of them will look nice with the slacks you bought last week."

Perhaps you have advance knowledge of a super sale to be promoted next week in your store. Your customers would be grateful if you told them about the sale ahead of time. It would mean that they might be able to postpone an intended purchase for a week in order to save money.

Suggestion selling, when done properly, is something we all appreciate. As a salesperson, never be ashamed to suggest additional purchases to your customers. Just make sure that what you suggest helps to fulfill your customers' wants and needs. Use reason and consideration as you make suggestions. Customers will appreciate your thoughtfulness.

Suggest Merchandise for Special Occasions

There are several special occasions during the year when a salesperson should use suggestion selling. The seasons of the year (spring, summer, fall, and winter) are ideal occasions to suggest merchandise. **Seasonal merchandise**, such as women's and men's apparel, lend themselves to suggestion selling. Sporting goods also change with the seasons. In these cases, suggestions from salespeople can result in increased sales. Purchases are also made for special occasions such as birthdays, weddings, anniversaries, graduations, and holidays such as Christmas, Easter, Hanukkah, Thanksgiving, Valentine's Day, Mother's Day, and Father's Day. Examples of suggestion selling for special occasions include:

"Frank, Mother's Day is only nine days away. Before you leave, take a look at our special display of gift ideas next to the register."

"Ms. Fleming, did you notice the new lightweight pants we are featuring for a Father's Day present?"

"Mrs. Perez, you may want to look at the luggage and briefcase specials we have for graduation. They would make a nice graduation present for Diego."

ILLUSTRATION 13-4
The Christmas season is a good time to suggest additional merchandise.

H. Armstrong Roberts, Inc.

HOW TO MAKE SUGGESTIONS TO YOUR CUSTOMERS

Suggestion selling is based on the idea that when salespeople offer suggestions at the right time, customers will respond favorably because the idea of buying the item is on their mind. Probably the easiest and most effective way of making suggestion selling work for you is to put yourself in your customer's place. If *you* had bought the item or the service just purchased by your customer, is there anything else you would like to have? At this point you, the salesperson, are in a better position than the customer to know what else should be purchased. You know your product or service line completely and you know, through questions you have asked, the wants and needs of your customer. Now it's just a simple matter of suggesting merchandise to satisfy those wants and needs. Here are four rules to follow in making suggestions to your customers:

1. Don't suggest additional merchandise to your customers while they are still considering the first purchase. Make sure you close the original sale before suggesting additional merchandise. After the customers have decided to buy, you should make the suggestion before the original purchase is wrapped and paid for. Make the suggestion while the customers are still thinking about their first purchase.

2. Make the suggestion from the customers' points of view. Suggest items that will benefit your customers. If you really listen to your customers during the sales presentation, you will have a good idea of their wants and needs. Avoid giving customers the idea that you are simply making suggestions to increase your sales. The suggestions should be sincere and should be made as a service to your customers.

3. Make a specific suggestion. After selling the customer the original purchase, make a specific, positive suggestion. For example, if your customer just bought a dress shirt, don't ask: "Is there anything else?" Instead say, "Here's our new line of ties. Wouldn't this one go well with your new shirt?" This suggestion reminds the customer of the need for a new tie to go with the new shirt.

4. Make sure you have demonstrated the suggested merchandise and have sold the benefits. If possible, demonstrate the suggested merchandise. For example, show how well the suggested tie goes with the dress shirt the customer just purchased. Let the customer use the suggested product or put the product in the customer's hands.

The salesperson who achieves the greatest success in selling is the one who knows how to sell additional suggested merchandise. Suggestion selling, if used correctly, will be well-received by your customers and will provide you with satisfied customers who will return to buy from you again and again.

GIVING REASSURANCE TO YOUR CUSTOMERS

Everyone likes to be right. **Reassurance** is the act of giving confidence to someone else. When a customer makes a buying decision, the salesperson should reassure the customer that a wise buying decision was made. If the reassurance is sincere, the customer will feel even better about the purchase.

"Will someone please tell me that I'm doing the right thing?" is the unspoken plea in the customer's mind. To this, the salesperson should answer: "Based on what you told me, I think you've made a very wise choice and this store will make sure that you are fully satisfied with your purchase." This reply, spoken sincerely, will reassure this customer.

Reassurance can be based on a number of things: business reputation, salesperson's knowledge, customer's expressed wants and needs, customer's knowledge, price, availability, quantity, quality, and manufacturer's reputation, to name just a few. As a salesperson, it is a part of your job to pick the appropriate way to reassure your customer that a wise buying decision has been made.

Providing customer reassurance is really very easy. After you have closed the sale and you have completed your suggestion selling, simply tell your customers that they have made a wise purchase. You should also thank your customers for their business and tell them that you have enjoyed serving them. Notice how the salesperson provides customer reassurance in this example:

Salesperson:	You will really like your new coat. It will keep you very warm and it certainly looks stylish.
Customer:	Thank you. I think I'll really like it.
Salesperson:	Well, thank you very much. I enjoyed waiting on you. Please come back and shop again.

Remember, in every sale the customers must be satisfied or the merchandise may be returned. To be certain that your customers are satisfied, provide customer reassurance by:

1. Explaining how to use and care for the product.
2. Reassuring your customers that they will be satisfied with the product.

SALES TERMS

gross sales

net profit

related merchandise

want lists

trading up

merchandise special

seasonal merchandise

reassurance

SALES QUESTIONS

1. Are the following statements true or false?

   a. Suggestion selling should be a service to your customers.

   b. Suggestion selling should be based on what customers tell you during the sale.

   c. Suggestion selling is high-pressure selling.

   d. Suggestion selling is an effective technique to increase sales.

   e. A suggested item should relate to the original purchase.

   f. Suggestion selling should benefit the business more than the customer.

   g. Product and service knowledge is a prerequisite for the effective use of suggestion selling.

   h. Gross sales are the profits left after subtracting the cost of merchandise and operating expenses from net sales.

   i. Net profit is the amount of dollars a business receives from the merchandise and services it sells.

   j. Every time you complete a suggestion sale it increases the net profit of the store.

   k. A want list is kept by salespeople to increase their sales with repeat customers.

   l. Trading up involves showing the customer one item and then showing a higher-priced item.

   m. Merchandise specials announced over a store speaker system are a form of suggestion selling.

   n. Suggestion selling should be attempted before closing the original sale.

   o. Suggestion selling should be based on product features.

   p. An effective phrase for suggestion selling is: "Is there anything else?"

   q. It is not necessary to demonstrate additional merchandise items in suggesting them to customers.

r. Most customers do not appreciate salespeople who use suggestion-selling techniques.

s. Reassurance and suggestion selling are the same selling techniques.

t. Reassurance should be provided before the salesperson closes the original sale.

2. Which of the following suggestion-selling statements should be used to increase your sales through suggestion selling? Write the letter of each statement which is an effective suggestion-selling statement.

a. May I help you with anything else today?

b. Would you like to look at some ties to go with your new dress shirt?

c. You don't need anything else today do you?

d. We have several purses which will match your new coat.

e. Did you notice our sale on stockings today?

f. What style of pants do you think might go with your new shirt?

g. Did you notice our sale on matching blouses for your skirt?

3. Read the following suggestion-selling statements and identify them as suggesting related merchandise, trading up, suggesting merchandise specials, suggesting larger quantities, suggesting new merchandise, or suggesting merchandise for special occasions.

a. These socks are three pair for $8.

b. This blouse would go well with the skirt you just bought.

c. Football season starts next week. Have you seen our stadium cushions?

d. That is a nice sport shirt for the money, but are you familiar with our shirt-sweaters? They are only $5 more.

e. Let me show you our merchandise special on wash-and-wear pants.

f. The handkerchiefs are $2 each or five for $7.50.

g. May I suggest that you buy your wife a comforter for Christmas?

h. The boots you're looking for are $39.95. I'd suggest that you buy the insulated boots for $44.95. They are a much better value.

i. Have you seen the new stadium blankets we received last week?

j. This is the last day of our special on radial tires. Did you see our best radial tire line that is featured in our display?

SALES ACTIVITIES

A. Using the following information, compute the net profit to a store when one, two, and three shirts are sold during the same sales transaction.

Cost of shirt   — $12.00
Retail price of shirt — $19.95
Operating expenses — $ 3.49

B. Select a product and describe how you would complete each of the following suggestion-selling techniques for that product.
a. Suggest related items
b. Suggest larger quantities
c. Suggest trading up

SELLING:

SPECIAL SKILLS NEEDED

UNIT

4

SELLING:

SPECIAL SKILLS NEEDED

CHAPTER 14: SALES FORMS
AND TRANSACTIONS
CHAPTER 15: CASH REGISTER OPERATION
AND HANDLING MONEY
CHAPTER 16: STORE LOSSES
CHAPTER 17: SALES-SUPPORTING SKILLS
CHAPTER 18: TELEPHONE SELLING

SALES FORMS AND TRANSACTIONS

Your Learning Goals

After studying this chapter, you should:

- *understand the importance of sales forms.*
- *know what information to put on a sales form.*
- *know how to prepare a sales form using an organized routine.*
- *be aware of mistakes to avoid when completing sales forms.*
- *understand the types of sales and nonsales transactions.*

Your customer has decided to make a purchase. The sale, however, is not finished. You must properly record the sale immediately after your closing. This recording must be done quickly and accurately. Once customers decide to buy, they become impatient to complete the sale, receive their purchases, and leave. How you record each sale is very important to you, your customers, and your company. Your customers want an accurate receipt of their purchases and the business wants accurate information about the sale.

Whether the business is large or small, a procedure for recording sales must be completed for every sale. This procedure will vary from business to business, but the basic procedure is the same. Salespeople must be familiar with their company's sales forms, cash register, method of making change, and all other specific procedures and policies of their company.

Beginning salespeople should learn their company's procedures before they begin selling. Customers become irritated when they receive an unreadable or inaccurate sales form, when they watch the salesperson correct an error on the cash register, or when they receive poorly wrapped merchandise. Don't lose the customers' confidence after you have sold them the product or service. Be prepared to record the sale quickly and accurately, to wrap the merchandise, and to thank the customers for shopping at your business.

SALES FORMS

A **sales form** is a written record of a sale. Sales forms are often referred to as sales slips, sales checks, or sales receipts. These forms are important to the operation of a business. They serve two functions: first, they give the customers a receipt that shows all the necessary information about the sale; second, they serve as a vital source of information to the business.

The majority of businesses use cash registers to record the necessary information for each sale. The cash register records the sale and prints a receipt. Some businesses require a handwritten sales receipt rather than the sales receipt produced by the cash register.

Customers should always be given some type of receipt for their purchases. Sales forms represent a very simple contract between the customer and the business. The customer agrees to purchase and the business agrees to sell the item at a mutually acceptable price. The sales form or receipt is the customer's copy of the simple contract.

Many businesses require that a copy of the sales receipt accompany any merchandise returned. This assures the business that the merchandise was purchased there. It also provides other necessary information such as the date of the sale, the identification of the salesperson, the exact amount of the sale, and the amount of sales tax charged.

The information recorded on a sales form is also useful to the business. Store buyers analyze sales forms to determine what colors, sizes, and styles of merchandise customers are buying. This information also helps buyers determine the quantity of these items to purchase in the future and when the merchandise should be ordered and delivered. Sales forms are used by the credit or accounting personnel to bill products or services to customers' charge accounts. If the business offers delivery service, the customers' correct names and complete addresses are needed to insure proper delivery. Management personnel use sales forms for several different reasons: to determine the productivity of a sales-

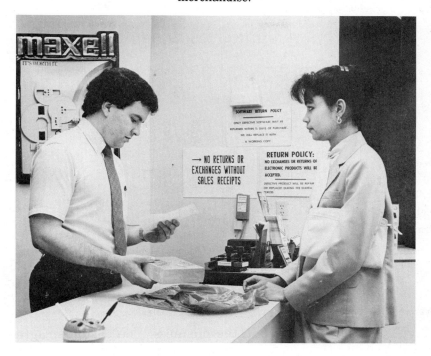

person, to control the budget, to keep inventory records up to date, and to analyze sales records to keep track of customers' buying and spending habits.

Information on a Sales Form

Different kinds of sales forms are used in different businesses. Each business form is designed to meet specific needs. While some businesses use many different forms, others may use the same form for every type of sale.

As a salesperson, you should know what information your business requires on each sales form. The arrangement may be different, but most sales forms require the same information: the date of purchase, the customer's name and address, the salesperson's identification, the type of sale or other transaction, the description of the merchandise or service, and the pricing information. The sample sales form in Illustration 14-2 is designed to record all types of sales on the same form.

ILLUSTRATION 14-2
Salespeople should know what information their business requires on the sales form.

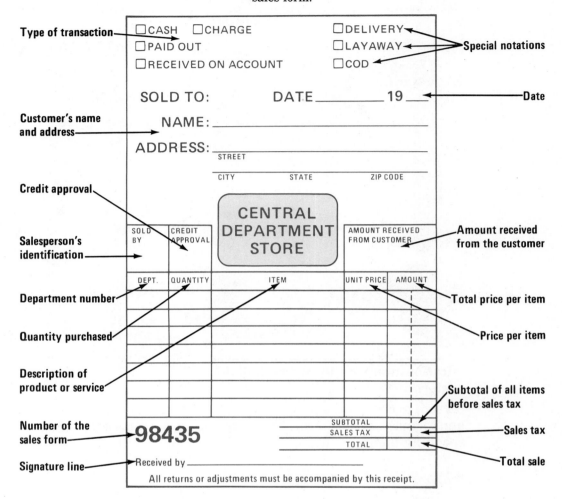

Date of Purchase. All sales records are kept by the date of purchase. This date must be on every sales form. Daily records are kept according to the date of the sale. In addition, returnable merchandise usually must be returned within a specific period of time. Because the date is on all sales forms, there is no doubt about when the sale took place.

Customer's Name and Address. The customer's name and address is placed on the sales form when the items are to be delivered, when sales are being charged to a customer's account, when a customer receives a cash refund for returned merchandise, or when a customer is paying on a charge account. Most businesses require the signature of the customer when merchandise is charged or when a cash refund is received for returned merchandise. A signature line is usually located on the bottom of the sales form.

Some businesses ask for the customer's name and address on sales forms for all types of sales. Salespeople can use the sales forms to learn the names of customers. Businesses also compile mailing lists from this information. Market surveys based on customer addresses can provide the store management with information on where to direct advertising in order to reach the store's customers.

Salesperson's Identification. Each salesperson is given an identification number or letter to be placed on each sales form. Rather than writing their complete names, salespeople use these letters or numbers to quickly record their identification. It is important that this identification be recorded on each sales form. This identification is needed when merchandise is returned or exchanged. If a customer has a question about the purchase, the numbers or letters will help to identify the salesperson who sold the item. If the accounting department or the delivery department has a question about the sale, the salesperson who sold the merchandise can be more easily located. Salespeople who receive a commission on their sales will want the sale recorded properly so that they will receive their commission. Sales managers will use the identification numbers to review individual sales performances and to determine sales quotas, bonuses, or promotions.

Type of Transaction. A **transaction** is the act of carrying on business between a customer and the store. Some businesses will use a single sales form with space to mark or record each type of transaction. If this type of form is used, salespeople must mark the type of transaction on each sales form. Other businesses may use several different forms, one form for each type of transaction. When different forms are used, the type of transaction is usually printed in bold letters at the top of each individual form. It is important to the customer, the salesperson, the credit department, the accounting department, and the store's management to know the type of transaction. The transaction designation may identify the transaction as a cash, charge, COD, or layaway sale; as an amount paid out of the register; or as a payment received on account.

Description of Merchandise or Service. On each sales form there is a line provided for the salesperson to record the description of the merchandise or service. Usually in a smaller business, only the quantity and the item are required. In medium-sized or larger businesses, a department number, the quantity of items, and a complete description of the merchandise being sold are usually needed. The description of the merchandise may include style numbers, sizes, colors, cost codes, or other information. Be sure you understand the order in which the information is to be written. If the description is detailed and specific, it will help store buyers plan future purchases; help eliminate any questions from the credit, accounting, or delivery departments; and help other salespeople if the customer wants to return the item at a later date.

Pricing Information. On some sales forms, a space to record the unit price per item and the total price of the item is provided on the same line as the merchandise description. On other sales forms, the space to record the unit price is omitted. In this case write the unit price immediately after the description of merchandise.

Here is where your math skills become important. After you have multiplied the quantity of the item times the unit price for that item, place the total in the amount column. Add all of the item amounts together. This is the subtotal before taxes. Record this figure toward the bottom of the sales form or on the line immediately after the last item listed on the sales form. Next, figure the sales tax and add the sales tax to the subtotal to determine the total amount of the sale. This is the amount the customer pays.

Correct pricing information is important. If you record an incorrect price or your arithmetic is wrong, you have either overcharged your customer or lost money for your business. As a result, your customers will lose confidence in you, the store's inventory records will be incorrect, and the business's profits will not be correct on the business's profit or loss statement. Daily sales records as well as other financial reports will also be incorrect. It only takes a few seconds to check the sales form to be sure everything is correct.

Preparation of a Sales Form

Good selling practices and good store operations depend upon accurate records. If the sale is not recorded properly, the business may suffer a financial loss. It is the salesperson's responsibility to fill out the required information on the proper form. Completing sales forms requires a complete understanding of the types of sales and the specific information demanded by the business. Customers expect salespeople to complete sales forms quickly and accurately. This may mean working under pressure when several customers are waiting to be served. Preparing sales forms correctly can be as important as selling your products or services.

Use Your Sales Book or Sales Register. Most sales forms are kept in a sales book or a sales register. A **sales book** is a pad of approximately 50 sales forms. After you write a sale using a sales book, remove the carbon paper and tear the copies out of the book. A **sales register** is a small metal or plastic container that will hold approximately 100 sales forms. After you fill out the sales form, eject the copies from the container. Regardless of which system your business uses, it is important that you always use the sales book or sales register assigned to you.

Each sales form is numbered in sequential order. Always write your sales in the numbered sequence. Your records are maintained by the accounting department according to the numbers printed in your sales book. This is the reason you should always use your own sales book. If you make an error while recording the sale and you want to start over, do not destroy the incorrect copy. Instead write *VOID* across the front of the form. The word **VOID** means that the sales form is canceled and cannot be used. Some businesses require the salesperson to provide a brief explanation for the error and then have the voided copy authorized by the store manager. After you have voided the sales form, use the next form in sequential order to write up the sale.

Most sales forms are written in duplicate by using carbon paper or the newer carbonless paper. The business keeps the original and the customer receives the carbon or second copy. Sales forms may be written with more than one copy depending upon the operation of the business. For example, in a larger business that offers its customers delivery service, the business may use four copies. The original or first copy is used for store records. The second copy is given to the customer as a receipt. The third copy is retained by the credit or accounting department to be sent with the customer's charge statement. The fourth copy is used as a delivery ticket for COD sales that must be delivered, or for merchandise that is placed on layaway. Some sales books also record the sale on a piece of tissue that stays in the sales book or sales register after the other forms have been used and removed.

Organize Your Routine. After you have closed the sale, you need to quickly record the sale. This process is easier if you are organized. Develop a system for writing the sales forms, ringing the sale on the cash register, and wrapping the merchandise. Always use the same procedure so it will become automatic. Being well-organized is an asset for every salesperson.

You will need to have a specific place to keep your sales book and pen. Place them next to the cash register or in some other designated area of the sales counter. Don't waste the customer's time while you try to locate your sales book. This will irritate your customer.

Every applicable blank on the sales form should be filled out at the time you record the transaction. Don't leave out information because it is not readily available, thinking you'll fill it in later. Often you will become busy and forget to write down this information. This causes problems for the accounting department, and the customer receives an incomplete sales receipt. Don't skip any information. If you are not sure, don't guess. Ask the store manager or supervisor for the information you need.

When completing the sales form, write the required information in the proper order. Start at the top of the sales form and work from left to right, top to bottom. Record the type of transaction and the date by using the number of the month. Some sales transactions will require the customers' names and addresses. Always write your identification. When writing the description of the merchandise, list the department, quantity, item, and other required information. Record the price per item as well as the total price for the items. Add the total amounts for each item to determine the subtotal. Figure the sales tax and add it to the subtotal. This will be the total the customer owes. If the sales transaction requires the customer's signature, have the customer sign the form. If there are special instructions, write them on the form. Finally, record the amount received from the customer on the sales form and ring it up on the cash register.

Be systematic when writing your sales forms. If you follow the same procedure each time, you will be less likely to make a mistake. It takes valuable sales time to void a sales form. Be right the first time. Develop the skill of filling out sales forms quickly and accurately.

Avoiding Mistakes on Sales Forms

Completing sales forms is an important responsibility of salespeople. Because store managers, buyers, and credit and accounting personnel use completed sales forms in their work, poorly completed sales forms can cause them many problems. There are four common types of mistakes salespeople make in completing sales forms:

1. handwriting is sloppy
2. required information is not recorded
3. abbreviations are used
4. arithmetic is poor

ILLUSTRATION 14-3
By following the same procedure each time you fill out the sales form, you will be less likely to make a mistake.

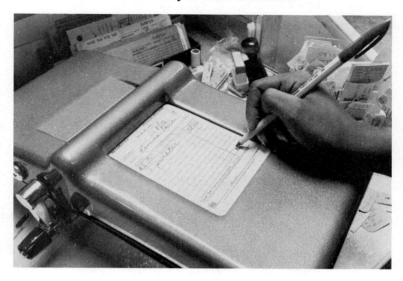

These problems cause others to have difficulty doing their jobs. Buyers have difficulty knowing what was sold. Accountants have difficulty keeping inventory records accurate. Customers become frustrated because they cannot read the sales form or they find an error on their sales receipt.

Write Legibly. Because sales forms are important business records handled by many people, salespeople must take a little extra time to write legibly. Most businesses want their salespeople to print using capital letters. It is easier and less confusing to read. If you have poor handwriting, practice to improve it. It may save you the embarrassment of trying to read your own poor handwriting at a later date.

In addition to providing readable sales information, you must also be sure that other people can easily read your sales figures. Does your "0" look like a "6," or your "7" look like a "1"? Can your customers tell the difference between your "7's" and your "9's"? Salespeople are often in a hurry and write their sales figures poorly. Then, because they cannot read the figures themselves, they make additional arithmetic errors. Don't be careless. Write your sales figures legibly.

Write Completely and Accurately. Information that you record on your sales forms must be complete and accurate. Be sure to complete every required part of the sales form. If information is not available at the time of the sale, take a few minutes to find it before proceeding with the next customer. If you wait until the end of the day, you will most likely forget to look up the information you need.

Be sure the information you are recording is accurate. If a customer thinks the charge account number is "01784" but is not sure, look it up. Never guess.

Avoid Abbreviations. Avoid abbreviations when filling out sales forms. Customers who, a month after making charge purchases, receive a bill for "3 sks" or "2 ln mws" may not remember what they purchased. If customers can't remember what they purchased, they will be reluctant to pay the bill. When filling out a sales form, be specific. Don't use abbreviations.

Check Arithmetic. Salespeople are expected to know how to add, subtract, multiply, and divide accurately. They should also know how to work with fractions, decimals, and percentages. Arithmetic errors are too common on sales forms. Your business and your customers expect you to be able to figure your sales correctly. For example, you should be able to figure how much the customer will pay if the customer buys three belts for a vacuum cleaner at 79¢ each, if the customer receives a 10 percent discount on hardware supplies, or if the customer buys one-fourth pound of candy at $1.88 per pound. If you charge the customer 79¢ total for all three vacuum cleaner belts, you will have lost $1.58 in sales for your company. If you charge 94¢ for the one-fourth pound of candy, you will have overcharged your customer 47¢.

Be careful to record your decimals in the correct place. There is a big difference if you charge your customer $1.50 for an item priced at $15.00. Also check your sales figures to be sure you did not reverse them. Don't write 78¢ when it should be 87¢. Remember, one mistake can often lead to another. If the unit price is wrong, the item total will be wrong, the sales tax will be wrong, and the total paid by the customer will be wrong.

Spend a few extra seconds on each sale to be sure your sales forms are accurate and legible and have all the required information written on them. You, your customers, and your company will be glad you did.

TYPES OF SALES TRANSACTIONS

A **sales transaction** involves the exchange of a product or service for the purchase price or the promise to pay the purchase price. Each sales transaction involves recording the sale on a sales form, the cash register, or both. It is necessary for salespeople to know the different types of sales transactions. Generally these are classified as cash sales, charge sales, COD sales, layaway sales, and discount sales.

In this section, the methods of recording each transaction will be explained. An example is presented for each transaction to help you understand it. Remember that each business has its own specific sales forms, its own methods for completing those forms, and its own requirements for information to supply on each form. Learn the specific forms and methods of completing these transactions for your company. In the following examples, you are employed as a salesperson for the Central Department Store. The Central Department Store will be used only as an example to help you understand how to record the different transactions.

The Central Department Store uses a three-part sales form. The first or original copy is kept by the business. The second copy is given to your customers as their sales receipt. The third copy is used to accompany a delivery or COD sale or is attached to a layaway sale. The Central Department Store uses one sales form for all transactions.

Cash Sales

A **cash sale** is made when the customer immediately pays for the product or service with money or a check. The majority of sales transactions in a business are cash sales. When customers make cash purchases, they should receive a sales form or a cash register tape. The sales form or cash register tape is the customer's record of the sales transaction and is known as a **receipt of purchase.** These receipts are necessary for customers who may want to return or exchange the items they purchased.

If the item is to be delivered, the sale is called a **cash-send** transaction. The sales form must have the customer's complete name and correct address on it.

A cash sale is the simplest transaction to record. After you have closed the sale, take the merchandise to the sales counter. Then complete the sales form in your sales book following your established routine. For example, a customer wants to purchase one electric drill for $34.95, six drill bits at 98¢ each, and one extension cord for $4.65 from the hardware department. This department's identification code is HW. Today's date is October 10. Your salesperson's identification number is 58. Starting at the top of the sales form, you would record the information required on the form as shown in Illustration 14-4.

ILLUSTRATION 14-4
A cash sale is the simplest transaction to record.

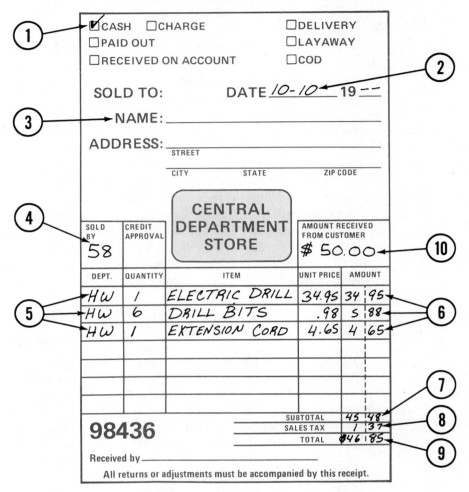

1. Check the type of transaction; in this case, a "CASH" sale.
2. Record the date.
3. You will not normally need the customer's name and address for a cash sale, although some businesses will require this information.
4. Write your identification number, 58.
5. Record the merchandise information. Write the department identification, the quantity of each item, the item name, and the unit price for each item.
6. Multiply the quantity times the unit price to determine the amount for each item listed.
7. Add the amounts together to determine the subtotal.

8. Figure your sales tax. For this example, use a 3 percent sales tax. Multiply the dollar figure of the subtotal times .03 and then add 1¢, 2¢, or 3¢ depending on where the cents figure of the subtotal falls on the tax chart below.

TAX CHART			
.01	to	.14	no tax
.15	to	.44	1¢
.45	to	.74	2¢
.75	to	.99	3¢

9. Add the tax to the subtotal to determine your total sale.
10. The customer gives you $50. Place this figure on the sales form in the box which is labeled, "Amount Received From Customer."

Now you are ready to record the sale on the cash register. After this is done, keep the original copy of the sales form and give the second copy to the customer. The third copy is thrown away unless the item is to be delivered or is a layaway sale.

If the sale is a cash-send sales transaction, you would record the customer's complete name and address and check "Delivery" in the upper right-hand corner of the sales form. After printing the customer's name and address, repeat the spelling to the customer or show the form to the customer and ask if it is correct. Follow this procedure for all deliveries. You would then tape or staple the third copy of the sales form to the wrapped merchandise for delivery.

Charge Sales

Charge sales transactions take place when customers charge products or services to their charge accounts in order to pay at a later date. Most customers, when using charge accounts, will take the purchases with them. These sales transactions are called **charge-take** transactions. However, if the business offers delivery service, customers may charge the items and have them delivered. These are called **charge-send** sales transactions.

There is a steady increase in the use of charge accounts by customers. Many customers find it more convenient to carry a few **charge cards**, also referred to as **credit cards**, rather than carry a large sum of money when shopping. Charge sales offer customers the opportunity to purchase something now and pay for it later.

Most businesses offer credit to their customers because they know that the customers will take advantage of this service. Charge accounts increase customer sales, increase the quantity customers buy, and increase the chance that customers will come back to the same business to shop.

There are two basic charge account systems available to businesses. Some businesses have their own charge system. Others offer charge accounts through a bank or other independent credit card plan. Some offer both. Businesses with their own charge system must keep extensive records, bill customers each month, and collect overdue charge accounts. These credit-related activities can be a very expensive part of a business operation. Businesses charge interest on overdue charge accounts to help pay for their extra expenses.

If the store accepts credit cards issued by a bank or other independent company, customers are able to charge their purchases, but the store sends the records of these charge sales to a central accounting office of the independent company. Billings, collections, and other transactions are handled by the company which issued the credit card. The independent credit card companies charge the store for the credit services.

Regardless of the plan used, customers are normally required to fill out a credit application. When the application is approved, a charge card is usually sent to the customers and a credit limit is set. The **credit limit** is the maximum amount customers can charge to their account. In our example, the Central Department Store accepts bank credit cards and also offers its own charge account to customers, but it does not issue its own charge cards. Salespeople must call the credit department for approval of each sale charged.

In completing a charge sale, follow your normal routine for completing the sales form. A sample charge sale on a Central Department Store's charge account is recorded on the sales form in Illustration 14-5. The numbered items on the sales form correspond with the numbered steps below for recording the charge sales information.

1. Check "CHARGE."
2. Record the date.
3. Write the customer's name and complete address.
4. Write your identification number.
5. Complete the merchandise description and pricing information. Recheck your figures for accuracy.
6. Ask for the customer's signature.

ILLUSTRATION 14-5
Information found on a charge sales form.

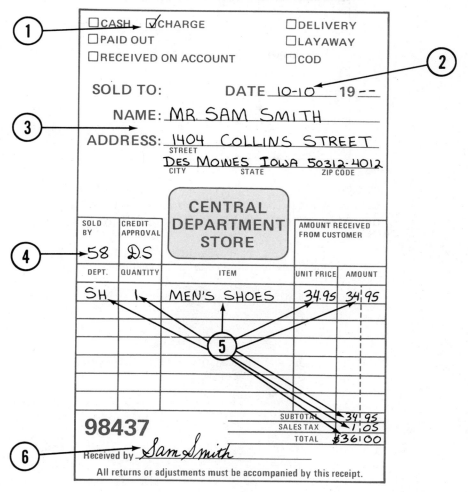

After you have completed the charge sales form, ask the customer to check the name and address as written to be sure it is correct. Then if necessary call the credit department or store manager for approval. Finally, ring the sale on the cash register as a charge sale.

When a customer wants to use a bank credit card, a different sales form is filled out. Although the form is different, it asks for the same information as the store's charge form. Read the form carefully. Neatly print all the information needed for the charge sale. A common bank charge form is shown in Illustration 14-6.

The customer will give you the bank charge card, and you will place it on a card embossing machine. This machine will record the

ILLUSTRATION 14-6
Typical charge form for a bank credit card.

SALES DRAFT		DEPT. NO.	CLERK'S NO.	CLERK'S INIT.	TAKE
					SEND
QUAN.	CLASS	DESCRIPTION		UNIT COST	AMOUNT
DATE		AUTHORIZATION CODE		SUB TOTAL	
				TAX	
	SALE CONFIRMED AND DRAFT ACCEPTED				
MasterCard X				TOTAL	
	CARDHOLDER'S SIGNATURE				

The Issuer of the card identified on this item is authorized to pay the amount shown as TOTAL upon proper presentation. I promise to pay such TOTAL (together with any other charges due thereon) subject to and in accordance with the Agreement governing the use of such card.

customer's name and account number from the card. Ask the customer to sign the form. On larger sales, either you or the credit department will need to call the bank for credit approval.

COD Sales

Some businesses will deliver merchandise to customers who place an order by telephone or mail. Even if the customer comes to the store, there are occasions when the customer would rather pay for the item when it is delivered. This type of sales transaction is known as a **COD sale** (Cash on Delivery or Collect on Delivery). If the item to be delivered is COD, the sales form must have the customer's name and correct address listed. Some businesses write a cash sales form and ring it up on the cash register after delivery is made. Other businesses write a charge sale and then, after the delivery, will credit the customer's account.

Regardless of the method used to record the sale, the customer pays for the item when it is delivered. Often, an additional delivery or handling charge is added. The COD charge is not taxed. Most businesses do not use COD sales frequently. With the increasing use of charge cards, customers can make purchases by charging them to their charge accounts.

Companies may use one of two procedures to record COD sales. The first example is written as a cash sale. To record this type of sale, you follow your normal routine for completing the cash sales form. For a COD cash sale, record the additional information as shown in Illustration 14-8.

1. Check "DELIVERY" and "COD" in the upper right-hand corner of the sales form.
2. Write the customer's name and address.
3. Add the COD delivery charges.

ILLUSTRATION 14-8
One way to record a COD transaction is as a COD cash sale.

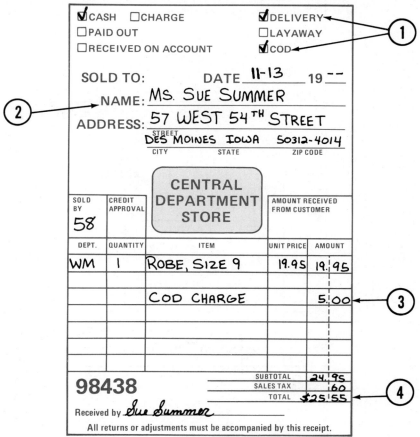

4. The customer pays the total and then signs the sales check when the item is delivered.

The customer's signature will verify that the customer has received the items ordered and has paid the bill. The customer keeps the second copy of the sales form. The original sales form and payment are then returned to the store and rung on the cash register as a cash sale.

The second method for recording a COD sale is to write it as a charge-send sales transaction. As well as following your normal routine for filling out the charge sales form, record the additional information as shown in Illustration 14-9.

ILLUSTRATION 14-9
A COD transaction may be recorded as a charge-send sales transaction.

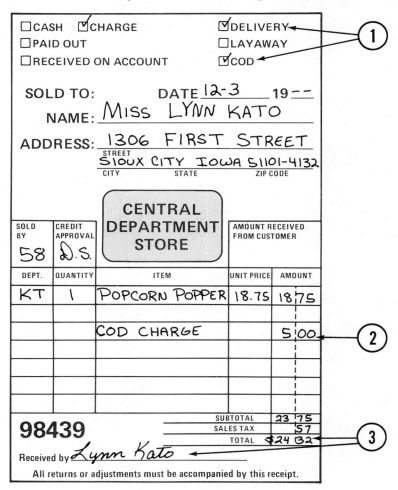

1. Check "DELIVERY" and "COD" on the sales form.
2. Add the COD delivery charge.
3. When the item is delivered, the customer pays the total and signs the sales check.

The sale is recorded on the cash register as a charge sale. Credit approval is obtained from the credit department. The original form is kept by the store. The second and third copies are delivered with the merchandise. Again, the customer's signature will verify that the customer received the items and paid the bill. The customer keeps the second copy of the sales form as a receipt. The person who delivers the merchandise should write "PAID" on the receipt. Later, the payment for the sale is recorded on the cash register as a received on account. (See Illustration 14-13, page 276, for use of the sales form as "received on account.")

Layaway Sales

Many businesses offer their customers the convenience of **layaway sales.** Layaway sales are sometimes referred to as "lay-bys" or "will-call" sales. In a layaway sales transaction, the salesperson will set aside an item of merchandise for the customer. A cash deposit is usually required at the time of sale. Then the customer can pay for the item over a specific period of time, usually not more than three or four months. Store policy may require salespeople to obtain credit approval for a layaway sale.

In most cases a layaway sale is written just like a charge sale, but the customer does not receive the item at the time of the sale. In a layaway sales transaction, the store keeps the item until the customer has completely paid for it. If the customer does not pay the balance during the specified time period, the item is returned to stock and made available for sale. The customer may also lose part and sometimes all of the deposit paid. Usually, though, businesses refund money paid on incompleted layaway sales.

There are several reasons why customers use layaway services. A customer may want to purchase an item before it is in season; for example, a customer may purchase a new winter coat in July. A customer may find that an item is hard to obtain or replace, so the customer will purchase one on layaway and will have it when it is needed; for example, the store has only one snow blower in stock for the season. Also, customers may purchase a more expensive item or take advantage of sale items. Perhaps a customer does not have enough money to pay the full price of an item at the time of purchase.

Both the customer and the store benefit from layaway sales transactions. The store benefits from the sale of the item, while the customer has the opportunity to purchase an item and pay for it over a period of time, thus being assured of buying the item wanted.

When writing up a layaway sale, follow your normal routine for completing sales forms and record the additional information as shown in Illustration 14-10.

1. Check "CHARGE" on the sales form.
2. Check "LAYAWAY" in the upper right-hand corner of the sales form.
3. Write any special instructions, such as when the final payment is due, on the sales form.
4. Have the customer sign the sales form.

ILLUSTRATION 14-10
Information found on a layaway sales form.

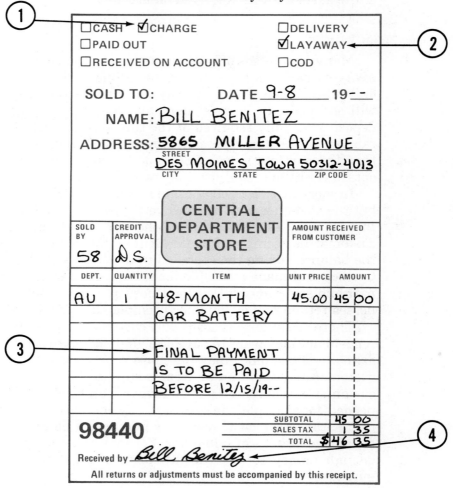

The business keeps the original copy of the sales form and records it on the cash register as a charge. The customer receives the second copy, and the third copy of the transaction is attached to the layaway item.

When the customer makes a payment on the item in layaway, fill out a new sales form. As shown in Illustration 14-11, the salesperson should:

1. Check "Received on account."
2. Fill in the "Amount received from customer."
3. Under "ITEM" write "layaway deposit" and the means of payment (cash or check).
4. Record the total payment.

ILLUSTRATION 14-11
When a customer makes a payment on an item in layaway, fill out a new sales form.

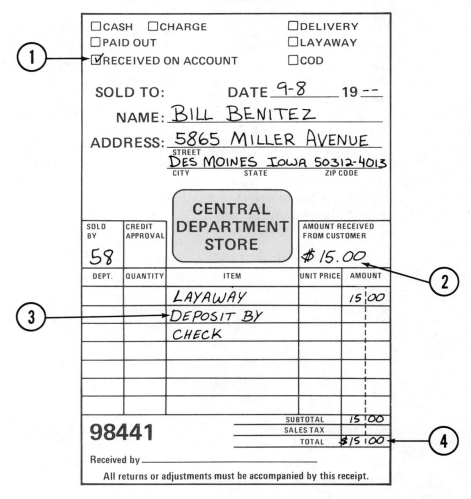

The customer pays toward the item over a period of time. When the item is completely paid for, it is given to the customer.

Discount Sales

When a person receives a reduction from the listed price of the product or service, this is known as a **discount sale.** Discounts are often given to employees and are occasionally given to certain customers. Discounts are usually given as a bonus to store employees. This also encourages them to purchase goods or services from their place of employment. Discounts may be given to certain groups of customers in order to gain steady, repeat business. When making a purchase, these customers should identify themselves.

Be familiar with your store's policies on offering discounts. If you are uncertain about your store's discount policies, ask your store manager or supervisor.

A **discount** is usually a percentage that is subtracted from the total price of the items purchased. This reduction from the price of merchandise can be written for any type of sales transaction, such as a cash sale, a charge sale, or a layaway sale. Illustration 14-12 is a cash sale with a discount.

To figure a discount, multiply the total price of the items purchased (include both dollars and cents even if the cents is .00) times the discount figure. In the answer, count four numerals from the right and place a decimal point. Drop the last two numerals in this answer, rounding up to the next highest number when the two numerals being dropped are fifty or more. This figure is the discount allowed on the sale.

Total of items	$ 50.95
Discount	× .15
Discount figure	$7.6425

After the discount has been determined, subtract the discount from the total price of the items. This figure is the subtotal.

Total of items	$50.95
Discount figure	− 7.64
Subtotal after discount	$43.31

Next, figure the sales tax. In this example, a 3 percent sales tax is used. Add it to the subtotal. This total is the amount the customer pays. Most businesses will also have the customer or employee sign for all discounts.

ILLUSTRATION 14-12
A discount sale may be any type of sales transaction, such as a cash sale.

☑CASH ☐CHARGE	☐DELIVERY
☐PAID OUT	☐LAYAWAY
☐RECEIVED ON ACCOUNT	☐COD

SOLD TO: DATE _10-13_   19 _--_

NAME: _____

ADDRESS: _____
STREET

CITY   STATE   ZIP CODE

CENTRAL DEPARTMENT STORE

SOLD BY	CREDIT APPROVAL		AMOUNT RECEIVED FROM CUSTOMER
58			$45.00

DEPT.	QUANTITY	ITEM	UNIT PRICE	AMOUNT
AU	1	TIRE		35 95
AU	1	TOOL BOX		15 00
				50 95
		LESS 15% DISCOUNT —		7 64

	SUBTOTAL	43 31
98442	SALES TAX	1 30
	TOTAL	$44 61

Received by _Don Christensen_ _____

All returns or adjustments must be accompanied by this receipt.

OTHER TYPES OF TRANSACTIONS

There are other types of transactions that do not involve the direct sale of a product or service. These include payments received on account, gift certificates, and merchandise returns or exchanges.

Payments Received on Account

When customers want to pay a COD sale, pay amounts due on purchases they have charged to their accounts, or pay toward a layaway sale, the salesperson may be responsible for crediting their account. This transaction is known as a **received on account.** Payments received are usually recorded on a sales form and on the cash register. The transaction does not involve the sale of merchandise or a service, but rather the receipt of money from the customer toward a customer's previous purchase. In some stores these transactions are handled by a customer service or credit office rather than by the salespeople.

A received on account is a bookkeeping transaction. Its purpose is to deduct the amount being paid from what the customer owes.

ILLUSTRATION 14-13
Information found on a received-on-account sales form.

☐CASH ☐CHARGE	☐DELIVERY
☐PAID OUT	☐LAYAWAY
☑RECEIVED ON ACCOUNT	☐COD

SOLD TO: DATE 10-20   19--

NAME: BEN MATSUMI

ADDRESS: 2409 COLLINS AVENUE
STREET

DES MOINES IOWA 50312-4020
CITY   STATE   ZIP CODE

CENTRAL DEPARTMENT STORE

SOLD BY	CREDIT APPROVAL		AMOUNT RECEIVED FROM CUSTOMER
58			$20.00

DEPT.	QUANTITY	ITEM	UNIT PRICE	AMOUNT
		CASH		20 00

98443

SUBTOTAL	20 00
SALES TAX	
TOTAL	$20 00

Received by _____

All returns or adjustments must be accompanied by this receipt.

While a received on account seems like a simple transaction, it is important that the correct amount be deducted from the correct customer's account.

As shown in Illustration 14-13, the salesperson writes either "CHECK" or "CASH" in the "ITEM" column. The customer receives the second copy of the sales form as the receipt of payment. The salesperson then rings the payment received on account on the cash register. (Do not figure sales tax on a received on account transaction. This is not a sales transaction because no sale of merchandise or service is involved.)

Gift Certificates

When buying a gift for someone else, customers may choose to purchase a gift certificate rather than select a product or service. A **gift certificate** states that a specific person has a specified sum of money available from the business to spend on a product or service. If a store offers gift certificates through its sales staff, the salesperson must fill out the form for the gift certificate in addition to the normal sales form.

When writing out a gift certificate, use good handwriting. Remember, this is a gift. Be sure all the information is correct. Ask for the correct spelling of the person's name who is to receive the gift certificate. The amount of the certificate is not written in numbers but is spelled out. The certificate is dated and signed by the salesperson. Most gift certificates will also have a ticket stub that is kept by the business. Record the name of the recipient, the amount, the date, and your identification on the certificate. In addition, record on the ticket stub the name and address of the person or group buying the gift certificate. Then when the gift certificate is returned, all the necessary information is available on the ticket stub.

As a salesperson for the Central Department Store, you will need to fill out two forms. The first form is a sales form as shown in Illustration 14-14. A gift certificate is written like a received on account. Be sure to have the recipient's complete name and address on the form. Also include on the sales form the person or group who purchased the certificate and record the transaction on the cash register as a received on account.

The second form to be filled out is the gift certificate that will be given to your customer. As you can see in Illustration 14-15, all the required information is recorded on both the certificate and the ticket stub. Remember, this is a gift. Use your best handwriting. If you make a mistake, void the certificate and write a new one.

ILLUSTRATION 14-14
A gift certificate sales form is written like a received-on-account sales form.

☐ CASH	☐ CHARGE	☐ DELIVERY	
☐ PAID OUT		☐ LAYAWAY	
☑ RECEIVED ON ACCOUNT		☐ COD	

SOLD TO: DATE _4-6_   19 _--_

NAME: _KENTON ZIEGLER_

ADDRESS: _814 3RD STREET_
STREET
SPERRY   IOWA   52650-4355
CITY   STATE   ZIP CODE

CENTRAL DEPARTMENT STORE

SOLD BY	CREDIT APPROVAL		AMOUNT RECEIVED FROM CUSTOMER
58			$20.00

DEPT.	QUANTITY	ITEM	UNIT PRICE	AMOUNT
		GIFT CERTIFICATE		20|00
		# 5843		
		PRESENTED BY:		
		ACE FLYING CLUB		
		DES MOINES, IOWA		
		JIM CLASEN, PRES.		

98444

SUBTOTAL	20|00
SALES TAX	
TOTAL	$20|00

Received by _____

All returns or adjustments must be accompanied by this receipt.

ILLUSTRATION 14-15
Information on the gift certificate is recorded on both the certificate and the ticket stub.

5843
Date Issued _4/6/--_
To: _KENTON ZIEGLER_
814 3rd STREET
SPERRY, IA
From: _ACE FLYING CLUB_
DES MOINES, IOWA
JIM CLASEN, PRES.
Amount: _$20.00_

Central DEPARTMENT STORE
DES MOINES, IOWA
Gift Certificate   5843

Date Issued _4/6/--_
To _Kenton Ziegler_
in the amount of _Twenty and no/100_
Presented by _Ace Flying Club_

Returns

Customers return merchandise for many reasons — incorrect size, uncoordinated colors, or malfunction. You should know your store's policies on merchandise **returns.** Do customers need a sales form or cash register receipt to return purchases? Are customers allowed to exchange the unsatisfactory item for a more suitable replacement? If customers ask for a cash refund, can you give them their money back? Can your customers return the item for credit to their charge accounts? What do you do if the item looks like it has been used? These questions are important, particularly after a holiday season when customers may want to return items without receipts.

Be prepared to handle returned merchandise. Some businesses will give cash refunds, charge credits, or exchange items — even on sale merchandise. Other businesses will allow the exchange of items, but will not extend charge credits or give cash refunds. Before you begin selling, you should know your store's policies on returned merchandise.

Handling a Cash Refund. When customers return an unwanted item but cannot find a satisfactory substitute, a cash refund may be given. A **cash refund** means the customers will receive the money that they originally paid for the item. Cash refunds are given only if the original sale was a cash sale. Most businesses require a sales form from the purchase before they will accept merchandise returns.

A cash refund is written like a cash sale except that you check "PAID OUT" rather than "CASH." Store policies often require the sales form for a **paid out** to include the customer's name and address, the customer's signature, and approval initials of the store or department manager.

The information needed on the sales form for a cash refund should be recorded as shown on Illustration 14-16:

1. Check "PAID OUT."
2. Record the date.
3. Write the customer's name and address.
4. Record your employee identification.
5. Record the merchandise description (i.e., department, quantity returned, item, unit price, total amount).
6. Include any special notations; in this case, "cash refund."
7. Record the subtotal, sales tax, and total sale.
8. Have the customer sign the form.

After you have filled out the sales form, record the sale on the cash register as a refund or paid out.

ILLUSTRATION 14-16
Information found on a cash refund sales form.

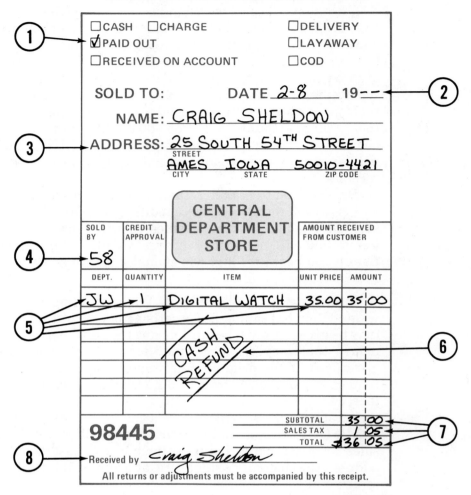

Handling a Charge Credit. Some stores issue charge credits to customers who cannot find a satisfactory replacement for the merchandise they return. For a **charge credit,** often referred to as a **charge return,** the business will record the amount of the original sale on a sales form as a received on account in the customer's name. The customer can use the charge credit like cash toward the purchase of other merchandise in the store. If the original purchase was a charge sale, the charge return can be used to credit the customer's charge account with the amount of the return. This credit will cancel out the amount that would have been due from the customer's original purchase of the merchandise.

To record a charge credit return on a sales form follow the procedure used in Illustration 14-17:

ILLUSTRATION 14-17
Information found on a charge credit return sales form.

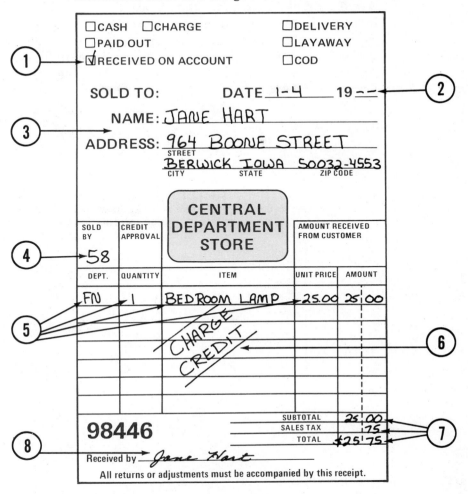

1. Check "RECEIVED ON ACCOUNT."
2. Record the date.
3. Write the customer's name and address.
4. Record your employee identification.
5. Record the complete merchandise description.
6. Include any special notations; in this case, "charge credit."
7. Record the subtotal, sales tax, and total sale.
8. Get the customer's signature.

You do not record a charge credit on the cash register because you have received no money.

Handling an Even Exchange. Exchanging one item for another is the most common method of accepting returned merchandise. An **even exchange** means that the item is exchanged for the same kind of item at the same price. The item may have been the wrong size or color. No money is exchanged. The price of the item is the same as the exchanged item. If the item information on the sales form remains the same, you do not need to fill out a new sales form. However, if the information is different, even when the price remains the same, you must fill out a new sales form.

Complete the sales form for an even exchange as shown in Illustration 14-18:

1. Check "CASH."
2. Record the date.

ILLUSTRATION 14-18
A sales form for an even exchange is filled out if the item information for the exchanged item differs from the item information for the original item.

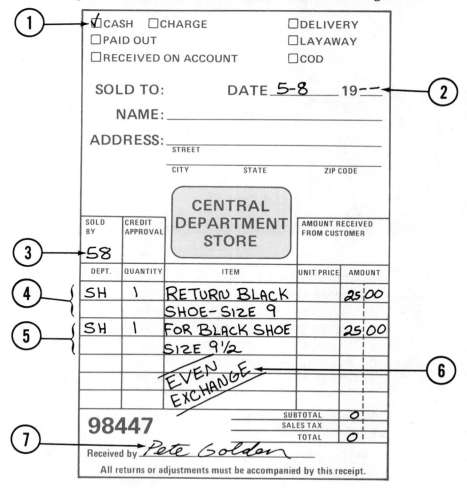

3. Write your employee identification.
4. Record the complete merchandise description and the total amount for the item being returned.
5. Record the complete merchandise description and the total amount for the exchange item.
6. Include the special notation; in this case, "even exchange."
7. Have the customer sign the sales form.

Since there is no money exchanged, you do not ring the sale on the cash register.

Handling an Uneven Exchange. An **uneven exchange** means that the customer returns an item and then selects another item for a different price. In this case, either the customer will pay more for the new item or the business will refund the difference in the prices. A new sales form will need to be written. Businesses use two methods to record uneven exchanges.

The first method requires two sales forms to be written, as shown in Illustration 14-19 below. First, write a cash refund

ILLUSTRATION 14-19
An uneven exchange may be recorded using two sales forms.

☐CASH ☐CHARGE		☐DELIVERY	
☑PAID OUT		☐LAYAWAY	
☐RECEIVED ON ACCOUNT		☐COD	

SOLD TO: DATE 4-8   19--
NAME: *LORI PETERSON*
ADDRESS: *2541 FIRST AVENUE S.W.*
                STREET
ANKENY   IOWA   50021-4620
CITY   STATE   ZIP CODE

CENTRAL DEPARTMENT STORE

SOLD BY	CREDIT APPROVAL		AMOUNT RECEIVED FROM CUSTOMER
58			

DEPT.	QUANTITY	ITEM	UNIT PRICE	AMOUNT
RC	1	RECORD ALBUM	5.95	5 95
		CASH REFUND		

	SUBTOTAL	5 95
98448	SALES TAX	18
	TOTAL	$6 13

Received by *Lori Peterson*
All returns or adjustments must be accompanied by this receipt.

☑CASH ☐CHARGE		☐DELIVERY	
☐PAID OUT		☐LAYAWAY	
☐RECEIVED ON ACCOUNT		☐COD	

SOLD TO: DATE 4-8   19--
NAME: _____
ADDRESS: _____
                STREET
_____
CITY   STATE   ZIP CODE

CENTRAL DEPARTMENT STORE

SOLD BY	CREDIT APPROVAL		AMOUNT RECEIVED FROM CUSTOMER
58			$10.16

DEPT.	QUANTITY	ITEM	UNIT PRICE	AMOUNT
RC	1	RECORD ALBUM	6.95	6 95

	SUBTOTAL	6 95
98449	SALES TAX	21
	TOTAL	$7 16

Received by _____
All returns or adjustments must be accompanied by this receipt.

for the returned merchandise, then ring a paid out on the cash register. Next, write a new cash sales form for the new item. Ring this cash sale on the cash register, also. If the new item costs more than the returned item, the customer must pay the difference. If the new item costs less than the returned item, the business refunds the customer the difference. In this example the customer owes the business $1.03.

The second method of recording an uneven exchange uses only one sales form. Write the more expensive item first on the sales form, and then write the less expensive item. Write "returned" before the returned item. Subtract the price of the less expensive item from the price of the more expensive item and record this

ILLUSTRATION 14-20
An uneven exchange transaction using one sales form.

☑CASH ☐CHARGE		☐DELIVERY		
☐PAID OUT		☐LAYAWAY		
☐RECEIVED ON ACCOUNT		☐COD		

SOLD TO: DATE __5-1__ 19 _-_

NAME: _TODD MEYERS_

ADDRESS: _463 SOUTH STREET_
STREET
DES MOINES IOWA 50312-4040
CITY   STATE   ZIP CODE

CENTRAL DEPARTMENT STORE

SOLD BY	CREDIT APPROVAL		AMOUNT RECEIVED FROM CUSTOMER
58			$ 7.25

DEPT.	QUANTITY	ITEM	UNIT PRICE	AMOUNT
MS	1	TRAVEL ALARM		
		CLOCK	15.00	15 00
MS	1	RETURNED:		
		PEN SET	10.00	10 00

98450

SUBTOTAL	5 00
SALES TAX	15
TOTAL	$5 15

Received by _Todd Meyers_

All returns or adjustments must be accompanied by this receipt.

amount on the subtotal line. Figure the sales tax and total. If the customer owes the business more money for the new item, check cash or charge depending on how the customer wants to pay for the balance owed. Illustration 14-20 shows a cash sale return written on one sales form. In this example the customer owes the business $5.15.

If the business owes the customer money for the returned item, check paid out.

In Illustration 14-21, the customer receives a cash refund for selecting merchandise which costs less than the original purchase. This is a paid out or refund transaction.

ILLUSTRATION 14-21
Information on a paid out or refund transaction.

DEPT.	QUANTITY	ITEM	UNIT PRICE	AMOUNT
CI	1	RETURNED PURSE	9.98	9 98
CI	1	PURSE	8.98	8 98

□CASH □CHARGE   □DELIVERY
☑PAID OUT   □LAYAWAY
□RECEIVED ON ACCOUNT   □COD

SOLD TO: DATE 5-2 19--
NAME: JUDY CORNFIELD
ADDRESS: 4 3RD AVENUE N.E.
   STREET
HAMPTON IOWA 50441-4032
   CITY   STATE   ZIP CODE

CENTRAL DEPARTMENT STORE

SOLD BY: 58
CREDIT APPROVAL:
AMOUNT RECEIVED FROM CUSTOMER

CASH REFUND

98451

SUBTOTAL	1 00
SALES TAX	03
TOTAL	$1 03

Received by *Judy Cornfield*
All returns or adjustments must be accompanied by this receipt.

SALES TERMS

sales form	charge-take	received on account
transaction	charge-send	gift certificate
sales book	charge card	returns
sales register	credit card	cash refund
void	credit limit	paid out
sales transaction	COD sale	charge credit
cash sale	layaway sale	charge return
receipt of purchase	discount sale	even exchange
cash-send	discount	uneven exchange
charge sale		

SALES QUESTIONS

1. What are three other names for sales forms?

2. Describe the two important functions of sales forms.

3. Explain the purpose of a sales receipt.

4. Explain how the information on a sales form is useful within the business.

5. Why do different businesses have different kinds of sales forms?

6. List the information that can be obtained from a sales form. Give the reason for each type of information.

7. Give several reasons why the customer's name and address should be written on a sales form.

8. Describe the importance of writing a sale in your own sales book rather than in someone else's book and why it is important to use forms in numeric sequence.

9. Describe how each copy of a four-copy sales form might be used in a business.

10. Explain why salespeople need an organized routine for recording sales.

11. What are the most common mistakes salespeople make when writing sales forms?

12. Why is it important to fill out a sales form legibly and accurately?

13. Explain why salespeople should avoid abbreviations on sales forms.

14. Arithmetic is important to salespeople, customers, and the operation of the business. Explain the problems caused by poor arithmetic by salespeople.

15. Describe each of the different types of sales transactions.

16. What advantages are there for businesses to extend charge accounts to their customers?

17. Explain the two methods businesses use to offer their customers charge accounts.

18. Why are COD sales becoming less common in business?

19. Why should customers be asked to sign each charge, refund, or discount sales form?

20. Give several reasons why customers use a store's layaway service.

21. What questions should a salesperson be able to answer about merchandise returns?

22. Why are charge credits and even exchanges not recorded on the cash register?

23. Explain the difference between an even and an uneven exchange.

SALES ACTIVITIES

A. When writing a sales form, in what order would you suggest the sales information be written?

B. A delivery was made to 28 North 4th Street and the merchandise was returned to the store. The address should have been 24 North 8th Street. How could this problem have been avoided? What can you do to find the correct address when items that cannot be delivered are returned?

C. Determine the total price of these items.

1. 2 sweaters @ $17.95 each
2. 12 lbs. nails @ $2.75 lb.
3. 3 pkgs. handkerchiefs @ $1.95 pkg.
4. 4 coffee cups @ $2.59 each
5. 6 coffee filters @ 3 for $2.99

D. Calculate a 3 percent sales tax for each of these items.

1. 2 records @ $6.00
2. 1 needle @ $5.75
3. 1 record stand @ $12.98
4. 3 posters @ $4.50

E. You are employed in a fabric shop. A customer, Kathy Sicurella, calls you on the phone. She has just received a bill from your company which lists a part of her purchase as "2 rem." and she can't remember what this means. Kathy is also upset because no receipt was enclosed with the fabric and other items she purchased. She would like to return a few of the items, but cannot because there is no proof of her purchase. Write a conversation you might have with Kathy Sicurella.

F. You are the manager of a gift shop. The business carries many expensive gift items. When you sell an item, you often reorder that item as soon as possible. You have found that one salesperson leaves descriptive information off the sales forms. This delays your reorders. The salesperson also makes arithmetic errors, but is an otherwise excellent salesperson. What possible solutions are there to this problem?

G. The following sales form was written for a charge sale with a discount. What are the errors in this sales form?

☐ CASH	☐ CHARGE		☐ DELIVERY
☐ PAID OUT			☐ LAYAWAY
☐ RECEIVED ON ACCOUNT			☐ COD

SOLD TO: DATE _____ 19 ___

NAME: JIM FRENCH

ADDRESS: _____
STREET

CITY   STATE   ZIP CODE

CENTRAL DEPARTMENT STORE

SOLD BY	CREDIT APPROVAL		AMOUNT RECEIVED FROM CUSTOMER

DEPT.	QUANTITY	ITEM	UNIT PRICE	AMOUNT
	2	DASH LIGHTS	12.00	20 00
		Less 10%		5 00

98452

	SUBTOTAL	25 00
	SALES TAX	
	TOTAL	$25 00

Received by _____

All returns or adjustments must be accompanied by this receipt.

CASH REGISTER OPERATION AND HANDLING MONEY

Your Learning Goals

After studying this chapter, you should:

- *understand the importance of the cash register.*
- *be able to identify the features of the cash register keyboard.*
- *be able to identify other cash register features.*
- *understand the operation of the cash register.*
- *be able to establish a cash register routine.*
- *understand the general change-making procedure.*
- *be able to prepare a change fund and balance the cash register.*

Most business managers would agree that, next to selling, operating a cash register and handling money are the most important responsibilities of salespeople. The successful operation of the business depends upon skilled salespeople who can accurately record information.

In many businesses, salespeople are responsible for operating cash registers and handling money. However, large businesses, particularly discount and self-service operations, hire and train specialized **cashiers** and checkout people. Their responsibility is to record the sale on the cash register, make change, and wrap the merchandise, while building a good relationship with the customer. Regardless of whether a business employs cashiers or salespeople to perform cashier duties, sales must be completed quickly and accurately.

FUNCTIONS OF CASH REGISTERS

Every time a sale is completed, the business must have a record of the sale and the customer must have a receipt of purchase. This recording procedure requires salespeople to accurately record the sale as quickly as possible. Whether or not sales forms are written, most businesses use a **cash register** to record the sale.

Businesses spend a considerable amount of money for their cash registers. They know that a cash register will provide them with accurate, detailed information that is essential to the operation of their business. In addition to providing a convenient money storage drawer, the cash register also serves as an information-gathering device.

A cash register may be an adding machine with a cash drawer. This type of cash register simply totals the sale and opens the cash drawer to receive the customer's money or to allow the salesperson to make change. A store which uses this type of cash register usually also uses sales forms so the business can collect important information concerning the sale and give the customer a detailed receipt.

In other businesses, particularly self-service businesses such as drugstores, grocery stores, or discount stores, the cash register is used to provide an itemized record of the sale. Since no sales form is written, the cash register must be able to record all the information that is usually recorded on a sales form. The cash register will also issue to the customer a detailed cash register receipt of the sales transaction. In fact, some cash registers will print the customer's receipt, compute the sale, sales tax, and total, transfer sales information to a computer, show the amount of change due to the customer, disperse change, issue trading stamps, approve charge cards, and perform several other important functions.

A current cash register design is actually a computer terminal that records sales. Some electronic cash register terminals are connected directly to a computer (referred to as "on-line"). Other terminals will store the information on a magnetic tape or disk that is later sent to the computer center to be processed.

Much information can be recorded in the electronic cash register terminal from a price ticket. This results in more accurate inventory control and purchasing procedures. By using a number code, a business can record the item, the manufacturer, the date the item was received, the cost of the item, and other necessary information. These electronic cash register terminals can also approve credit, compute discounts, figure sales tax, and calculate the entire sale and change due the customer. These cash register terminals can print a sales form or issue a detailed receipt.

ILLUSTRATION 15-1
Much information can be recorded in the electronic cash register terminal from a price ticket.

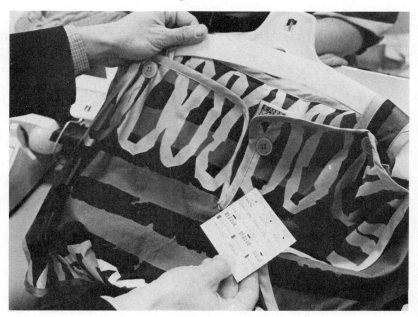

For faster information entry, an electronic wand can be attached to the cash register terminal. From the coded price ticket, the electronic wand reads the merchandise information and records it in the cash register terminal and in the central computer.

Some businesses use the "Universal Product Code" (UPC) developed for optical scanners. The code for each product is recorded in a central computer. When an item is purchased, the item is moved over a laser-beam scanner and the UPC is read by the scanner. After the code is read, the necessary item information is called up from the computer and is printed on the cash register tape and on a detailed audit tape (the tape which stays on the cash register and contains the same information as the tape which is given to the customers).

There are several major advantages to using an electronic cash register terminal. It speeds up checkout procedures. Arithmetic errors in calculating sales amounts, sales tax, and totals are mostly eliminated. Because the terminal can approve credit, the system reduces credit losses from poor-risk charge customers. Bookkeeping is automated. Inventory control is more accurate and up-to-date, so the business can purchase more merchandise when inventory levels become low. Electronic cash register terminals can also alert salespeople to entry errors when recording the items being purchased by a customer. Today, many businesses are investing in the minicomputer electronic cash register terminals because of their many advantages.

The cash register is a vital part of a business operation. As long as salespeople record accurate information, the cash register saves time when recording a sale. It provides valuable information to the business for future planning and buying. The business can record daily sales operations as well as determine which products or services are selling well, common price ranges in which customers purchase, what departments are more profitable than others, and which salespeople make the most sales.

ILLUSTRATION 15-2
Cash registers can provide valuable information to the business for future planning and buying.

KNOW YOUR CASH REGISTER

The type of cash register used depends upon the specific type of business, the sales volume, and the amount of information required for the business operation. Although there are many kinds of cash registers which perform different functions, they all have similar features. Learn the general features of any cash register. Your knowledge of cash register functions will help you to understand the importance of the cash register when you learn to operate one for a business.

The Cash Register Keyboard

Become familiar with the cash register keyboard. The keyboard may contain amount keys, salesperson's identification keys, department or classification keys, transaction keys, a no-sale key, a correction key, a subtotal key, sales tax and total keys, and amount-received and change-due keys. These keys are not placed in the same location on every cash register. Beginning salespeople should become familiar with the cash register they use, its operation, and the information they need to record on it.

The Amount Keys. The **amount keys** record the purchase price of the product or service. They are generally located in the center of the cash register keyboard. The capacity of the amount keys depends upon the cash register and the sales volume of the business. Some businesses may have the capacity to record up to $999,999.99 on their cash registers.

There are two arrangements for the amount keys on the keyboard of a cash register. The keys may be arranged in rows or in a ten-key arrangement, as shown in Illustration 15-3.

ILLUSTRATION 15-3
Cash register keys may be in rows (a) or in a ten-key arrangement (b).

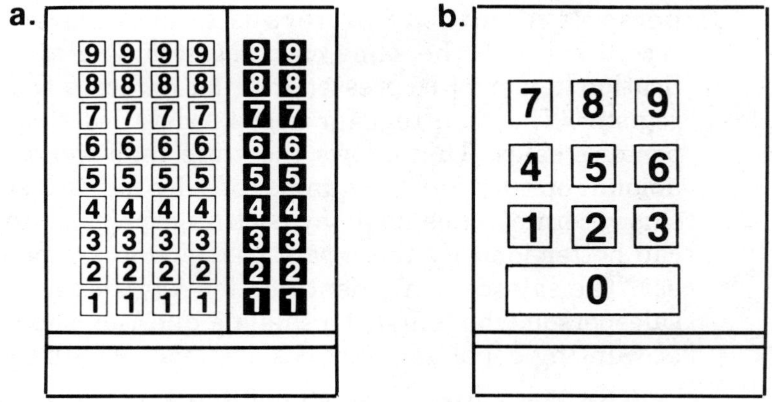

When the amount keys are arranged in rows, the ones are located at the bottom of the keyboard and nines at the top. Usually the dollar keys are one color and the cent keys are a different color. There are no zero keys on this keyboard arrangement. When no key is pressed in that row, the zero is printed automatically. For example, to record a sale of $15.09, the $10-key (fourth column from right), the $5-key (third column), and the 9¢-key (first column) are pressed. No key should be pressed in the second column from the right. Then when the motor bar, transaction key, or subtotal key is pressed, the amount of $15.09 will be recorded on the cash register.

When the ten-key arrangement is used for the amount keys, there is no distinction between dollar and cent keys. To record the purchase price of $15.09, you would press the 1-key, the 5-key, the 0-key, and the 9-key. The cash register will automatically place the decimal before the last two digits pressed on the keyboard. If the figure is an even dollar amount, you must record the cents as two zeros. For $21.00 you must press a 2, a 1, and two zeros. If you do not press the two zeros for cents, the sale will be recorded as 21¢ rather than $21.00.

Many businesses use the ten-key arrangement on their cash register keyboards. They want their salespeople to be able to press the correct keys without looking at the keyboard. This method is called the **touch system.** It enables salespeople to record the sale without looking at their fingers, so their eyes are free to look at the price ticket, the merchandise, and the customer. The touch system can be difficult for beginning salespeople to use. However, with frequent use of the ten-key keyboard arrangement, salespeople are less likely to make errors and will be able to record sales more quickly.

Salesperson's Identification Keys. The purpose of the **salesperson's identification keys** is to allow several salespeople to record sales on the same cash register. The salesperson's identification key must be pressed in order to record the sale on the cash register. The cash register keeps a detailed record of each salesperson's sales. This allows the store manager to know the total amount of sales and the number of sales for each salesperson. With this record of sales made by each salesperson, store management can better identify those salespeople who are productive employees. The salesperson's identification key also helps to identify the salesperson who handled a sale if a question should arise from the accounting department or if a customer wants to return an item.

The Department or Classification Keys. Many businesses record sales information according to a department or classification system. Letters, numbers, or even the title of the department may be listed on the cash register's **department or classification keys.** Grocery stores may use the department classifications of produce, meat, dairy, grocery, deli, and bakery. A shoe store may use the department classifications of slippers, dress shoes, sport shoes, boots, and general merchandise. In a hardware store, department one may be assigned to plumbing materials; department two, electrical supplies; department three, lawn and garden supplies; and department four, small appliances.

The purpose of pressing the department keys is to record sales information that is used for inventory control, future buying, and future planning such as expanding a profitable department or reducing inventory in a less profitable department. Usually the department or classification information is on the price ticket of the merchandise so that salespeople can locate the information quickly and record it accurately on the cash register.

Transaction Keys. Transaction keys record each kind of sale. The classification of transactions is usually cash, charge, received on account, and paid out or refund. Some cash registers may also record cash-send, charge-send, cash-take, or charge-take transactions. One of these transaction keys must be pressed to properly record the sale. All types of transactions are recorded on the customer's cash register receipt and the cash register detailed audit tape.

The accuracy of daily sales records depends upon salespeople recording the proper information. At the end of the sales day, the cash register's cash and charge sales are totaled. If the salesperson made an error on the cash register during the day, the sales information will be wrong. This causes problems that must be corrected by the accounting department.

No-Sale Key. Occasionally a salesperson may need to open the cash drawer without recording a transaction. For example, a customer may want change for a large bill. In another instance, if the cash drawer is low on $1 bills, the salesperson may take out a $20 bill and put in twenty $1 bills. To open the register's cash drawer, press the **no-sale key.** On cash registers without a no-sale key, a salesperson must press the salesperson's identification key and the total key. Either way, the cash drawer opens without ringing up a sale.

Some businesses require that the store manager or supervisor approve the salesperson's opening of the cash drawer with the no-sale key. This protects the business and the salesperson from possible wrongdoing. Even if the business does not require approval, it is best to have another salesperson know your reason for using the no-sale key.

Correction Key. If you press an incorrect key, press a *clear* key, release lever, or **correction key** to correct the error. When the correction key is operated, the incorrect entry is removed. This allows you to press the correct keys before the sale is recorded on the cash register. If you find that you are pushing the correction key often, you need to slow down when entering the information on the register and concentrate on entering the correct information. Try to catch errors before they are entered on the cash register.

Subtotal, Sales-Tax, and Total Keys. Once all the items are properly recorded on the cash register, the salesperson will need to press the **subtotal key.** This gives the total amount of all items before sales tax. If the cash register does not automatically calculate sales tax, the salesperson should know how to figure the correct sales tax. This figure is then entered on the amount keys of the keyboard and the **sales-tax key** is pressed. This procedure will add the sales tax to the subtotal. The **total key** is then pressed as the final procedure in recording the sale.

Amount-Received and Change-Due Keys. Not all cash registers have amount-received and change-due keys. However, with these keys the cash register can figure the customer's change. The purpose of the **amount-received key** (sometimes called the *amount-tendered key*) and the **change-due key** is to remove the possibility of change-making errors. This procedure for making change is faster and more accurate than making change yourself.

After the sale has been totaled, enter on the keyboard the amount of money received from the customer. Press the amount-received key and then press the change-due key. At this point the cash drawer will open and the customer's receipt will be issued by the cash register. The indication window will show the exact change to be given to the customer. This information is also recorded on the detailed audit tape.

Other Cash Register Features

There are several other important cash register features that salespeople need to be aware of: the indication window, the detailed audit tape, the autographic window, the receipt slot or printer, the motor bar, the cash drawer, the change plate, and the date-setting mechanism.

Indication Window. The **indication window** is a glass window usually located on the top of each cash register. The indication window allows the customer to watch what the salesperson is recording on the cash register. A salesperson can also look at the indication window to verify that the information was correctly recorded. The information found in the indication window will usually include the salesperson's identification letter, the type of transaction, the price of the item, and the department or classification information. Whatever information is shown in the indication window is also permanently recorded on the customer's cash register receipt and on the detailed audit tape.

Detailed Audit Tape. A **detailed audit tape** is the permanent record of all cash register transactions. Anytime the cash register drawer is opened, it is recorded on this tape. Almost all cash registers have paper tape inside the machine that records this information. In addition, the newer electronic cash register terminals record this information in a computer. The detailed audit tape serves as the legal, permanent record of all transactions for each business day.

Know how to change the tape in your cash register. This procedure may require the approval of the store manager or supervisor. Usually a red, green, or blue line will appear on the tape as it nears the end of the roll of paper. This means that it is time to replace the roll. Because this procedure takes time, change the tape before you handle the next transaction. Avoid making a customer wait for you to replace the tape.

Autographic Window. On most cash registers the detailed audit tape can be seen through the **autographic window.** This window allows the salesperson to see the information recorded for the last sale. The window opens to allow the salesperson or store manager to make any necessary notations on the detailed audit tape. Perhaps you are to note all bank charge cards, or approvals for refunds, or errors that will need to be corrected. The autographic window allows notations to be made on the detailed audit tape.

Receipt-Tape Slot and Receipt Printer. The customer must receive a receipt of purchase. This may be a sales form, a cash register receipt, or both. When sales forms are not used, the cash register will have a **receipt-tape slot.** The receipt is printed by the cash register and issued from this slot. This tape contains the same information that is printed on the detailed audit tape.

Some cash registers are designed to automatically receive a special sales form. This form is inserted into the **receipt printer.** As the salesperson records the information on the cash register, the register will print this information on the sales form. When the sale is recorded, the salesperson removes the sales form. The original is kept by the business and the duplicate is the customer's receipt of the purchase.

Motor Bar. Most cash registers have a **motor bar** or entry key located on the keyboard. The purpose of the motor bar is to activate the cash register to record whatever information you have entered

ILLUSTRATION 15-4
The receipt is printed by the cash register and contains the same information
as the detailed audit tape.

on the keyboard. Any errors should be corrected with the correction
key before the motor bar is pressed. When the motor bar is pressed,
the information is recorded on the permanent detailed audit tape
and on the customer's receipt. Unless the salesperson's identification key and department key are also pressed, the motor bar will
not operate the cash register.

Cash Drawer. The **cash drawer** provides for an organized
system of receiving and dispersing money. The cash drawer is located at the base of the cash register. When the sale is recorded
properly and entered into the cash register, the cash drawer will
open. The cash drawer contains a **cash tray** for the currency and
coins. As shown in Illustration 15-5, this removable tray is organized with the bills and coins arranged from right to left. The
lowest denomination is placed at the far right. The bills are placed
face up.

Some cash drawers only have a four-slot cash tray. In this case,
the checks and larger denominations of bills are placed under the
tray in the cash drawer. In some businesses, the checks and larger
bills are always placed under the cash tray.

An orderly cash drawer is important. It will allow you to make
change quickly and accurately. Straighten all bills before you place
them in the cash drawer. Be sure that the coins are placed in the

ILLUSTRATION 15-5
A typical cash tray arrangement.

E M P T Y	$20	$10	$5	$1
50¢	25¢	10¢	5¢	1¢

correct pocket of the cash tray. It is important to know the organization of the cash drawer. Making correct change from the cash drawer is an important responsibility.

Change Plate. The **change plate** is a small shelf located directly above the cash drawer. Always place the customer's money on the change plate while making change. If you place the customer's money in the cash drawer immediately and then remove the customer's change, the customer may claim he or she gave you a larger bill and that you did not return enough change. The proper use of the change plate is to place the customer's money on the change plate, make change from the cash drawer, count the change to the customer, and then place the customer's money immediately into the cash drawer and close it. This standard procedure for using the change plate will help you and save your business money.

Date-Setting Mechanism. Every cash register receipt and detailed audit tape will have the day, month, and year recorded on it. The **date-setting mechanism** is located inside the cash register. If you are responsible for preparing a cash register for the day, you must know how to change the date. It is important that the date-setting mechanism be set for the correct day, month, and year.

YOUR CASH REGISTER ROUTINE

Organize a systematic method of recording a sale on the cash register. Develop a step-by-step procedure to follow. Always use the same procedure so it will become automatic. Be prepared to quickly and accurately ring each sale on the cash register so your customers are not detained. However, never **"bunch" sales;** that is, never record several sales at once on the cash register. Too often errors are made and your customers do not receive a receipt for their purchase. Follow this cash register routine:

1. Beginning at the left of the keyboard, press the correct sales-person's identification key and the proper transaction key.
2. Look at the price ticket of the merchandise; then record the following information from the ticket: department code, item numbers, and the price of the item.
3. Press the item key or motor bar to ring each item on the cash register.
4. After all items have been recorded, press the subtotal key.
5. Determine the sales tax and enter the figure on the amount keys; then press the sales-tax key.
6. Press the total key. This will add the sales tax to the subtotal. If your cash register does not figure the customer's change, the cash drawer will open when you press the total key. Announce to the customer the total sale.
7. If your cash register figures the customer's change, enter the amount of money received from the customer on the amount keys and press the amount-received key.
8. Press the change-due key. This will automatically subtract the sale from the amount received from the customer. When the change-due key is pressed, the cash drawer will open.

If you make an error before you have rung it on the cash register, press the correction key and reenter the correct information. Occasionally you may ring the wrong information into the cash register. When you enter a larger amount than the price of the item, this is known as an **over-ring.** When you enter on the cash register an amount that is less than the price of the item, this is known as an **under-ring**. Know how to immediately correct these errors. Each business has its own method of correcting errors. For an over-ring the entry will probably be voided and the correct amount rerung. For an under-ring, the entry may be voided and rerung or the difference may be added to the under-ring. Whether the store procedure is to void the incorrect amount and rering the correct amount or to write a note to the accounting department explaining the error, correct the error immediately. If a sales form or cash register receipt is to be voided, write *void* across it in large letters. Have it approved by the store manager and then place it in the cash drawer.

Be systematic when ringing a sale on the cash register. If you follow the same procedure each time, you will be less likely to make a mistake. Correcting an error takes time, so be right the first time. Develop the skill of quickly and accurately recording sales on the cash register.

Remember to follow this routine procedure: Write your sales forms, record the sale on the cash register, and then wrap the customer's merchandise. With this procedure you will be less likely to make an error.

HANDLING MONEY

Salespeople constantly receive and exchange money. Your job requires you to accurately handle money. This is an important responsibility. Your employer expects you to correctly handle and protect the business's money. Customers expect to receive the correct change. Don't disappoint them. Knowing how to handle money will save you time and will strengthen your customers' confidence in your ability to serve them.

The Change Fund

At the beginning of each business day, a change fund must be counted into the cash drawer. As sales are recorded on the cash register during the day, salespeople may have to make change for their customers. At the end of the business day a tally of the day's sales and money must be calculated.

The **change fund** is the supply of money that is counted into the cash drawer at the beginning of each business day. The amount to be placed in the cash drawer will depend upon the kind of store and the sales volume expected. This change fund is a constant amount; it does not change from day to day.

Salespeople should know the procedure for establishing the change fund. This procedure should be completed before the start of the business day. The cash register and money should be ready before the day's first sale is recorded.

Throughout the business day you should anticipate the need for additional money in the cash drawer. Occasionally you will find that you are short of a particular denomination of a coin or currency. When this situation occurs, you will need to buy change. **Buying change** means that you take a large bill from the cash register to the accounting office or to another cash register, and exchange the large bill for the desired coin or currency needed. Always buy change in even amounts, for example: a $20 bill for twenty $1 bills; a $1 bill for two 50¢ rolls of pennies. Never lend or borrow from the cash register. Always exchange even money. This way you will not change the total money in the cash drawer, but rather exchange a larger bill into smaller denominations of coins or currency of equal value.

On busy days you may find an excess of cash in the cash drawer. Having too many coins or too much currency in the drawer poses

Change Fund Procedure

1. Pick up the change fund from the appropriate person or location within the business and take it to the cash register.

2. Check to be sure that the cash register totals are reset to zero. Also be sure the date is correct.

3. Press the salesperson's identification key and either the no-sale key or the total key to open the cash register drawer.

4. Remove the coins from the change fund and place them on the sales counter or on a piece of cardboard covering the bill compartment of the cash tray.

5. There is a specific compartment in the cash tray for each denomination of coins and currency. Beginning at the right, count the number of pennies into a coin pocket of the cash tray. Then write the total on a piece of paper. Follow this same procedure for nickels, dimes, quarters, and half dollars.

CHANGE FUND

The change fund should be $_____.

pennies	_____.__
nickels	_____.__
dimes	_____.__
quarters	_____.__
half dollars	_____.__
$1 bills	_____.__
$5 bills	_____.__
$10 bills	_____.__
$20 bills	_____.__
Total	$_____.__

Counted by:_____

Date:_____

---

6. Now count the currency into the appropriate longer compartments. One-dollar bills are located behind the pennies, the fives are behind the nickels, the tens are behind the dimes, and the twenties are behind the quarters. If larger bills are used, they are usually placed

under the cash tray in the cash drawer. List the currency on the piece of paper.

The usual arrangement of the cash drawer is:

EMPTY	$20	$10	$5	$1
50¢	25¢	10¢	5¢	1¢

Occasionally new bills are used in the change fund. New bills have a tendency to stick together and as a result, you may give the customer too much change. It is recommended that you crumple each new bill and then straighten it out or put an old bill between each newly crumpled bill before putting them into the cash drawer. This will help to eliminate the problem of handling new bills that may stick together.

7. Verify the total of the change fund. Add all coins and bills together. If the money in the change fund is equal to the amount originally planned for the cash drawer, the change fund is said to be *even*, and you are now ready to begin the sales day.

However, if the change fund has more money than originally planned, the change fund is said to be *over*. If the change fund has less money than originally planned, the change fund is said to be *short*. In either case, you may want to recount the coins and currency and also recheck your arithmetic on the piece of paper. When the change fund is not even, notify the accounting department and the store manager immediately. You are responsible for the accuracy of the change fund. Correct an error before the cash register is used to record a sale.

a difficulty in making change. If the nickels are overflowing into the next coin pocket or there are too many $1 bills in the cash tray compartment, remove some of them. Count out the excess money, put it in the change-fund bag or box and take it to the accounting office. Most businesses want a note placed under the cash tray stating the amount of excess cash removed. Another note, signed by the store manager or supervisor, should be placed with the excess cash. These notes will protect you from suspicion of removing cash for your own personal use. They are also needed to help balance the cash register detailed audit tape with the cash drawer at the end of the business day.

Making Correct Change

All salespeople must know how to make change. While some cash registers figure and dispense the customer's change automatically, every salesperson must still be able to make correct change. It is an important part of recording the sale, because customers seldom give the exact amount for a purchase. Knowing the procedure for making change will help reduce errors as well as build customer confidence.

General Change-Making Procedure. Salespeople should know how to operate the cash register and to make change quickly and accurately. Here is a summary of the basic procedures to follow in making change.

General Change-Making Procedure

1. Always state the total of the sale to the customer.

2. Always state the total amount received from the customer.

3. At this point, *never* put the customer's money into the cash register drawer. *Place the money on the cash register change plate.* This allows you to have both hands free and prevents you from forgetting the amount the customer gave you.

4. Finish recording the sale on the cash register and open the cash drawer. Quickly look at the indication window to be sure the sale was recorded correctly on the cash register.

5. If a sales form is used, place the original in the designated location.

6. Using the fewest possible coins and currency, silently count the customer's change to yourself from the cash drawer.

7. Push the cash drawer in, but do not close it. Turn to your customer, who should be standing next to the cash register; repeat the sales amount and the amount received from the customer. Now count the correct change out loud to the customer. By counting the change to yourself from the cash register and then out loud to the customer, you should eliminate any errors in making change.

8. Remove the customer's money from the change plate and place it into the cash register drawer.

9. Always close the cash register drawer after every transaction. Finish one money-handling matter before starting a new one. Keep your cash drawer closed when not in use.

10. While the customer is putting away the change, neatly wrap the merchandise along with the customer's copy of the receipt and then thank the customer.

ILLUSTRATION 15-6
Every salesperson must be able to make correct change.

While it may take a little extra time, this general procedure for making change will help safeguard against store losses. Concentrate on properly recording and handling money. You will be a more valuable salesperson if you can skillfully ring the sale on the cash register and give the customer correct change.

Addition Method of Counting Change. The **addition method of counting change** is also known as the *manual method* or *counting-forward method*. It is a simple, yet accurate, method of counting change. The customer will give you the money for the purchase. State out loud the amount of the purchase and the amount received from the customer. After you have placed the money on the change plate, count the customer's change to yourself. Starting with the sales amount, add the fewest possible coins and currency until you have built up to the amount the customer gave you. For example, assume the sale is $12.34 and the customer gives you a $20 bill. You say to the customer, "That was $12.34 out of $20.00." Then beginning with $12.34, take the change from the register and count to yourself: a penny, $12.35; a nickel, $12.40; a dime, $12.50; two quarters, $12.75, $13.00; two dollars, $14.00, $15.00, and a five, makes $20.00.

Now count the correct change out loud back to the customer. Never dump the coins and currency into the customer's hands or on the sales counter. This is rude and often allows errors to be made. A customer doesn't want to recount change because the salesperson was either too lazy or in a hurry. Be courteous and helpful; count the change to each customer coin by coin and bill by bill. In the example, you would turn to the customer and say: "The sale was $12.34 out of $20.00." Giving the coins and currency in order, say: "$12.35, $12.40, $12.50, $12.75, $13.00, $14.00, $15.00, and $20.00." Notice that each amount was mentioned when counting the change to the customer. By following this procedure, the change will have been counted twice by you and once by the customer.

Subtraction Method of Counting Change. Cash registers which compute change will automatically subtract the total sale from the amount received from the customer. Using the **subtraction method of counting change,** with the total of the sale visible in the indication window of the cash register, say to the customer, for example, "That is $12.34 out of $20.00." Place the customer's $20 bill on the change plate. Press "$20.00" on the amount keys and then the amount-tendered key. To finish the transaction, press the change-due key. The correct change amount will appear in the indication window, $7.66.

Count the change from the cash register drawer using the fewest number of coins and currency possible and then count it to the customer. Say, "Your change is $7.66. That is $5, $6, $7, $7.25, $7.50, $7.60, $7.65, $7.66." Place the $20 bill from the change plate into the cash drawer and close it. The entire sales transaction will have been recorded on the customer's cash register receipt.

If the exact amount is given, enter the exact amount on the cash register. Press the correct amount received, the amount-tendered key, and then the change-due key. No change due will be shown in the cash register indication window.

Some change-computation cash registers are connected to a coin-dispensing machine. If so, the change-due key is pressed and the correct change is shown in the indication window. The fewest number of coins are automatically dispensed into the coin cup. The salesperson needs only to remove the correct bills, if any are needed, from the cash register drawer. As a courtesy to your customers, remove the coins from the coin cup (if they haven't already done so), give the coins to your customer, and count the currency: "That was

$12.34 out of $20.00. Your change makes $13.00, $14.00, $15.00, and $20.00." Coin-dispensing machines save the salesperson time and help reduce errors.

Handling Odd-Cent Transactions. An **odd-cent transaction** means that the total of the sale ends in an uneven amount, such as $12.34, and the customer gives you the change for the odd cents in addition to the money for which you are to make change. In this example the customer gives you a $20 bill, a quarter, a nickel, and four pennies. In this case you should cancel out the 34¢ as you make the change from the cash drawer. You should say, "$12.00 out of $20.00; $13, $14, $15, and $20."

If the customer had given you two quarters and a $20 bill, make the odd-cent change first. While giving the customer the change say: "$12.34 out of $20.50." Give a penny: "That's 35¢." Give a nickel: "40¢." Give a dime: "50¢." Then give the $1 bills and say: "and $13, $14, $15, and a $5 bill makes $20.00"

Remember this general rule: The extra money is used to cancel the odd cents of the sale to make the sales figure even. While it may be confusing, most customers give this extra change so as to receive the fewest possible coins as change. If you become confused about how much change to give, write it as a subtraction problem on a piece of paper or even on the sales form. Subtract the total sale from the money given to you by the customer. By doing this, you and your customer will be able to check for any errors.

If You Made Incorrect Change. Occasionally when counting change to a customer, you may have extra money or be short money in your hand. An error has been made. You don't know if the customer has been short-changed or if you made an error when counting money from the cash drawer.

Don't panic. Be courteous and ask that all the customer's change be returned to you; then recount it. Say, "I'm sorry, I have made an error. Let me start over to be sure you receive the correct change." Correct your error and recount the correct change to the customer. If the customer refuses to return the change, let someone in authority handle the situation.

Never give the customer any extra money you may have in your hand. If you were short, never take more money from the cash drawer without knowing where the error was made. Correct the error yourself. Don't let the customer tell you what to do. A dishonest customer may have recognized that you gave too much change and may say to you, "That's okay. Mistakes happen," and walk away.

Balancing the Cash Drawer

At the end of each business day the cash drawer must be balanced with the cash register. A daily balance form is prepared. This form shows the summary of the day's sales and money received. The **daily balance form** is a written report which compares the balance of the cash drawer to the cash register reading of the detailed audit tape. A sample daily balance form is shown in Illustration 15-7.

The procedure of balancing the cash drawer and the audit tape is often called **cashing out** or **proving cash.** To prove cash, begin by counting and removing all coins, currency, and checks from the cash drawer. Write the total amount for each denomination on the daily balance form. Add any refunds and subtract your daily change fund amount to find the net cash received during that business day.

Next, find the total cash sales and received on accounts from the cash register detailed audit tape. Subtract any COD's or returned merchandise to find your net cash register reading. Determine if cash is even, short, or over by taking the difference between net cash received and the net cash register reading. If net cash received is more than the net cash register reading, your cash is **over**. If the net cash received is less than the net cash register reading, your cash is **short**. After you determine the net cash register reading, be sure to sign and date the daily balance form.

Some businesses require that the next day's change fund be counted and put into a separate money bag. This can be done before or after you count the money from the cash drawer. Other businesses may have the accounting department count the next day's change fund.

When you have completed your report, turn it and the money into the accounting department or the store manager. Never let someone else turn the money in for you if you are the person responsible for the money and the summary report.

Prepare your cash register for the next business day. First, check to be sure there is an ample supply of detailed audit tape and customer receipt tape in the cash register. Second, reset all total and activity counters to zero, unless they are read on a monthly or quarterly basis. Third, change the date-setting mechanism to the next business day. Fourth, keep the cash drawer open overnight. This will reduce the risk of possible damage in case of burglary. No records or money are to be stored in the cash register overnight. When you have completed the daily balance form and prepared your cash register for the next business day, you have completed the cashing-out procedures.

ILLUSTRATION 15-7
A daily balance form is a summary of the day's sales and money received.

Daily Balance Form

Number	Denomination	Amount
_____	**Pennies**	_____
_____	**Nickels**	_____
_____	**Dimes**	_____
_____	**Quarters**	_____
_____	**Half dollars**	_____
_____	**$1 bills**	_____
_____	**$5 bills**	_____
_____	**$10 bills**	_____
_____	**$20 bills**	_____
_____	**Checks**	_____

Total cash in drawer _____
ADD: Cash paid out _____
Total cash _____
LESS: Change fund _____
    Net cash received _____
*Cash register reading _____
LESS: CODs and returns _____
    Net cash register reading _____
Cash over _____
Cash short _____
Cash even ☐

*Cash sales and received on accounts as shown on detailed audit tape.

Completed by: _____

Date: _____

SALES TERMS

cashier

cash register

amount keys

touch system

salesperson's
   identification key

department or
   classification key

transaction key

no-sale key

correction key

subtotal key

sales-tax key

total key

amount-received key

change-due key

indication window

detailed audit tape

autographic window

receipt-tape slot

receipt printer

motor bar

cash drawer

cash tray

change plate

date-setting mechanism

"bunch" sales

over-ring

under-ring

change fund

buying change

addition method
   of counting change

subtraction method
   of counting change

odd-cent transaction

daily balance form

cashing out or
   proving cash

(cash) over

(cash) short

SALES QUESTIONS

1. Why do businesses record sales on a cash register?

2. Explain the advantages to businesses of using electronic cash register terminals.

3. What three factors determine the type of cash register a business will use?

4. Explain the two types of cash register key arrangements.

5. When operating a ten-key cash register, what are the advantages of using the touch system?

6. Explain the purpose of using (a) the department or classification key, (b) the transaction key, (c) the amount-received and change-due keys, (d) the detailed audit tape.

7. List the reasons for writing on the detailed audit tape.

8. When operating a cash register, why is it important to have a specific routine?

9. How do you correct an over-ring or an under-ring on the cash register?

10. How can you eliminate the problem of new bills sticking together?

11. What should you do if the change fund is not "even"?

12. Why should you "buy change" in even amounts?

13. How should you handle excess cash from the cash register drawer?

14. Why should you always place the customer's money on the change

plate before you count the customer's change?

15. List the step-by-step procedure for making change.

16. Describe the two methods of counting change: (a) the addition method and (b) the subtraction method.

17. Why should you always count out loud the change you give back to your customers?

18. How do you make change when the customer gives you an odd-cent amount?

19. What should you do if you think you have made an error when counting change out loud to your customer?

SALES ACTIVITIES

A. Identify where the different denominations of coin and currency should be placed in the cash drawer, using the letters from the illustration below.

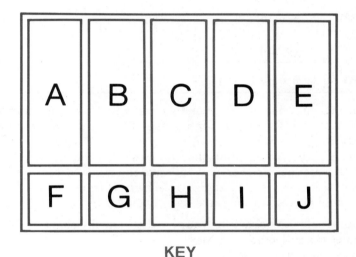

KEY

1. 1¢
2. 5¢
3. 10¢
4. 25¢
5. 50¢
6. $1
7. $5
8. $10
9. $20

B. Today you are responsible for placing the change fund in the cash drawer. You have picked up the change bag from the store manager's office. The change fund should be $200.00. You have the following coins and currency: 25 pennies, 25 nickels, 25 dimes, 24 quarters, 20 one-dollar bills, 8 five-dollar bills, 4 ten-dollar bills, and 4 twenty-dollar bills. Is the change fund: (a) even, (b) over, or (c) short? If the change fund is over or short, what should you do?

C. Write how many of each coin and/or currency you will need to make change for each sale found on page 312. Use the fewest number of coins and currency possible.

Sale Amount	Amount Received	Denominations								
		1¢	5¢	10¢	25¢	50¢	$1	$5	$10	$20
$12.68	$20.00									
$ 9.32	$10.00									
$ 6.94	$ 7.00									
$28.37	$40.00									
$52.48	$55.50									
$24.63	$25.75									
$ 2.28	$20.30									
$ 5.03	$ 5.05									

D. It's been a busy day. Earlier you had many customers waiting to be helped, and you ran out of $1 bills for making change. The cashier next to you quickly gave you twenty $1 bills. Now the cashier says you forgot to exchange a $20 bill for the twenty $1 bills. You explain that you can't remember, but if you are over when you balance your cash drawer, you will give the other cashier twenty dollars. The other cashier becomes insulted and says, "The next time you need change, don't ask me." How could this situation have been avoided?

E. Obtain a sales tax chart for your locality. On the chart, mark each point at which the sales tax collected increases to the next highest amount. Using the chart, figure the sales tax to be collected on the following sales amounts:

1. 79¢
2. $6.95
3. $1.00
4. $3.75
5. 10¢
6. $19.50
7. $4.49
8. $2.77
9. 87¢

STORE LOSSES

Your Learning Goals

After studying this chapter, you should:

- *be able to recognize the methods of shoplifting.*
- *know how to apprehend a shoplifter.*
- *be able to identify money manipulation schemes.*
- *know how to prevent money manipulators from stealing.*
- *know how to distinguish a counterfeit bill from a genuine bill.*
- *know the causes of other store losses.*
- *understand the procedures that help prevent employee thefts.*

Loss of money and merchandise because of dishonest customers and employees has become a serious concern to many businesses. These store losses cost American businesses billions of dollars in lost profits each year—profits that could be used for store improvements, salaries, and business expansions. Store losses are also responsible for increased prices to honest customers.

Dishonest employees who steal from their stores are responsible for large losses. In addition, losses from shoplifters, money manipulators, and counterfeiters are increasing every year. Theft of money and merchandise, however, is not the only cause of store losses. Careless errors by employees are also very costly. All of these store losses are expensive. Store losses in the United States amount to millions of dollars each day.

313

The purpose of this chapter is to identify the methods that contribute to the problem of store losses. It is not to teach someone how to shoplift or how to become a money manipulator. Awareness of the problems of store losses will help you to be alert and to prevent the loss of money or merchandise. Be a responsible employee. Learn how you can help to reduce store losses.

SHOPLIFTING

Shoplifting is an alarming problem in retail businesses. Whether it is called shoplifting, theft, pilferage, or stealing, taking merchandise without paying for it is a crime. This costly crime accounts for billions of dollars in reduced inventories each year. Each year, losses by shoplifting amount to more than all of the nation's bank robberies, holdups, and burglaries combined.

The theft of merchandise by customers or employees is a serious concern to businesses. Whether a customer steals an item of merchandise or a salesperson pockets an item without paying, these thefts account for a reduction in inventories as well as in store profits. In order to protect the store's merchandise, every employee needs to recognize shoplifters and the methods they use.

The Shoplifter

A **shoplifter** is a person who takes merchandise from a business without paying for it. Shoplifters may be amateurs or professionals. Appearance, age, and personality offer no clues to pinpoint shoplifters. A shoplifter could be a pleasant-looking older lady, a gentleman who looks trustworthy, a mother with an infant child, or a teenager. Shoplifters come from all walks of life. They steal inexpensive as well as expensive items.

Losses from shoplifting increase every year. For every one male shoplifter, there are approximately 20 female shoplifters. More than half of all shoplifting apprehensions involve people in the 13- to 19-year-old age group. Nearly half of all shoplifting losses take place during the Christmas shopping season.

Professional Shoplifters. There are fewer professional shoplifters than amateur shoplifters, but thefts by professionals usually amount to a much greater total loss. **Professional shoplifters** are people who make a living by stealing items that they can resell. The professional shoplifter steals to make a profit.

For example, you may say to an acquaintance that you would like to have a new CB radio like the one on display in the local department store. This person may tell you that you could buy one just like it for half that price. A few days later you may be offered the same CB radio stolen from the department store display. It is illegal to steal an item or to knowingly purchase stolen merchandise.

Some professional shoplifters operate as a team. They enter the store at the same time. While one occupies a salesperson with a sale, the other person steals. Sometimes, rather than look at merchandise, a professional shoplifter will cause a disturbance — pretend to faint or have an accident. These types of distractions are very common techniques used by professional shoplifters.

Amateur Shoplifters. Amateur shoplifters outnumber professional shoplifters. These shoplifters have a strong desire to steal. Rather than steal for a profit, they steal items they want for themselves. These shoplifters may steal just for the fun of trying to "get away" with a dishonest act. Very few amateur shoplifters take things they physically need but cannot afford.

If you ask shoplifters why they steal, you will usually hear these answers: "Just for the fun of it." "Everybody does it." "I was bored." "Someone dared me." "No one would help me." Regardless of the excuse, most items are taken because of an impulse to have the item.

Recognizing Methods of Shoplifting

How can a salesperson determine if a customer is dishonest? It is not easy to recognize shoplifters. However, the behavior of a customer can provide clues. An honest customer is interested in the merchandise — its price, color, and quality. A shoplifter is more interested in what is going on around the store. The shoplifter looks all around to see if anyone is watching and may show nervous behavior.

While the behavior of a potential shoplifter is one indication that a customer may be a thief, salespeople must also be aware of some common methods used by shoplifters. By being familiar with the general behavior and the methods shoplifters use, you will be able to determine if someone is attempting to steal from you.

Be aware of customers who are dressed out of season, such as wearing a heavy coat in the summer or a raincoat on a clear day. Bulky clothing on customers might be another clue. Bulky clothing is a favorite place to hide merchandise. Sometimes shoplifters use a coat with a slit in a pocket leading to a bag which is fastened inside.

Be aware of anything in which merchandise can be concealed. Favorite items that shoplifters use to hide things include a baby blanket, a camera bag, a coat, an umbrella, or a large shopping bag.

Watch for Unusual Customer Behavior . . .

- **people who show no interest in what is for sale.** These people linger in the store but seem to have no intention of making a purchase.

- **people who avoid salespeople.** Shoppers who turn and walk away when salespeople approach may be trying to steal.

- **people who spend an excessive amount of time in the store.** If a customer is spending an excessive amount of time in a department, you should be concerned that the customer may be waiting for just the right moment to steal.

- **people who come in at closing time to "just look around."** Shoplifters know that at closing time salespeople are very busy getting ready to close the store. They know that salespeople are too busy to watch for shoplifters. Be aware of "just-looking" customers at this time.

- **people who pick up an item several times or leave and come back to an item.** These may be undecided customers, but don't count on it. Shoplifters may pick up an item and set it down several times. Then when the time is right, they will pick it up and leave.

- **people who drop and pick up items.** This is particularly true if a person drops several items. Remember the hand is quicker than the eye: What you may see is a customer who dropped two items, when in fact the customer dropped three, putting two back while keeping the other one.

- **people who walk behind counters or into storerooms.** Customers who are found in the storeroom without a salesperson may be lost, but more likely they are looking for something to steal.

- **people in groups.** People who enter in groups should be watched more carefully, particularly if the group separates throughout the department or area.

Don't be fooled by a wrapped gift box (sometimes called a booster box), or a bag that seems to be stapled shut with a price ticket attached. A customer who comes into a store without jewelry or some other accessory and wears or carries the items out of the store may be a shoplifter. Customers may try on several clothing items and then put their own clothes back on over the store's clothes and walk out.

One thing is clear: shoplifting methods are almost endless. A busy store, open displays, dressing rooms, items displayed near an

ILLUSTRATION 16-1
Shoplifters may look around to see if anyone is watching and show nervous behavior.

exit, poor lighting, blind spots in stores, few salespeople, or salespeople too busy to help customers are all problems that give shoplifters an opportunity to steal. Salespeople must be able to recognize a shoplifter's behavior and methods so they can be aware of potential thefts.

Your Responsibility to Prevent Theft

While the store may use two-way mirrors, movie cameras, electronic tags, alarm systems, security stations, and other security devices, these are not enough to catch all shoplifters. It is your responsibility to help prevent thefts from occurring. Alert salespeople who are courteous to customers are the key to preventing thefts. If salespeople do their jobs well, shoplifters will find it difficult to steal.

Be aware of customers. Know when customers are around. When a customer comes into your selling area, offer prompt service. The stock work can wait until after you have offered your help. Prompt, friendly service will signal a potential shoplifter that this is not the right place nor time to steal.

Always acknowledge the presence of a customer. Customers want to be recognized, particularly if they are in a hurry or want immediate attention. If you are busy with one customer, at least recognize the other customers. The best way to stop shoplifters is to recognize them. Potential shoplifters know that you have seen them and that you are aware of them as they walk around. Say, "I'll be with you in a few minutes." "Do you need any help finding something?" or "Someone will help you soon." Honest customers will appreciate this, while dishonest customers will become fearful of being watched and caught.

Be helpful to customers. If you see a customer handling merchandise, use the merchandise approach to begin a sales conversation. If a customer is carrying items from one area of the store to another, offer to set them by the cash register or to hold them for the customer. Again, honest customers will appreciate your concern and dishonest customers will be discouraged from stealing.

Prevention is the key to successfully controlling thefts. Salespeople who care about their work do a better job discouraging dishonest customers. Shoplifting is everyone's problem. Part-time salespeople should also know how to effectively prevent shoplifters from stealing. It is everyone's responsibility, and it begins with you!

Apprehending a Shoplifter

Consider the following situation: As you are putting away stock, you look up and see a customer pocket an item of merchandise. You become very nervous and say to yourself, "Why did I have to see that?" You cannot ignore it because you are positive the customer took it. What should you do?

It is surprising how many salespeople, or occasionally even department managers, really don't know what to do, what to say, or what the laws are in their state concerning a shoplifting situation. While the law may vary from state to state, in every shoplifting situation you must know the following five points:

1. What merchandise was taken.
2. Location in the store from which the item was taken.
3. How it was taken (method used).
4. Where it was concealed.
5. Whether the merchandise is still concealed on the shoplifter or is among the shoplifter's belongings.

When you see someone take something, be sure you know these five points. Don't assume that you saw someone take something. Don't guess it is in the customer's right coat pocket. Be sure. It is embarrassing to you and to the store if you cannot give these five points of information to the store manager or police.

When a shoplifter is spotted, employees should always follow the guidelines and procedures for their individual store. However, many businesses neglect to train store employees on how to apprehend a shoplifter until after a shoplifting crime occurs. Unfortunately, many businesspeople feel that shoplifting doesn't happen in their store and they aren't prepared for it when it does happen.

There is a general procedure to follow when you see a shoplifter. Remain calm; don't panic. Don't leave the area to get help. The shoplifter may see you leave in a hurry and, as a result, get rid of the item as fast as possible. Try to keep the shoplifter in sight at all times.

At this point, you must know without any doubt what was taken, the area of the store from which it was taken, how the item was taken, where it was concealed, and if the shoplifter still has the item.

Don't approach suspected shoplifters until after they have left the immediate area, since you don't know for sure if they actually intend to pay for the item. Perhaps the customer intended to pay for the item, but because there were several items in the customer's hands, the item was placed in a pocket. The intent of the customer to take the item without paying for it is an element of the crime of shoplifting. In order to prove shoplifting intent, the question you must be able to answer without any doubt is: Did the customer intend to steal, rather than pay for, the item?

It is for this reason that some authorities suggest that you wait until after potential shoplifters leave the store before you stop them. However, this is not always necessary. Once shoplifters pass through a checkout lane, walk by the cash register, or begin to walk toward the exit, you may stop them. If a person has an opportunity to pay for the item but doesn't, that person may be guilty of shoplifting.

After you are sure that the customer does not intend to pay for the item, you must take action. It is strongly suggested that you let the store manager handle the situation. However, if you must apprehend the shoplifter yourself, signal another employee to get the store manager while you keep the suspect under careful watch.

When you approach a shoplifter, don't grab the individual. Just say very firmly, "Excuse me, do you have something that does not belong to you?" or "I would like the things you took from the store." If the person denies taking anything, you might say, "I would like the (item) you have hidden under your coat." Never threaten the suspect or say the words "steal," "stolen," "You are under arrest," or "Do you plan to pay for the item?" Do not allow the person to pay for the item nor make the promise not to prosecute. When you detain the shoplifter, authorities strongly suggest that you have a witness to back up your findings.

Most states have **merchant protection laws** which offer some protection to store owners against false arrest suits. These laws protect merchants who detain suspected shoplifters if the merchant has reasonable cause for suspicion and if the suspects are detained in a reasonable way and for a reasonable length of time.

When approached, most shoplifters realize they are caught and will usually offer to pay for the item or put it back. Don't allow them to do either. Ask the shoplifter to accompany you to the manager's office. Let the store manager or local police handle the situation.

If a shoplifter runs away, it is best to have someone call the police while you follow. Try to get a detailed description of the person, where the person fled, description of any car used, the license number, and so forth. Don't try to be a hero by physically holding or detaining a suspect.

After the apprehension, write a summary of what happened for the store manager and local police. This summary should include the following:

1. What was taken.
2. The value of the item.
3. Location in the store where the theft occurred.
4. How the item was taken.
5. Where it was concealed.
6. Description of the person involved.
7. What you said to the person.
8. The suspect's reactions and comments.
9. Witnesses to the apprehension and shoplifting.
10. Date and time of the shoplifting.

There are a few things you should NEVER do in a shoplifting situation. These include:

1. Never approach the suspect until he or she has left the immediate area.
2. Never let the shoplifter pay for the items.
3. Never promise not to prosecute.
4. Never use physical force to hold the suspect.
5. Never create a scene in the store.
6. Never say "arrest," "steal," or "stolen."
7. Never search the suspect or the suspect's belongings.
8. Never force the suspect to sign a confession of guilt.
9. Never make any deals with the suspect.

10. Never be with a shoplifter in a closed room or store office without a witness.
11. Never discuss the situation outside the store.

Neglect of customers is the greatest cause of shoplifting. Be alert. Greet customers promptly. If you see someone shoplift, know what action to take. Follow store policies and procedures. Be prepared to give the store manager or local police the information they need to apprehend a shoplifter. Know the shoplifting laws in your state.

MONEY MANIPULATORS

Handling money accurately is a required skill for salespeople. Making change for customers is an important responsibility. If you make an error in handling money, either the store or the customer suffers a loss. If you give too little change, the customer is cheated; if you give too much change, the store loses profits. Therefore, if you think you made an error in counting change, courteously ask that the customer return all the change so you can recount it.

An honest error is only one of several ways that businesses lose money in making change. Dishonest customers who use techniques of confusion when a salesperson is making change are called **money manipulators.** These people deliberately steal money from businesses. Money manipulators will usually avoid alert salespeople who correctly make change.

Careful handling of money begins by letting the customer know you are careful. Salespeople who are clumsy with ringing sales on a cash register, who don't seem to concentrate on doing a good job, or who look and act inexperienced are prime targets for money manipulators. Salespeople who place customers' money in the cash drawer first, rather than on the change plate, are also easy targets.

Protect yourself from money manipulators. Because there are several types of money manipulators, salespeople should learn to recognize them by their dishonest methods of operation which include: causing confusion, passing money back and forth several times, smooth conversation, and the right situation. Money manipulators prefer busy checkout counters during noon hours or at the end of the day. They are watching for young or inexperienced store employees and can strike at any time and any place.

Change Bluffers

One mistake customers often make is to think they gave you more money than they actually did. This may be an honest mistake, but **change bluffers** purposely use this technique.

For example, change bluffers might make a small purchase and give the salesperson a $5 bill. The salesperson gives the correct change from the $5 bill to the change bluffer, who then takes the purchased item and starts to slowly walk away. Now the change bluffer deliberately waits until the salesperson has closed the cash register drawer and starts to help another customer. Then the change bluffer turns back to the salesperson and says, "Excuse me, but you only gave me change for a $5 bill. I'm sure I gave you a ten." At this point most store employees, feeling they have made an error, would give the change bluffer another $5 bill and apologize.

Change bluffers usually operate during busy times of the day. Salespeople are less likely to concentrate on each sale if they are in a hurry to help the next customer. This is why change bluffers select busy checkout counters. They want to embarrass the salesperson into correcting the so-called error immediately. The busy salesperson might do so to avoid causing a disturbance in front of the other customers; this is exactly what change bluffers want!

Stop the change bluffers! Don't let them push you into giving them more money. Protect yourself by calling for the store manager or supervisor right away. The customer will probably demand an immediate adjustment, but calmly explain that it will only take a minute to see if an error was made.

The store manager has three options to handle the situation. Depending upon how busy the store is or how upset the customer appears, these options are available:

1. If the amount is small, some store managers may give the customer the change requested. If this happens, pleasantly apologize to the customer for the inconvenience. You may be right and the customer wrong, but under the circumstances it is not worth losing your job.
2. The store manager could take the customer's name, phone number, and address, explaining that when the cash register drawer is cashed out at the end of the day, the store will call if an error was made.
3. The best solution is to close down the cash register and immediately cash out to determine if an error has been made.

Never accuse a customer of shortchanging you. If you are alert, you should know if you made an error. Honest mistakes do happen. Let someone in authority handle the situation. Don't handle it alone.

Marked-Bill Passers

Another method used by money manipulators is the marked-bill routine. **Marked-bill passers** work in pairs. One bill passer will enter the store, and the second bill passer will enter a few minutes later. To a salesperson they will appear as two separate customers. The first bill passer will make a small purchase with a marked, large denomination bill, such as a $20 bill. The marking on the bill may be a cigarette burn, a torn corner, a bill that has been partly torn and then taped, a bill with a number or address written on it, an ink spot, or some other distinctive mark.

The first bill passer purchases an item and leaves the store. The second bill passer waits a few minutes before going into action. Then, walking up to the same cash register (but to a different salesperson if possible), the second bill passer purchases an item of merchandise with a smaller denomination bill. The store employee records the sale on the cash register and returns the correct change. The bill passer starts to put the money away and picks up the package to leave but deliberately waits until the cash drawer has been closed. Then turning back to the salesperson, the marked-bill passer, with a puzzled look, says, "You only gave me change for a $5 bill." The bill passer pulls out the change and holds it up. "See. I'm sure I gave you a $20 bill," claiming that you, the salesperson, are dishonest.

If you accept the customer's word, you must give the extra change. However, a confident salesperson should say, "I'm sure you only gave me a five." The customer will, of course, insist that a $20 bill was given. "I know I had a $20 bill in my billfold before I came in here and now it's gone. In fact, I remember that $20 bill had a red ink spot on the front of it." At the person's insistence, you open the cash register drawer to prove that there is no ink spot on the top $20 bill. However, when you pull out the top $20 bill, it has a large red ink spot on the front, just as the individual said.

You must admit that the evidence in this case seems clear. The person told you there was a bill with a red ink spot and you found the marked bill. Because you can see the apparent proof and probably feel embarrassed, it is only natural to apologize and give the customer more change. But don't take the customer's word for it. Be confident that you did not make an error.

Marked-bill passers work in pairs so the first person can give the salesperson the marked bill to provide so-called "proof" for the second person who claims to be shortchanged. This situation is similar to a change bluffer except that the marked-bill passer will apparently have proof—the marked bill.

Stop the marked-bill passer! Be alert and concentrate on each sales transaction. Again, as in the case of the change bluffer, call the store manager or supervisor immediately. Do not give the marked bill back to the person even if requested. If the customer demands immediate adjustment, the manager can close down the cash register and cash out to see if an error was made. The manager can also take the customer's name, address, and phone number, and call the customer if any error was made after the cash drawer is cashed out at the end of the day.

In the case of change bluffers and marked-bill passers, be sure you are right. You could lose a potentially good customer if it was indeed an honest mistake. If you are wrong, sincerely apologize rather than make up excuses. Leave no doubt in the customer's mind that you are sorry for the error and inconvenience.

Shortchange Artists

Shortchange artists often use a routine called the **hustle**, which is a method used to steal money from a salesperson or cashier. The shortchange artist passes money back and forth several times to the salesperson. This dishonest person does this to create confusion so the salesperson will lose track of whose money it is. Shortchange artists may ask several questions, fumble with packages, scold a child, or ask for a roll of coins rather than bills — anything to confuse you. The shortchange artist will sense when the salesperson seems confused or thrown off guard.

For example, a shortchange artist enters the store and makes a small purchase totaling less than $1. The person uses a $5 bill to pay for the item. The salesperson gives the customer four $1 bills and some change. As the change is accepted, the shortchange artist looks surprised. The person takes out a $1 bill and says, "I'm sorry, I wanted to pay you with a $1 bill." Adding the $1 bill to the four received as change, the shortchange artist asks for the $5 bill back. At this point, the shortchange artist deliberately waits until the salesperson takes the $5 bill out of the cash register and lays it on the counter. Then the shortchange artist slowly counts the five ones back to the salesperson.

So far no money is lost; the store and customer are even. But before the salesperson has a chance to put the five $1 bills back in the cash drawer, the shortchange artist says, "I guess you can always use smaller bills to make change, can't you?" The salesperson usually responds, "Sure." "Well, then," the shortchange artist says, "just take this $5 bill of mine and give me back a ten. I always like to have one for emergencies." The shortchange artist is assuming that the salesperson will mentally (but mistakenly) add this $5 bill to the five singles, thus making a total of $10.

Most salespeople, particularly inexperienced salespeople, will give the shortchange artist the $10 bill and, because the transaction went so smoothly, they will never even know they lost money. Even though small denomination bills were used in this example, the shortchange artist can use large denomination bills to steal even more.

Shortchange artists pass money back and forth several times. They rely on confusion. Using the power of suggestion, they tell you what to do: "Take this $5 bill of mine and give me back a ten." Shortchange artists' methods don't always work. If the methods fail, the dishonest person will simply admit an error was made and try to pass it off as an honest mistake.

Another trick shortchange artists use is interrupting the salesperson. They will ask you to make change for a larger bill before you have finished the first change-making transaction. Again, this dishonest person will try to throw you off guard with the interruption. This person will try to confuse you and then will offer to clear the matter up for you. Of course, the person's solution to the problem will always result in a gain for the short-change artist and a loss to the store.

Be alert for the shortchange artist. If the customer interrupts you, politely acknowledge the request and continue to complete the first transaction. After you have handled the first transaction, thank the customer for waiting and then handle the second request. Shortchange artists cannot steal from you if you follow the correct procedure for handling money.

Split-Bill Passers

The split-bill passing technique is used by professional money manipulators. The **split-bill passer** takes a larger denomination bill, such as a $20 or a $50 bill, and actually divides and strips apart the two sides of the bill, separating the face from the back. By doing the same thing to a smaller denomination bill, the split-bill passer can then carefully glue the separated halves together. Thus, a $20 bill and a $1 bill become a $40 swindle.

Cutting money in half is another method of alteration used. The split-bill passer attaches the left half of a larger denomination bill to the right half of a smaller denomination bill. When presenting these split bills, the split-bill passer will present several bills or money that has been folded in order to hide the altered money.

Follow Correct Change-Making Procedures . . .

- always receive the customer's money first.
- never be in a hurry to make change.
- state the amount of the sale and the amount given to you by the customer.
- always place the customer's money on the change plate of the cash register.
- count the money from the cash drawer and then to the customer.
- immediately place the money from the change plate into the cash drawer.
- close the cash drawer.
- complete each money transaction before handling another.
- always close the cash register drawer after each money-handling transaction.

The split-bill passer will come into the store and make a small purchase, giving the salesperson the split bill with the larger denomination part showing. In most cases the salesperson will not detect the split bill. It is difficult to notice because the bill looks like genuine money. It is for this reason that salespeople should always turn over each bill received as they place it on the change plate of the cash register. By following this simple procedure, salespeople will be sure that it is the same on both sides.

If you should notice a split bill, calmly make change. Put the bill in the cash register, close the cash drawer, and give the merchandise to the customer. After the customer leaves, call the store manager and police immediately. Give them a detailed description of the individual. Never give the split bill back to the customer. The split bill should only be given to the police or store manager.

Till Dippers

Till dippers are people who steal money directly from cash registers. Usually till dippers work in pairs. One customer will make a purchase. When the salesperson has opened the cash drawer to make change, the second customer will create a disturbance. This second customer will do anything to get the salesperson to focus attention away from the cash register: faint, start an argument, shout for the salesperson, tip over a counter display, spill food on the floor, or try any other diversion technique. The first customer then reaches into the open cash register and removes money.

Never turn your back to the cash register when the cash drawer is open. If it is necessary to leave when the cash drawer has been opened, close it first. This will prevent a customer from reaching in and taking the bills. You can always reopen it when you return.

More recently, till dippers have been using another technique. Because many cash registers have similar operation, a till dipper watches the salesperson open the cash drawer. Later, when the salesperson is busy, the till dipper returns to the sales counter, quickly opens the cash register, and leaves with the money. Till dippers usually operate in large city department stores — stores too large for all the salespeople to know each other. The till dipper, dressed like a salesperson, is seldom recognized. Till dippers may also work as a team, one acting like a customer who makes what appears to be an honest purchase.

COUNTERFEITING

Counterfeiting has become a serious problem. Not only must businesses be aware of counterfeit money, but also fake money orders, gift certificates, and payroll and traveler's checks. The incidence of counterfeiting is increasing because of the sophisticated photo-offset printing and color-photocopying equipment now available.

People who pass counterfeit currency are difficult to track down. They know that they only have to pass the money once to make a profit. Counterfeiters appear and act as honest customers. Since counterfeiters show no unusual behavior, salespeople must know the differences between genuine and counterfeit money. Be familiar with each denomination of bills. While the most frequently passed counterfeit bills are tens and twenties, fives, fifties, and one hundreds can also be used.

Know your money. Because salespeople handle a great deal of money every day, they need to handle it with care. Study the bills you receive so you become familiar with the workmanship on them. The best way to determine if a bill is counterfeit or genuine is to compare it with a bill you know is genuine.

The Portrait

Look at the portrait. On counterfeit bills the portrait is dull, smudgy, or unnatural-looking. The oval background is often dark with irregular and broken lines. However, on a genuine bill the portrait stands out distinctly from the oval background. Eyes appear lifelike. The background is a fine screen of regular dotted lines. Clarity and sharpness of detail will give you a clue to the genuineness of the bill. Be familiar with the portrait on each bill. A genuine bill may have been altered to boost the amount. For example, a $1 bill may have been changed to a $10 bill, but the portrait is still of George Washington.

Denomination	Portrait
$1	George Washington
$2	Thomas Jefferson
$5	Abraham Lincoln
$10	Alexander Hamilton
$20	Andrew Jackson
$50	Ulysses S. Grant
$100	Benjamin Franklin

The Seal

Check the colored seal. The sawtooth points around the rim are usually uneven or broken on counterfeit money. The sawtooth points on a genuine bill are even and sharp. The seal and numbers may be printed in green, red, or blue ink. Federal reserve notes, which are printed in green, are the most common. United States notes are printed in red, and silver certificates are printed in blue.

The Border

Look closely at the borders. On genuine bills the lines and swirls should be distinct, not muddy. Again, this is difficult to reproduce on counterfeit money. Usually the border margins are uneven on genuine bills.

The Serial Numbers

To an expert, the serial numbers on a bill may be a clue as to whether or not the bill is counterfeit. They may be misplaced, unevenly printed, or the wrong color. If you receive several bills that are questionable, look to see if each bill has a different serial number. If not, they are counterfeit.

The Paper

Paper money is printed on special U.S. Government paper. Look for very fine red and blue lines on the paper. Counterfeit money is often missing these colored lines because they are difficult to reproduce by ordinary printing processes. However, the colored threads are not always noticeable on genuine bills that are badly soiled or worn.

ILLUSTRATION 16-2
Genuine currency is printed on special paper containing fine red and blue fibers.

BUREAU OF ENGRAVING AND PRINTING

Compare Bills

Your best guide is to compare a suspicious bill side by side with a genuine bill. Look for differences, not similarities. You will find many similarities, but if you find just a few differences, have the bill checked by an expert.

Follow the procedure given on page 330 if you feel that a gift certificate is a fake or a payroll check appears unusual. *Always* have someone in authority approve it. Don't accept the responsibility yourself. If you accept counterfeit money, a fake money order, or a forged traveler's check, the business must take the loss. A business that operates on a 2 percent net profit and accepts a counterfeit $20 bill must then sell $1,000 worth of merchandise to pay for this loss.

Be alert. Learn what to look for when accepting money. You must be able to make a decision quickly. Is it genuine or is it counterfeit? Be familiar with money. Chances are that the money is genuine, but you should know the procedure to follow if the bill looks questionable.

If You Believe You Have Been Given Counterfeit Money . . .

- remain natural and calm.
- never give the money back to the customer, even if requested.
- excuse yourself from the customer.
- ask the store manager or supervisor to approve the bill. (If the customer sees you talking to the manager and starts to leave, you can be sure that something is wrong.)
- if the store manager approves the bill, complete the transaction. If there is a strong doubt, it is best to complete the transaction or try to delay the customer. Never accuse the customer of giving you a counterfeit bill. The customer may be completely honest and not realize that the bill is counterfeit.
- while you complete the transaction or delay the customer, the store manager should call the police and a bank officer to come to the store.
- if the customer leaves, write a description of the person. If the person leaves in a car, write a description of the car and the license number.
- place the suspicious bill in an envelope to be sure it is not confused with other money. Write the date, your name, and the denomination on the envelope.
- when police and a bank officer arrive, ask them to determine if the bill is genuine.

OTHER STORE LOSSES

There are several ways businesses lose money other than through shoplifters, money manipulators, and counterfeit money. These other losses happen because store employees do their jobs carelessly. There seems to be almost no limit to the number of possible errors that store employees can make, all of which cause a loss to the store. Most are simple mistakes which can be avoided.

Accepting personal checks without identification or authorization is one of these simple mistakes. Many salespeople don't take the time to obtain the proper identification or authorization because they are in a hurry or they want to make the sale. When accepting a personal check from a customer, quickly look to see if it is dated, if the numerals match the written figures, if it is signed by the customer, and if it is made payable to the business. Every business has established procedures to follow. Correctly follow this procedure when accepting personal checks.

Losses can occur if a salesperson accepts a customer charge without checking to see if the customer has an established account. Don't accept charges without authorization. When filling out charge forms, be sure the customer gives you the correct name and address. Spell everything correctly. Ask the customer to sign the form. Losses also occur when charges are written to the wrong accounts, charge cards are used by unauthorized customers, or salespeople are in such a hurry that they omit the customer's name and address from the charge form.

Salespeople also make errors when they fill out cash sales forms. Salespeople may forget to record all the required information, such as the date, the department, the name of the salesperson, the type of transaction, the listing of items sold, and other important information. Store losses also occur when the information is so poorly written that the accounting department cannot read it. Wrong merchandise numbers, wrong prices, incorrect calculation of figures on multiple purchases, inaccurate addition, or incorrect sales tax are all common errors. All of these errors require extra work in the accounting department to make the necessary corrections. Use common sense to avoid careless mistakes. Be alert enough to catch simple errors in figuring and recording prices or stock numbers. Never guess about the price of an item. Write neatly and record all the necessary information.

Store losses can result from improper operation of the cash register. If an error is made in recording a sale on the cash register, the error should be corrected immediately. If the error is not corrected, customers may pay the wrong amount for the sale. If an incorrect sale is not voided, the store will appear to be short of cash at the end of the day. Be alert and record sales on the cash register properly. If you make an error, correct the mistake immediately.

Every business has procedures for receiving merchandise. Some salespeople neglect this important responsibility by not following these procedures. They may sign for unauthorized merchandise. They may not count the number of items received; for example, sign for four cartons when only three are received. They may check off the wrong item received; for example, check item number 699 for item 696. They may sign and accept damaged boxes of merchandise without first checking the contents. Because salespeople are anxious to make a sale, they may take an item from the stockroom before it is checked in and priced. All of these are avoidable mistakes.

Pricing errors account for many store losses. When merchandise is received, the invoice should be checked against the purchase order. The merchandise is then marked with the price. Common pricing errors include marking the incorrect price on the item, failing to place the necessary price-coding information on the ticket, or putting the right price on the wrong items. Many errors are the result of poor figuring. Poor handwriting will also cause pricing errors. The salesperson who cannot read someone else's handwriting and is unsure of the price should always ask rather than guess. Pricing errors are very costly to the store.

Store losses also result from delivering an item to the wrong address, attempting to deliver an item when no one is home, and delivering an item more than once to the same address because the first delivery was not checked off. Deliveries that are undeliverable can triple handling costs: once for trying to deliver, twice for having to return them to the store, and three times when they are finally delivered. A phone call before attempting to deliver an item will assure that the customer is home to accept the delivery and that the address is correct.

Improper care of merchandise results in store losses. If merchandise becomes torn, dirty, or used looking, it must be sold at a reduced price or thrown away. Customers usually don't buy items that have been improperly cared for.

It takes only a few minutes to handle an item properly. Be careful when putting merchandise away or when moving items in and out of stock. Keep the merchandise looking new and clean.

Finally, show enough interest in your job to be helpful to customers. The stock work can wait. The conversation with another employee can wait. The customer cannot wait. If a customer walks out of the store because the salespeople were too busy to be helpful, the store will have lost a sale; and this means a loss of store profits.

Many of these mistakes can be avoided. It is your responsibility to help reduce store losses. Write clearly and accurately. Recheck all figures. Check to be sure you have the correct spelling of a customer's name and address. Learn and follow store procedures and policies. Care enough about your job to want to do it better. Assume the responsibility yourself to help reduce store losses.

DISHONEST EMPLOYEES

Theft of merchandise and money is not limited to dishonest customers. Nationally, dishonest employees take almost twice as much as dishonest customers. Because store employees know their business's operations, a dishonest employee can find ways to turn a situation into an opportunity to steal. Once employees begin stealing, they will usually continue to steal. While a dishonest customer may steal only once, a dishonest employee could steal from a business every day.

Employee thefts are a serious problem because employers must entrust employees with merchandise, money, and other business matters. It is difficult for a store manager to accept the fact that a "loyal" employee is actually guilty of stealing. "I just can't believe it!" is a typical reaction. The dishonest employee who steals is often a well-liked and trusted employee.

When caught stealing, most employees will blame it on the company they work for. The dishonest employee will usually try to justify the theft by saying, "I deserve the merchandise (or money)" or "It's your fault for not paying me more." These employees have the feeling that they are overworked and underpaid. "Besides," they tell themselves, "the company will never miss it."

The success of any program designed to curb employee thefts depends upon employee morale. Employees must feel that they are an important part of the business. They want to be paid a fair wage and to be treated fairly. While the desire to steal the item may still be tempting, an employee who feels important to the success and operation of the business will seldom steal.

Policies to Discourage Employee Thefts

To help discourage employee thefts, the opportunity to steal must be eliminated as much as possible. Small as well as large companies should follow established company policies and procedures. Every company should have guidelines on what to expect from employees. These guidelines and procedures should be the same for everyone. The employer should set a good example for employees to follow. A system that requires everyone to use standardized procedures will help to eliminate the opportunity for an employee to steal.

The following policies will discourage employee thefts:

1. A procedure should be established for receiving, checking, and marking merchandise.
2. Pricing machines rather than handwritten price tickets should be used.
3. All sales transactions should be handled the same way.
4. No employee is to make personal change from the cash register.
5. All refunds and exchanges must be approved by the manager, and the customer should sign the form. This will indicate that the customer received the refund.
6. All personnel should enter and leave the business by the same entrance.
7. All employee purchases should be written up by the manager during working hours or, preferably, just before leaving the store.
8. All employee packages and personal belongings should be kept in one place.
9. All packages must contain a sales receipt of the contents.
10. Each salesperson should use a sales book. The sales forms should be numbered and used in sequential order.
11. If possible, each employee should have a cash drawer from which to make change. Some businesses use a central checkout counter to reduce the number of people making change from the same cash register.

The important thing to remember is this: Store policies are established to help a business operate more efficiently. These policies will discourage dishonest employees and will help honest employees do a better job.

Managers are in the best position to detect and stop employee thefts. The store manager is the key to prevention. Supervision and constant awareness of the actions of employees will help store managers to be aware of opportunities for employee theft. If store management operates a loosely organized business and has an easygoing attitude about the operation of the business, employees will realize this. This may encourage employees to consider stealing because they feel they won't get caught. Managers must make it known from the time an employee is hired that both shoplifters and dishonest employees will always be dealt with severely.

An employee caught stealing can be fired immediately. In addition to being fired from the job, the employee loses any future job recommendations and job benefits and now has a poor reputation. Some businesses also call local police to arrest dishonest employees. As a result of legal prosecution, the employee's name is generally published and a police record is started.

Dishonest Co-workers

What should you do if you see a co-worker take merchandise or money? This can be a difficult situation for you. What if the store manager sees you as you observe another employee stealing — and you don't report it? The store manager may think that you steal, too, or have helped others steal. Or the store manager may believe that you don't care enough about the success of the business to report a dishonest employee. What if the co-worker realizes you saw the theft and didn't report it? That employee may assume that you are guilty of stealing, too.

If another employee suggests to you that you work together to steal either merchandise or money, tell the employee that you want absolutely nothing to do with the scheme, because your job, work record, and reputation are too important to you.

If you actually see a co-worker steal either money or merchandise, follow the same procedure as if the co-worker were a dishonest customer. Be absolutely sure that you saw the theft. There may be a simple explanation, but it is best to alert the store manager or supervisor. Explain what you saw and then let the store manager apprehend the employee. Avoid taking direct action yourself. You should be prepared to explain what you saw to the store manager and the employee.

SALES TERMS

shoplifting	money manipulators	hustle
shoplifter	change bluffer	split-bill passer
professional shoplifter	marked-bill passer	till dipper
amateur shoplifter	shortchange artist	counterfeiting
merchant protection laws		

SALES QUESTIONS

1. Explain the difference between professional and amateur shoplifters.

2. Describe the behavior of a customer who may really be a shoplifter.

3. Describe some common methods used by shoplifters.

4. What types of security devices are used by businesses to detect shoplifters?

5. How can salespeople help prevent thefts?

6. List five points of information you must know before apprehending a shoplifter.

7. Explain what the "intent" of a customer means as it relates to shoplifting.

8. Describe the procedure to follow when apprehending a shoplifter.

9. During the apprehension of a shoplifter, why should you have a witness?

10. Describe what you must never do in a shoplifting situation.

11. What protection do merchants have from false arrest suits by suspected shoplifters who have been detained for questioning?

12. What should you do if you feel you have made an honest error when making change for a customer?

13. Why are salespeople who place the customers' money into the cash drawer first, rather than on the change plate, easy targets of money manipulators?

14. What three options does the store manager have when there appears to be a mistake in making change?

15. Describe the methods used by: a change bluffer, a marked-bill passer, a shortchange artist, a split-bill passer, and a till dipper.

16. Describe how a salesperson can prevent the following money manipulators from stealing: a change bluffer, a marked-bill passer, a shortchange artist, a split-bill passer, and a till dipper.

17. Describe the correct change-making procedure.

18. What should you look for when comparing a genuine bill with a bill you believe to be counterfeit?

19. If you believe you have received a counterfeit bill, what procedure should you follow?

20. How can businesses discourage employee thefts?

21. What should you do if you see a co-worker steal either money or merchandise?

SALES ACTIVITIES

A. List some of the possible errors by salespeople that cause store losses.

B. You are employed in the shoe department of Central Department Store. A customer is trying on a pair of shoes. While the customer is walking in them to determine if the shoes fit correctly, you glance over at Sally, who works at the cosmetic counter, and you see her drop a tube of lipstick into her purse. What action should you take and when?

C. Obtain from your instructor or retail Chamber of Commerce a copy of the current shoplifting laws or theft laws in your state. After reading the laws, write a report suitable for presentation at a store meeting on shoplifting.

D. You are working in a camera specialty shop. A customer has just purchased two rolls of film. You are counting the customer's change when the customer interrupts and asks you how long the film will remain on special. You have an extra dollar bill in your hand when you finish counting the change to the customer. What should you do? The customer insists that you did not return enough change. What three options are available to you or the store manager?

17
SALES-SUPPORTING SKILLS

Your Learning Goals

After studying this chapter, you should:

- *know the sales-supporting duties performed by salespeople.*
- *be aware of the importance of a neat and clean store.*
- *understand the types of information found on merchandise tags.*
- *understand the purpose of window and interior displays.*
- *know the rules for building displays.*
- *understand the ways of developing product knowledge.*
- *know how to handle a customer complaint.*
- *be able to plan work using a daily TO DO list.*

The salesperson's most important function is selling products or services to customers. A salesperson, however, does have other duties. These duties are called sales-supporting duties.

SALES-SUPPORTING DUTIES

Sales-supporting duties are tasks which salespeople perform when they are not involved in personal selling with their customers. As a salesperson in a retail business, you will probably spend about half of your time actually selling. The other half of your time will be spent performing nonselling duties: stocking shelves; keeping your selling area neat and clean; receiving, checking, and

ILLUSTRATION 17-1
Salespeople perform sales-supporting duties when not involved in
personal selling.

marking merchandise; building displays; maintaining adequate
merchandise stock; studying merchandise information; taking inventory; and handling customer complaints.

Stocking Shelves

Stocking shelves, or **stockkeeping**, is an important duty for
two reasons. First, merchandise that is neatly arranged and in good
condition makes a favorable impression on customers. Salespeople
usually start each sales day by checking the merchandise to make
certain it is properly displayed. You may have to replenish the
current stock of some items. Stock is normally stored under the
merchandise display or in a stockroom. You should make certain
that you have enough merchandise on the sales floor for your customers at all times.

Second, stocking shelves makes you aware of the location of
your merchandise. It is very important that you, the salesperson,

have access to all the merchandise and know the exact location of each item. When you want to sell customers a related item to go with their original purchase, you must know the exact location of the related item.

Know what is being advertised, too. When customers request merchandise featured in an advertisement, you should be able to take the customer directly to that merchandise. Customers can become very annoyed with salespeople who cannot provide merchandise information upon request.

A Salesperson's Stockkeeping Duties Include...

- keeping a complete assortment of merchandise in stock on the sales floor.
- keeping merchandise clean, neat, and orderly.
- making sure the merchandise is properly marked.
- knowing the location of all merchandise.

Keeping Your Selling Area Neat and Clean

Customers enjoy shopping in stores which are neat and clean, stock quality merchandise, and have friendly, courteous salespeople. One of the first and most important impressions customers have of a business is its physical appearance. Customers expect a neat and clean store. Few customers will pay the full retail price for merchandise which looks dirty or damaged.

All salespeople should be responsible for basic housekeeping duties within their sales area. Start each day by making sure your displays, merchandise shelves, and merchandise are clean, neat, and orderly. If you have time between customers, check to see that your sales area is still orderly. Make sure the sales floor is free of any paper, boxes, or litter. Pick up fallen merchandise and straighten displays so your sales area is not only clean but is in good order for customers to find the merchandise they want. Remove any damaged or soiled merchandise from the sales area. Make certain that the area around your cash register is also neat and clean.

An attractive store will help to put customers in a favorable buying mood. Businesses spend millions of dollars in creating a favorable store atmosphere for customers. Part of your job as a salesperson is to maintain that atmosphere by keeping the store neat and clean.

Location courtesy of Fabric Circle U.S.A., Hyde Park Plaza, Cincinnati, Ohio

Receiving, Checking, and Marking Merchandise

When a business buys merchandise for resale, a salesperson must complete three functions before placing the merchandise in stock to sell to customers. These three functions are receiving, checking, and marking.

Receiving is the process of taking possession of the merchandise. Most stores have a receiving department or area where incoming merchandise is delivered. Larger stores receive merchandise at a warehouse. When the merchandise arrives, a receiving clerk or salesperson counts and inspects the condition of the packages.

After the merchandise has been received, a salesperson checks it into the store. **Checking** involves opening the packages, removing the merchandise, and inspecting the shipment to make certain it includes all the merchandise that was ordered. The salesperson then sorts the merchandise, making certain that the quality is satisfactory. The major function the salesperson performs in the checking process, therefore, is inspecting the new merchandise.

Once the merchandise has been checked, the salesperson usually marks it before putting it on the sales floor. There are two reasons for **marking** merchandise. First, the merchandise is marked to provide the customer with information about each item. Customer information may include the retail price, the size or weight, the stock number, and the color of the merchandise. Second, marking merchandise provides the store with information such as the retail price, the cost price, the merchandise classification, the stock number, and the date of receipt. This information provides the store with needed data to keep accurate records for sales and inventory control.

Most merchandise tags are put on the product by the manufacturer or wholesaler. Many small stores hand mark merchandise price tags. Larger stores may use a machine for marking prices. A salesperson may mark the merchandise with the original price or remark the merchandise when the price is increased or reduced.

Building Displays

Displays attract the customers' attention with the hope of creating interest in the displayed merchandise. The two most common forms of displays are window displays and interior displays. An **interior display** is a merchandise display within the store. These can be built on counters, tables, racks, walls, or in special display cases.

Most large retail institutions, such as department stores or variety stores, have **display specialists** who plan and build window and interior displays. Specialty shops may hire independent display consultants to build their displays. In small retail businesses, salespeople often assist in building displays. The salesperson may help to build a display as well as to suggest merchandise which should be featured.

To Build a Successful Display...

- select merchandise customers want.
- decide on a central theme for the display.
- make certain the display is attractive.
- match the display to your store's image.
- show how the merchandise can be used.

There are five rules to follow in building effective interior displays. These rules apply to displays in all types of stores.

Rule 1: Select merchandise your customers want. Don't expect a display to sell merchandise that customers do not want or need. The primary purpose of a display is to attract the customers' attention and interest to the product. It is the salesperson's job to sell the merchandise to customers.

Rule 2: Decide on a central theme or sales story for your display. Once you have decided on the theme, select merchandise for the display which relates to that theme. For example, you may wish to have summer vacation as a theme for a women's sportswear specialty shop. Build a summer vacation display using related merchandise items such as T-shirts, shorts, swimsuits, sandals, tote bags, beach towels, and sunglasses. All of these items might be needed for a summer vacation. Merchandise items featured in interior displays may also be featured in window displays or retail advertisements in the newspaper or special spring and summer catalogs.

Rule 3: Make certain that your display is attractive and pleasing to the customer's eye. It should not appear cluttered, so do not include too many items. Select a feature item and then select other items which are directly related. Once the display has been built, it is important to keep the display fixtures and merchandise clean at all times.

Rule 4: Make the display match your store's image. It is important that your displays contain the quality of merchandise that best represents your store's image. For example, an exclusive gift shop should feature top-quality merchan-

ILLUSTRATION 17-3
Displays attract customers' attention and create interest in the merchandise.

dise in its displays. Displays, store layout, and store advertisements should all emphasize the excellent quality of merchandise the store sells.

Rule 5: Show how the merchandise is used. If possible, the display should be built to help the customer visualize how the product can be used. If the display features paint, it might show items which have been painted. Clothing may be displayed on mannequins. Furniture may be displayed in a room arrangement.

Maintaining Adequate Stock

Successful stores must keep accurate records of what merchandise is in stock, what merchandise has been sold, and what merchandise is on order. This information is determined in different ways by various stores. Stores using electronic cash registers can utilize the central computer for stock-control information. When a sale is rung on a computer register, the computer automatically computes the necessary stock-control information. It shows how much merchandise is on hand and how much merchandise has been sold.

If you work in a store that does not have computer registers, you may be asked to make certain the store has enough merchandise in stock. At the end of each sales day, you may have to replenish the merchandise on the sales floor. You may also be asked occasionally to take a physical count of the merchandise on the sales floor and in the storage area. Based on this inventory, or the amount of merchandise on hand, you may be asked to determine how much merchandise needs to be purchased.

You may also be asked to make a **competitive shopping trip** to determine the types of merchandise, prices, displays, selling procedures, and other merchandising policies of competitors. These trips can also furnish ideas for your store on how to sell merchandise more effectively.

Learning About Your Merchandise

Manufacturers, wholesalers, and retailers are all looking for salespeople who have product knowledge and can use effective selling techniques. A salesperson has many uses for product knowledge. If you are well-informed about your product or service, you will enjoy your work more, you will have confidence in what you are doing, and you will make more sales. To give an effective sales demonstration, a salesperson should know the following things about the product or service:

1. the product features
2. how the product will perform
3. uses of the product
4. care for the product
5. benefits the customer receives from the product
6. knowledge of competing products
7. product guarantees and warranties.

As a salesperson, there are several ways you can develop product knowledge. You should constantly be looking for the product knowledge you need for selling. You should learn about the new products which come in. You can learn about your merchandise by studying what you sell, talking to and watching other salespeople, studying your store's publications and advertising, listening to your customers, and attending sales training programs.

Study What You Sell. When you are not involved in personal selling, take time to study your merchandise. Do this when you are performing stockkeeping or housekeeping duties. Notice how the merchandise is constructed and make comparisons between the features of differently priced merchandise. Learn the benefits customers receive from the better quality merchandise, so you may use that information in assisting your customer to purchase the right merchandise. You should also study the merchandise labels and tags. This will tell you what the product is made of, how the product should be used, and how to care for it.

Learn from Other Salespeople. New salespeople should observe more experienced salespeople to learn how they use product knowledge. Take advantage of your co-workers' knowledge, and learn from their experiences. You can also gain product knowledge from the store's owner or buyer. The buyer knows the merchandise and can help you to learn about it. The buyer also can use your help as a salesperson to learn which products sell best and which products your customers like and dislike.

Study Product Literature. Your store probably receives a variety of publications which provide information about products it stocks. Large chain stores often develop their own company training manuals containing product information on their merchandise. Also, most manufacturers publish pamphlets about their products. These are excellent sources of information about product features and product uses. You may also want to read trade magazines such as *Consumer Reports*. Each of these publications contains valuable

ILLUSTRATION 17-4
New salespeople can gain product knowledge from the store's buyer.

information you can use in your sales presentation. Ask your manager where to find these publications.

Study Store Advertising. Carefully read all of your store's advertising. The advertisements give you good product descriptions to use in your sales presentation. Good salespeople read all the store's ads so they can answer any questions customers ask.

Learn from Your Customers. Customers are excellent sources of product information. Customers will often know more than you do about how a product performs and how the product can be used in new ways. Note the types of questions your customers ask about your product. By studying these questions, you can learn which features customers are interested in. This information provides a guideline on what type of product information to study and what benefits you should sell your customers.

Once you have product knowledge, use it. Make it a part of each sales presentation. Customers like salespeople who can explain the benefits received from purchasing a product. Salespeople should use product knowledge to back up the claims they make about buyer benefits.

Attend Sales Training Programs. Enrolling in a **sales training program** is an excellent way to obtain product knowledge and to learn selling techniques. Courses offered by the store, the chamber of commerce, and community colleges are all excellent sources for obtaining product and selling knowledge. Manufacturers also offer courses and printed materials presenting information about the products they produce and sell. Distributive education programs in high school and post-secondary institutions are designed to prepare students for careers in marketing, sales, and management.

Taking Inventory

Salespeople may be asked to take a physical count of the merchandise in the store. This is called a **physical inventory.** The purpose of the physical inventory is to determine the exact amount of merchandise the business has on hand.

Information received by taking a physical inventory is very important. It provides the data needed to help determine the store's profits or losses. An inventory also shows what merchandise has been selling well and provides information on what merchandise to reorder. Stores that use electronic cash registers can keep accurate, up-to-the-minute information on sales and the amount of merchandise in stock. These stores may not need to have salespeople take physical inventory very frequently.

ILLUSTRATION 17-5
A salesperson takes a physical inventory to determine the exact amount of merchandise the business has on hand.

Handling Customer Complaints

A **customer complaint** is an expression of dissatisfaction about a product, service, or store policy after the sale. Salespeople must handle customer complaints very carefully. If a customer's complaint is handled poorly, the customer may never return to shop at the store. If the complaint is handled correctly, this can build customer goodwill and do much to make certain the customer will return to shop at the store again.

The first step in handling a customer's complaint is to let your customer explain the complaint thoroughly without interruptions. If you have questions, wait to ask them until the customer is finished explaining. Never argue with your customer. You may win the argument but lose the customer.

The second step in handling customer complaints is to restate the major points of the complaint to the customer, so you are certain you understand the complaint and the facts. If your store policy allows you to make an adjustment, you may do one of two things. If the item is inexpensive, you may wish to replace it without further discussion. It is more important to keep your customer happy so that the person will return to buy from you again, than to lose the sale of an inexpensive merchandise item. If the merchandise the customer is complaining about is expensive, your manager or store owner should handle the customer's complaint.

A technique often used by businesses is to ask what the customer feels would be an acceptable solution or adjustment. If the customer's suggestion for an adjustment is within reason, you may have the authority to accept it. The adjustment is usually less costly than losing the customer completely.

To Handle Customer Complaints. . .

- listen to the customer.
- restate the customer's complaint.
- ask the customer for a solution.
- take action.

Handling customer complaints is not easy. It is much easier to handle a complaint, however, after you get all the facts and understand your customer's feelings. Customers who have been treated poorly will not return to shop and will also tell their friends about the poor treatment they received. It is possible to lose several customers because one customer's complaint was handled poorly.

Whatever action you take, be friendly, courteous, and fair to your customer. You may want to follow up each customer complaint to make certain your customer is satisfied with your adjustment. The goodwill created by handling customer complaints properly can insure a satisfied customer who will come back again to buy.

USING NONSELLING TIME WISELY

About half of your sales time will be spent in personal selling. The other half should be spent in sales-supporting activities. Salespeople, like all businesspeople, should use their time wisely. An excellent technique for effectively managing your time is to start each day by listing the sales-supporting duties you want to complete for the day. Illustration 17-6 provides an example of a daily TO DO list which a salesperson may use.

An important purpose of the daily **TO DO list** is to make certain that your time is spent increasing your sales productivity. Here is

ILLUSTRATION 17-6
A "TO DO" list helps salespeople to manage their time effectively.

TODAY'S "TO DO" LIST

Priority	Date 6/3
3	1 Select products for window display.
1	2 Mark down prices of long-sleeved dress shirts.
2	3 Proofread newspaper ad to be run in next week's paper.
4	4 Call Supplier to see when new catalog is available.
	5
	6
	7
	8
	9
	10
	11
	12
	13
	14
Notes	

a list of things you can do in your nonselling time to increase your sales:

1. Study your merchandise to determine selling features and develop buyer benefits.
2. Keep your selling area neat and clean.
3. Study your selling area so you know the location of all your merchandise.
4. Talk with other salespeople about your merchandise and how to sell to different types of customers.
5. Read training manuals and trade magazines to learn more about selling.
6. Check with your local telephone company to learn about telephone selling.
7. Call regular customers to inform them of the arrival of new merchandise or a special sale.
8. Call customers who have not shopped in the store recently to suggest that they come in and look at a new line of merchandise in the store.

These are all suggestions which may increase your sales. Any of these activities are items you may want to put on your daily TO DO list. Once you have completed all the items on your list, take time to plan additional nonselling duties by making a new TO DO list.

SALES TERMS

sales-supporting duties

stockkeeping

receiving

checking

marking

interior display

display specialist

competitive shopping trip

sales training program

physical inventory

customer complaint

TO DO list

SALES QUESTIONS

1. List eight sales-supporting duties performed by a salesperson.

2. What are the benefits to the store from having salespeople effectively perform each of the eight sales-supporting duties?

3. What benefits can salespeople receive from stocking shelves?

4. What benefits do salespeople receive from studying the retail store's advertisements?

5. Explain the functions performed by

salespeople in:

    a. Receiving merchandise
    b. Checking merchandise
    c. Marking merchandise

6. What is the purpose of an interior display in a retail store?

7. What are the five rules for building a successful display?

8. What three stock-control functions are performed by electronic cash registers?

9. Why should managers and salespeople make competitive shopping trips?

10. Discuss five ways that salespeople can learn more about the products they sell.

11. Where can salespeople enroll in sales training programs?

12. Explain the following statement: "Customer complaints can be good opportunities for salespeople."

13. List four general steps in handling a customer complaint.

14. List at least six things a salesperson should do in nonselling time.

15. Explain the benefits of completing a "TO DO list."

TELEPHONE SELLING

Your Learning Goals

After studying this chapter, you should:

- *understand the advantages of telephone selling over person-to-person selling.*
- *know how to plan an effective telephone sales presentation.*
- *know the steps of a telephone sales presentation.*
- *understand common buying motives.*
- *be able to complete an effective telephone sales presentation.*
- *be able to overcome customer objections in a telephone sales presentation.*
- *be able to develop an effective closing for a telephone sales presentation.*

The telephone is a very important means of communication for all businesses. A business may use the telephone to order merchandise, to seek new customers, to make appointments with new and established customers, to inform customers about new merchandise, to sell products and services to customers, to follow up a sale, to follow up an advertisement, and to build customer goodwill.

The telephone offers several advantages over person-to-person selling. A salesperson can contact customers by telephone without having to travel to the customers' homes or businesses. Many more customers can be contacted in a day by telephone. Using the telephone can save a business time and money.

Because of these advantages, many firms are increasing their use of the telephone. Retailers, especially, are expanding their use of the telephone to sell both products and services. For example, retailers call customers when new fashion merchandise arrives at the store. Retailers also call customers who have recently purchased major appliances such as televisions, air conditioners, washers, and dryers because they want to sell maintenance and service contracts for the appliances. Insurance agents and real

ILLUSTRATION 18-1
Securities salespeople conduct much of their business over the telephone.

estate agents use the telephone to gain new customers and to set up appointments with customers. Colleges, churches, and other public service organizations use the telephone to raise money.

Although there are advantages to telephone selling, it is more difficult than personal selling because there is no personal contact with the customer. The customer cannot see the product nor observe how it works. In addition, a telephone salesperson cannot observe the customer's reactions nor get the customer personally involved in the sales presentation. To overcome these disadvantages, the salesperson must be well-trained in telephone selling techniques.

To be an effective telephone salesperson, you should receive special training. Your sales vocabulary must be specific. Your lis-

Businesses Use the Telephone to...

- order merchandise.
- seek new customers.
- make appointments with customers.
- inform customers about new merchandise.
- sell products and services.
- follow up a sale.
- follow up an advertisement.
- build customer goodwill.

tening skills must be good because you have to hear your customer's objections and overcome those objections with positive selling techniques.

THE TELEPHONE SALES PRESENTATION

An effective telephone sales presentation involves careful planning and the effective use of selling techniques. The telephone sales presentation involves two major parts: the preplanning and the actual telephone sales presentation. The following outline describes the steps of a telephone sales presentation.

Steps of a Telephone Sales Presentation

PREPLANNING

- Study your product or service.
- Develop a sales vocabulary.
- Outline your sales call.

THE TELEPHONE SALES PRESENTATION

- Give an opening statement.
- Establish rapport with your customer.
- Provide feature-benefit statements.
- Ask qualifying questions.
- Overcome customer objections.
- Close the sale.

Preplan the Sales Call

Making a successful telephone sale involves more than just picking up the telephone and dialing a prospective customer. Like a personal sales presentation, telephone selling involves gathering information about the product or service, developing a sales vocabulary, preparing an opening statement, creating a rapport with your customer, developing feature-benefit selling statements, preparing qualifying questions, determining how to overcome customer objections, and developing techniques to close the sale. In Chapter 3, you learned that personal selling is 90 percent preparation and 10 percent presentation. Telephone selling requires the same amount of preparation. There are three major steps in planning a telephone sale.

1. Study your product or service.
2. Develop a sales vocabulary.
3. Outline your sales presentation.

Study Your Product or Service. The initial step in developing your sales presentation is to study what you are selling. You should know the product's features, what the product is made of, how the product will perform, how the product is used, how to care for the product, the product's guarantees, and the benefits customers will receive from owning the product.

Emphasis should be on developing that last point—customer benefits. Customers who buy over the telephone are no different than customers who buy in the store. All customers buy products and services because of the benefits they will receive from owning that product or service. To make sure you know your product or service adequately, you should understand the buyer benefits your customers will receive from owning the product you're selling. Customers buy a product or service because of rational or emotional buying motives. The benefits you sell in your telephone sales presentation should relate to the customer buying motives listed on page 356.

Appeal to these customer buying motives. As you plan your telephone sales presentation, list the features of your product or service and translate each one into a customer benefit.

Develop Your Sales Vocabulary. Since you cannot demonstrate your product over the telephone, it is very important that you provide the customer with a positive visual image of the product through the words you use. Some words have more sales power than others. Since your customer can't see, touch, or smell the product, you must develop customer interest and desire by using a

Buying Motives

Rational	Emotional
• saves money	• pride and prestige
• saves time	• love
• guaranteed	• fear
• economical	• comfort
• low maintenance cost	• convenience
	• safety
	• satisfaction
	• pleasure

colorful **sales vocabulary.** Telephone companies recommend the use of the following terms to help the customer *see* the product over the telephone:

1. **Expressive adjectives** — luxurious, lovely, efficient, time-saving, economical, dependable, delectable, elegant, coordinated, brilliant, beautiful, genuine, practical, stylish, efficient.
2. **Forceful words** — value, popular, quality, modern, guaranteed satisfaction, powerful, recommended, unlimited, heavy-duty, reputation, energy-saving, rugged.
3. **Personal words** — you, we, us, your, our.
4. **Picture phrases** — a wide range of vibrant colors; luxurious and easy to care for; comfortable and long-wearing; helps you save energy and money; a symbol of quality, dependability, and value; easy to install and use.

Here are two examples of telephone sales presentations which use sales sentences to help the customer *see* the product or service over the telephone:

1. "You'll never have to worry about the high cost of repair if you own our satisfaction-guaranteed maintenance and service agreement. The agreement guarantees you the best service available on your new air conditioner. Our service department is as close as your telephone, and we have developed a reputation of quality service at a low cost. The agreement gives you an unlimited number of service calls and an annual preventive maintenance checkup at your convenience."
2. "Victor, I'm calling back to talk to you about some new ties we just received which are coordinated with the new line of dress

shirts you ordered last week. You will appreciate how well the ties coordinate with the shirts. The ties are stylish and come in beautiful colors which will blend well with the summer shades of your new dress shirts. To make certain the ties sell, I'll send along our sales promotion kit that includes how to set up a window display to show your customers how the ties coordinate with the shirts. Do you think you'll sell ten dozen or twelve dozen ties?"

Outline Your Sales Presentation. To make certain that you are ready to sell over the telephone, you should develop an outline for your sales presentation. One more advantage of telephone sales is that you may use notes to serve as a guide for your sales presentation. Although you should avoid a canned sales talk, you should plan each part carefully. A **canned sales talk** is a sales presentation read or memorized word for word. Illustration 18-3 outlines the parts of a typical telephone sales presentation.

ILLUSTRATION 18-2
When selling by telephone, you may use notes to serve as a guide to your presentation.

Make the Sales Presentation

To complete a successful telephone presentation: speak clearly, listen to your customer's responses to determine the person's reaction to the presentation, and sell specific benefits which interest

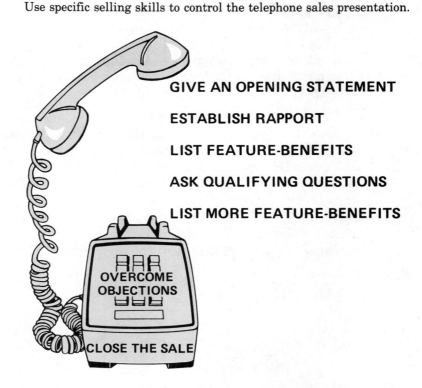

ILLUSTRATION 18-3
Use specific selling skills to control the telephone sales presentation.

GIVE AN OPENING STATEMENT

ESTABLISH RAPPORT

LIST FEATURE-BENEFITS

ASK QUALIFYING QUESTIONS

LIST MORE FEATURE-BENEFITS

OVERCOME OBJECTIONS

CLOSE THE SALE

your customer. Since there is no personal contact with your customer, it is important that you utilize specific selling skills to control the sales presentation. Your goal is to establish rapport with your customer, interest the customer in your product or service, and create customer desire to purchase the product or service.

The telephone sale begins with an opening statement. This statement should help to develop rapport with your customer. You can develop rapport by commenting about something of interest to the customer or by asking a question. Once you have the customer's attention, you can begin the actual sales presentation. The telephone presentation, like a personal sales presentation, should be based on the customer's interests. It should include a series of feature-benefit statements followed by questions to determine the customer's reaction to the statements.

The typical telephone sales presentation may be divided into several parts which include giving an opening statement, establishing rapport, using feature-benefit statements, asking questions, providing additional feature-benefit statements, overcoming objections, and closing the sale.

Give an Opening Statement. The **opening statement** in a telephone sales presentation is just as important as the approach in a personal sales presentation. The first 10 to 15 seconds are an extremely important part of your sales call. As in personal selling, the purpose of your opening statement is to put the customer in a receptive mood and focus the customer's attention on your sales presentation.

The Purpose of the Opening Statement Is to...

• put the customer in a receptive mood.

• focus the customer's attention on your sales presentation.

First, you should introduce yourself and the business you represent. Make your opening statement slowly and clearly so your customer is sure to understand your name and business. Your remarks should be friendly and designed to gain the customer's attention. Speak naturally, pleasantly, and confidently. The following statements are examples of effective opening statements:

"Mr. Cousteau? I'm Bill Anderson, an interior designer with Cole's Home Decorating Service."

"Hello, Mr. Klein. This is Judy Semes of Judy's Fabric Shop."

"Hello, Mrs. Bennett. This is Dave Rogers of Seneca Home Appliance."

Establish Rapport with Your Customer. After the introduction, you should attempt to develop some **rapport**, or a pleasant relationship, with your customer. The purpose of the rapport is to put the customer in a receptive mood. Rapport can be developed by mentioning something you have in common with the customer or something in which you're sure the customer is interested.

The following statements illustrate ways of developing rapport with a customer:

"Mr. Alvarez, your friend Dave Lyle suggested that I call you about our new bookkeeping system. He said you were interested in improving your bookkeeping procedures."

"Mr. Porter, I'm calling to follow up on the letter we mailed to you last week about our new, simplified gourmet cookbook."

Start Your Sales Message with a Feature-Benefit Statement. Products and services have both features and benefits. Features, in themselves, have no sales impact. It is your job to change the product features into buyer benefits. Since benefits are what the customer buys, every telephone sales message should be based on feature-benefit statements. For example, if you are selling to a business account, you will need to explain how that business will benefit from your product or service. Your sales message should explain how your product or service will help the business obtain more customers, sell more products at less cost, and earn the business a greater profit.

If you are selling for a retail store, your sales message should explain to your customers how your product or service will benefit them. For example, if you are selling a maintenance and service contract for an air conditioner over the telephone, your sales message should stress buyer benefits. Notice how the following sales message stresses a buyer benefit.

Telephone
Salesperson: Hello, Mrs. Bennett, this is Dave Rogers of Seneca Home Appliance. I'm calling about the air conditioner you purchased last year from us. How did the air conditioner work for you last summer?

Customer: Fine!

Telephone
Salesperson: I'm sure you really enjoyed it. We sure had hot weather last summer. The reason I'm calling, Mrs. Bennett, is that the one-year guarantee on the parts and service for the air conditioner expires in two weeks. I wanted to make certain that you have

the same continuous guarantee on your air conditioner for another full year. Our maintenance and service contract provides you with full coverage of all parts and labor on the air conditioner. It will insure you the same cool, comfortable, and relaxing temperature you enjoyed last summer.

The buyer benefit stressed in the sales message is that the customer will enjoy a cool, comfortable, relaxing summer at home.

Ask Your Customer a Qualifying Question. The next step in the sales message is to get the customer's reaction to the buyer benefit statement. An easy way to do this is to ask a qualifying question. A good qualifying question should be used to get your customer involved in the sales presentation and to get a reaction to your sales message. The qualifying question is used to determine your customer's reactions to buyer benefits. A good qualifying question should begin with: who, what, where, when, or how.

A qualifying question for the maintenance and service contract for the air conditioner sales message could be:

Telephone
Salesperson: How does that sound, Mrs. Bennett?

Customer: Okay, I guess. How much does the service cost?

The better the qualifying question, the more you'll learn about your customer's buying motives. In the example above, the customer told the salesperson that she was concerned about the cost of the service. The more you learn about your customer's needs and wants, the easier it will be to continue the sale. Other qualifying questions might include: "How is your air conditioner working?" "When was your air conditioner last serviced?" "When were the condenser, coils, and controls of your air conditioner checked?"

Provide Additional Feature-Benefit Statements. The sales message should be based on the benefits your customer wants from the product or service. Each feature-benefit statement should translate the feature into a buyer benefit. Many salespeople who are familiar with the features of their product or service mistakenly assume that the customer will also understand these values. As a result, the salesperson does not effectively translate the product features into buyer benefits. Don't assume your customer will understand the benefit of owning the product or service. Your job as a salesperson is to translate the product feature into a buyer benefit for your customer. For each feature you identify, you should also explain the buyer benefit your customer will receive.

Once you have stated the benefit, use a qualifying question to determine the customer's reaction. An example of additional feature-benefit statements which may be used to sell the maintenance and service contract on the air conditioner include:

"Mrs. Bennett, the service contract is $24.95 and it covers anything that can go wrong with your air conditioner. Plus, the service contract includes a preventive maintenance service call, so that you can have the unit completely checked to make certain it's operating properly. For $24.95 you get complete coverage for the full year. That means you won't have to worry about any expensive service or repair bills on the air conditioner for one full year. Doesn't that sound like a wise investment, Mrs. Bennett?"

Notice that the salesperson has provided the additional feature, translated it to a buyer benefit, and followed it with a qualifying question. The question is a way to determine the customer's reaction to the presentation.

Overcome Objections. No matter how well you have pre-planned the sales message, you should expect your customer to offer some objections. A good telephone salesperson will anticipate possible objections and work out answers to the objections in advance.

Customer objections usually fall into one of four categories: a product or service objection, a postponement objection, a price objection, or a personal objection.

1. **Product or Service Objection.** Customers may feel that your product or service will not fulfill their needs. Customers may be reluctant to buy your product or service because they feel there is something wrong with it.
2. **Postponement Objection.** The postponement objection is a very common customer objection. It is the customer's way of avoiding the decision to buy your product or service. An effective way of overcoming this objection is to stress the benefits the customer will receive from buying now rather than later.
3. **Price Objection.** Customers may feel that the price of the product or service is too high. They may not be aware of the value they will receive for the money they spend. Point out the extra benefits provided by your product or service.
4. **Personal Objection.** A personal objection is one in which customers object either to you personally or to your business. Cus-

tomers may have reservations about buying something over the telephone without seeing the product. They may also have had bad personal experiences with telephone salespeople. It is important to develop customer trust through warm, friendly, confident conversation with your customers. To handle personal objections, you must know your company, your products and services, and the buyer benefits of what you are selling.

It is important that you not feel threatened or worried by your customer's objections. An objection is not a rejection of your product or service. It is simply the customer's reason for not buying your product or service now. Many times objections are requests for more information. Think of your customer's objections as both a lack of understanding by your customer and an opportunity to sell the benefits of your product or service.

To overcome customer objections, use the following four-step process.

To Overcome Your Customer's Objections...

- understand the real objection.
- welcome the objection.
- answer the objection.
- offer an additional buyer benefit.

Step 1: Understand the Real Objection. The first step in overcoming your customer's objection is to make sure you understand the real objection. In many cases your customer may not give you the real reason for objecting.

A good technique to use in understanding your customer's objection is to either ask a question or restate the objection until you are sure you understand it. Some examples of this technique are:

"What is it that concerns you about the service contract, Mrs. Bennett?"

"Do you feel that the service contract is too expensive, Mrs. Bennett?"

"Do I understand you correctly, Mrs. Bennett? You feel that the service contract is too expensive."

All three of these questions should get the customer to confirm or correct your understanding of the objection.

Courtesy of Government Development Bank for Puerto Rico

Step 2: Welcome the Objection. The purpose of welcoming the objection is to avoid an argument with the customer. Since an objection represents a stumbling block in making the sale, it cannot be ignored. A good salesperson recognizes the objection in a diplomatic manner by agreeing with the customer and then selling the customer the benefits of the product. Here are some examples:

"Mrs. Bennett, I certainly understand why you feel the service contract may be too expensive."

"Mrs. Bennett, I'm glad you mentioned that you think the price is too high."

"Yes, this service contract may seem expensive, but do you realize the benefits you'll receive from this agreement?"

Step 3: Answer the Objection. You already have worked out answers to customer objections in preplanning your sales call. Now is the time to use them. The key to effectively handling your customer's objections is to reduce or eliminate the disagreement or objection to your product or service.

It is important that you listen to and answer all of your customer's objections. Don't argue with your customer — you may win the argument but lose a customer. Instead, you should answer the customer's objection completely, and then continue your sales message. There are several ways to answer your customer's objections.

- Use the *yes, but* method.
- Use the *superior point* method.
- Give an additional benefit.
- Change the objection into a benefit.

Two examples of the techniques for answering objections are:

"*Yes,* I can understand why you feel the service agreement may seem expensive, *but* have you considered all the benefits you'll receive? You'll receive a full year of complete coverage on all parts and labor. One service call to your home normally costs at least $20 and that doesn't include any parts or labor. So you are really paying very little to insure continuous maintenance and service on your unit. It is very easy to spend at least twice that amount on one service call. So it really is a wise investment, wouldn't you agree?"

"You know, Mrs. Bennett, you are right about the price of the service agreement. At first it does seem very expensive. Let me explain, though, why the $24.95 for the agreement is really rather inexpensive. If you have had any repairs recently on your TV, refrigerator, washer, dryer, or any major appliance, you'll realize how expensive service costs can be. In fact, most businesses charge at least $20 just to come to your house for repair service on an appliance. Well, in addition to the service call, our agreement provides complete coverage of all parts and labor on anything that might go wrong for one complete year. So you can see, Mrs. Bennett, that this is really a good investment, isn't it?"

Step 4: Offer an Additional Benefit. Once you have answered your customer's objection, offer an additional benefit and continue the sale. For example, if a customer objects to the cost of a service contract, answer the price objection and offer an additional benefit. In the next example, note how the telephone salesperson answers the price objection and then offers the additional benefit of a free maintenance-service checkup.

"I can understand why you are concerned about the cost of the service agreement. I am, too. It seems all repair services are extremely expensive. In this case, however, I'm glad you mentioned the service costs. The agreement covers all the parts and labor on any repairs you may need during the year. In addition, you will receive one maintenance-service call during the year to make certain the unit is operating properly. You can have the maintenance-service checkup at any time during the year at your convenience to insure that your air conditioner will continue to operate correctly. You won't have to worry about your air conditioner failing to provide you cool, comfortable, and relaxing living conditions during the heat of summer. Now when you consider all those benefits, Mrs. Bennett, isn't that a wise investment?"

Once you have overcome your customer's objections, continue with your sales message. When the customer reacts positively to your benefit statements or qualifying questions, attempt to close the sale.

Close the Sale. The purpose of your telephone sales presentation is to sell the product or service to your customer. It is important that you be able to use good closing techniques if you expect to sell to your customer. Too many times salespeople use good opening statements, establish good rapport with the customer, ask good qualifying questions, use good buyer benefits, and effectively overcome the customer's objections, but they fail to close the sale.

You cannot be an effective salesperson if you cannot ask for the order and close the sale. You need to be alert and ready to close the sale when your customer is ready to buy. When the customer seems sold on a benefit, agrees with your sales message, and seems ready to buy, try to close the sale.

Here are three common closing techniques you may use to ask for the sale.

1. **The Choice Close.** The choice close is designed to ask the customers which of two alternative products or services they would like to buy. Examples of the choice close include:

   "Mrs. Bennett, now that you understand all the benefits you will receive from our service agreement, would you like a one-year or two-year service agreement on your air conditioner?"

   "Mrs. Bennett, do you want to put this service contract on your account, use a credit card, or pay cash?"

2. **Summary Close.** A good way to lead into a close is to review or summarize the customer's positive reactions to the feature-benefit statements.

"Mrs. Bennett, you said you were concerned about the cost of the service agreement. But now you can see how many benefits you will receive and how you will really save money by owning the guaranteed service agreement. In fact, if you only need one service call, you will be saving money by purchasing the service agreement. So the service agreement is really a good investment, don't you agree?"

The summary close is achieved by summarizing for the customer the reasons and major benefits of buying your product or service. After reviewing the benefits, ask the customer to buy. It will naturally follow the positive responses to your benefit statements.

3. **Assumed Close.** If you are doing a good job during the sales presentation, you are asking questions that seek agreement from your customer. If the customer is interested and has agreed with your benefit statements during the sales presentation, you may close the sale by assuming the customer is buying. You may use either a statement or a question to close the sale using this technique.

"Mrs. Bennett, I'm sure you'll be pleased with the protection offered in this service contract. I will mail the agreement out this week."

"This is without question one of the best service agreements you can own. You will enjoy the cool comfort of your home this summer even on days which are 105 to 110 degrees. When do you want me to mail the agreement to you?"

The close should be completed with warm, friendly confidence. You're not applying pressure to your customers but are assisting them in buying a good product or service which will provide many benefits. If your customers are going to say yes to your close, they must have confidence in you, your products, and your services.

The telephone can be a very successful tool for selling products and services. It is extremely important that you spend a considerable amount of time preparing your sales presentation. Remember, selling over the telephone requires that you sell customers the benefits they want. Since you are not personally in touch with the customer, you must use feature-benefit statements and qualifying questions to guide your verbal sales presentation.

SALES TERMS

sales vocabulary	canned sales talk	price objection
expressive adjectives	opening statement	personal objection
forceful words	rapport	summary close
personal words	product or service objection	assumed close
picture phrases	postponement objection	

SALES QUESTIONS

1. Give two advantages of telephone selling over personal selling.

2. List at least five functions businesses perform by the telephone.

3. Give at least two disadvantages of telephone selling.

4. List the two major parts of a telephone sales presentation.

5. List the steps involved in preplanning a telephone sales presentation.

6. What is the difference between a rational and emotional buying motive?

7. Why is sales vocabulary so important in telephone selling?

8. What are the limitations of using a canned sales talk for a telephone sales presentation?

9. List the steps involved in making a telephone sales presentation.

10. What is the purpose of the opening statement of a telephone sales presentation?

11. What are six ways you can develop rapport with your customer over the telephone?

12. Why should the telephone sales presentation be based on feature-benefit statements?

13. What is the purpose of a qualifying question?

14. List the four categories of customer objections.

15. Explain the four steps you should follow in overcoming customer objections.

16. Explain the difference between the choice close, the summary close, and the assumed close.

SALES ACTIVITIES

A. Some merchandise is easier to sell over the telephone than other merchandise.

1. List four products or services you might easily sell over the telephone.

2. For each product, list three expressive adjectives which will help the customer to "see" the product over the telephone.

3. For each of the products listed in Question 1 above, develop sales sentences which include a feature-benefit statement and a qualifying question to determine the customer's response.

5

SELLING:
YOUR FUTURE

SELLING:
YOUR FUTURE

CHAPTER 19: IMPROVING YOUR
SELLING SKILLS
CHAPTER 20: CAREER OPPORTUNITIES
IN SELLING
CHAPTER 21: HOW TO GET
A SELLING JOB

IMPROVING YOUR SELLING SKILLS

Your Learning Goals

After studying this chapter, you should:

- *understand how to evaluate your sales personality.*
- *be able to identify your personality strengths and those traits which need to be improved.*
- *be able to evaluate the planning procedures you use in the pre-approach.*
- *be able to evaluate your ability to approach customers.*
- *be able to evaluate your ability to qualify your customers.*
- *be able to evaluate your ability to give a feature-benefit sales presentation.*
- *be able to evaluate your ability to handle your customers' objections.*
- *be able to evaluate your ability to close the sale.*
- *be able to evaluate your ability to use suggestion selling and customer reassurance.*

A person needs to master many skills to be successful in a particular area. Baseball players, guitarists, golfers, pianists, tennis players, gymnasts, and salespeople develop successful skills in similar ways. Before a pro tennis player can become a tennis superstar, he or she has to learn the correct way to hit the tennis ball and how to play the game. Then thousands of hours must be spent hitting forehands, backhands, volleys, overheads, and serves

ILLUSTRATION 19-1
Like a pro tennis player, a salesperson must learn the proper
techniques and then practice them.

© Kathryn Dudek/PHOTO NEWS, 1985

to perfect the game. To be a superstar salesperson (or just an effective salesperson), you need to follow the same procedure. You must learn the proper methods and then perfect them. You must understand the correct selling techniques. You must practice and use those techniques and analyze your sales performance. You must identify techniques which need improvement, and continue to improve those skills. This formula will work whether you are selling cars, insurance, houses, clothes, appliances, furniture, or stocks and bonds.

EVALUATING YOUR SALES PERSONALITY

Many people think that an individual is born with either a pleasing or a poor personality. This is not true. Personality is what people see when they look at you, what they hear when you speak, and what they feel in your presence. It is the sum of all your attitudes, habits, and feelings. These traits can be developed and improved. To improve your sales personality, rate yourself on the following traits and identify which ones you need to improve.

Personal Appearance

First impressions with customers are usually lasting ones. Conscientious salespeople make every effort to present themselves in a favorable manner to each customer. A good physical appearance is an important first step in serving your customers well. Most customers are critical of salespeople who are not neat in appearance, clean, and dressed appropriately for the store and the job. A poor personal appearance may cause the salesperson to lose sales.

Enthusiasm

Do you enjoy spending time with dull and boring people? Probably not. Customers don't enjoy buying products or services from dull salespeople either. Enthusiasm in selling means you enjoy explaining your products or services and showing the benefits your customers will receive from owning them. If you show enthusiasm, it's a lot easier for your customers to get excited about owning the product or service you are selling. Successful salespeople show enthusiasm every day.

Service Attitude

Do you convey the message that your job is to assist the customer? Is your customer convinced that you sincerely want to help? Or do you feel that as long as the customer buys something, you've done your job? Repeat customers come back to a salesperson because they feel that the salesperson is "customer-oriented." If you don't feel your job is to assist customers in making a wise buying decision, your customers will not develop any loyalty to you. If

ILLUSTRATION 19-2
When a salesperson shows enthusiasm it's easier for customers to get excited about owning the product.

Rick Norton/Kings Island

you're not concerned about your customers, they will easily detect your lack of concern. Successful salespeople are sincere in wanting to help their customers.

Honesty

Being honest with your customer can build sales. There may be times when your product or service is not what the customer needs or wants; in these situations, it's best to tell the customer just that. You may miss one sale, but more than likely you will build customer trust. The customer will come back to you again because you have been honest. Being honest creates customer confidence in you.

Confidence

A lack of confidence in your ability to sell will be very evident to your customer. You acquire confidence when you know your product, you have faith in your own sales ability, and you believe your customer will receive benefits from owning the product. Confidence is acquired through positive experiences. Experience provides you with the opportunity to evaluate your own strengths and weaknesses. Sales weaknesses should be thought of as areas which need improvement. The way to improve is to know your strengths and work on the areas in which you need improvement. Self-confidence leads to customer confidence. Customers will more often buy from a salesperson who demonstrates confidence than from one who lacks confidence.

How do you measure up? Have you acquired these important personality traits? Answer the following questions to evaluate your sales personality traits.

Evaluate Your Sales Personality

- Are my clothes always neat and clean?
- Do I dress appropriately for my job?
- Do I show enthusiasm toward the products and services I sell?
- Do I show a sincere concern for my customers?
- Am I honest in dealing with my customers?
- Have I developed a service attitude toward my customers?
- Am I confident in my ability to assist customers?
- Do I remain poised in my sales presentation to customers?

EVALUATING YOUR SALES SKILLS

An effective salesperson controls the sales presentation by successfully completing each of the following seven steps of the sale: the preapproach, the approach, determining needs and wants, the feature-benefit presentation, handling customer objections, closing the sale, and suggestion selling and reassurance.

The Preapproach

In Chapter 3 you learned that selling is 90 percent preparation and 10 percent presentation. The preapproach is your preparation for the sale. It involves the planning you do to better understand your product or service, your customers' buying motives, and the selling skills you should use. How effective are you in preplanning your sales presentation?

Evaluate Your Preapproach

- Have you identified the features of your product?
- Do you know why each product feature is important?
- Can you translate each product feature into a buyer benefit?
- Do you know how your product operates and performs?
- Have you developed at least five qualifying questions to determine your customers' buying motives?
- Have you developed your selling techniques to effectively:

    approach your customers?

    determine your customers' needs?

    demonstrate your product using feature-benefit statements?

    handle any customer objections?

    use trial closing skills?

    use suggestion selling skills?

    provide reassurance to your customers?

In addition to preplanning the techniques to use in your sales presentation, you must also have a positive attitude about selling. In fact, most sales trainers feel that, to be an effective salesperson, you must have a positive attitude toward your business and your products. The list on page 376 identifies attitudes you should possess to be a successful salesperson.

The Approach

The sale begins when the salesperson approaches the customer. The approach should be warm, sincere, genuine, and friendly. A good approach gains the customer's attention and directs it to the roduct. How effective is your approach?

Determining Needs and Wants

Selling involves gaining information from your customers. This information is important to determine what your customers need or want in a product or service. This is called qualifying your customers. You can do this by asking a qualifying question, giving a selling statement, listening to your customers' responses, and observing your customers. It's easy to satisfy your customers' needs and wants once you determine what they are. How effective are you at qualifying your customers?

Evaluate Your Ability to Qualify Your Customers

- Have you developed the ability to begin the sale with a statement or question to get the customers' responses?
- Can you ask good qualifying questions which begin with *what, which, where, when,* or *how*?
- Have you developed the ability to determine your customers' needs by listening to your customers?
- Have you developed the ability to determine your customers' reactions by observing them?

The Feature-Benefit Sales Presentation

The sales presentation should be based on the benefits your customers want from the product or service. A good feature-benefit presentation reassures your customers that you are knowledgeable. Remember to use specific benefit statements so that your customers understand the benefits which are important to them. How do you rate your ability to give a feature-benefit sales presentation?

Evaluate Your Ability to Give a Feature-Benefit Sales Presentation

- Have you developed a list of features for each product or service you sell?
- Have you learned the buyer benefits your customers will receive from each of these features?
- Have you developed the ability to determine your customers' specific buyer benefits by asking qualifying questions?
- Have you learned how to involve your customers in your sales presentations?
- Does your sales presentation appeal to your customers' senses?
- Have you learned how to properly handle the products you sell?
- Can you base your sales demonstration on your customers' buyer benefits?

Handling Customer Objections

No matter how effective a salesperson you are, you should expect objections from your customers. They can be product or service objections, price objections, postponement objections, or personal objections. Remember, try not to be threatened by your customers' objections. Think of them as a lack of understanding by your customers and an opportunity for you to sell them buyer benefits. How well do you handle customer objections?

Evaluate Your Ability to Handle Your Customers' Objections

- Have you developed the ability to welcome your customers' objections?
- Have you developed the ability to listen to your customers' objections?
- Have you developed the ability to show empathy for your customers?
- Can you use the following methods effectively in overcoming your customers' objections?

yes, but	question
direct denial	demonstration
superior point	third party
boomerang	close on an objection

Closing the Sale

From the very beginning of the sale, you should be ready to close. It is your job to help make the buying decision easier for your customers. The close should be based on your customers' responses. Customers usually will give you some type of buying signal when they are ready to buy. Closing techniques include: the ask-your-customer-to-buy close, the choice close, the assumed close, the advantages-and-disadvantages close, the premium close, the standing-room-only close, the last-chance-to-buy close, the testimonial close, the objection close, and the suggestion-selling close. How effective are you at closing the sale?

Suggestion Selling and Reassurance

Suggestion selling is a personal service for your customers. It is suggesting merchandise which relates to your customers' original purchase or other items they may need. It should not be done to push something on your customers that they do not need or want. The suggestion should be based on what your customers tell you

Evaluate Your Ability to Close the Sale

- Have you learned how to listen for and recognize customer buying signals?
- Have you developed the ability to narrow the customers' choice of products?
- Can you get agreement from your customers?
- Have you developed the ability to determine which products you should show your customers?
- Can you use the following closing techniques?

ask-your-customer-to-buy close	standing-room-only close
choice close	last-chance-to-buy close
assumed close	testimonial close
advantage-disadvantage close	objection close
premium close	suggestion-selling close

during the sale. The suggestion can be a related-merchandise item, a new merchandise item, larger quantities of the same item, a better quality item, a merchandise special, or an item for a special occasion. How effective are you at suggestion selling?

Evaluate Your Ability to Use Suggestion Selling

- Do you close the original sale before suggesting additional merchandise?
- Do you make suggestions from the customers' point of view?
- Do you make a specific suggestion using one of the following techniques?

a specific related-merchandise item	a better quality item — trading up
a new merchandise item	a merchandise special
larger quantities of merchandise	merchandise for a special occasion

- Do you provide customer reassurance after the suggested sale is completed?

EVALUATING YOUR SALES DEMONSTRATION

Salespeople who are willing to work hard to improve their sales techniques will become good salespeople. The first step in improving your selling skills is to understand your selling strengths and the skills which you need to improve. You may wish to have your teacher, supervisor at work, fellow employees, or other students evaluate your sales presentation by answering the following questions. The answers to these questions will help you to understand your selling strengths and the skills which you need to improve.

Evaluate Your Sales Demonstration

APPROACH

- Did the salesperson use an appropriate approach?
- Did the approach direct the customer's attention to the product?

SALES PRESENTATION

- Did the salesperson ask questions to get the customer involved in the sale?
- Did the salesperson listen to the customer and show an interest in the customer as an individual?
- Was the salesperson able to determine the customer's needs?
- Did the salesperson demonstrate adequate knowledge of product features?
- Did the salesperson handle the product with care and respect to increase its value to the customer?
- Did the salesperson demonstrate and explain the buyer benefits the customer would receive from the product?

HANDLING OBJECTIONS

- Did the salesperson welcome the customer's objections and listen to them with interest?
- Did the salesperson handle and overcome the objections with respect?

TRIAL CLOSE

- Did the salesperson take advantage of the customer's reactions and attempt a trial close at the appropriate time?
- Was the sale closed?
- Did the salesperson provide suggestion selling as a service to the customer?
- Did the salesperson provide customer reassurance?

SALES QUESTIONS

1. List four steps you can use to become an effective salesperson.

2. Respond to the following statement: "Salespeople are born, not made."

3. Why are the following personality traits important in becoming a successful salesperson?

   a. personal appearance
   b. enthusiasm
   c. service attitude
   d. honesty
   e. confidence

4. Which of the following steps of a sale are the most difficult for you to complete and why?

   a. preapproach
   b. approach
   c. determining needs and wants
   d. feature-benefit sales presentation
   e. handling customer objections
   f. closing the sale
   g. suggestion selling and reassurance

5. Explain the statement: "To be an effective salesperson, you must have a positive attitude toward your business and your products."

6. List at least seven attitudes needed for successful selling.

7. How does the salesperson benefit from qualifying the customer?

8. Why should a sales presentation be based on the customer's needs rather than on product features?

9. Why shouldn't a salesperson become upset by a customer's objections?

10. When should a salesperson attempt a trial close?

11. What should be the basis of the salesperson's suggestion selling during the sales presentation?

12. What questions should you ask to evaluate selling techniques at each of the following steps of a sale:

    a. approach
    b. sales presentation
    c. handling objections
    d. trial close

SALES ACTIVITIES

A. Rate your personality traits on a scale from 1 to 3 (1 = excellent, 2 = okay, 3 = needs improvement).

personality traits:

appearance
enthusiasm
service attitude

honesty
confidence

For each personality trait you rated *needs improvement,* list the specific steps you should take to improve that trait.

B. Rate your performance of the following sales techniques using the scale given in Part A.

selling techniques:

preapproach

approach

determining need and wants

feature-benefit sales presentation

handling objections

closing the sale

suggestion selling and reassurance

For each selling technique you rated *needs improvement,* list the specific steps you should take to improve that technique.

CAREER OPPORTUNITIES
IN SELLING

Your Learning Goals

After studying this chapter, you should:

- *know the three major types of businesses which employ salespeople.*
- *understand the difference between personal selling and self-service selling.*
- *be able to explain the difference between the major types of retail stores.*
- *know the types of job opportunities in wholesale selling.*
- *know the types of job opportunities in manufacturers' selling.*
- *understand the benefits of a career in selling.*

Are you interested in a career with many challenging and interesting job opportunities? Are you interested in a career in which you can make a very good salary? Are you interested in a career which is constantly growing? If you are, you should learn more about the career opportunities in selling. The purpose of this chapter is to identify the major employment opportunities in selling and to describe the characteristics of the selling jobs within those employment areas.

WHERE SELLING TAKES PLACE

Selling is one of the few occupational areas which is always looking for new people. Selling is done from retail stores, wholesale distribution centers, manufacturers' sales offices, and private homes. Some salespeople have offices in their homes and sell in local areas. Other salespeople travel extensively, selling their products and services in two or three states or throughout the country.

Everything you own was at one time sold by someone. The clothes you wear, the food you eat, the house in which you live, the car you drive, and the records or tapes you listen to were all sold to you by someone. Some salespeople sell **tangible products** or items which you can see or touch such as clothes, food, books, houses, automobiles, and computers. Other salespeople sell **intangible items** or things which cannot be seen or touched such as insurance, stocks and bonds, advertising, and financial and credit services.

Selling offers a wide variety of challenging and interesting career opportunities. Capable and talented salespeople are constantly sought by every type of manufacturer, wholesaler, and retailer. Currently there are more than 12 million people employed in sales jobs. More than seven million salespeople are employed by retailers; more than one and one-half million salespeople are employed by wholesalers; over one and one-half million are involved in selling real estate, insurance, and financial services; and over one-half million people are employed as manufacturers' salespeople.

Sales Employees in the United States in 1985

Occupational Area	Number of Salespeople
Retail Salespeople	7,228,000
Wholesale Salespeople	1,727,000
Finance, Insurance, and Real Estate Agents and Brokers	1,659,000
Manufacturers' Salespeople	735,000
Service Salespeople	702,000

Source: U.S. Department of Labor

About 12 percent of our total work force is currently employed in sales occupations. The Department of Labor estimates that employment in most sales jobs will rise about as fast as the average for all jobs through 1995. Faster than average growth is expected for wholesale, travel, real estate, and securities sales opportunities.

If you are thinking about a career in selling, you can see that there are many career opportunities available to you. You will have a choice of working in many different industries selling the products or services of your choice. If you enjoy clothes, you may want a job in the fashion business. If you enjoy music, you may want to sell in a music-related business. You may consider selling automobiles, sports cars, or recreational vehicles if you enjoy cars. If you are good at math, you may want to consider selling computers, electronic equipment, or other technical products.

Selling jobs may be classified by the types of businesses that employ salespeople, the types of products or services the salesperson sells, and the type of buyer the salesperson calls upon. For this chapter, selling jobs will be explained according to the types of businesses that employ salespeople.

TYPES OF BUSINESSES THAT EMPLOY SALESPEOPLE

There are three major types of businesses that employ salespeople: retailers, wholesalers, and manufacturers. Retailers hire salespeople to sell merchandise and services to consumers. Wholesalers hire salespeople to sell products to retailers, other wholesalers, industrial firms, or other businesses. **Manufacturers** employ salespeople who sell products to other manufacturers or directly to wholesalers or retailers.

Retailers

You are probably very familiar with retail store selling. Department stores, variety stores, discount stores, and specialty shops are types of retail stores. Supermarkets, drugstores, service stations, and restaurants are also retail stores. There are more sales jobs in retailing than in manufacturing and wholesaling combined. A retail salesperson sells merchandise and services to the ultimate consumer or user of the product or service.

The success of any retail business depends on how effective the salespeople are in selling their products and services to customers. The amount of personal selling skills that retail salespeople need depends on the approach the store decides to take with its customers. Even though contact with the customer is a part of all sales jobs, the selling skills, duties, and responsibilities of retail salespeople are different in each store. Some retail stores, like department stores, specialty shops, and appliance stores, hire salespeople to sell products and services. These stores rely on the salespeople to personally sell the products and services to customers.

Other retail stores, like discount stores, variety stores, supermarkets, and drugstores, are considered **self-service** operations and hire clerks, order-takers, or cashiers.

In stores which use a personal selling approach, the salesperson's major tasks are to create an interest in the product and to stimulate the customers' desire to purchase the products. The personal selling skills salespeople need include approaching the customers, giving feature-benefit sales presentations, answering customers' questions, overcoming customer objections, closing sales, and using suggestion-selling skills. The salesperson's job is to satisfy the needs and wants of the customer by utilizing personal selling skills.

Professional retail salespeople consider themselves both problem-solvers and creative salespeople. Salespeople who sell major appliances, automobiles, furniture, women's and men's apparel, and other relatively expensive products or services must use personal selling skills. They must know their products, know how to analyze their customers' needs, know how to sell customers the benefits they will receive from owning the product or service, and be able to close the sale. In performing these skills, the salesperson is assisting the customers in making a wise buying decision.

ILLUSTRATION 20-1
Salespeople who sell expensive products such as automobiles need personal selling skills.

In contrast, salespeople who work in self-service stores like supermarkets, drugstores, discount stores, and variety stores often do little more than take the customers' money. These people are essentially **clerks** or order-takers and do not have a great need for personal selling skills. The self-service stores rely on in-store displays and promotions to create customer desire for the merchandise. Little, if any, personal selling takes place in self-service stores.

In addition to selling, most retail salespeople perform sales-supporting duties like writing sales slips, operating the cash register, wrapping merchandise, and keeping their work area neat and clean. They may also order merchandise, stock shelves, mark prices, build displays, and assist in taking inventory.

Employers generally prefer salespeople who have at least a high school education. Young people interested in a career in retail selling will benefit from enrolling in a high school or post-high school marketing and distributive education program. Students in these programs receive classroom instruction in marketing, retailing, and management and often work part-time at a local business. The classroom instruction and practical on-the-job training should help to provide the needed experiences for a successful sales career.

ILLUSTRATION 20-2
Little personal selling takes place in self-service stores.

Retail selling is one of the few occupations in which qualified salespeople may advance to executive jobs regardless of their educational background. However, retailers prefer to hire people who have had previous sales experience and college courses in management programs or a college degree in marketing, retailing, or management. Illustration 20-3 shows the career path a salesperson can follow into a management position.

ILLUSTRATION 20-3
Career path a salesperson can follow into management positions.

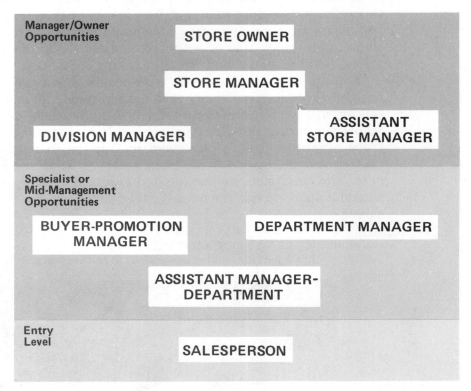

Most of the selling that retail salespeople perform occurs within a retail store. Almost all retail salespeople, therefore, are involved in over-the-counter, or **internal selling.** There has been, however, an increased use of **external selling** in retailing in the past few years. External salespeople sell products or services outside the store environment. Examples of external retail sales include telephone sales, catalog sales, life insurance sales, interior decorating sales, home remodeling sales, and home demonstrations. Since retail selling is primarily in-store selling, the following information describes the stores in which retail selling takes place.

Department Stores. Department stores are large retail stores that handle a wide range of merchandise including clothing, shoes, furniture, housewares, sporting goods, toys, fabric, cosmetics, automotive parts, cameras, and jewelry. These stores may also have catalog and telephone sales departments, and some may sell insurance and beauty shop services.

Department stores are divided into several separate departments. Each department has a department manager and department salespeople. Some departments may have an assistant department manager. Department stores stress customer service by offering services such as free delivery, installation, credit, telephone and mail-order departments, gift wrapping, the opportunity to return merchandise, alterations, and restaurants. Nationally known department stores include J.C. Penney; Sears, Roebuck; Montgomery Ward; Macy's and Bloomingdale's in New York; Marshall Field in Chicago; Neiman Marcus in Dallas; and Bullock's in Los Angeles.

Department stores hire more salespeople than any other type of retail store. Salespeople are hired for all departments in the store. Successful salespeople are often promoted to positions such as assistant department manager, department manager, buyer, store division manager, and store manager.

Variety Stores. Variety stores handle a wide variety of merchandise such as toys, housewares, candy, clothing, small electrical appliances, paper and school supplies. Variety stores were originally known as "five-and-tens" because all the merchandise in these stores was priced at either five or ten cents. These stores are now known as limited-price variety stores, since the prices of merchandise range from ten cents to $25 or more.

These stores have in past years sold merchandise on a cash-and-carry basis, but today most of them offer credit services. Salespeople do little selling in variety stores. In this type of store most of a salesperson's time is spent in sales-supporting duties such as stocking merchandise, operating a cash register, answering customer questions, and wrapping merchandise. Well-known variety stores include F.W. Woolworth Co. and the Ben Franklin Stores.

Discount Stores. Discount stores carry a wide variety of general merchandise. They operate on a self-service basis and stock merchandise which is usually sold for lower-than-normal prices. The lower prices are made possible by their large volume of sales and by the elimination of elegant decor, personal selling, and other services offered by department stores. Although name brands are

available in appliances, cameras, toys, and health and beauty aids, most of the merchandise sold in a discount store is not name brand. Prices on name-brand merchandise are normally higher than nonname-brand merchandise. Well-known discount stores include K-Mart, Zayre's, and Target.

Specialty Shops. Stores that sell a single category of merchandise are called **specialty shops.** An office supply specialty store may sell typewriters, file cabinets, desk organizers, typing paper, envelopes, note pads, and bulletin boards. Other specialty shops include men's and women's clothing stores, jewelry stores, shoe stores, florists, luggage stores, automotive parts stores, sporting goods stores, and greeting card stores. Specialty shops are relatively small and are found in both downtown and shopping center locations. Often they are locally owned and operated and emphasize personal service to the customer.

Characteristics of Retail Selling. Retailing offers many job opportunities for people interested in selling. Salespeople who sell major appliances or other expensive merchandise often work on a **commission** basis. They are paid a percentage of the amount of merchandise they sell.

Two of the disadvantages of a retail selling career are the number and irregularity of hours some salespeople must work. Retail salespeople may work 45 to 55 hours per week. Some evening and weekend work is usually required. However, many people find

it interesting and challenging to work with new merchandise and to assist a variety of customers in making wise buying decisions.

Wholesale Selling

Wholesalers are middlemen who sell to retailers, manufacturers, and other wholesalers. Wholesale salespeople may be classified in several ways. When they are classified according to the types of merchandise they sell, they are called technical and nontechnical salespeople.

Technical salespeople sell highly technical products such as machinery, electronic equipment, printing equipment, and computers. **Nontechnical salespeople** sell food, drugs, hardware, furniture, and products which are not so complex.

Wholesale salespeople may also be classified as inside or outside salespeople. **Inside salespeople** work in the wholesaler's office and telephone their customers. **Outside salespeople** travel to their customers' businesses and personally sell their products.

Businesses which buy products from wholesalers may use the products in the operation of their business or in manufacturing finished products. They may also resell the products to customers for a profit. Many job opportunities exist in the field of wholesale selling. Wholesale representatives call on retailers, hotels, restaurants, hospitals, schools, building contractors, lumberyards, beauty salons, and manufacturers. Wholesale representatives sell products including machinery, lumber and building materials, electronic equipment, drugs and pharmaceutical products, textiles, apparel items, food products, hardware, chemicals, automotive parts, electronic parts, and appliances. The following sections describe the common types of job opportunities in wholesale selling.

Wholesale Sales Representatives. Wholesale sales representatives work for wholesalers and sell to retailers. They may be either inside or outside salespeople. The most common products handled by wholesale representatives are food products, drugs, textiles, automobile parts, and small appliances. Wholesale representatives perform many important services for retailers, such as checking the store's stock and ordering items that the store will need before the next sales call. Wholesale representatives may also provide advice and assistance in advertising, display, retail selling, and merchandising techniques.

Wholesaler representatives may handle from 400 to 50,000 items. Because they handle so many items, they usually sell from a catalog or several catalogs. It is not uncommon for a wholesale salesperson to represent two or more competitive firms. For example, a pharmaceutical sales representative may sell over 8,000 items and represent 50 or more different companies.

Wholesale representatives perform many marketing services for customers. First, and most important, they sell products and services. In addition, they have large stocks of products, make frequent sales calls, provide finance and credit services, provide sales promotion aids, and provide prompt delivery. Wholesaling is very competitive because many businesses sell competitive products at similar prices. Therefore, it is important that wholesale representatives be service-oriented and provide many ideas on business operation to their customers.

Wholesale representatives provide services such as **merchandise plans** to their retail customers. For example, when sales representatives sell a product to a drugstore, they also provide the customer with a complete merchandise plan. The plan includes an advertising program for the product, display techniques, aids to promote the product in the store, and product information needed to sell the product. Wholesale representatives who sell technical products also provide many services to their customers, including analyzing the business to determine its technical equipment needs. After the equipment is sold, the representative supervises the installation of the equipment and usually trains the customers' employees to operate the equipment. Wholesale representatives may also be asked to provide advice on business practices such as pricing, buying, taking inventory, and offering customer services. Because sales representatives are asked to help their customers, they must be up-to-date and well-informed on successful business practices. The wholesale representative really serves as a consultant to customers in helping them to merchandise and sell their products.

Rack Jobbers. Rack jobbers sell items such as beauty aids, panty hose, magazines, stationery, hand tools, small household utensils, and other nonfood items. This merchandise is usually displayed on a rack within the store. Rack jobbers commonly display their products in the nonfood departments of supermarkets. Rack jobbers usually own both the merchandise and the display rack. The primary duties of a rack jobber are replenishing the store's stock as needed and pricing the merchandise. The store receives a percentage of the retail price of the merchandise sold.

Wholesale Route Salespeople. Wholesale route salespeople have assigned delivery routes and regular accounts. There are two types of route salespeople: those that service commercial or industrial businesses, and those which deliver to retail businesses. Commercial and industrial accounts buy tools, cleaners, janitorial supplies, office supplies, and other items used in the operation of their business. In contrast, route salespeople who deliver to retail businesses sell merchandise which is resold to the consumer. For example, route salespeople deliver candy, soft drinks, milk, and bakery goods to supermarkets. One retail route salesperson may call on over 35 stores per day.

ILLUSTRATION 20-6
Wholesale route salespeople who deliver to retail businesses sell merchandise which is resold to the consumer.

Ford Truck Operations

Industrial Wholesale Salespeople. Industrial wholesale salespeople sell industrial goods. **Industrial goods** are products purchased and consumed by manufacturers. Some manufacturing firms may not have their own sales departments and salespeople. Instead, they contract with wholesale salespeople to represent them.

Industrial salespeople may be classified according to the type of merchandise they sell. Industrial wholesale sales representatives sell technical and nontechnical products. Typical **technical products** include machinery, electronic equipment, building materials, plumbing and heating equipment, printing and copy equipment, and computer equipment. Technical salespeople give technical assistance to industrial users. This assistance might include selecting the equipment which best fits the needs of the customer, installing and maintaining the technical products, and training the employees to use that equipment. Technical sales representatives need extensive training because of the complexity of the products they sell. Many technical sales representatives are college graduates with special training in engineering, chemistry, biology, or pharmaceuticals.

ILLUSTRATION 20-7
Technical sales representatives give technical assistance including selecting the equipment which best fits the needs of industrial users.

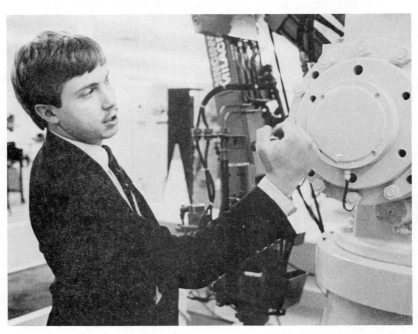

Experienced wholesale salespeople who have leadership qualities may advance to supervisor, sales manager, or executive positions. Employment opportunities for salespeople in wholesaling are excellent for those with product knowledge and selling ability. A person's success in wholesale selling greatly depends on his or her ability to locate new customers and to persuade them to buy.

Manufacturers' Selling

All manufacturers employ salespeople. Large manufacturing firms like General Electric, IBM, Procter and Gamble, General Mills, and Kellogg employ large full-time sales forces. Smaller manufacturers hire representatives who sell products for several different manufacturers. The manufacturers' representatives are paid a commission on sales and do not receive a salary from the manufacturing firms. There are currently about 414,000 manufacturers' salespeople and representatives.

Manufacturers' salespeople and manufacturers' representatives sell both technical and nontechnical products. Technical products include computers, heavy-duty machinery, transportation equipment, copy machinery, professional and scientific instruments, and electronic equipment. Most manufacturers' salespeople sell **nontechnical products.** The majority of nontechnical manufacturers' salespeople sell food products. Other nontechnical products include furniture, appliances, paper, health and beauty aids, school and hospital supplies, and printing supplies and materials.

A manufacturer's salesperson is assigned to a sales territory. It may be a large metropolitan area, part of a state, or one or more states. The size of the territory is usually based on the number of accounts or customers found within that geographic area. The salesperson is usually the only representative of the manufacturer who calls on the customer.

The duties that manufacturers' salespeople perform vary depending on the nature of the products they sell. Salespeople who sell technical products are referred to as technical experts or sales engineers. They perform very different functions from retail or wholesale salespeople. Sales engineers possess a high degree of technical product information. For example, computer salespeople may spend months or years trying to sell a complex computer system to one customer. These salespeople must be experts in computer applications. Their duties include determining the specific needs or computer applications for the customer and developing computer programs for the customer. After the computer equipment is installed, the salespeople would also make certain that the system is working properly and even provide training to the customer's employees on computer operation.

Salespeople who sell technical products are usually college graduates who have received specialized technical training and practical experience in using their products. Manufacturers' salespeople should be aggressive, able to communicate well with the customer, able to manage time, and capable of making decisions. They must possess a wealth of product information and understand a variety of product applications. Manufacturers' salespeople must also be able to use rational selling benefits in their sales presentations. Their customers want to know how the product will save them time and money. Manufacturers' salespeople may work for the company in its plant before becoming salespeople. Illustration 20-8 shows the career path manufacturers' salespeople of a nontechnical product may follow.

ILLUSTRATION 20-8
Career path manufacturers' salespeople may follow into management positions.

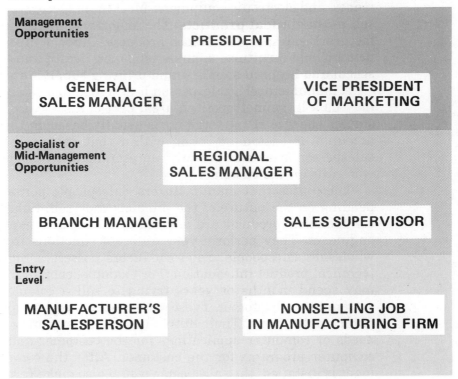

The following section describes the common types of job opportunities in manufacturers' selling.

Manufacturers' Salespeople. Manufacturers' salespeople work full-time for only one manufacturer and are paid a salary and commission on sales. Manufacturers' salespeople call on customers at the customers' places of business and use personal selling skills. Manufacturers' salespeople are also asked to perform other duties for their customers. These duties vary with the type of product or service they sell.

Sales Engineers. A special type of manufacturers' salesperson is the **sales engineer.** Sales engineers sell highly technical products such as heavy equipment, heavy machinery, computer equipment, transportation equipment, scientific instruments, and complex electronic equipment. They are usually well-educated with a college degree in science, math, engineering, or electronic data processing.

Companies who buy from manufacturers who employ sales engineers expect the engineers to spend a considerable amount of time setting up a system specifically designed for their use. Among the specific duties sales engineers perform are product installation, product use, employee training, and cost and efficiency procedures for best utilization of the product. Because of the complexity and cost of the technical product, sales engineers will spend months working with a customer to obtain the sale and to make sure the product is being used efficiently.

Manufacturers' Representatives. Hired by manufacturers who do not employ full-time salespeople, **manufacturers' representatives** usually work for several different manufacturers and are paid on a commission basis. These representatives usually handle hundreds of products. Their major duties include contacting customers on a regular basis, determining products which best fulfill the customers' needs, and providing assistance in solving the customers' business problems.

Missionary Salespeople. Missionary salespeople provide nonselling services to customers to build goodwill for the manufacturer. They call on wholesalers, retailers, and other manufacturers to make certain that customers are happy with the manufacturers' products. Missionary salespeople are also used to find out what problems their customers are having and to help customers improve their business practices. They suggest ways for customers to improve their sales, advertising and display, buying, pricing, and other merchandising practices.

Other Sales Career Opportunities

Most of the selling jobs discussed in this chapter have pertained to selling products. Not all salespeople sell products, however; some salespeople sell services. In fact, there has been an increase in the number of services sold in this country in the past decade. Service selling involves the sale of intangibles such as insurance, real estate, stocks and bonds, advertising services, finance and credit services, travel and transportation services, and business and educational consulting services. Two of the major occupational areas in service selling are insurance and real estate selling.

Insurance Agents and Brokers. Policies that protect an individual or a business against future losses are sold by **insurance agents and brokers.** You can buy insurance protection for your home, your car, your business, other property, and your life. Agents sell three basic types of insurance: life, property, and health insurance. There are two types of insurance agencies. The first type, an agency that sells insurance for one company, would include insurance companies like Metropolitan Life, New York Life, Prudential, Equitable Life Assurance Society, and Aetna Life & Casualty. The second type of insurance agency is the independent agency which is authorized to sell insurance for one or more insurance companies. There are over 600,000 agents, brokers, and underwriters in the insurance business. Insurance agents spend most of their time prospecting for new customers and discussing insurance policies with existing and prospective customers. Some agents do most of their selling in their own business offices, while others spend most of their time calling on the customer at the customer's home or business. Other duties performed by insurance agents include preparing reports, maintaining records, planning insurance programs for prospective customers, and updating the insurance programs of existing customers. Most insurance agents are paid a sales commission on the policies they sell.

Real Estate Agents and Brokers. For most people, buying a house is the single most expensive purchase they ever make. Salespeople who represent customers in buying and selling houses are called **real estate agents and brokers.** Real estate agents arrange and conduct the meetings between the buyer and seller of a house or commercial property. They also arrange for loans from finance companies or banks for their customers and perform other duties to insure customer satisfaction with the real estate purchase.

Real estate agents spend most of their time prospecting for customers, showing and selling real estate, handling rental proper-

ILLUSTRATION 20-9
In addition to selling policies, insurance agents maintain records and update
the insurance programs of existing customers.

ties, and obtaining property listings. A **property listing** is the
process of announcing that a house or other real estate property is
for sale or rent. In obtaining a property listing, the real estate
agent enters into an agreement to sell or rent the owner's property.
Agents usually receive a commission from a real estate broker for
obtaining property listings and for selling real estate. They may
show several houses to a prospective buyer before the customer
decides to purchase a particular property. Because customers may
invest $50,000 or more in a house, they are usually very careful
in studying the house and its features before they purchase the
property.

BENEFITS OF A CAREER IN SELLING

Salespeople can achieve tremendous rewards in selling: advancement, interesting and challenging work, financial benefits,
security, steady employment, and personal satisfaction. In a vigor-
ous, expanding economy, the salesperson will have work and security because the demand for good salespeople is always greater
than the supply.

Very often the sales organization *is* the company. The men and women of the sales force generate the company's sales and in turn contribute to keeping the other employees—the production workers, shipping and receiving employees, office employees, and engineers—working at their jobs.

Selling offers an opportunity limited only by the salesperson's own ability and ambition. In the eyes of the corporate personnel managers, selling experience is impressive when it appears on a job applicant's resume. In some companies, it often improves an applicant's chances for getting nonselling as well as selling jobs. Selling is considered to be a basic, grass-roots experience essential for the understanding of any company's business.

Perhaps the major benefit of a selling career is the money you can earn. Some sales jobs pay very good salaries. If you are paid on a commission basis, the more you sell, the more you earn. In selling, your income is usually based on your productivity. If your sales increase, your salary increases. In addition, many salespeople become sales managers, vice-presidents of sales, and even corporate presidents. So a career in selling provides the potential for a very good income as well as many opportunities for promotion into executive positions.

SALES TERMS

tangible products	nontechnical salespeople	nontechnical products
intangible items	inside salespeople	manufacturers'
manufacturers	outside salespeople	salespeople
self-service	wholesale sales	sales engineers
clerks	representatives	manufacturers'
internal selling	merchandise plan	representatives
external selling	rack jobbers	missionary salespeople
department stores	wholesale route salespeople	insurance agents and
variety stores	industrial wholesale	brokers
discount stores	salespeople	real estate agents and
specialty shops	industrial goods	brokers
commission	technical products	property listing
technical salespeople		

SALES QUESTIONS

1. Explain the difference between tangible products and intangible items.

2. List at least seven occupational areas which employ salespeople in the United States.

3. List the three major types of businesses which employ salespeople.

4. Explain the difference between retail selling, wholesale selling, and manufacturers' selling.

5. What is the difference between personal selling and self-service operation?

6. Explain the difference between:

   a. Department stores and specialty shops
   b. Variety stores and discount stores
   c. Department stores and variety stores

7. Explain the difference between inside and outside wholesale salespeople.

8. What are five services wholesale sales representatives provide to their customers?

9. What is the difference between a rack jobber and a wholesale route salesperson?

10. Explain the difference between a wholesale sales representative and an industrial wholesale salesperson.

11. What is the difference between technical and nontechnical products?

12. Explain the difference between a manufacturer's salesperson and a manufacturer's representative.

13. What is the difference between a sales engineer and a missionary salesperson?

14. Explain why the sale of insurance, stocks and bonds, advertising, and finance and credit are called service selling.

SALES ACTIVITIES

A. There are many challenging and interesting jobs in selling. In selecting a career, you should match your interest with the opportunity and experience available in a particular occupation. List the factors which you feel are important to consider in selecting an occupation.

B. List the benefits offered by a career in selling. Which ones match what you feel are very important factors in selecting an occupation?

C. Rank the following sales jobs in the order of your preference. Rank the jobs from 1 to 12. Number 1 is the job you like best and number 12 is the job you like least.

department store salesperson

sales engineer

insurance agent

real estate agent

speciality shop salesperson

rack jobber

wholesale route salesperson-industrial

wholesale route salesperson-retail

industrial wholesale salesperson

missionary salesperson

manufacturer's representative

manufacturer's salesperson

Explain the reasons you ranked your top three jobs as those you like the best. What benefits of those jobs appeal to you?

HOW TO GET A SELLING JOB

Your Learning Goals

After studying this chapter, you should:

- *be able to take an honest look at your qualifications.*
- *know the sources for finding a job.*
- *be able to write a resume and a letter of application.*
- *know how to complete an application form.*
- *know how to prepare for an interview.*
- *be able to sell yourself in an interview.*
- *know the importance of the follow-up.*
- *understand how to succeed in a new job.*

You want a sales job. You know that somewhere, some employer has exactly the sales job you want — one that will use your knowledge and abilities and provide challenges and opportunities for advancement.

To find that job, you need to carry out a well-planned job search. You already have a product to sell — you — your knowledge, skills, and experience. Now you need to know how to market your product most effectively. Whether you are in school, just out of school and ready to start a career, or looking for a new sales position after years of experience, the job-seeking techniques presented in this chapter will help you to secure the position you want.

Take your future seriously. Prepare yourself to get the sales position you want rather than to accept a job just because it is available. Too often people accept any job just to earn money. Realize that your first sales job is an important step in developing a good work record.

A job is more than a way to earn a living; it is a way of life. Knowing how to obtain a job, knowing what your job is, being prepared to work, and following company policies are the ways you become a valuable employee. If you give an honest share of yourself, you will receive in return not only a salary, but also many fringe benefits. You have learned how to successfully sell products and services; now you will learn how to sell yourself.

Getting the right sales job is a job in itself—a job that requires careful thought and planning. There are many job opportunities. You need to find the job you want and then demonstrate that you are the right person for that job. This idea must be communicated to the interviewer. You have to sell yourself. You must know the best methods of applying for a sales job. Be prepared to get the job you want.

TAKE A LOOK AT YOURSELF

As the first step in preparing to apply for a job, you should decide exactly what your qualifications are. You will need to prepare a detailed inventory of your background and experience so that you will know exactly what assets you have to offer an employer.

No matter what type of job you are seeking, your personal inventory will become a basic guide in your search. Your personal inventory will help you decide how to present your qualifications, and it will be your source for the facts, dates, and other information you will need to give an employer.

Your Education

Do you have sufficient educational training to secure the sales job you want? Most sales positions require at least a high school education. But just because you have graduated from high school does not mean that you are qualified for the job. A high school diploma only indicates to an employer that you have kept your commitment to complete high school.

While in school, take advantage of every opportunity to learn. Explore and enroll in courses that are related to a vocation which interests you. After you have finished a course, you may find that you really liked it and want to learn more about that particular area. You may also discover that a particular course or career area does not interest you.

Discuss career areas with your high school guidance counselor. Many schools offer career guidance. Take advantage of these resources. Guidance counselors can also give you vocational interest and aptitude tests. The results of these tests may help you find your career interest.

For some jobs a high school diploma will get you started, but you may need further education and training to advance. Look at your career interests and consider how much education is required.

Your Personality

Your personality includes those traits which set you apart as an individual. No two people are exactly alike. We all have good and bad personality traits. Your personality is made up of how you look, what you say, how you feel, and what you do.

Personal appearance is important. Your clothing should fit your personality and the kind of sales job you are applying for. Even the way you wear your clothes reflects your personality. Are your clothes neat, clean, and properly fitted, or are they wrinkled, dirty, sloppy, or too tight? A good rule to follow when selecting the appropriate clothing for an interview is to dress the way the employees dress for the sales job you are seeking. By following this rule you will avoid underdressing or overdressing for the interview.

Not only are the clothes you wear important, but good grooming and health also are essential for a good appearance. A daily bath, deodorant, clean and combed hair, clean teeth, and clean fingernails all add to your personal appearance. You will be judged by that first impression — your appearance.

Your personality also includes what you say and how well you listen. Being a good listener is just as important as being a good talker. So, be interested and pay attention to what is being said. Think before you speak and have something worthwhile to say. The tone of your voice also plays an important part in what you say. A loud, boisterous tone of voice is not appropriate for an interview.

How you feel is reflected by the way you act. The way you act — your behavior — is an important part of your personality. How do you act in a stressful situation? Are you courteous and well-mannered? Do you smile? Are you generally in a good mood? How do you react to people? Can you visit with people you have never met? The way you feel about other people and the way you treat other people are important parts of your personality.

Assessing your personality is very important when exploring a selling career. Know your personality strengths and weaknesses. Be honest with yourself. What jobs are you best suited for? Would you rather work with people or work with things? If your personality does not fit the job, chances are you will be unhappy in that job.

Your Work Experience

What work experience have you had that qualifies you for a sales job? Work experience includes paid jobs and voluntary activities. Employers are interested in knowing that you have worked, regardless of whether you were paid. Even if a job you have had seems entirely unrelated to the job you are applying for, the employer will be interested. Many job activities can be related to other positions. Working with people, being responsible, and establishing good work habits are all characteristics employers are looking for. By taking a personal inventory of your activities, accomplishments, and work experience, you will be better able to sell yourself to an employer.

Because students may be applying for their first job, employers are interested in their in-school as well as out-of-school activities. Does your involvement show that you have initiative, leadership potential, ability to organize, a willingness to follow orders, an interest in details, and the ability to work with people? Your achievements in and out of school can demonstrate that you have sufficient ability and interest to perform the responsibilities involved in the work you select. Your school courses; your extracurricular school activities, clubs, and organizations; your community involvement; and your willingness and ability to learn the job are of great interest to employers.

WHERE TO FIND A JOB

After you have decided what kind of sales job you want and what you have to offer, you are ready to find that job. The key to getting a sales job is locating job openings. Most employers do not have to search for workers to apply for job openings, especially beginners. It is up to you to find the job opportunity. However, you will save a lot of time and have a better chance of obtaining a sales job if you plan your job search. Before you start, know what types of jobs interest you most; then compile a list of job sources. Here are some of the more common types of sources for job leads:

1. *Friends and Relatives.* Friends and relatives are probably the best source for job leads. An employer is more likely to interview you if you have a personal referral for a job.
2. *School Placement Services.* Talk to your school guidance counselor. Some schools offer placement services.
3. *Employment Agencies.* Job seekers can go to employment agencies to find job listings. Employment agencies are either public or private. Public agencies do not charge a fee for their placement services. Private agencies are businesses that charge a fee for helping you secure a job.
4. *Newspaper Advertisements.* The classified section of the newspaper will list job openings for full- and part-time jobs. The newspaper also reports on new and expanding businesses in the community that may be hiring additional employees.
5. *Telephone Directory.* Different types of businesses are listed in the Yellow Pages of the telephone directory. Skim through the Yellow Pages to get an idea of the types of businesses to which you may apply.
6. *Direct Application.* You may want to start with a door-to-door canvas of businesses and eventually hope to find a job. This is probably the poorest method because the employer knows that you are just looking for any job available.
7. *Other Sources.* Other sources of information about jobs include unions, trade associations, the chamber of commerce, public libraries, and specialty magazines.

ILLUSTRATION 21-1
The classified section of the newspaper is a good source for job leads.

PREPARING YOUR RESUME

After you have completed your personal inventory, you should prepare a **resume**. This personal data summary is an outline of factual information about you. It includes personal information, education, work experience, references, and other information. A resume is not always required for a sales job. However, your resume will be an organized source for the facts, dates, and other information you need to give a prospective employer.

Write your resume yourself. It will help you to organize the material you need for an interview or application form. Leave a copy of your resume with the interviewer or enclose it in a letter of application. Remember, you are selling yourself.

Your resume should be typed. If you need more than one copy, have it duplicated. The number of copies you make depends upon the type of sales job you will be seeking and the number of businesses at which you will be applying. Never give a carbon copy to an employer. This tells the employer that you are looking for just any job.

The resume should be typed without error. Organization and details do make a difference. If your resume is sloppy and poorly written, the employer will think that you don't really care about the sales position and that you are a careless and sloppy person. First impressions are important.

In a resume, give the employer all the personal information that you feel is important to the job. While employers cannot require certain types of information (a picture, for example), you may voluntarily include one with your resume.

There is no one standarized form of resume. Your resume simply needs to be well-written, organized, and error-free. It is best done in outline form. This makes it more concise and easier to read. Illustration 21-2 a and b are samples of well-written resumes.

Personal Information

Begin with your name, address, telephone number, and social security number. Include your area code when giving your telephone number. Always use ZIP Codes when giving addresses in the resume.

You may want to include other personal information such as your age, date of birth, marital status, height, weight, health, and so forth. If you include this information, it is better to place it after the more important facts, such as your education, activities, and work experience.

ILLUSTRATION 21-2a
A well-written, organized, error-free resume will give prospective employers a
good first impression of you.

PERSONAL DATA

NAME	John D. Busemeyer
ADDRESS	1301 First Street Webster City, IA 50595-4063
TELEPHONE	(515) 832-3057
SOCIAL SECURITY	478-58-0875
EDUCATION	To be graduated from Webster City High School, Webster City, IA 50595-4076, on May 20, 19--.

Business courses studied include:

    selling
    advertising
    business law
    typewriting

ORGANIZATIONS	basketball team, captain, 19-- band, 19-- to present art club, 19-- to 19--
WORK EXPERIENCE	Jack's Clothing Store: Webster City, IA 50595-4055, June, 19-- to present. Sales- person, some window and interior displays, housekeeping duties.

Feldman Business Machines: Cedar Falls, IA
50613-4264, May, 19-- to June, 19--. Courtesy
help, cash register operation, stockkeeping.

INTERESTS	golf, reading
PERSONAL INFORMATION	Age: 18 Date of Birth: July 7, 19-- Height: 6'2" Health: Excellent
REFERENCES	(by permission)

Mr. Charles Shore, President, Vick's Oil
Company, Waterloo, IA 50501-4087.

Dr. Rebecca S. Jones, medical doctor, Webster
City, IA 50595-4042

Mr. Doug Osbourne, salesperson, Modern Farm
Systems, Webster City, IA 50595-4066.

ILLUSTRATION 21-2b
A resume is best done in outline form; it is more concise and easier to read.

```
                       LINDA JOHNSON
                    468 South First Street
                 Webster City, IA  50595-4082


PERSONAL INFORMATION:

     Telephone:        (515) 832-2232
     Social Security:  584-68-1274
     Date of Birth:    September 5, 19--

EDUCATION:

     To be graduated from Webster City High School, 1001 Lynx
     Avenue, Webster City, IA  50595-4076, on May 18, 19--.

     Business Courses Studied:

     Selling
     Business Management
     Advertising
     Retailing
     Distributive Education

ORGANIZATIONS:

     Art Club, 19-- to 19--
     Basketball Team, 19-- to 19--
     Debate Team, 19-- to 19--

WORK EXPERIENCE:

     Hy Vee Food Store, 3117 Beach Street, Webster City, IA
     50595-4032, October, 19-- to present, Mr. Robert Zellweger,
     manager.  Checker-cashier, ordered candy, and general house-
     keeping duties.

REFERENCES:  (by permission)

     Ms. Gloria Thomas
     Employee, Hy Vee Food Store
     3186 Madison Road
     Webster City, IA  50595-4044
     (515) 832-5551

     Mr. Juan Garcia
     9834 South Street
     Webster City, IA  50595-4062
     (515) 832-8907

     Mr. Cliff McNally
     51 Parkshore Drive
     Webster City, IA  50595-4054
     (515) 832-5937
```

Education

If you are still in school, write: "To be graduated from . . . ." After you have graduated, you should write: "Graduated from . . . ." When listing your education, give the name and address of the school, and the date you graduated. If you graduated from a technical school or college, include the degree you received. If you have taken courses that relate to the position for which you are applying, include them.

Special Information

There are several categories of special information you may include, such as awards, hobbies, school activities, interests, organizations, and others. You may also wish to combine some of these areas into one category, for example, "Hobbies and Other Interests." List at least two items under each category. Be specific. Rather than writing "sports" under the category of "interests," write your specific interest, such as "basketball" or "swimming."

Work Experience

In listing your work experience, begin with your present job. Again, be specific. A statement such as "worked in a clothing store" does not give enough information. Write the name and address of the business, the dates you worked there, and your major duties. You may also want to include your employer's name, address, and telephone number.

Remember, work experience is not limited to paid jobs. Include experiences that were voluntary and those experiences in which you have worked with people; for example, "School Newspaper, Webster City High School, Webster City, Iowa 50595-4083, 19-- to 19--. Photographer, Writer, Editor."

References

The last category of your resume is a listing of your references. Include at least three people who know you well enough to recommend you.

Contact your references before you include their names on your resume. This is the reason "by permission" is given after the title on the resume. Employers will then know that the people listed on your resume have agreed to give you a reference.

LETTER OF APPLICATION

Writing a **letter of application** is the customary way to ask a business for a personal interview, although direct personal applications or telephone inquiries are acceptable in some cases. The basic purpose of any letter of application is to obtain an interview, not a job. The letter you use to sell yourself to an employer is a sales letter. It should sell an employer on the fact that you have the qualifications necessary to fill the sales job. An employer reads your letter and resume to decide whether or not to grant you an interview. If your letter is poorly written and does not stand out from other letters, the employer will probably not give you an interview.

Plan your letter carefully. It must be well-written, without spelling, punctuation, vocabulary, or typing errors. It should be typed in a proper business-letter style on quality, letter-size paper. Limit your letter to one page.

A letter of application should have three sections. The first section indicates the exact purpose of the letter. It should state the position for which you are applying and how you learned of the vacancy. This section should attract the interest of the employer. Carefully word what you want to say. Don't say, "I saw your ad in last night's paper for a salesperson. I think I can handle the job." Instead, say, "I am interested in the position of salesperson as advertised in the *Des Moines Register* on March 18. Please consider me to be an applicant for this position." If the beginning of the letter is poorly written, chances are the employer will not finish reading your letter. Remember, as the employer reads your letter, you are being evaluated.

The second section of your letter should state your qualifications for the job. Depending upon your qualifications, you may need to write two or three paragraphs. In this section, describe your education and work experience that make you qualified for this position. Even though this information is on your resume, this will give you an opportunity to further explain your qualifications. Use short paragraphs. Group your ideas together in a logical manner.

The third section should request an interview. It need only be a few sentences. Make it sound like you expect a reply. Tell how and when the employer may reach you. After reading your letter, the employer may want to contact you immediately. Make this as convenient as possible by including your telephone number.

Illustration 21-3 is a **letter of inquiry.** It is not written in reply to a specific job vacancy. Rather, it is written to inform an employer that you wish to be employed in a position in the business. This

ILLUSTRATION 21-3
A letter of inquiry informs an employer of the applicant's desire to work for
the firm in a certain position.

2514 North Main Street
Webster City, IA 50595-4036
June 15, 19--

Mrs. Charlene Bailey
Personnel Director
B. R. Fisher Company
2150 Ridge Avenue
Webster City, IA 50595-4082

Dear Mrs. Bailey:

As a high school graduate interested in retailing, I am writing
to you regarding the possibility of my being employed at the B. R.
Fisher Company.

For the past six months I have worked as a salesperson after
school and on Saturdays at the Star Sales Company, 1561 Brown
Street, Webster City, IA 50595-4022. During July and August of
last year, I worked in the receiving room of William Stewart &
Sons, 6220 Frankford Avenue, Webster City, IA 50595-4034. In these
positions I learned modern procedures for handling incoming ship-
ments and a great deal about merchandise and how to sell. I was
especially successful in selling house furnishings and toys.

During the past year, as part of my work in retailing at
Webster City High School, I made a study of merchandising methods
in department stores. My courses in English and art in high school
have also helped my work in retailing.

I would appreciate the opportunity to talk with you. My
telephone number is (515) 832-2222.

Sincerely,

Rachel Bishop

Rachel Bishop

Enclosure

---

letter is written in a modified block style. Notice how the writer's return address, the complimentary close, and the signature line begin at the horizontal midpoint of the paper.

Illustration 21-4 is a specific letter of application. It is written in reply to a specific sales job opening. Notice that both letters have the word "Enclosure" typed at the bottom. The word **enclosure** means that something is enclosed with the letter of application. In this example, the job applicant has enclosed a resume.

Address your letter to a specific person if possible. This will make your letter more personal and easier to write. If no name is given in a job advertisement, you may want to call the company and ask to whom a letter of application should be addressed. If it is not possible to obtain a name for the letter, you may want to omit the greeting and use a subject line. For example, rather than typing "Dear Sir or Madam," or "Ladies and Gentlemen," you could type "Letter of Application" in capital letters.

After you have typed an error-free letter of application, you will need to fold the letter properly and place it in a typed envelope. You have spent a great deal of time and care in typing your letter. The same care should be taken when typing the envelope and folding the letter. Always use a number ten, business-size envelope. See Illustration 21-5 for directions on addressing envelopes and folding letters.

THE APPLICATION FORM

The **application form** is similar to a resume. It gives employers the information they need to evaluate each applicant. The application form is a summary of information written by the job applicant on a form provided by the employer. Most job applicants are required to complete an application form before they have an interview. When applying for a job by letter, you may receive the application form by mail with a request that it be filled out and returned. However, many job applicants are given the application form when they come in for an interview.

Filling out your application form is just as important as writing your resume and letter of application. Read the application form completely. Never leave a blank space empty. If the question does not apply, write "does not apply," "none," or another appropriate response. Even if you draw a line across the blank, the employer will know you have read the question. This will show that you did not omit an answer and that you are not hiding any information. If in doubt about anything on the form, ask about it.

4208 Vernon Avenue
Webster City, IA 50595-4057
May 18, 19--

Mr. Frederick M. Monroe
J. C. Penney Company
Crossroads Shopping Center
Fort Dodge, IA 50501-4535

Dear Mr. Monroe:

I am interested in the position of salesperson as advertised in the Fort Dodge Messenger on Friday, May 17. Because of my background in selling and the successful completion of my high school salesmanship course, I feel that I would be qualified for this sales position.

I am presently a junior at Webster City High School. My major subjects in school are salesmanship, retailing, and business law, and next year I will be enrolled in business management and the distributive education program. In addition to my regular school work, I served on the student council for two years and was vice-president my sophomore year. I am a member of the school jazz band, art club, and drama club.

For the past two summers and on Saturdays during the past school year, I have worked as a cashier at the Colonial Store, 1908 First Street, Webster City, IA 50595-4058. This type of work experience has been valuable in developing my ability to serve customers.

I hope to secure an interview for the position that you have available. My telephone number is (515) 832-2222.

Sincerely,

Ann Neal

(Miss) Ann Neal

Enclosure

ILLUSTRATION 21-5
Take time to properly fold the letter and type the envelope.

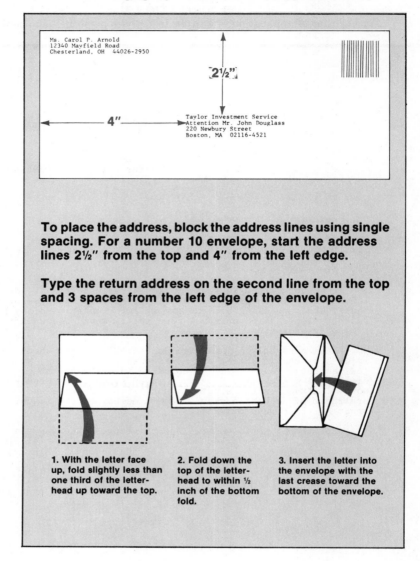

To place the address, block the address lines using single spacing. For a number 10 envelope, start the address lines 2½" from the top and 4" from the left edge.

Type the return address on the second line from the top and 3 spaces from the left edge of the envelope.

1. With the letter face up, fold slightly less than one third of the letterhead up toward the top.

2. Fold down the top of the letterhead to within ½ inch of the bottom fold.

3. Insert the letter into the envelope with the last crease toward the bottom of the envelope.

Fill out the application form neatly. If you make a mistake and cannot erase it neatly, ask for another application form. Never cross out mistakes. Use your best handwriting or print neatly. If possible, type the application. Always have a pen and pencil with an eraser in case the employer wants the form written in pen or pencil.

Answer all questions accurately and honestly. All the information you give in the application form should correspond with the information in your resume. Have a copy of your resume with you when you fill out the application form. Be sure to spell names and addresses correctly. Your resume will also give you the correct dates, telephone numbers, and other information you will need.

Concentrate when completing an application form. Fill it out slowly and carefully so it will be complete, accurate, and neat. Reread your application form. When you are sure it is filled out properly, return it to the employer. Illustration 21-6 on page 418 is a sample application form.

YOUR APPOINTMENT

You have requested an interview. If the employer calls you to make an appointment, be sure to write down the information given about the interview. Repeat it to the employer so you are sure it is correct. Know where and at what time you are to have the interview. If possible, learn the name of the person who will interview you. If you received a letter in reply to your letter of application, the letter should clearly give you this information. If you have any questions, call the employer and ask for additional information, but don't wait until the day of the interview.

Before you go to the interview, review the information you have on your resume. This preparation enables you to answer questions quickly and accurately. Also, find out all you can about the business firm which will be interviewing you. This enables you to ask intelligent questions. It also shows the interviewer that you are interested in that particular firm.

Dress appropriately for the interview. Your personal appearance will reflect your personality. Look your best. Be conservative in style and color. The interviewer should focus attention on you, not on your clothes.

Be on time for your appointment. Know where you are going and how long it will take to get there. Give yourself plenty of time. Start early for the appointment and go alone. Don't take a friend or relative with you. If someone drives you to the interview, arrange to meet later. Never be late for the appointment. A late start is a poor start. If for some reason you have a problem keeping the appointment, call the employer before the time of your appointment. Explain the reason for not being able to keep the appointment, apologize for any inconvenience, and request another appointment, although you may not get one.

If you are making a direct application in person where an appointment is not necessary, introduce yourself to the employer and

ILLUSTRATION 21-6
The information you give on the application form should correspond with the information on your resume.

APPLICATION FOR EMPLOYMENT

We are an equal opportunity employer, dedicated to a policy of non-discrimination in employment on any basis including race, creed, color, age, sex, religion or national origin.

PERSONAL INFORMATION

Date _____   Social Security Number _____

Name _____
Last _____ First _____ Middle _____

Present Address _____
Street _____ City _____ State _____ Zip _____

Permanent Address _____
Street _____ City _____ State _____ Zip _____

Phone No. _____

EMPLOYMENT DESIRED

Position _____   Date You Can Start _____   Salary Desired _____

EDUCATION

	Name and Location of School	Circle Last Year Completed	Did You Graduate?	Subjects of Special Study
Grammar School			☐ Yes ☐ No	
High School		1 2 3 4	☐ Yes ☐ No	
College		1 2 3 4	☐ Yes ☐ No	
Trade, Business or Correspondence School		1 2 3 4	☐ Yes ☐ No	

What Foreign Languages Do You Speak Fluently? _____

Activities Other Than Religious (Civic, Athletic, etc.) _____
EXCLUDE ORGANIZATIONS, THE NAME OR CHARACTER OF WHICH INDICATES THE RACE, CREED, COLOR OR NATIONAL ORIGIN OF ITS MEMBERS.

FORMER EMPLOYERS List Below Last Three Employers, Starting With Last One First

Date Month and Year	Name and Location of Employer	Salary	Position	Reason for Leaving
From To				
From To				
From To				

REFERENCES Give Below the Names of Three Persons Not Related To You, Whom You Have Known At Least One Year.

	Name	Address	Business	Years Acquainted
1				
2				
3				

In Case of Emergency Notify _____
Name _____ Address _____ Phone No. _____

I authorize investigation of all statements contained in this application. I understand that misrepresentation or omission of facts called for is cause for dismissal. Further, I understand and agree that my employment is for no definite period and may, regardless of the date of payment of my wages and salary, be terminated at any time without any previous notice.

Date _____   Signature _____

ILLUSTRATION 21-7
Dress appropriately for the interview.

ask if this would be a good time for you to apply for a job. If the employer is busy, request an appointment at the employer's convenience.

As you walk in, try to be relaxed and confident, but not overconfident. Smile! Remember, the impression you give the person who receives you is very important. If you are greeted by a receptionist, give your name, the time of your appointment, and the person whom you are to see. For example, "Good morning. My name is Chris Olson. I have an appointment for a job interview at 10 o'clock with Mr. Don Perry." You will probably be asked to wait until the interviewer is free. If you have not filled out an application form, ask the receptionist if you are to do so.

Don't bother the receptionist with general conversation. Instead, think about what you want to say to the interviewer. Don't chew gum, smoke, comb your hair, or slouch in your chair. Maintain your best composure while you wait. Your actions are likely to be observed and possibly reported to the interviewer as part of your evaluation.

If you have been unable to obtain the name of the person who will interview you, ask the receptionist. Know how to pronounce the interviewer's name correctly so you can use it during the interview. Also, if possible, leave your coat in the receptionist's office. You should never have any packages with you. You don't want to give the impression that the main purpose of this trip was to go shopping.

THE INTERVIEW

The purposes of an **interview** are for the interviewer to get information from you, for you to get information from the interviewer, and for each of you to form an opinion — the interviewer to form an opinion about you and you to form an opinion about the job. You are prepared for this interview. You are ready to sell yourself. Your attitude should be: "Here's what I have to offer this company!" Remember, the interviewer is employed to hire people, not to turn them away.

Smile as you greet the interviewer. Use the interviewer's name: "Hello, Miss Abel. I'm Kelly Peterson." If the hand of the interviewer is extended, shake hands firmly. Remain standing until you are told where to sit, and then sit with your body facing the interviewer. This will get you off to a good start.

What do you say after you have said hello? Let the interviewer take the lead. The interviewer will ask most of the questions and you will provide most of the answers. When answering questions, be specific and to the point. Think before you talk. Don't ramble, but don't answer with a simple yes or no. Have a conversation, not a question-and-answer session with the interviewer.

Be honest and sincere when answering questions. Give the interviewer your attention by looking into the interviewer's eyes. Don't look around the room, on the interviewer's desk, or at the floor. Speak distinctly using good English and don't mumble. Don't interrupt or argue with the interviewer. Don't beg for a job. Avoid

ILLUSTRATION 21-8
Give the interviewer your attention by looking into the interviewer's eyes.

talking about personal problems or criticizing past employers. Remember, you want to stress your qualifications, not your problems. If the interviewer tells you that you would be working with people, for example, emphasize any work experience or courses you have had that would help to qualify you. Listen carefully to the interviewer's questions in order to understand what is being asked of you. If you are not sure you understand a question or you don't know the answer, don't try to bluff an answer.

Some Typical Questions Asked in an Interview Are. . . .

- tell me about yourself.
- describe your education.
- how does your experience fit the requirements for this job?
- in what type of school activities did you participate?
- why do you think you might like to work for our company?
- describe your work experience.
- what do you know about our company?
- how was your attendance in school and on other jobs?
- what would you look for in a good employee?
- how do you feel about performance evaluation of your work?
- why are you leaving your present job?
- how would you handle this situation? (Interviewer gives an example of a sales situation.)
- career-wise, where would you like to be in five years?
- this position requires a few nights and some weekend work. Will this be a problem?
- if selected, how much time will you need to give notice to your present employer?

It is permissible to ask questions of the interviewer. In fact, questions will show that you are interested in learning about the job. You may want to know more about the position, job responsibilities, and the company. Don't be afraid to ask what you need to know. If an employer offers you a job, be sure you understand exactly what will be expected of you and the salary you will earn. If salary has not been mentioned, ask what the beginning salary would be for the position. Avoid giving the impression that you are interested only in the pay.

Watch for clues on how you are doing during the interview. Is the interviewer relaxed? alert? interested? following you? encouraging you with nods, smiles, and comments? Size up the interviewer. If the interviewer seems puzzled by a comment, say, "Have I covered that point adequately?" or "Let me state it a different way." While the interviewer is watching you, you should be watching the interviewer. You have approximately 15 to 30 minutes to talk with someone who has the power to decide whether or not to hire you for a particular job. Analyze the interview as you are sitting there. This will help you realize if you are selling yourself well.

The interviewer will indicate when the interview is over. At this point, don't start an idle conversation. Instead, you should stand and thank the interviewer for the opportunity to talk about the job. Don't say, "Thank you for your time." The interviewer's time is your time. You were not an interruption of the interviewer's work. One purpose of the interviewer's job is to interview and hire people.

If you are not offered the job, ask if you can check back soon. You can usually tell from the way the interviewer responds to this question whether you have a chance for this job or any other job with the company. Don't show disappointment if you are not offered the job at the end of the interview. The employer may want to check references or interview other applicants. If the employer asks you to call back, make a written note of the time, place, date, telephone number, and whom to call. Then leave promptly. Many job applicants lose jobs because they do not leave promptly. The interviewer has other applicants to interview or other business to complete. Don't cause a delay in the interviewer's schedule.

AFTER THE INTERVIEW

Now is the time to analyze the company, the position, and the salary, and to decide if you want the position. Give it careful thought. You must decide if you want to be employed with the company just as the company must decide if they want to hire you. This is an important decision.

After you have carefully considered the job, write a thank-you letter to the interviewer (see Illustration 21-9) or phone the interviewer if you were told to do so. Express your feelings about the job. You can either express continued interest in the job if it has not been offered to you, or let the person know you are no longer interested and you want to withdraw your application. Remember, you don't have to accept the first job you are offered.

ILLUSTRATION 21-9
After you have carefully considered the job, write a thank-you letter
to the interviewer.

1308 Second Street
Webster City, IA 50595-4066
April 6, 19--

Mrs. Jane Fowler
Personnel Director
A. C. Hart Company
Webster City, IA 50595-4032

Dear Mrs. Fowler:

    Thank you for the opportunity to talk with you about the
salesperson's position available in your shoe department.

    After discussing this job with you, I am interested in your
company and in the salesperson's position. I feel that my retailing and selling courses along with my part-time work experience
at the B. L. Black Company have prepared me for this job.

    If you need any additional information, I can be reached at
the above address or by telephone (515) 832-2224. I hope to hear
from you soon.

        Sincerely,

        Dan Fort

        Dan Fort

Do's and Dont's for Job Seekers

Do...

- stress your qualifications and abilities for the job opening.
- give experiences you have had which would qualify you for the job.
- indicate your stability, good attendance record, and good safety record.
- use proper English. Speak enthusiastically and distinctly.
- try to learn about the company and its products and services before the interview.
- address the interviewer by name.
- approach the employer with respect and courtesy.
- be optimistic in your attitude.
- be courteous to receptionists.
- use good posture.
- be polite and sincere.
- apply for a specific job.
- answer questions honestly and straightforwardly.
- apply for the job in person and alone.
- have available a list of former employers, periods of employment, wages, nature of work, and reasons for leaving.
- be well-groomed and appropriately dressed.
- smile.

Don't...

- keep stressing your need for a job.
- discuss past experiences which have no application to the job situation.
- chew gum or smoke during the job interview.
- apologize for your age.
- lean over or sit on the corner of the interviewer's desk.
- display a feeling of inferiority.
- attempt to read or pick up any personal papers on the interviewer's desk.
- speak with a muffled voice.
- criticize former employers.
- hedge or lie in answering any questions.
- ask the employer about salary early in the interview.
- take a newspaper or packages with you to the interview.
- discuss your personal or financial problems.
- arrive late for the interview.
- be a "know-it-all" or a person who can't take instructions.
- argue with an interviewer.
- yawn or slouch in your chair while being interviewed.
- become discouraged in your search for a sales job.

If you do not receive a letter or telephone call within approximately five days after the interview and you are still interested in the job, call the employer. Ask if the position for which you applied has been filled or if you are still being considered. Tell the employer you are interested in the job. The follow-up after the interview is important. The interviewer may be waiting to see if you are interested enough in the job to call or write. A follow-up call or letter is a courtesy that may win you the job you want.

If you fail to get the sales job, don't become discouraged. Keep looking. The next job for which you apply may be perfect for someone with your qualifications. Don't feel that just because you were turned down, you have nothing to offer. Employers are always looking for job seekers who have the necessary qualifications for a job. Maybe the first interview didn't go well. You may have been too nervous and afraid to speak up. Maybe you lacked confidence.

Don't give up. The key to a successful interview is preparation, organization, and planning. Review the do's and don'ts for job seekers. Practice answering typical questions. Be prepared and ready for your next job interview. Believe in yourself.

YOUR JOB

The way you start your new sales job can mean future success or failure. Accept your responsibilities from the beginning. Report to work on time. Be loyal to your employer and co-workers. Be helpful to others. Be willing to do more than you are asked to do. Show initiative by anticipating things to be done without waiting to be told. Ask questions, listen, and remember the answers. Be observant. Try to learn quickly.

Give your best to your job. You will improve your chances for advancement and continuous employment. If your job is right for you, it can be an enjoyable, rewarding experience which could lead to a lifetime career.

SALES TERMS

resume	letter of inquiry	application form
letter of application	enclosure	interview

SALES QUESTIONS

1. Why is your first job important?

2. What information should you include in your personal inventory?

3. What four factors contribute to your personality?

4. When selecting the appropriate clothing for an interview, what rule should you follow?

5. When reviewing the work experience of job applicants, what do employers look for?

6. What sources can you use to obtain a job?

7. What general topics are frequently included in a resume?

8. Why should a resume and letter of application by typed and error-free?

9. Before including the names of references in your resume, why should you contact these people?

10. What is the purpose of a letter of application?

11. What information should you include in each of the three sections of a letter of application?

12. What is the difference between a letter of inquiry and a letter of application?

13. Explain the meaning of the word *enclosure* at the bottom of a letter.

14. How can you obtain the name of the person to whom a letter of application should be addressed?

15. Give several suggestions on how to complete an application form.

16. After the employer has called to arrange an interview, what information should you know about the scheduled interview?

17. Give several suggestions on how to prepare for a successful job interview.

18. While waiting to see the interviewer, what should you do? What should you not do?

19. What are the purposes of the interview?

20. Give several questions job applicants might ask an interviewer.

21. List several important do's and don'ts for a job interview.

22. As soon as the interview is over, what should you do?

23. How should you follow-up with the employer after the interview is over?

24. Explain this statement and give examples: "The way you start your new sales job can mean success or failure."

SALES ACTIVITIES

A. Interview a new teacher in your school. Ask this teacher to explain how the interview for the teaching job was conducted, the types of questions asked, the preparation necessary for the interview, and any general suggestions for having a successful job interview. Write a report on your interview and then turn it in to your instructor.

B. Prepare a resume similar to the two samples on pages 409 and 410. Include all the necessary information about yourself on the resume, and then type it and turn it in to your instructor.

C. Visit the guidance office in your school. What information do they have on sales careers and preparing for job interviews?

D. Write a letter of application for a sales position. You may select the type of business and the job interviewer's name. This letter should be typed and error-free.

INDEX

A

Acceptance, as a buyer benefit, 150
Action: defined, 37; stage in the buying process, 37-40
Addition method of counting change, 305-306; defined, 305
Adjectives, expressive: for use in telephone sales, 356
Advantages-and-disadvantages close, 219-220; defined, 219
Advertising: as an influence on customers, 54; store, as a source of merchandise information, 346
Aetna Life & Casualty, 398
Affection and love, as a buying motive, 73
Agents: insurance brokers and, 398; real estate brokers and, 398-399
Amateur shoplifters, 315
Ambition, 18
Amount keys: defined, 293; as part of the cash register keyboard, 293-294
Amount-received keys: change-due and, as part of the cash register keyboard, 296; defined, 296
Amount-tendered key. *See* Amount-received key
Appearance: as a buyer benefit, 150; personal, as part of sales personality, 372-373
Appearance of products, as product information, 93
Application, letter of, 412-414; illustration of, 415

Application form, 414, 416-417; defined, 414; illustration of, 418
Appointment for an interview, 417, 419
Approach(es), 107-116; defined, 41; evaluating the salesperson's, 376, 380; example of an, 168; features of a good, 109; focus, on the customer, 109-112; importance of, 108; the merchandise, 113-114; select the appropriate, 112; the service, 115-116; as step of a sale, 41-42; types of customer, 112-116; the welcome, 114
Ask-your-customers-to-buy close, 215-216; defined, 216
Assortment of merchandise, as patronage buying motive, 83
Assumed close, 367
Assume-they-are-buying close, 218-219; defined, 218
Attention: defined, 32; stage in the buying process, 32-34
Attitude, service: as part of sales personality, 373-374
Autographic window, 297

B

Benefits. *See* Buyer benefits
Benefits of product or service knowledge to salespeople: earn a promotion, 90-91; enjoy job more, 88; gain confidence, 88-89; organize sales presentation, 89-90; overcome sales resistance, 90
Ben Franklin Stores, 389

Bloomingdale's, 389
Boomerang method of answering customer objections, 198
Boss, customer as, 52-53
Brand of products, as product information, 96
Brokers: insurance agents and, 398; real estate agents and, 398-399
Building displays, five rules to follow when, 342-344
Bullock's, 389
Bunch sales, 299
Business(es): bread and butter of, 4; customer-oriented, 9; eleven commandments of good, 9; repeat customers needed by, 4; retail, 385-391 (*see also* Retail business); selling skills in, 4; telephone use in, 354; types that employ salespeople, 385-399; *U* comes before *I* in, 46
Buyer benefits: chart of product features, performance, and, 155; common types of, 150; defined, 5; demonstration of, 175-176; formula for translating product features and performance into, 156; illustration of gain to customers from owning the product through, 157; translating product features into, 153-161; what is a, 150-153
Buying change, 301
Buying decision(s): customer, 63-65; five, 189; helping the customer make an easy, 208-212; helping the customer make a wise, 5; illustration of selling techniques and mental stages of, 40; techniques for helping the customer make an easy, 212
Buying decision objections, customer. *See* Customer buying decisions
Buying motives, 68-69, 145; classifications of, 75-84; common, 74 (*see also* Common buying motives); customer, 67-84; defined, 69; emotional, 79-81, 356; patronage, 82-84 (*see also* Patronage buying motives); primary, 76; product, 81-82; rational, 78-79, 356; selective, 76-78; use of, in preplanning sales call, 356; using, to sell, 84
Buying process, customers', 32-40; illustration of five mental stages in the, 33
Buying and selling process, 30-47; illustration of, 31
Buying signals, 212-213, 214; defined, 137; recognizing customer, 137-140

C

Camera: example of trading up and, 240-243; feature-benefit chart of, 160

Canned sales talk, 357
Care of products, as product information, 96
Cash: handling new bills, 303; over, in balancing the cash drawer, 308; proving, or cashing out, 308; short, in balancing the cash drawer, 308
Cash drawer: balancing the, 308-309; as cash register feature, 298-299; defined, 298
Cashiers, 289
Cashing out or proving cash, 308
Cash on delivery. *See* COD sale
Cash refund: defined, 279; handling a, as type of return transaction, 279-280; illustration of a, transaction, 280
Cash register: defined, 290; functions of, 290-292; illustration of key arrangements on the, 293; the salesperson's routine for the, 299-301; salespeople should know their, 292-299; types of, 290-292
Cash register features: autographic window, 297; cash drawer, 298-299; change plate, 299; date-setting mechanism, 299; detailed audit tape, 297; indication window, 296-297; motor bar, 297-298; receipt-tape slot and receipt printer, 297
Cash register keyboard: amount keys, 293-294; amount-received and change-due keys, 296; correction key, 295-296; department or classification keys, 294-295; no-sale key, 295; salesperson's identification keys, 294; subtotal, sales-tax, and total keys, 296; transaction keys, 295
Cash register operation, handling money and, 289-309
Cash sale: defined, 263; illustration of a, 264; as a type of sales transaction, 263-265
Cash-send sales transaction, 263
Cash tray: defined, 298; illustration of a typical arrangement of the, 299
Cassette recorder, feature-benefit chart of, 159
Casual looker, 61
Change: addition method of counting, 305-306; general procedure for making, 304-305; making correct, 304-307; if the salesperson made incorrect, 307; subtraction method of counting, 306-307
Change bluffers: defined, 322; as money manipulators, 321-322; three options of handling, 322
Change-due keys of a cash register keyboard, 296

Change fund, 301-303; defined, 301; handling new bills in the, 303; procedure for, 302-303

Change-making procedures, follow correct, 326

Change plate as a cash register feature, 299

Charge accounts. *See* Charge sales

Charge cards, 265

Charge credit: defined, 280; handling a, as type of return transaction, 280-281; illustration of a, transaction, 281

Change form, illustration of, 268

Charge return, 280

Charge sales: defined, 265; illustration of, 267; as type of sales transaction, 265-268

Charge-send sales transaction, 265

Charge-take sales transaction, 265

Check(s), sales. *See* Sales forms

Checking: defined, 341; merchandise as sales-supporting duty, 341-342

Choice close, 217-218; defined, 217; in telephone sales, 366

Classification keys: of a cash register keyboard, 294-295

Clear key, as a correction key, 295-296

Clerks, 387

Close: advantages-and-disadvantages, 219-220; ask-your-customers-to-buy, 215-216; assumed, in telephone sales, 367; assume-they-are-buying, 218-219; choice, 217-218; choice, in telephone sales, 366; conditional, 225; credit, 225; defined, 43; delivery, 225; errors made in, 225-226; evaluating the salesperson's trial, 380; exclusive-line-of-merchandise, 225; failure in, 227-228; last-chance-to-buy, 221; narrative or testimonial, 222; natural, 207-208; objection, 222-223; premium, 220; price, 225; sale, 206-228; six reasons salespeople hesitate to ask customers to buy when making a, 210-211; standing-room-only, 221; success in making a, 227; suggest-related-merchandise, 223-224; summary, in telephone sales, 366-367; testimonial or narrative, 222; trial, 140, 214-215; trial order, 225; when salespeople should make a, 212-214

Closing the sale, 43-44, 179; evaluating the salesperson's ability in, 378, 379; in telephone sales presentation, 366-367

Closing the sale techniques: ask customers to buy, 210-211; be confident, 211; find out why some customers resist buying, 211; narrow the selection, 209-210; stop showing new merchandise, 209; talk about customer ownership, 210; use buying signals, 212-213, 214

Closing the sale techniques in telephone sales: assumed close, 367; choice close, 366; summary close, 366-367

Close-on-an-objection method: answering customer objections by the, 201-202; defined, 202

COD sale: defined, 268; illustration of a cash, 269; illustration of a charge-send, 270; as type of sales transaction, 268-271

Collect on Delivery. *See* COD sale

Comfort, as a buyer benefit, 150

Comfort and convenience, as buying motives, 71-72

Commandments of good business, eleven, 9

Common buying motives: comfort and convenience, 71-72; gain or economy, 69; health, 70-71; prestige and recognition, 73-74; safety and protection, 72-73; variety and recreation, 74-75. *See also* Buying motives

Commission, 390

Competition of products, as product information, 97

Competitive shopping trip, 344

Complaints: handling customer, as sales-supporting duty, 348-349; techniques for handling customer, 348

Computer register, as an electronic cash register, 344

Computer terminals, as cash registers, 290

Conditional close, 225

Confidence: as a benefit salespeople gain from product or service knowledge, 88-89; as part of sales personality, 374; salespeople having, to make the buying decision easier, 211

Consideration: defined, 19; as a personality trait, 18

Consumer Product Safety Commission, 72

Consumer Reports, 345

Consumers, 6

Consumption, 6

Control, sales, 110; take, during the approach, 110-111

Convenience, as a buyer benefit, 150

Convenience and comfort, as buying motives, 71-72

Conversation, 128

Conviction: defined, 36; stage in the buying process, 36-37

Cooperation, 18

Correction key: defined, 295; as part of cash register keyboard, 295-296

Counterfeiting, 327-330; defined, 327

Counterfeit money, what to look for: border, 328; discrepancies when comparing bills, 329-330; paper, 329; portrait, 327-328; seal, 328; serial numbers, 328

Counting change: addition method of, 305-306; subtraction method of, 306-307

Counting-forward method of counting change, 305-306

Courtesy: defined, 19; as a personality trait, 18

Credit: handling a charge, as a type of return transaction, 280-281; illustration of a charge, transaction, 281

Credit cards: defined, 265; illustration of a charge form for, 268

Credit close, 225

Credit limit, 266

Criticism, ability to accept, 26-27

Customer(s), 51-65; answer the objections of, 194-195; appeal to five senses of, in making a feature-benefit sales presentation, 172; asking, to buy, 210-211; ask the telephone, a qualifying question, 361; assisting the, 4-5; benefits of involving the, in making the feature-benefit sales demonstration, 170; as boss, 52-53; buyer benefits received by, 150-153; buying decision objections of the, 189-191; buying process, 32-40; as a casual looker, 61; check the understanding of, to qualify, 166-167; check for wandering mind of, in making a sales presentation, 167-170; decided, 58-59, 120-122; determining needs and wants of, 42, 119-140; determining what product features will do for, as a step of translating product features into buyer benefits, 153-161; determining what to say to, in making a feature-benefit sales presentation, 146-147; establish rapport with, in telephone sales presentation, 359-360; evaluating the salesperson's ability to qualify the, 377; finding out why some, resist buying, 211; five buying decisions made by, 189; focus the approach on the, 109-112; four rules to follow when suggestion selling to, 246; general procedures for answering objections from, 192-195; get the opinion of the, with qualifying questions, 166; handling objections of the, 181-202; helping, make a wise buying decision, 5; how salespeople make suggestions to, 246-247; how to sell to different types of, 120-125; illustration of buying and selling process between salesperson and, 31; involve the, in making the feature-benefit sales presentation, 170-179; just-looking, 60-62, 124-125; is king, 9; listen to objections from, 192-193; make the buying decision easy on, 208-212; making the feature-benefit sales presentation by qualifying the, 165-170; making a feature-benefit sales presentation for the, 163-179; meet your, 58-62; moods of the, 62-63; never returns to shop, 24; objections (See Objections); objections or excuses from the, 183-187; observe the, 126-128; pause before answering objections from, 193; planning a feature-benefit sales presentation for, 143-161; prepare to answer objections of, 187-189; qualify 125-134; reassuring, 247-248; recognizing buying signals of, 137-140; repeat, 8; select the item to show the, 134-137; as shoplifters, 314-315; show empathy for, 193; six reasons salespeople hesitate to ask, to buy, 210-211; as source of merchandise information, 346; as a source of product or service information, 100; talking about ownership to make the buying decision easier for, 210; techniques for answering objections from, 199-202; three types of, 121; translating product features into buyer benefits for, 153-161; treat your, like a friend, 53; types of, 58-62; types of merchandise to suggest to, 234-245; undecided, 60, 122-124; use the name of the, during the approach, 111-112; wants and needs of the, 57-58; watching for unusual behavior in, 316; ways salespeople can assist, 4; welcome objections of the, 182-183; what they buy, 145-146; what they expect from salespeople, 22-25; when to answer objections from, 191-192; why they buy, 69-75

Customer approaches: merchandise, 113-114; service, 115-116; welcome, 114

Customer buying decisions: place, 64, 189, 190; price, 65, 190; product, 64, 189; quantity, 65, 190-191; time, 65, 190

Customer buying motives, 67-84

Customer complaints: defined, 348; handling, as sales-supporting duty, 348-349; techniques in handling, 348

Customer empathy, 47

Customer influences: advertising, 54; displays, 54-55; merchandise available, 56-57; previous experience, 53-54; service, 55-56; store image, 53; store interior, 55

Customer moods, 62-63; how to respond to, 63

Customer objection(s): defined, 43; evaluating the salesperson's handling of, 378, 380; general procedure for answering, 192-195; handling, 43; techniques for answering, 195-202. *See also* Objection

Customer-oriented businesses, 9

Customer-oriented selling, 14

D

Daily balance form: defined, 308; illustration of, 309

Date-setting mechanism as a cash register feature, 299

Decided customers, 58-59, 120-122; defined, 58

Delivery, cash on or collect on. *See* COD sale

Delivery close, 225

Demonstration: defined, 200; evaluating the salesperson's ability in the sales, 379-380; feature-benefit sales, 175-178; product, 170; as rule of suggestion selling, 246

Demonstration of buyer benefits, 175-176

Demonstration method: answering customer objections by the, 200-201; defined, 200

Department or classification keys: defined, 294; as part of the cash register keyboard, 294-295

Department of Labor, 384

Department stores, 389

Dependability: defined, 19; as a personality trait, 18

Desire: defined, 35; stage in the buying process, 35-36

Detailed audit tape as cash register feature, 297

Determining customer needs and wants, 119-140; evaluating the salesperson's ability in, 376-377; as a step in the sales process, 42

Determining what to say, as a part of the feature-benefit sales presentation, 146-161

Direct-denial method of answering customer objections, 197

Discount, 274

Discount sale: defined, 274; illustration of, 275; as type of sales transaction, 274-275

Discount stores, 389-390; defined, 389

Dishonest co-workers, 335

Dishonest employees, 333-335

Displays: building, as sales-supporting duty, 342-344; building a successful, 342; five rules to follow when building, 342-344; as an influence on customers, 54-55

Display specialists, 342

Does, what each feature: as a step in translating product features into buyer benefits, 154

Do's and don'ts for job seekers, 424

Dramatization: defined, 173; use, to involve the customer in the feature-benefit sales presentation, 173-174

E

Economic activity, customers' needs and wants as basis of, 67-68

Economy or gain, as a buying motive, 69-70

Electronic cash registers, three stock control functions of, 344

Eleven commandments of good business, 9

Empathy, 47; customer, 47; defined, 19; as a personality trait, 18; reflective statements of, 193; show your customer, 193

Employees: dishonest, 333-335; number of sales, in the U.S. in 1985, 384; policies to discourage theft by, 334-335

Employers: loyalty to, 27; what they expect from salespeople, 25-27

Emotional buying motives, 79-81, 356; defined, 79

Enclosure, 414

Engineer, sales, 397

Enjoyment, as a buyer benefit, 150

Enthusiasm: defined, 19; as part of sales personality, 373; as a personality trait, 18

Envelope, illustration of how to fold letter and type, 416

Equitable Life Assurance Society, 398

Even cash, in change fund, 303

Even exchange: defined, 282; handling an, as type of return transaction, 281-283; illustration of an, transaction, 282

Exchange: handling an even, as type of return transaction, 281-283; handling an uneven, as type of return transaction, 283-285; illustration of an even, 282; illustration of a paid out or refund transaction as type of uneven, 285; illustration of an uneven, using one sales form, 284; illustration of an uneven, using two sales forms, 283

Exclusive-line-of-merchandise close, 225

Excuses: defined, 184; objections or, 183-187

Expressive adjectives, 356
External selling, 388

F

Feature(s): chart of performance, buyer benefits, and product, 155; chart of performance and product, 154; chart of product, 153; defined, 148; determining what the product, do for the customer as a step of translating product features into buyer benefits, 153-161; illustration of product, 149; listing the product, as a step of translating product features into buyer benefits, 153; product, 148; translating product, into buyer benefits, 153-161; what is a product, 148-149
Feature-benefit charts: camera, 160, cassette recorder, 159; girl's denim jeans, 156; quartz watch, 158; stereo receiver, 161
Feature-benefit sales demonstration, 177-178; appeal to the customer's senses to involve the customer in the, 172-173; benefits of involving the customer in the, 170; defined, 175; determine what to do in a, 164-165; involve the customer in the, 170-179
Feature-benefit sales presentation: check the customer's understanding with qualifying questions during the, 166; check for a wandering mind with qualifying questions when making a, 167-168; defined, 43; determine what to do in making a, 164-165; determine what to say in making a, 146-161; evaluating the salesperson's, 377, 380; example of an approach in the, 168; example of qualifying the customer in the, 168-170; get the opinion of the customer with qualifying questions during the, 166; give selling statements as qualifying questions during the, 167; handle the product properly to involve the customer in the, 174-175; illustration of seven steps in the, 41, 164; importance of the, 144-145; making a, 163-179; making a, as a step in the sales process, 42-43; outline of a, 147; planning a, 143-161; qualify the customer to begin the, 165-170; use selling aids to involve the customer in the, 175; use showmanship or dramatization to involve the customer in the, 173-174. *See also* Feature-benefit sales demonstration
Feature + performance = buyer benefit, 156
Five buying decisions, 189

Five senses, appealing to customers', in making a feature-benefit sales presentation, 172-173
Forceful words, 356
Forms, sales, *See* Sales forms
Formula for translating product features into buyer benefits, 156
F. W. Woolworth Co., 389

G

Gain or economy, as a buying motive, 69-70
General Electric, 395
General Mills, 395
Gift certificate: defined, 277; illustration of a, 278; as type of transaction, 277-278
Goods, industrial, 394
Gross sales, 233

H

Hair dryer: buyer benefit and buyer benefit statement for, 152; illustration of product features for, 149; product features and feature statement for, 148
Handwriting, importance of legible, on sales forms, 261
Health, as a buying motive, 70-71
Hearing, 172
Hidden objections, 184
Honesty: defined, 19; as part of sales personality, 374; as a personality trait, 18
How, as a qualifying question, 168
Human relations: defined, 25; importance of, in selling, 8-9; the salesperson and, 12-27
Humor, sense of: as personality trait, 21
Hustle routine used by shortchange artists, 324

I

IBM, 395
Identification keys, salesperson's: as part of the cash register keyboard, 294
Image, store: as an influence on customers, 53; as a patronage buying motive, 82
Indication window: as cash register feature, 296-297; defined, 296
Industrial goods, 394
Industrial wholesale salespeople, 394-395; defined, 394
Initiative: defined, 20; as a personality trait, 18

Inquiry, letter of, 412, 414; illustration of, 413

Inside salespeople, 391

Insurance agents and brokers, 398

Intangible items, 384

Intangible products, 10

Intangible services, 10

Interest, 34; stage in the buying process, 34-35

Interior display, 342

Internal selling, 388

Interview: after the, 422-425; defined, 420; job, 420-422; typical questions asked in an, 421

Inventory, taking: as sales-supporting duty, 347

Is, what each feature: as a step in translating product features into buyer benefits, 153

J

Jeans, feature-benefit chart for girl's denim, 156

Job: common sources for leads about, 407; how to get a selling, 403-425; how to succeed in a new, 425; salespeople need to look at themselves to prepare for a, 404-406; the salesperson's, 12-16; where to find a sales, 406-407

Job seekers, do's and don'ts for, 424

Jogging shoes: chart of product features for, 153; chart of product features and performance for, 154; chart of product features, performance, and buyer benefits for, 155

Just-looking customer, 60-62, 124-125; defined, 60

K

Kellogg, 395

Keyboard, cash register. *See* Cash register keyboard

King, customer is, 9

K-Mart, 390

Know-it-all, salesperson should not be a, 102-103

L

Last-chance-to-buy close, 221

Layaway sales: defined, 271; illustration of, 272; illustration of a payment made on a, 273; as type of sales transaction, 271-274

Lay-bys. *See* Layaway sales

Letter: illustration of thank-you, 423; illustration of how to fold, 416

Letter of application, 412-414; defined, 412; illustration of, 415

Letter of inquiry: defined, 412, 414; illustration of, 413

Listener, be a good, to qualify customers, 132-134

Love and affection, as a buying motive, 73

Loyal, 20

Loyalty, 20; to employer, 27; as a personality trait, 18

M

Macy's, 389

Management, illustration of career path salespeople can follow into, 388

Manipulators, money, 321-327

Manual method of counting change. *See* Addition method of counting change

Manufacturers, 385

Manufacturers' representatives, 397

Manufacturers' salespeople, 397; defined, 397; illustration of career path, may follow into management, 396

Manufacturers' selling, 395-397

Manufacturers' selling job opportunities: manufacturers' representatives, 397; missionary salespeople, 397; sales engineers, 397

Manufacturing process of products, as product information, 94

Marked-bill passers: defined, 323; as money manipulators, 323-324

Marketing, 6

Marking: defined, 342; merchandise as sales-supporting duty, 341-342

Marshall Field, 389

Material composition of products, as product information, 93-94

Means, what each feature: as a step in translating product features into buyer benefits, 150, 155

Mental stages of the customers' buying process, 32-40

Merchandise: better quality, 239-243; care and use of, as knowledge salespeople should have, 92; carried by store, as knowledge salespeople should have, 91; carried in other departments, as knowledge salespeople should have, 91; as an influence on customers, 56-57; larger quantities of, 238-239; learning about, as sales-supporting duty, 344-347; location in store of, as knowledge salespeople should have, 91; narrowing the selection of, to make the buying decision easier, 209-210; not carried by store, as knowledge salespeople should have, 91; promoted, as knowledge salespeople should have, 92; quality and price of, as a patronage buying motive, 83; related, 235-237; reserve stock and location of, as knowledge salespeople should have, 91; salespeople should stop showing customers new, to make the buying decision easier, 209; seasonal, 245; as a source of product or service information, 99-100; special occasion, 245; special occasion, as type to suggest to customers, 244-245; special ordered, as knowledge salespeople should have, 92; specials on, 243-244; suggesting new, examples of, 238; talking about customer ownership of, to make the buying decision easier, 210; what to learn about the, 345

Merchandise approach, 113-114; defined, 113

Merchandise assortment, as a patronage buying motive, 83

Merchandise plan, 392

Merchandise returns. *See* Return

Merchandise special, 243

Merchandise tags, information found on, 342

Merchant protection laws, 320

Metropolitan Life, 398

Missionary salespeople, 397

Money: cash register operation and handling, 289-309; how salespeople should handle, 301-309; making correct change, 304-307; if salesperson receives counterfeit, 330; table of portrait and denominations of, 328

Money manipulators, 321-327; change bluffers as, 321-322; defined, 321; marked-bill passers as, 323-324; short-change artists as, 324-325; split-bill passers as, 325-326; till dippers as, 326-327

Money savings, as a buyer benefit, 150

Montgomery Ward, 389

Motive(s), buying, 68-69, 145. *See also* Buying motives; Common buying motives; Patronage buying motives

Motor bar, as cash register feature, 297-280; defined, 297

Motorcycle, illustration of buyer benefits of owning, 157

Narrative close, testimonial or, 222

Natural close, 207-208

Neatness: defined, 20; as a personality trait, 18

Need, 68

Needs and wants: determining customers', 42, 119-140; evaluating the salesperson's ability to determine, 376-377

Neiman Marcus, 389

Net profit, 233

New York Life, 398

Nonselling duties, 16. *See also* Sales-supporting duties

Nonselling time: list of items to do in, 350; using, wisely, 349-350

Nontechnical products, 395

Nontechnical salespeople, 391

No-sale key as part of the cash register keyboard, 295

Objection(s): answer the, in telephone sales, 364-365; buying decision, 189-191; customer, 43; defined, 182; evaluating the salesperson's handling of customer, 378, 380; excuses or, 183-187; general procedure for answering customers', 192-195; handling customer, 43, 181-202; hidden, 184-185; listen to customer's, 192-193; making customer's, work for salespeople, 202; overcoming, in telephone sales presentation, 362-366; pause before answering, 193; prepare to answer customer, 187-189; promptly answering customers', 194-195; real, 184; restate the, 194; show empathy for the customer, 193; summary of procedure for answering customer's, 195; techniques for answering, 197-202; techniques for answering, in telephone sales, 365; understand real, to overcome objections in telephone sales, 363; welcome the, to overcome objections in telephone sales, 364; when to answer, 191-192

Objection close, 222-223; defined, 223

Objections in a telephone sale, types of customer: personal objection, 362-363; postponement objection, 362; price objection, 362; product or service, 362

Occupational areas, number of salespeople employed in, 384

Odd-cent transactions, 307

One-stop shopping, 56
Opening statement: as approach in telephone sales presentation, 359; defined, 359; purpose of the, in telephone sales presentation, 359
Opinion questions, 43
Order-taker, 13
Outside salespeople, 391
Over in balancing the cash drawer: cash in change fund is, 303; defined, 308
Over-ring, 300

P

Paid out: defined, 279; illustration of a refund or, transaction as a type of uneven exchange, 285
Patronage motives, 23
Payments received on account, as type of transaction, 275-277
Penney, J.C., 389
Performance, product: chart of product features and, 154; chart of product features, buyer benefits, and, 155; defined, 154; formula for translating, into buyer benefits, 156; as product information, 95
Personal appearance, as part of sales personality, 372-373
Personal benefits, five: of product or service knowledge, 88-91
Personal experience, as a source of product or service information, 100-101
Personal information, as part of a resume, 408
Personal inventory, for job search, 404-406
Personality: defined, 17; developing a sales, 22; as qualification for sales job, 405-406; questions for evaluating the sales, 374; traits needed by salespeople's, 16-22
Personal objection, 362-363
Personal selling, 15
Personal words, 356
Person-to-person communication, 128, 129, 131, 134
Phrases, picture: for use in telephone sales, 356
Physical inventory, 347
Picture phrases, 356
Place: as a buying decision objection, 189-190; as a customer buying decision, 64
Pleasure, as a buyer benefit, 150
Poise: defined, 20; as a personality trait, 18
Postponement objection, 362

Preapproach: defined, 41; determining what to do for the feature-benefit presentation as the, 164-165; evaluating the salesperson's, 375-376; as step of the sales process, 41
Premium close, 220
Preplan the sales call, as step of telephone sales presentation, 355-357
Prestige: as a buyer benefit, 150; defined, 73
Prestige and recognition, as buying motive, 73-74
Price: as a buying decision objection, 190; as a customer buying decision, 65; merchandise quality and, as a patronage buying motive, 83
Price close, 225
Price objection, 362
Price of products, as product information, 96-97
Pride of ownership, as a buyer benefit, 150
Primary buying motives, 76
Procter and Gamble, 395
Product(s): as a buying decision objection, 189; as a customer buying decision, 64; intangible, 10; involve the customer in the feature-benefit sales presentation by properly handling the, 174-175; nontechnical, 395; study the service or, to preplan the sales call, 355; tangible, 10, 384; technical, 394; what salespeople should learn about services or, 93-99
Product appearance, as product information, 93
Product brand, as product information, 96
Product buying motives, 81-82; defined, 81
Product care, as product information, 96
Product competition, as product information, 97
Product demonstration, 170
Product feature(s): chart of, for jogging shoes, 153; chart of performance and, for jogging shoes, 154; chart of performance, buyer benefits, and, for jogging shoes, 155; defined, 148; determining what the, does for the customer as a step of translating product features into buyer benefits, 153, 154; explain how customers can benefit from, as a step of translating product features into buyer benefits, 153, 155-156; formula for translating, into buyer benefits, 156; illustration of a, 149; listing the, as a step of translating product features into buyer benefits, 153; translating, into buyer benefits, 153-161; what is a, 148-149

Product information, 87-103; benefits of, 88-91; don't be a know-it-all about, 102-103; knowledge of, makes a difference, 91-93; sources of, 99-102 (*See also* Sources of product information); what to learn about services and, 93-99

Production, 6

Product knowledge, benefits of. *See* Benefits of product or service knowledge to salespeople

Product knowledge needed by salespeople: appearance, 93; brand, 96; care, 96; competition, 97; manufacturing process, 94; material composition, 93-94; performance, 95; price, 96-97; related items, 97; service, 96; uses, 94-95. *See also* Merchandise information, salespeople's

Product literature, as source of merchandise knowledge, 345-346

Product manufacturing process, as product information, 94

Product material composition, 93-94

Product objection, 362

Product performance: defined, 154; as product information, 95

Product presentation. *See* Feature-benefit sales presentation

Product price, as product information, 96-97

Product-related items, as product information, 97

Product service, as product information, 96

Product uses, as product information, 94-95

Professionalism, 18

Professional shoplifters, 314-315; defined, 314

Profit, net, 233

Proper timing, 109

Property listing, 399

Protection and safety, as buying motives, 72-73

Proving cash, cashing out or, 308

Prudential, 398

Publications, as a source of product information, 101-102

Punctuality: defined, 20; as a personality trait, 18

Purchase: date of, as information on a sales form, 256; receipt of, 263

Q

Qualify customers, 125-134; ask questions to, 129-132; defined, 125; be a good listener in order to, 132-134; make a sell-ing statement to, 128-129; observe and, 126-128

Quality, merchandise price and: as a patronage buying motive, 83

Quantity: as a buying decision objection, 190-191; as a customer buying decision, 65

Question method: answering customer objections by the, 199-200; defined, 199

R

Rack jobbers, 393

Rapport: defined, 359; developing, with telephone customers, 360; establish, with customer in telephone sales presentation, 359-360

Rational buying motives, 78-79, 356; defined, 78

Real estate agents and brokers, 398-399; defined, 398

Real objections, 184

Reassurance: defined, 247; evaluating the salesperson's ability for suggestion selling and, 378-379; giving, to customers, 247-248; suggestion selling and, 44, 231-248

Receipt printer: defined, 297; receipt-tape slot and, as cash register feature, 297

Receipt of purchase, 263

Receipt-tape slot: defined, 297; receipt printer and, as cash register feature, 297

Received on account: defined, 276; illustration of a, sales form, 276; payments, as type of transaction, 275-277

Receiving: defined, 341; merchandise as sales-supporting duty, 341-342

Recognition, 74

Recognition and prestige, as buying motive, 73-74

Recreation and variety, as buying motives, 74-75

References, as part of a resume, 411

Reflective empathy statements, 193

Refund: handling a cash, as type of return transaction, 279-280; illustration of a cash, 280

Register, cash. *See* Cash register

Register, sales, 259

Related merchandise, 235

Related-merchandise sales, examples of, 235

Release lever, as a correction key, 295-296

Repeat customers, 8

Reserve stock, location of, as knowledge salespeople should have, 91

Resistance, sales, 183-184

Resume: defined, 408; illustrations of a, 409, 410; parts of, 408-411; preparing the, 408-411

Retail businesses, 385-391; department stores as, 389; discount stores as, 389-390; specialty shops as, 390; variety stores as, 389

Retailers: defined, 6; as type of business employing salespeople, 385-391

Retail selling, characteristics of, 390-391

Return, 279-285; charge, 280; defined, 279

Routine for preparing a sales form, 259-260

S

Safety, as a buyer benefit, 150

Safety and protection, as buying motive, 72-73

Sale(s): the approach as a step of the, 107-116; cash, 263-265; charge, 265-268; close, in telephone sales presentation, 366-367; if you closed the, 227; closing the, 179, 206-228; closing the, by making the buying decision easy, 208-212; COD, 268-271; determining customer needs and wants as a step in the, 119-140; if you didn't close the, 227-228; discount, 274-275; errors in closing the, 225-226; evaluating the salesperson's ability to close the, 378, 379; getting the, off to a good start, 116; gross, 233; layaway, 271-274; summary of steps of a, 44, 45; techniques to close more, 215-225; types of, transactions, 262-275; when salespeople should close the, 212-214

Sales book: defined, 259; salespeople should use the sales register or, in preparing a sales form, 259

Sales career, other opportunities for a, 398

Sales check. *See* Sales forms

Sales control, 110

Sales demonstration, evaluating the salesperson's ability in the, 379-380

Sales employees, number of, 384

Sales engineers, 397

Sales form(s), 254-262; avoiding mistakes on, 260-262; defined, 254; four common mistakes made on, 260; preparation of a, 258-260; transactions and, 253-285

Sales form illustrations: cash refund transaction, 280; cash sale, 264; charge credit transaction, 281; charge sale, 267; COD cash sale, 269; COD charge-send sale, 270; discount sale, 275; even exchange transaction, 282; gift certificate transaction, 278; layaway sale, 272; layaway sale payment, 273; received on account transaction, 276; with required information, 256; uneven exchange transaction, as a paid out or refund, 285; uneven exchange transaction, using one sales form, 284; uneven exchange transaction, using two sales forms, 283

Sales job qualifications: education, 404-405; personality, 405-406; work experience, 406

Salesperson (salespeople): and avoiding mistakes on sales forms, 261-262; as bread and butter of a business, 4; change-making procedures for, to follow, 326; closing the sale by, 206-228; defined, 12; employers' expectations of salespeople, 25-27; evaluating the sales personality of, 372-374; evaluating the sales skills of, 375-379; five personal benefits of product or service knowledge received by, 88-91; and focusing the approach on the customer, 109-112; general procedure to follow for answering customer objections by, 192-195; handling customer objections by, 181-202; helpful, as a patronage buying motive, 82; human relations and, 12-27; identification of, as information on a sales form, 257; illustration of buying and selling process between customer and, 31; illustration of career path, can follow into management, 388; illustration of career path manufacturers', may follow into management, 396; illustration of sales-supporting duties performed by, 339; improving the selling skills of the, 371-380; industrial wholesale, 394-395; inside, 391; job of, 12-16; knowing services, 97-99; loyalty to employer and the, 27; making customer objections work for, 202; manufacturers' 397; merchandise knowledge, how salespeople gain, 344-347; missionary, 397; new job of, 425; nontechnical, 391; other, as source of merchandise knowledge, 345; outside, 391; personality traits needed by, 16-22; preparation to answer customer objections by, 187-189; qualifications for sales job, 404-406; if, receives counterfeit money, 330; responsibility of the, to prevent theft, 317-318; sales-supporting duties of the, 16; selecting the appropriate sales approach, 112; selling as the most important function of, 13-15; as a source of product or service information,

100; take a look at yourself, 404-406; taking control of the sale by the, 110-111; technical, 391; techniques for answering customer objections used by, 195-202; types of businesses that employ, 385-399; using the customer's name in the sales approach, 111-112; ways customers can be assisted by, 4; welcoming customer objections by, 182-183; what customers expect from, 22-25; what to learn about their merchandise, 345; when to answer customer objections by, 191-192; where to find a job, 406-407; wholesale route, 393; willingness to follow directions and the, 26

Sales personality: developing a, 22; evaluating the saleperson's 372-374; questions for evaluating the, 374

Salesperson's identification keys, 294

Sales presentation. *See* Feature-benefit sales presentation; Telephone sales presentation

Sales process, illustration of seven steps in, 41

Sales receipt. *See* Sales form

Sales register: defined, 259; salespeople should use the sales book or, in preparing a sales form, 259

Sales representatives, wholesale, 392

Sales resistance: defined, 183-184; salespeople can overcome, as a benefit from product or service information, 90

Sales skills, evaluating the salesperson's, 375-379

Sales steps: approach, 41-42; closing the sale, 43-44; determining customer needs and wants, 42; evaluating the, 375-379; handling customer objections, 43; illustration of seven, 41, 164; making a feature-benefit presentation, 42-43; preapproach, 41; suggestion selling and reassurance, 44; techniques and seven, 45

Sales-supporting duties, 338-349; illustration of, 339; of the salesperson, 16

Sales-supporting skills, 338-350

Sales talk, canned, 357

Sales tax chart, three percent, 265

Sales-tax key, 296

Sales training program: defined, 346; as source of merchandise information, 346-347

Sales transaction: defined, 262; sales forms and, 253-285; types of, 262-275. *See also* Transactions, illustrations of

Sales vocabulary: defined, 356; to preplan the sales call, 355-357; terms recommended for use on telephone, 356

Seal, on currency, 328

Sears, Roebuck, 389

Seasonal merchandise, 245

Security, as a buyer benefit, 150

Security devices, to prevent shoplifting, 317

Selective buying motives, 76-78; defined, 76

Self-confidence: defined, 20; as a personality trait, 18

Self-control, defined, 21; as a personality trait, 18

Self-service, 386

Selling: benefits of a career in, 399-400; in business, 4; career opportunities in, 383-401; characteristics of retail, 390-391; contributions of, 6-7; customer-oriented, 14; defined, 4; developing the *You* attitude in, 44-47; evaluating the preapproach through attitudes for, 376; examples of merchandise to use for suggestion, 235; external, 388; how to get a job in, 403-425; the importance of human relations in, 8-9; importance of suggestion, 232-234; internal, 388; introduction to, 3-10; manufacturers', 395-397; 90 percent preparation and 10 percent presentation is, 146; opportunities in, 10; personal, 15; reassurance and suggestion, 44, 231-248; as the salesperson's most important function, 13; salesperson's willingness to learn more about, 26; in our society, 7; telephone, 352-367; what is, 4-5; what is suggestion, 232; where, takes place, 383-385; wholesale, 391-395. *See also* Suggestion selling

Selling aids: defined, 175; involve the customer in the feature-benefit sales presentation using, 175-179

Selling attitude, 102-103

Selling process: the approach and the, 107-116; buying and, 30-47; illustration of buying and, 31

Selling skills: in business, 4; improving the salesperson's, 371-380; in your personal life, 3

Selling statement: make a, to qualify your customers, 128-129; as qualifying questions, 167

Selling techniques, illustration of customers' mental stages and, 40

Sense of humor: defined, 21; as a personality trait, 18

Senses, customer's five, as used in a feature-benefit presentation, 172

Serial numbers on currency, 328

Services: intangible, 10; merchandise or, description as information on a sales form, 257-258; salespeople should know, 97-99; store, as an influence on customers, 55-56; store, as a patronage buying motive, 83-84; study the product or, to preplan the sales call, 355; what salespeople need to learn about products or, 93-99

Service approach, 115-116; defined, 115

Service attitude, as part of sales personality, 373-374

Service knowledge, benefits of product or, 88-91. *See also* Benefits of product or service knowledge to salespeople

Service objection, product or, 362

Service of products, as product information, 96

Service selling, 398-399

Shops, specialty, 390

Shoplifter, 314-315; amateur, 315; apprehending a, 318-321; defined, 314; intent of, 319; professional, 314-315

Shoplifting, 314-315; defined, 314; list of what not to do in situation of, 320-321; recognizing methods of, 315; recognizing methods of, by watching for unusual customer behavior, 316; security devices to prevent, 317; summary written in situation of, 320

Shopping, one-stop, 56

Shopping trip, competitive, 344

Short: in balancing the cash drawer, defined, 308; cash in change fund is, 303

Shortchange artists: defined, 324; as money manipulators, 324-325

Showmanship: defined, 173; use dramatization or, to involve the customer in the feature-benefit sales presentation, 173-174

Show me attitude, 145

Sight, 172

Signals, buying, 137, 212-213, 214

Skills: evaluating the salesperson's sales, 375-379; improving the salesperson's selling, 371-380; sales-supporting, 338-350

Smell, 172

Sources of product information: customers, 100; merchandise, 99-100; other sources, 102; personal experience, 100-101; publications, 101-102; salespeople, 100

Specialty shops, 390

Split-bill passer: defined, 325; as money manipulators, 325-326

Sports car: buyer benefit and buyer benefit statement for, 152; product features and feature statement for, 148

Stages in customer buying process, 32-40

Standing-room-only close, 221

Steps of a sale: the approach, 107-116; evaluating the, 375-379; illustration of seven, 41, 164; seven techniques and, 45; summary of, 44, 45. *See also* Sales steps

Stereo receiver: buyer benefit and buyer benefit statement for, 152; feature-benefit chart of, 161; product features and feature statement for, 148

Stock: maintaining adequate, as sales-supporting duty, 344; location of, as important knowledge for salespeople to have, 91

Stocking shelves, as sales-supporting duty, 339-340

Stockkeeping: defined, 339; duties of a salesperson when, 340

Stores, reasons why customers enter, 119-120. *See also* Retail businesses

Store advertising, as source of merchandise information, 346

Store image: defined, 53; as influence on customers, 53; as a patronage buying motive, 82

Store interior, as influence on customers, 55

Store location, as a patronage buying motive, 84

Store losses, 313-335; other, 330-333

Store services: as an influence on customers, 55-56; as a patronage buying motive, 83-84

Subtotal key, 296

Subtraction method of counting change, 306-307; defined, 306

Suggestion selling: defined, 44; evaluating the salesperson's ability for reassurance and, 378-379; examples of merchandise to use for, 235; four rules to follow when, 246; how to make suggestions to customers for, 246-247; importance of, 232-234; reassurance and, 44, 231-248; what is, 232; what to suggest to customers, 234-245

Suggestion selling merchandise, types of: better quality merchandise, 239-243; larger quantities of, 238-239; merchandise for special occasions, 244-245; merchandise specials, 243-244; new merchandise, 238; related merchandise, 235-237

Suggest-related-merchandise close, 223-224; defined, 223

Summary close, 366-367

Superior-point method of answering customer objections, 198

T

Tact: defined, 21; as a personality trait, 18

Tangible products, 10, 384

Taste, 172

Tax chart, three percent sales, 265

Technical products, 394

Technical salespeople, 391

Telephone, use of, in business, 354

Telephone customer, developing rapport with the, 360

Telephone sales presentation, 357-367; asking your customer a qualifying question, 361; closing the sale in, 366-367; establishing rapport with the customer in, 359-360; giving an opening statement in, 359; illustration of selling skills to control, 358; overcoming objections in, 362-366; preplanning in, 355-357; providing additional feature-benefit statement in, 361-362; starting your sales message with a feature-benefit statement in, 360-361; steps of a, 354

Telephone selling, 352-367

Testimonial, 201

Testimonial close, 222

Thank-you letter, illustration of, 423

Theft: policies to discourage employee, 334-335; responsibility of salesperson to prevent, 317-318

Third-party method of answering customer objections, 201

Till dipper: defined, 326; as money manipulators, 326-327

Time: as a buying decision objection, 190; as a customer buying decision, 65

Time savings, as a buyer benefit, 150

Timing, proper: for making the approach in a sale, 109

To do list, 349

Total key, 296

Touch, 172

Touch system, 294

Trading up: defined, 239; example of camera and, 240-243; suggest better quality merchandise by, 239-243

Training programs, sales: as source of merchandise information, 346-347

Trait(s): defined, 18; evaluating five personality, 372-374; personality, needed by salespeople, 18

Transaction(s): cash sales, 263-265; charge sales, 265-268; COD sales, 268-271; defined, 257; discount sales, 274; gift certificates, 277-278; handling odd-cent, 307; layaway sales, 271-274; other types of, 275-285; payments received on account, 275-277; return or exchange, 279-285; sales, 262; type of, as information on a sales form, 257; types of sales, 262-275

Transaction keys: defined, 295; as part of the cash register keyboard, 295

Transactions illustrations of: cash refund, 280; cash sale, 264; charge credit, 281; charge sale, 267; COD cash sale, 269; COD charge-send sale, 270; discount sale, 275; even exchange, 282; gift certificate, 278; layaway sale, 272; layaway sale payment, 273; received on account, 276; uneven exchange, as a paid out or refund, 285; uneven exchange, using one sales form, 284; uneven exchange, using two sales forms, 283

Trial close, 140, 214-215; defined, 140; evaluating the salesperson's, 380

Trial order close, 225

U

Undecided customer, 60, 122-124; defined, 60

Under-ring, 300

Underwriters Laboratory, 72

Uneven exchange: defined, 283; handling an, as type of return transaction, 283-285; illustration of a paid out or refund transaction as type of, 285; illustration of an, transaction using one sales form, 284; illustration of an, transaction using two sales forms, 283

Universal Product Code (UPC), 291

Uses of products, as product information, 94-95

V

Variety and recreation, as buying motives, 74-75

Variety stores, 389

Vocabulary, develop sales, to preplan the sales call, 355-357

Void, 259

W

Want, 68

Want lists, 238

Wants and needs: customers', 57-58; determining customers', 119-140; evaluating the salesperson's ability to determine, 376-377

Watch, feature-benefit chart for quartz, 158
Welcome approach, 114
What, as a qualifying question, 168
When, as a qualifying question, 168
Where, as a qualifying question, 168
Who, as a qualifying question, 168
Wholesale route salespeople, 393
Wholesalers, 6
Wholesale sales representatives, 392
Wholesale selling, 391-395
Why, as a question to find out why some customers resist buying, 211
Will-call sales. *See* Layaway sales
Winter coat: buyer benefit and buyer benefit statement for, 152; product features and feature statement for, 148
Woolworth Co., F. W., 389

Words: forcefuls, for use in telephone sales, 356, personal, for use in telephone sales, 356
Work experience: as part of a resume, 411; as qualification for sales job, 406
Writing, importance of legible, on sales forms, 261

Y

Yes, but method of answering customer objections, 196-197; defined, 196
You attitude, developing, in selling, 44-47

Z

Zayre's, 390